Applied Ethics

An Impartial Introduction

Applied Ethics

An Impartial Introduction

Elizabeth Jackson

Tyron Goldschmidt

Dustin Crummett

Rebecca Chan

Hackett Publishing Company, Inc.
Indianapolis/Cambridge

24 23 22 21   1 2 3 4 5 6 7

For further information, please address
   Hackett Publishing Company, Inc.
   P.O. Box 44937
   Indianapolis, Indiana 46244-0937

   www.hackettpublishing.com

Cover and interior design by E. L. Wilson
Composition by Aptara, Inc.

Cataloging-in-Publication data can be accessed via the Library of Congress
Online Catalog.
Library of Congress Control Number: 2021936826

ISBN-13: 978-1-64792-011-1 (pbk.)
ISBN-13: 978-1-64792-014-2 (PDF ebook)

The paper used in this publication meets the minimum requirements of
American National Standard for Information Sciences—Permanence of Paper
for Printed Library Materials, ANSI Z39.48–1984.

∞

Contents

Acknowledgments

Even though our names appear in order—reverse alphabetical!—on the cover, the authors each contributed equally to the book. Each of us focused a bit more on certain chapters, but all the chapters are the work of multiple hands. Still, each of us blames the others entirely for any infelicities or blunders.

We all thank Deborah Wilkes of Hackett Publishing for her encouragement, advice and patience.

Liz and Ty thank the Eudaimonia Institute at Wake Forest University for a grant to work on this project over the summer of 2018 and to purchase many books.

Dustin received funding for this project from the European Research Council (ERC) under the European Union's Horizon 2020 research and innovation programme (grant agreement No. 786762).

Rebecca thanks David (aka #1) with whom she participated in a reading group on punishment. Though all of his reading was done *a priori*, his lived example modeled the real value of applied ethics.

Dustin also thanks Alex Rausch. Alex did not contribute to this book in any way, but did beat Dustin in an arm wrestling contest—the stakes being that the loser had to thank the winner in the acknowledgments of a publication.

4. Argumentation

In addition to exploring applied ethics, we want to leave you with an additional gift that you can take with you even if you forget everything about applied ethics after reading this book. (But we still really hope you don't forget about applied ethics!) This gift is **argumentation**, or the ability to present and analyze arguments well. We think that argumentation is an especially valuable gift to impart because it is transferable to other fields of study and areas of your everyday life.

In each chapter we give reasons for and against the views we discuss. In philosophy when we present premises (or claims or reasons) for a conclusion in a methodical way, we call this an 'argument.' An argument is a collection of premises and the conclusion the premises support. **Arguments** have two parts: **premises** and a **conclusion**. The premises are supposed to support the conclusion. In a good argument, the premises are (1) plausible and (2) support, or even guarantee, the conclusion.

Philosophers often number premises and preface the numbers with a 'P' to signify that it's a premise. Conclusions are signified with a 'C' and often start with a verbal cue as well, such as "therefore" or "thus." Here's an example of how this might go:

(P1) All cats are cute.

(P2) Ponyo, Artemis, and Apollo are cats

(C) Thus, Ponyo, Artemis, and Apollo are cute.

Sometimes an argument isn't very good, either because a premise isn't plausible or because the premises don't lead to the conclusion. For instance, you may look at the above argument and doubt (P1) because you find hairless sphynx cats unattractive. A bad argument does not mean that the conclusion is automatically false. It just means that the argument is bad or that it does not provide a good reason to think that the conclusion is true. The conclusion might still be true for some other reason. We assure you that even if (P1) is false, Ponyo, Artemis, and Apollo are in fact cute.

Figure 1. A sphynx cat.   Figure 2. Ponyo.   Figure 3. Apollo (left) and Artemis (right).

Moral arguments often have some premises that are moral claims and some premises that are non-moral claims. In applied ethics, people will often disagree about both types of claims. For example, look at the argument below about the death penalty:

(P1) If the death penalty prevents future murders, then it is morally justified.

(P2) The death penalty prevents future murders.

(C)   Therefore, the death penalty is morally justified.

Premise 1 is a **moral claim**, that is, it involves a moral position—it is about whether an action is justified by a future consequence. Premise 2 is a **non-moral claim**—it does not involve a moral position. Often, but not always, non-moral claims also will be **empirical**, meaning they are subject to observations about the world. In this argument, Premise 2 is both a non-moral and an empirical claim.

Suppose two pundits are arguing on television about the moral status of the death penalty. They might both disagree on premise 1, which claims that a future good (preventing murders) morally justifies putting someone (say, a murderer) to death. One of the pundits might think that a good consequence always justifies an action, while the other might hold that there are factors other than good consequences that morally matter. Perhaps intentionally taking life is wrong, regardless of the good consequences it may cause or whether the person deserves to die.

Or, the pundits might disagree on premise 2, with one person believing that the death penalty does prevent future murders and the other believing that it has no effect on future murders or perhaps even makes them more likely. Notice that whether premise 2 is true is an empirical matter. If a matter is empirical, this means that we know about it by making observations about the world. Thus, to figure out if the death penalty is wrong, we might consult social scientists investigating the effects of the death penalty to compare murder rates in societies before and after the abolition of the death penalty.

When doing applied ethics, it is important to pay attention to both moral and non-moral claims. It is also important to be able to tell the difference between them, since we turn to different kinds of experts and evidence when investigating the truth of those claims. For instance, if we want to figure out whether premise 1 is true, we should probably consult people who study ethics. But if we want to know whether premise 2 is true, we should probably ask sociologists who have studied the relevant data. The beauty of applied ethics is that it unites these different fields of specialty to provide us with guidance in everyday decisions.

After we present some influential arguments, we then consider objections to the arguments and replies to the objections.

- **Objections:** objections target the argument at various points. In explaining what arguments are, we earlier pointed out that good arguments have (1) plausible premises that (2) lead to or support the conclusion. Thus, most of the objections we consider target a premise, showing that it is not plausible or ill-supported, or the reasoning, showing that the premises do not really lead to or support the conclusion.

- **Replies:** replies to objections are supposed to show that the objection is mistaken; there may also be a reply to the reply, and so on.

You can imagine these arguments, objections, and replies going similarly to opposing lawyers making their cases in court. We recommend you play the juror, subjecting the arguments on all sides to the most critical scrutiny. You can also leap out of the jury box to present a case of your own. You may think of an argument, an objection, or a reply of your own that we have not included!

As we proceed, we will introduce you to different patterns of argument and teach you how to evaluate such arguments. You'll also get used to analytic thinking as you read through our own presentations and criticisms of arguments. Our hope is that practicing reasoning about the topics in this text will give you the skills to think carefully and clearly about other moral questions—including questions you face in your own life not covered in this textbook.

5. Conclusion

Hopefully, you now have a better idea of what you're in for! We look forward to exploring applied ethics with you.

Further Reading

Each chapter contains a little section on further reading on the argument covered and closely related topics. Other textbooks on applied ethics are Singer (2011) and Oderberg (2000). The reader will discover how often our treatment is indebted to Singer in particular. There are many anthologies on applied ethics. We especially recommend Boonin and Oddie (2009), LaFollette (2014), and Timmons (2019). Timmons (2019) is an introduction to normative ethics, and Chrisman (2017) is an introduction to metaethics. Shafer-Landau (2017) is an introduction to normative ethics, as well as some metaethics. Lyons and Ward (2018) is an introduction to arguments and critical thinking.

Section 1

Abortion

Chapter 2

The Sanctity of Life Argument

1. Introduction

Is abortion morally **wrong**? **Abortion** is the intentional termination of a pregnancy, which almost always causes the death of the fetus. For simplicity, **fetus** covers the zygotic, embryonic, and fetal stages of the organism—though, as we'll see, some take the stage of the organism to matter in the debate.

The **pro-life position** *is that abortion is wrong*—usually or always. The **pro-choice position** *is that abortion is not wrong*—usually or always. Some pro-life positions allow exceptions, for example, when abortion is performed because the mother's life is at risk, or the pregnancy results from rape, or the fetus is anencephalic (without a brain). And some pro-choice positions allow exceptions, for example, when the abortion is performed very late in pregnancy (and many pro-choice positions are against late-stage abortions that would not provide a significant benefit that birth would not). Depending on how many exceptions are allowed, positions might be more or less pro-life or pro-choice—there's a continuum.

> Do you have beliefs about the morality of abortion? Do you support a pro-life or pro-choice position? What exceptions, if any, do you allow?

We'll cover one pro-life and one pro-choice argument in this chapter: the sanctity of life and personhood arguments, respectively. These two arguments are paired together because they focus on *whether the fetus is the kind of thing that has a right to life*. We won't *directly* apply them to rare cases. Then in the following chapter, we'll turn to a pro-life argument that focuses on why **killing** a fetus would be wrong even if it is not a person. Finally, in the last abortion chapter, we'll turn to a pro-choice argument that says abortion is permissible even if the fetus does have a right to life.

2. Sanctity of Life: A Pro-Life Argument

A traditional pro-life argument—sometimes called the **sanctity of life argument**—emphasizes the value of all human life (see Singer 2011, chap. 6; cf. Lee and George 2005). The core idea of this position is that *there is something special about humans*, and that *specialness gives humans a right to life*. What exactly is special about humans? Well, different thinkers and traditions give very different answers.

For instance, some theistic traditions hold that humans are special because they are created in God's image. But you don't have to believe in God to think that humans are special. Others think that humans are special because they are the only ones endowed with souls, or morality, or rationality. For the purposes of this argument, it doesn't matter *why* humans are special, it just matters that they are and that their specialness means that their lives are valuable—so valuable that they have a right to life. This is the first premise of the argument:

(P1) All humans have a right to life.

What is a right to life? A right to life is a certain kind of moral right. Moral rights allow us to make *legitimate demands on others; they create obligations for others to do or not do certain things on our behalf.* These obligations may not always be absolute. If I'm lost in a blizzard and the only way I can save my life is to break into your cabin (you aren't there to let me in, and I can't get permission), breaking in may infringe your property rights, but it also seems morally okay (Feinberg 1978). However, in the vast majority of cases, infringing a right is wrong: if you can ever permissibly infringe rights, it's only in exceptional cases. Bob's right to life means that we should not kill him, exceptional cases aside (e.g., self-defense). Bob's right to property means that we should not take or break his stuff, exceptional cases aside (e.g., breaking into his cabin). Moral rights also could mean even more: that we have to protect Bob's life and properties from others.

> Do you think that humans are special? If so, what makes them special?

We'll see later (e.g., Chapters 5 and 6) that some ethical theories, such as **utilitarianism**, either do not make much use of rights or reject the existence of rights altogether. However, belief in moral rights is certainly popular, and we'll take the notion for granted for right now.

This discussion of rights brings us to our second premise:

(P2) If something has a right to life, then intentionally killing that
        thing is impermissible.

If someone has a right to life, then intentionally killing them wrongs them. So killing is impermissible. Putting (P1) and (P2) together, we get our first conclusion and mini-argument:

(P1) All humans have a right to life.
(P2) If something has a right to life, then intentionally killing that
        thing is impermissible.
(C)   Intentionally killing humans is impermissible.

At this point, you may be looking at the argument and thinking about cases in which intentionally killing humans seems permissible—consider intentionally killing someone who is threatening your life. Slightly more controversially, many people think that it is permissible to intentionally kill humans in the context of a just war, or if they deserve death for some horrible crime. Notice that in these cases, the humans being killed are not "innocent." Plausibly, their right to life is suspended because they are infringing upon someone else's rights. To account for these cases, we can think of the argument as being a little more specific:

(P1)   All (innocent) humans have a right to life.

(P2)   If something has a right to life, then intentionally killing that thing is impermissible.

(C)   Intentionally killing (innocent) humans is impermissible.

From here, we can quickly complete the argument to arrive at our pro-life conclusion:

(P3)   Fetuses are (innocent) humans.

(C2)   Therefore, intentionally killing a fetus is impermissible.

This, in a nutshell, is the sanctity of life argument.

Now that we've presented the argument, it's time to investigate whether it has any weaknesses. Perhaps you find yourself thinking, "(C2) is implausible! That's what's wrong with the argument!" Even if that's the case, it's important to be able to explain *how* the argument goes wrong. After all, we have carefully presented the reasoning behind the conclusion. If you disagree with the conclusion, it's important to identify where this reasoning goes wrong. (If you agree with the conclusion, it's still important to carefully examine the reasoning, either to establish additional support for your belief in the conclusion or to discover whether you believe the conclusion for different reasons.)

Recall from the introduction that a good argument has two things: (i) plausible premises that (ii) support or guarantee the conclusion. These premises, if true, lead to the conclusion, so we're good on (ii). What remains to be seen is whether the argument has plausible premises. This means we need to turn our attention to (P1), (P2), and (P3). Virtually no one disagrees with (P3). The fetuses in question are organisms of the species *Homo sapiens*, that is, the human species. They are also innocent.

This leaves us with (P1) and (P2) as possible weaknesses. We've already seen that (P2)—the claim that if something has a right to life, then killing that thing is impermissible—raises some questions when it comes to self-defense, just war, and punishment. It may be that even in the case of innocent humans, (P2) is questionable. (For instance, if someone innocently presents an imminent threat to your life and killing them is the only way to survive, it may still be permissible to kill them even though they are innocent.) We'll talk more about (P2) in Chapter 4, which focuses on a famous pro-choice argument that says it is permissible to kill a fetus *even if* it has a right to life. This leaves us with (P1).

3. An Argument from Elimination in Defense of Premise 1

While both pro-lifers and pro-choicers agree that fetuses are humans, pro-choicers (but not all of them!) tend to hold that there is a difference between a human fetus and a post-birth human that is *morally relevant* when it comes to killing. People who hold this position deny (P1), which claims that all humans have a right to life. They hold that fetuses are not *enough* like me and you, that there's some morally relevant difference between us and fetuses: maybe birth, maybe viability, maybe sentience—something. This difference makes it permissible to kill a fetus, but not permissible to kill you, me, or other post-birth humans.

Pro-lifers respond with an **argument from elimination** to show that birth, viability, sentience, and whatnot do not make any difference. An argument from elimination starts by listing all of the possible options. It then eliminates all but one of the options, thus concluding that the last option standing must be the case. For instance, suppose we care about who the best NBA team in California is. We can use an argument from elimination. We'll start by listing all of the possible options:

(P1)   Either the Warriors are the best NBA team in California, or the Kings are, or the Lakers are, or the Clippers are.

Then, we can start eliminating the options:

(P2)   The Warriors are not the best NBA team in California.

(P2)   The Kings are not the best NBA team in California.

(P3)   The Lakers are not the best NBA team in California.

This brings us to our last option, the Clippers, and allows us to conclude:

(C)   The Clippers are the best NBA team in California.

If all the premises are true—if we correctly identified all of the options and correctly eliminated the ones that don't work—we're left with a true conclusion.

The pro-life position utilizes this type of argument. The argument lists all of the potential morally relevant differences between human fetuses and post-birth humans, plus the possibility that there is no morally relevant difference. It then *eliminates* each of the potential morally relevant differences until it is left only with the no difference option. The argument then concludes that there is no morally relevant difference between human fetuses and post-birth humans. This in turn supports (P1) of the original pro-life argument: that (innocent) humans have a right to life, which includes both human fetuses and post-birth humans.

To make things more concrete, let's look at some of the potential morally relevant differences that pro-choicers propose and why pro-lifers eliminate those options:

- **Birth:** There are two problems with this difference. If killing becomes wrong at birth, then the location—inside versus outside the mother's body—makes a difference. But location does not typically make such a difference in whether someone has a right to life: for example, I have a right to life whether I'm in my office or in my car. Second, there is no determinate stage of the birth process in which the right to life kicks in. Would the right kick in once the head emerges? Or only once most of the body emerges? Or only once the whole body emerges?

- **Viability:** Viability is the point when a fetus can survive outside the womb. People who think that viability is the morally relevant difference think that abortion is permissible in earlier stages of a pregnancy but impermissible after that. (These days, viability is often located around twenty-four weeks, though some premature infants survive when born as early as twenty-two weeks after pregnancy and others die when born after twenty-four weeks.) So it doesn't provide a very robust pro-choice criterion. But it's still worth considering if viability separates those who do not have a right to life (earlier-stage fetuses) from those who do (later-stage fetuses and post-birth humans). One problem is that if the right to life kicks in at viability, then medical technology makes a difference: abortion is wrong only once medicine would allow the fetus to survive outside the womb. However, it is not plausible that whether someone has a right to life depends on the available medical technology.

- **Sentience:** Something is *sentient* if it has subjective experiences, that is, if there's "something it's like" to be it. There's something it's like to be you, or the authors of this book, or a cat. You have feelings, sensations, etc., and are therefore sentient. There's nothing it's like to be a rock or a mushroom, so these aren't sentient. Like viability, sentience typically occurs partway through pregnancy, so if this is the morally relevant distinction, it implies that abortion is permissible in earlier stages and impermissible in later ones. But there are two further complications. First, if sentience is the morally relevant difference, then it seems humans who are not sentient don't have a right to life. Some post-birth humans, like ones in temporary comas, are not sentient, but they still have a right to life. Maybe it makes a difference that they have been sentient in the past, or maybe they still have the capacity for sentience in some way that an organism without a developed brain doesn't, but showing that would require further argument. Second, there is disagreement about when the capacity for sentience develops. Most scientists believe this doesn't happen until about midway through pregnancy or later—perhaps around twenty or twenty-four weeks, or even later—but others think it happens as early as twelve weeks

(Derbyshire & Bockmann, 2020). Even if we take the twelve-week figure, in the United States more than 90 percent of abortions occur at or before thirteen weeks (Kortsmit et al. 2020). However, it's hard to say exactly what's necessary for sentience, and some people think it could develop even earlier. (Initial brain activity has been detected between six and ten weeks, when many women still don't know they're pregnant.) If it turns out that sentience develops very early in pregnancy, many pro-choice people would probably still think abortion was permissible at that stage. So by their own lights, sentience doesn't seem to be the morally relevant difference.

- **Consciousness:** People disagree about the definition of consciousness. Some people think consciousness is sentience (see the previous bullet point). Others think consciousness is *self-awareness*. Given this definition, newborns and infants do not have a right to life, since they do not yet have self-awareness. But this is not plausible, and virtually all pro-lifers and pro-choicers agree that newborns and infants have a right to life. Thus, consciousness cannot be the morally relevant difference.

If these are all of the potential morally relevant differences, and the pro-lifer is right to eliminate them, then the only remaining option is that *there is no morally relevant difference between a human fetus and post-birth human.* Here's what this pro-life argument from elimination looks like in premise-conclusion form:

(P1) Either birth is a morally relevant difference between a human fetus and a post-birth human, or viability is, or sentience is, or consciousness is, or there is no morally relevant difference.

(P2) Birth is not a morally relevant difference.

(P3) Viability is not a morally relevant difference.

(P4) Sentience is not a morally relevant difference.

(P5) Consciousness is not a morally relevant difference.

(C)   Therefore, there is no morally relevant difference between a human fetus and post-birth human.

> Can you think of another potential morally relevant difference between human fetuses and post-birth humans? If this difference is in fact morally relevant, which premise does it call into question?

This argument supports (P1) of the original sanctity of life argument. And as we noted, (P2) in that argument is uncontroversial. If this is right, then the conclusion follows and all innocent humans have a right to life.

At this point, we have an argument that all innocent humans have a right to life. Let's now turn to some objections.

Objection 1:

If there is no morally relevant difference between a fetus (even right after conception) and a post-birth human, then a zygote (super-early-stage fetus) dying is as bad as any other human dying. But this is implausible. For example, suppose you are in a burning hospital and can save either a frozen zygote in a canister or an infant—but not both. If letting a zygote die is as bad as letting an infant die, then you could save either. However, you definitely should save the infant over the zygote—even over a number of zygotes (see Greasley 2017, 108).

This objection doesn't obviously challenge one of the premises. It does precisely what we earlier said was a bad way of responding to an argument: it challenges the conclusion. But let's think a little bit harder about what this objection might be suggesting about the premises. It doesn't challenge (P2) to (P5). So perhaps it is challenging (P1). The objection is suggesting that there must be an overlooked morally relevant difference between a zygote and a post-birth human that explains why we should definitely save the infant over the zygote. In other words, (P1) is false because it is missing a potential morally relevant difference.

Reply:

Even if both a zygote and infant have an equal right to life, *there might be other reasons for why letting a zygote die is not as bad as letting any other human die.* For instance, the infant would experience incredible pain and distress before dying, and that, coupled with the death, would be worse than the zygote dying without experiencing pain or distress. In addition, the family of the infant who loves it very much would be incredibly devastated by the infant's death, probably much more so than the family of the zygote, who probably does not love it in this way.

> Many pro-lifers hold that *only* humans have a right to life. Suppose this is right; then animals like cats and dogs don't have a right to life. A beloved cat who burns to death would experience incredible pain and distress before dying and have a family who would be devastated by its death. If you were forced to save either the beloved cat or the zygote, which should you save? What might this imply for the significance of the right to life of the zygote?

Objection 2:

Pregnancies often end in miscarriage—estimates are between 20 percent and 89 percent (Nepomnaschy et al. 2006). If fetuses have a right to life because of the specialness associated with being human, then we should think that the death of a fetus is as bad as the death of an infant. This means that *the rate of miscarriage would*

be catastrophic—easily the biggest public health crisis of
our time. But this is implausible: miscarriages are not
as bad as famines or tsunamis that kill thousands of
people (which kill far fewer than the number of miscar-
ried fetuses). Indeed, barely any attention is devoted to
reducing the number of miscarriages (see Berg 2016).

> This second objection is similar to the first. Which premise does it challenge?

Reply:

Sometimes we do not perceive things to be as bad as they in fact are. Many of us
do not donate to or help famine victims, even though we are aware that people are
dying of poverty every day. Miscarriages are, in fact, a tragedy, but we often don't
perceive them to be for a number of reasons—for example, they happen subtly and
we are often unaware when they occur. Further, many women who miscarry are
devastated and feel as though they have lost a child. Thus, the objection doesn't
show that there isn't a relevant difference between a fetus and post-birth human—
it shows that *those who raise the miscarriage objection have not grasped the weight of
the miscarriage tragedy.*

Objection 3:

Like the first two objections, this third objection denies (P1). Unlike the first
two objections, it has a positive proposal for what the morally relevant difference
is: *ensoulment*. Ensoulment occurs when a human organism is connected with a
soul, that is, the special immaterial part that makes humans special. You might
have thought that people who believe in souls think that all human organisms
have them from the moment of conception—but this is not necessarily so! While
many do think that ensoulment could occur during conception, others think it
occurs later. For instance, some people thought that ensoulment could not occur
before twinning—the stage at which a zygote divides into two if there are going
to be identical twins (which usually happens within
two weeks of conception). This is because it would be
weird to have two souls in the pre-division zygote.
Instead, ensoulment occurs after there are two sepa-
rate zygotes. But if ensoulment occurs after twinning,
it would also probably occur after that time for single
births and non-identical twins as well.

> Suppose ensoulment occurs within the first two weeks of pregnancy. If it is wrong to kill beings with souls, would this support a pro-life or pro-choice view?

Aristotle and some prominent medieval Christian philosophers, such as the Catholic saint Thomas
Aquinas, believed that *fetuses don't have complete human
souls until a few months into pregnancy* (Swinburne
2007, 315n47). Today, the prominent Christian philosopher Richard Swinburne
argues that ensoulment probably doesn't occur until after the fetus becomes

sentient (2007, 315–16). (See the discussion of sentience earlier in this chapter for considerations about when this might happen.) If the possession of a soul is what makes it wrong to kill humans and fetuses don't possess souls until they become sentient, abortions performed before that point would seem to be morally permissible.

Reply 1:

Because souls are immaterial, we can't observe when ensoulment occurs. This makes it tricky to know for sure when a fetus has a soul. Perhaps we can make an educated guess: maybe, as Swinburne says, it occurs when the fetus becomes conscious. Even so, because we're not sure whether ensoulment has occurred, we might want to exercise caution since violating the right to life is so serious. This is an instance of the **precautionary principle**: when the stakes are high, it's better to err on the side of caution.

> Do you buy the precautionary principle? If so, what does it imply about the morality of abortion?

Reply 2:

This objection relies on the existence of souls, and *there are no souls*. There are various arguments for and against the existence of souls. Descartes famously argues that we are souls (also see Lee and George 2005 for an argument against the existence of souls in the abortion debate). A powerful response to Descartes comes from a contemporary, Princess Elisabeth of Bohemia (1643):

> I ask you please to tell me how the soul of a human being . . . can determine the bodily spirits, in order to bring about voluntary action. For it seems to me that all determination of movement is made by the impulsion of the things moved, by the manner in which it is pushed by that which moves it, or else by the particular qualities and shape of the surface of the latter.

Supposedly then your soul interacts with your body—your soul gets your body moving. The problem is understanding how an immaterial soul could interact with a material body. How deep this problem is—or whether it is a real problem at all—is way beyond the scope of this book. But both proponents and opponents of the soul threshold must get entangled in the debate.

> Do you believe in souls? Given how controversial the existence of souls is, does it seem wise to rely upon the existence of souls in the context of arguing about the right to life?

Reply 3:

Suppose that early-stage fetuses don't have souls and thus don't have a right to life. There might still be some independent reason for why it is impermissible to terminate a pregnancy. For instance, Swinburne himself thinks that early fetuses, lacking souls, do not have a right to life, so that killing them is not equivalent to murder. However, he also suggests that God might forbid abortion anyway because God has ordained pregnancy to produce new human beings, and abortion frustrates this purpose (Swinburne 2007, 316–17). Abortion would then be wrong, not because it violates the fetus's right to life, but because it violates a divine command. So even if ensoulment is a morally relevant difference and (P1) of the original sanctity of life argument is false, the conclusion of that argument—that killing a fetus is impermissible—could still be true. Notice that if this reply is correct, it is an instance of a bad argument that still has a true conclusion (see Chapter 1, p. 16).

4. Personhood: A Pro-Choice Argument

Compare the following two arguments:

Argument 1	Argument 2
(P1) All humans have a right to life.	(P1*) All persons have a right to life.
(P2) If something has a right to life, then killing that thing is impermissible.	(P2*) If something has a right to life, then killing that thing is impermissible.
(C) Killing humans is impermissible.	(C) Killing persons is impermissible.

Argument 1 should look familiar. It is the first part of the sanctity of life argument, which we've discussed at some length in the previous two sections. Argument 2 is almost identical—the only difference is that it replaces *humans* with *persons*. Perhaps this doesn't seem like a very big difference to you. But philosophers argue that *there is an enormous difference between humans and persons*. And in the context of abortion, the difference between humans and persons is key. To see this, let's look at the full sanctity of life argument and then the "persons" version of it:

Argument 1	Argument 2
(P1) All humans have a right to life.	(P1*) All persons have a right to life.
(P2) If something has a right to life, then killing that thing is impermissible.	(P2*) If something has a right to life, then killing that thing is impermissible.
(C) Killing humans is impermissible.	(C) Killing persons is impermissible.
(P3) Fetuses are humans.	(P3*) Fetuses are persons.
(C2) Therefore, killing a fetus is impermissible.	(C2*) Therefore, killing a fetus is impermissible.

In Argument 1, (P3) is uncontroversial. (P3*) in Argument 2 is more controversial, especially if 'person' and 'human' don't refer to the same beings. Some philosophers argue that 'human' is a species-specific term that picks out *Homo sapiens*, while 'person' is a term that picks out beings with special traits (we'll get to these traits in a moment). On this view, while many (or perhaps most) humans qualify as persons, not all do. And as it turns out, many people who recognize the difference between persons and humans think that *fetuses do not qualify as persons though they are humans*. (It's also possible that some non-human entities can qualify as persons, but that's not as important in this context.) Here's a way to visualize this view of humans, persons, and fetuses:

Figure 4

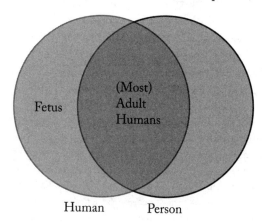

The distinction between humans and persons is at the heart of the pro-choice **personhood argument**. In a nutshell, this argument says that only persons have a right to life, and that since fetuses are not persons, they do not have a right to life. This means that the personhood argument denies (P1) of the sanctity of life argument: *not all humans have a right to life; only the ones who are also persons do*. But before spelling out the argument in detail, let's get clearer on the distinction between persons and humans.

4.1. Personhood

The distinction between person and human has been around for a while. The early modern philosopher John Locke (1689) said that a person is a "forensic" entity that "is a thinking intelligent being, that has reason and reflection, and can consider itself, the same thinking thing, in different times and places; which it does only by that consciousness which is inseparable from thinking." He argued that this person was different from the human organism and even allowed for cases in which one human organism might house two persons:

> If it be possible for the same *man* to have distinct incommunicable consciousness at different times, it is past doubt the same man would

at different times make different *persons*; which, we see, is the sense of mankind in the solemnest declaration of their opinions, human laws not punishing the mad man for the sober man's actions, nor the sober man for what the mad man did, thereby making them two persons. (335)

The scenario Locke envisions is similar to the twist in *Fight Club* (spoiler alert!) where it turns out that Tyler Durden and the unnamed narrator are two distinct personalities (and perhaps persons) who share the same body. Here's an important point to note from the end of Locke's passage: *persons are moral agents*. Part of what motivates the judgment that the mad man and sober man (e.g., Tyler Durden and the narrator) are different persons is the fact that they are not morally responsible for the same actions (e.g., Tyler is responsible for blowing up a building but the narrator is not).

This core idea, that persons—but not humans—are necessarily moral agents is also echoed by the more contemporary philosopher Harry Frankfurt (1971):

There is a sense in which the word 'person' is merely the singular form of 'people' and in which both terms connote no more than membership in a certain biological species. In those senses of the word which are of great philosophical interest, however, the criteria for being a person do not serve primarily to distinguish the members of our own species from members of other species. Rather, they are designed to capture those attributes which are the subject of our most humane concern with ourselves and the source of what we regard as most problematic in our lives. . . . Our concept of ourselves as persons is not to be understood, therefore, as a concept of attributes that are necessarily species-specific. It is conceptually possible that members of novel or even familiar non-human species should be persons; it is also conceptually possible that some members of the human species are not persons. (6)

Frankfurt goes on to suggest that many people mistakenly think 'person' and 'human' are interchangeable terms because plausibly, the only persons we've encountered are humans. However, on his view, many humans are not persons because persons have freedom of the will and non-persons don't, and not all humans have freedom of the will. This difference is significant because having free will makes one a moral agent.

Like Locke, Frankfurt holds that *persons* and *humans* are distinct concepts, and that being a person is intimately connected with being a moral being. This idea, that persons are moral beings, spans different cultures as well as times. According to traditional African thought, *personhood is something*

Do you think it's plausible that some humans are not persons? Do you think it's plausible that some persons are not humans? If yes, try to think of examples of each case.

that is achieved (Menkiti 1984). What marks this achievement is becoming fully incorporated into the community, which involves participating in communal life, fulfilling various obligations, and becoming ethically mature. Though each account of personhood varies slightly, all maintain that persons are not the same as humans and that being part of the moral community is an important part of being a person.

4.2. The Personhood Argument

Our version of the personhood argument is inspired by Mary Anne Warren's famous argument. Warren (1973) picks up on the distinction between persons and humans we've been exploring. She suggests that "the moral community consists of all and *only* people, rather than all and only human beings." She argues that *rights arise from a moral community*. So one is entitled to the right to life **if and only if** one is in the moral community. To support this claim, Warren asks us to consider a space traveler who encounters an alien species. Suppose the space traveler is trying to figure out how to interact with them and whether they have moral rights, such as the right to life. If all and only humans are members of the moral community, the answer is easy: the aliens are not humans, so they are not members of the moral community and do not have rights! But this is clearly not correct, and torturing E.T. for fun seems to violate his rights. Plausibly, some aliens do have rights.

> Suppose you encounter an alien species. What traits would you look for in trying to determine whether they are members of the moral community?

Warren suggests that persons, or members of a moral community, share some central traits:

- **Sentience:** the ability to feel pleasure or pain
- **Reasoning:** the ability to solve new and complicated problems
- **Agency:** the ability to act independently and control the environment
- **Language:** the ability to communicate on different topics
- **Consciousness:** self-awareness

These traits enable participation in the moral community, which explains why only persons are members of that community. And again, being a member of that community is what gives one rights, such as the right to life.

We're now ready for our argument:

(P1) All and only persons have moral rights, such as the right to life.

(P2) Fetuses are not persons.

(C)   Fetuses do not have moral rights, such as the right to life.

We've discussed the motivation for (P1), so let's now look at (P2). Consider the traits that persons have: participating in the moral community, sentience, reasoning, agency, language, and consciousness. *Fetuses do not have any of these traits.* Indeed, when we encounter non-human animals that have the same traits as fetuses, we do not think of them as persons who have a right to life.

> Look closely at the conclusion of the personhood argument. Suppose it's true that fetuses do not have moral rights, such as the right to life. Does that mean that abortion is permissible?

Recall that the pro-choice position is that abortion is always or usually permissible. (C) does not quite get us to that conclusion. An additional premise is required:

(P3) If something does not have a right to life, then it is permissible to kill it.

(C) It is permissible to kill a fetus.

Before turning to objections, let's take stock of our premises. If we define persons as beings that can fully participate in a moral community and that have at least some of the aforementioned traits, then it's clear that fetuses are not persons, and (P2) is true. While many accept (P1), some people do reject it. For instance, someone who holds the sanctity of life argument because they think there is something special about the human *species* would likely reject the claim that all and only persons have moral rights since they would want to hold that even non-person humans have rights. Since we've already touched on these sorts of positions in the sanctity of life argument, we won't rehash them here.

The remaining potential weak point of this argument is (P3), the claim that if something does not have a right to life, then it is permissible to kill it. This is the one we'll focus on in the next section.

> Before reading on, consider whether (P3) is plausible. Is it always permissible to kill things that lack a right to life? To put it another way, is it always permissible to kill things that aren't persons?

5. Objections to Premise 3 of the Personhood Argument

Objection 1:

There are beings that are not persons that it would be wrong to kill. For instance, it would be wrong for you to kill my cat, even though my cat probably is not a person and does not have a right to life. It may even be wrong to kill things like the Great Barrier Reef or a rain forest. Thus, even if fetuses are not persons and do not have a right to life, it might still be impermissible to kill them.

Reply:

Even if the aforementioned things do not have a right to life, *it might be wrong to kill them for other reasons.* Specifically, even though the things themselves do not have a right to life, some person might have a right that's connected to their life. For instance, many people think that killing someone's pet is impermissible because the pet has tremendous value to its person. Similarly, people have some collective right to the Great Barrier Reef or a rain forest or other features of the natural world because they play a crucial role in keeping the Earth habitable or have tremendous natural beauty. Notice that the value to some person(s) makes it wrong to kill these things.

There are situations in which it is wrong to kill a fetus. For instance, it clearly would be wrong to kill your neighbor's fetus. But this is because doing so would violate *your neighbor's right to their fetus.* Things might be different when it comes to your own fetus since *you* are the one who has rights in connection to that fetus. Thus, if you waive your right, it would not be wrong to kill your fetus. Similarly, if a pet owner waives their rights, it may not be wrong to kill their pet. If all members of the moral community got together and unanimously agreed to relinquish their rights connected to the Great Barrier Reef and the world's rain forests, it might not be wrong to kill those, either.

> Suppose your friend gives you permission to kill her puppy. Does this make killing it okay? What does your answer imply about the personhood argument?

Objection 2:

Animal activists insist that killing any animal is wrong. Many people become vegetarians or vegans for precisely this reason. But humans are animals too. So *killing fetuses is wrong, because fetuses are animals—human animals—*even if they are not persons. (For a discussion of animal rights, see Chapter 6.)

Reply 1:

We should ask *why* killing animals is wrong, even if they are not persons and do not have rights. Jeremy Bentham (1789), a philosopher we'll return to later, said, "The question is not, *Can they reason?*, nor *Can they talk?*, but rather, *Can they suffer?*" (1988 [1789], 311).

> As we noted above, some people define 'consciousness' as "the ability to feel pain," rather than as self-awareness. What might this alternative definition of consciousness imply about whether fetuses are persons? What might it imply about the morality of abortion?

Killing animals, especially in painful ways, is wrong. Crucially, as Bentham points out, the reason it is wrong to kill animals is that animals can suffer. But notice that this leaves room for the possibility of killing animals humanely. It also means that it might be okay to kill fetuses, if you can do so painlessly.

Reply 2:

Even if it is generally wrong to kill animals, it is not always wrong. For instance, killing an animal out of necessity to prevent starving is permissible. It can also be permissible to kill animals to prevent them from devouring our crops or infesting our homes. The main point to take away is that reasons that support not killing animals can be outweighed by other factors. Typically, women do not have abortions for fun, but for a pressing need: for their physical or psychological health, or for their financial **well-being**, or the financial well-being of their families. These factors might outweigh whatever reason weighs in favor of refraining from killing a fetus. We'll return to this point in Chapter 4.

Objection 3:

Recall that (P3) says that if something does not have a right to life, then it is permissible to kill it. Also recall that by the lights of the personhood argument, only persons have a right to life. Like fetuses, infants are not persons: they do not have any of the traits central to personhood until they are several months (or even years) old. They thus do not have a right to life. But even if this is true, it's obviously wrong to kill an infant! So (P3) must be false. There are non-person humans—namely, infants—that are clearly impermissible to kill.

Reply 1:

Biting the bullet is a metaphor for accepting a wild implication of an argument rather than attempting to explain why the argument does not have that implication (or just rejecting a premise of the argument). Surprisingly, some proponents of the personhood argument bite the bullet on this argument and accept that it is not wrong to kill infants (see, e.g., Tooley 1973; Warren expresses some sympathy toward this view). From ancient Greece to China under the one-child policy, many cultures have practiced infanticide. However, most of us will think this is an unacceptable—in fact, completely horrendous—bullet to bite, and any view that implies we can kill infants should be rejected. This brings us to a second reply.

Reply 2:

Like the reply to objection 1, there might be independent reasons that it is wrong to kill infants. Typically, infants are loved by their families, and their families have rights connected to them. Killing those infants would be impermissible not because it violates a right that the infant has, but because it violates a right the family has.

Reply to the reply:

But what if the family wants to waive their rights connected to their infant? It's still not permissible to kill their infants. (P3) allows for this possibility, so we should reject (P3).

Reply to the reply to the reply:

One critical difference between the fetus and infant is that the infant can survive being separated from its family while the fetus cannot. This means that the infant can be *adopted* while the fetus can't. As it turns out, there are many people who want to adopt children, and killing an infant instead of giving it up for adoption deprives those people of a tremendous opportunity and joy.

Reply to the reply to the reply to the reply:

This seems to imply that *it is still wrong to kill a fetus if it can survive outside the mother's body.* Recall that most fetuses can survive outside the womb at twenty-four weeks—and sooner and sooner as our technology improves. This suggests that any abortions after twenty-four weeks are still immoral (note that the average pregnancy lasts forty weeks).

> Do you think the personhood argument can adequately explain why killing infants is wrong? Why or why not?

Reply 3:

Even if killing an infant doesn't violate any rights, there might still be reasons not to do it. Plausibly, normalizing infanticide will affect us in other ways. In particular, it would likely be bad for our character and make us more vicious people.

Objection 4:

Some argue that abortion as well as infanticide are wrong, not because of the personhood of the fetus or infant, but because of their *potential personhood*: in the normal and natural course of things, the fetus and infant will develop into persons. One might even say that they are bound to have a future like ours (see Chapter 3). In virtue of this potentiality, perhaps they also have rights.

Reply 1:

Potential beings do not generally have the same rights as actual beings. After all, a prince—a potential king—does not have the same rights as a king, and a fertilized egg—a potential chicken—does not have the same rights as an actual chicken; boiling a chicken while it's alive is wrong, but boiling a fertilized egg is not (see Singer 2011, 138). Similarly, potential beings do not have the same right to life as actual beings: killing an actual person is impermissible, but killing a potential person is not.

Reply 2:

This reply is similar to reply 2 to objection 2. Even if there are reasons to let potential persons develop into actual persons, these reasons are not as strong as the right to life. That means that it is easier to find factors that outweigh whatever reasons there are to preserve potential persons than it is to find factors that outweigh an actual person's right to life. The reasons a mother has for wanting an abortion might very well outweigh the reasons in favor of preserving potential persons, even if those factors do not outweigh an actual person's right to life. We'll revisit this issue of weighing in Chapter 4.

6. Conclusion

We have seen various arguments for and against the claim that fetuses have a right to life, and that this makes it wrong to kill them. Now, we will turn to one of the most influential pro-life arguments: the future like ours argument. This argument claims that it is impermissible to kill fetuses (regardless of whether they are persons) because even though they are not yet like us, they will be in the future.

Further Reading

For defenses of traditional pro-choice arguments, see Warren (1973, 2000), Tooley (1973), Harman (1999, 2003), and Singer (2011). For defenses of traditional pro-life arguments, see Stone (1987), Lee and George (2005), and Kaczor (2015). Relevant readings also include English (1975), Engelhardt (1974), Greasley and Kaczor (2017), and Schouten (2017). For an argument for the view that we are souls, see Swinburne (2013), and for an argument for the view that we are organisms, see Olson (2007).

Chapter 3
The Future of Value Argument

In the last chapter, we investigated whether a fetus has a right to life. Now we turn to what is often taken to be the most powerful contemporary pro-life argument: the **future of value argument**. Originally presented by Don Marquis (1989, 2007), the future of value argument tries to show not only that abortion is **wrong**, but that it is very seriously wrong—that it is as wrong as murder. Interestingly, the argument explains the wrongness of **killing** without appealing to personhood. If successful, it demonstrates that the pro-life position is correct even if the sanctity of life argument fails. It also provides an answer to the personhood argument: it explains why it could be wrong to kill a fetus even if a fetus is not yet a person. As usual, we will first present the argument, and then we will consider some objections and replies.

1. The Argument

The future of value argument makes use of a *general theory of the wrongness of killing*. Killing is uncontroversially wrong in many cases. Killing in self-defense (or perhaps in the context of just war or punishment) is commonly thought to be an exception, but *not the general rule*. Marquis asks why killing us or other people is generally wrong. Presumably killing us or other people does not just happen to be wrong; it is not a cosmic coincidence or brute inexplicable fact that it is wrong. *What then makes killing wrong?* This question is at the heart of the argument. Marquis first presents a general theory of what makes killing wrong, and then he applies this theory to the killing of a fetus to arrive at the conclusion that killing a fetus is wrong.

> Before reading ahead, list some answers of your own to the question: What makes killing wrong? Compare these to the answers considered below.

Here are some candidate answers to the question:

- Killing is wrong because it *causes the victim physical pain.*
- Killing is wrong because it *causes family and friends of the victim emotional distress.*
- Killing is wrong because it *interferes with the victim's preference to continue on living.*

These are natural answers. After all, causing someone physical pain or emotional distress or interfering with their preference is usually wrong. If the idea is that these ingredients are essential to the wrongness of killing—that without them killing wouldn't be wrong—then we can actually construct some pro-choice arguments, quite contrary to Marquis. For example, we could construct this pro-choice argument:

(P1) Killing is wrong only when it interferes with the victim's preferences.

(P2) Abortion does not interfere with the fetus's preferences (since the fetus lacks the ability to form preferences).

(C)   Therefore, abortion is not wrong.

> Can you construct pro-choice arguments for the other candidate explanations of why killing is wrong? You can use the "interfering with the victim's preference" argument as a model.

Alternatively, if killing is wrong only when it causes physical pain or only when it causes family and friends emotional distress, abortion would not be wrong where the fetus doesn't feel pain (in early enough stages of neuronal development) or where the family and friends won't be distressed (in cases where they want the abortion).

Marquis points out that though these candidate explanations can be used to construct pro-choice arguments, the arguments aren't actually good. This is because the candidate explanations they are based on are not actually good explanations for the wrongness of killing. To demonstrate why this is, Marquis makes use of counterexamples.

> Can you think of counter-examples to the following claims?
>
> • All cats are cute.
> • If you study hard, you will get an A.
> • Good things happen to good people.

A **counterexample** is an example designed to *show that there is something wrong with a proposed definition, claim, or principle.* For example, if someone claimed that all mammals live on land, whales and dolphins would be counterexamples to that claim because they are mammals that live in the ocean.

Now that we know what counterexamples are, let's return to Marquis's counterexamples to the candidate explanations for the wrongness of killing. In order to construct counterexamples to those candidate explanations, Marquis looks for cases of *wrongful killing in which there is no physical pain, emotional distress, or preference interference.*

• Why think that causing physical pain is not essential to the wrongness of killing? Imagine a case in which *we are anesthetized*. You slip sleeping pills into our milkshakes, wait until we pass out, and then quickly behead us. That is wrong. But there is no physical pain. Indeed, the murder is not much less wrong than if you had simply stabbed us to death without anesthetic. So physical pain is not essential to the wrongness of killing.

- Why think that causing family or friends emotional distress is not essential to the wrongness of killing? Imagine a case in which *we have no family or friends*. We might be orphaned hermits living a solitary, spiritual life in a desert monastery. Along you come. You might even slip the pills into our milkshakes first. You behead us. That is wrong. But there is no emotional distress caused to family or friends. So causing emotional distress is not essential to the wrongness of killing.

- Why think that interfering with the victim's preferences is not essential to the wrongness of killing? Imagine a case in which *we have no preference to continue living*. We might be lovestruck teenagers, like Romeo and Juliet. We're in love with a guy or a girl, but they reject us. We're in deep despair and enlist your help to end it all. You bring along the milkshakes and pills. You behead us. That is wrong. But there is no preference interference. On the contrary, you helped us realize our preferences. So preference interference is not essential to the wrongness of killing.

Marquis instead answers that killing is wrong because it *deprives the victim of a future of value*. A **future of value** consists in the positive experiences and opportunities

> Can you think of any other answers to the question of what makes killing us wrong? Can you come up with counterexamples to these?

a being has to look forward to. These include creative projects, deep relationships, character development, and moral growth. The idea is that killing is wrong when and because it deprives its victim of all of these things.

Marquis sometimes describes a future of value as a **"future like ours"** (2007, 140). Not just any valuable future counts as a future of value in the relevant sense. For example, fish, chickens, and cows have some value in their futures—some positive experiences—but they do not have the range of experiences and opportunities (including moral opportunities) we do. So it would not be bad—or at least not as bad—to kill them. That's intuitive. Though some animal rights activists might argue that killing animals still deprives them of enough value to make killing them wrong.

But why think that depriving a being of a future of value—a future like ours—is what makes killing wrong? Because *this explanation makes sense of various things*, such as the

- **wrongness of killing us:** if depriving a being of a future of value makes killing wrong, then depriving us of a future of value would make killing us wrong. And killing us would indeed be wrong.

- **wrongness of killing relevantly similar beings:** if depriving us of a future of value makes killing us wrong, then depriving any being that resembles us in having a similar future of value would be wrong too. And it would indeed be wrong to kill other people— or even other extraterrestrials, like E.T., who have similar positive experiences and opportunities to look forward to.

- **degree of the wrongness of killing:** depriving us of a future of value is to deprive us of everything we have to look forward to— it inflicts the greatest possible loss we can suffer. Depriving us of everything we have to look forward to is very seriously wrong. So if depriving us of a future of value makes killing us wrong, then it would make killing us seriously wrong. And killing us would indeed be seriously wrong.

The idea also fits in with our intuitions about the badness of death generally. We fear death—and especially a premature death—because of all the good experiences and opportunities we'd be deprived of: "People with AIDS or cancer who know they are dying believe, of course, that dying is a very bad thing for them. They believe that the loss of a future to them that they would otherwise have experienced is what makes their premature death a very bad thing for them" (Marquis 1989, 190). If this is what makes death bad, then it should also make being killed, a particular kind of death, bad—and the action of killing wrong for bringing about such badness.

Marquis's answer also does better than all the other answers. It makes sense of the wrongness of killing in all the counterexamples: it makes sense of why killing would be wrong in the cases where we are anesthetized, have no family or friends, and are suicidal; suicidal people do have positive experiences and opportunities to look forward to, even though they don't realize it in their distraught state.

Next Marquis contends that *fetuses, in the usual and natural course of things, also have futures of value.* Indeed, they have futures quite like ours—after all, we were once fetuses ourselves. So it follows that killing fetuses is wrong. And not only is killing fetuses wrong. Killing fetuses is wrong for the same reason that killing us would be wrong. Killing fetuses is about as wrong as killing us would be. Since killing us would be very seriously wrong, killing fetuses turns out to be very seriously wrong too. Marquis (1989) concludes that abortion is very seriously wrong:

> The claim that the primary wrong-making features of a killing is the loss to the victim of the value of its future has obvious consequences for the ethics of abortion. The future of a standard fetus includes a set of experiences, projects, activities, and such which are identical with the futures of adult human beings and are identical with the futures of young children. Since the reason that is sufficient to explain why it is wrong to kill human beings after the time of birth is a reason that also applies to fetuses, it follows that abortion is prima facie seriously wrong. (192)

We can simplify the future of value argument as follows:

(P1)   Depriving a being of a future like ours is wrong.

(P2)   Abortion deprives a being of a future like ours.

(C)   Therefore, abortion is wrong.

(P1) is based on Marquis's theory of the wrongness of killing. (P2) is supported by the fact that in the usual course of nature fetuses will develop into people like us, with experiences and opportunities like our own.

We note some rare exceptions. Fetuses with severe defects, like anencephaly, will not naturally develop into people like us. They will die shortly after or even before birth. They do not have futures of value. So abortion in such cases would not be wrong—at least not for the main reason that killing us would be wrong. This verdict is quite intuitive; even many pro-lifers will agree that abortion in the case of such severe defects is not wrong. Marquis advertises his argument as a pro-life argument in cases that lack the complications of severe birth defects, or where the pregnancy threatens the life of the mother, or is the result of rape.

> Let's think about a couple of these complicated cases. Do you think that abortion is permissible when pregnancy threatens a mother's life? How about when the pregnancy is the result of rape? Do you think that Marquis's argument can yield a pro-life answer in these cases? (For more on these questions, see Card 2006.)

The future of value argument has to do with the potential of the fetus—the future and opportunities in store for it makes killing it wrong. Nevertheless, it is quite different from the potentiality argument we saw in Chapter 2. Recall that argument depended on the general idea that potential X's have the same rights as actual X's—so that if killing an actual person is wrong then killing a potential person (a fetus) is also wrong. This turned out to be false; recall the chicken and egg counterexample. But the future of value argument does not assume any such ideas: *it argues that killing the potential person is wrong, not on the grounds that potential X's have the same rights as actual X's, but on the grounds that killing the potential person deprives it of a future of value.*

> Recall that good arguments have plausible premises that lead to the conclusion. So an objection to an argument must either challenge the premises or show that the premises don't lead to the conclusion. Before reading ahead, can you think of any objections to the future of value argument?

2. Objections and Replies

It looks like (P1) and (P2) lead to the conclusion of the future of value argument. If the argument goes wrong, then something must be wrong with one or both of the premises. Has Marquis provided adequate support to these premises? Are there any reasons for thinking the premises false? We will consider objections against each premise in order.

2.1. Objections to Premise 1

Objection 1:

The first objection is known as the *contraception objection.* The objection is that if depriving a being of a future of value is wrong, then contraception is wrong, because by using contraception we prevent the conception of a fetus and thus deprive it of a future of value. But contraception is not wrong. So depriving a being of a future of value is not wrong. The objection essentially mirrors the future of value argument. Here is an argument with the same shape:

(P1) Depriving a being of a future of value is wrong.

(P2*) Contraception deprives a being of a future of value.

(C*) Therefore, contraception is wrong.

Since the conclusion is wrong, the argument must go wrong. Given that the entire point of contraception is to prevent a life, which will have a future of value, it seems like (P2*) is pretty plausible. That leaves us with (P1) as the only culprit.

Reply 1:

Some people (e.g., many Catholics) think contraception is wrong. In other words (C*) is true. Since the argument gets the conclusion right, there's no reason to think that either (P1) or (P2*) are false.

Reply to the reply:

Even among those who think that using contraception is wrong, most do not think that *contraception is as wrong as abortion*. So we could construct the contraception objection against them this way:

(P1) If depriving a being of a future of value makes abortion wrong, then it makes contraception as wrong as abortion.

(P2) But contraception is not as wrong as abortion (even if both are wrong).

(C) Therefore, depriving a being of a future of value does not make abortion wrong.

Reply 2:

Marquis replies that *there is a relevant difference between abortion and contraception*. While abortion deprives a being of a future of value, contraception does not. Marquis thus rejects (P2*) of the contraception argument, while he accepts (P2) of the future of value argument.

> It's often said that abstinence is the most effective form of contraception. Can we construct an "abstinence objection" that mirrors the contraception objection to object to the future of value argument?

Why does contraception not deprive a being of a future of value? Because *there is no determinate being on the scene to be deprived*. What could count as the being deprived of a future of value in the case of contraception? A sperm cell? An egg cell? No particular sperm cell is deprived of a future of value: no sperm cell on its own in the usual and natural course of things has a future like ours. No particular egg cell is deprived of a future of value: no egg cell on its own in the usual course of things has a future like ours. And there's no reason that the sperm cell rather than the egg cell is the being deprived of the future of value—and vice versa.

Marquis considers further possibilities. One might attempt to avoid these problems by insisting that contraception deprives both the sperm and the egg separately of a valuable future like ours. On this alternative, too many futures are lost. Contraception was supposed to be wrong because it deprived us of one future of value, not two. One might attempt to avoid this problem by holding that contraception deprives the combination of sperm and ovum of a valuable future like ours. But here the definite article misleads. At the time of contraception, there are hundreds of millions of sperm, one or so egg(s), and millions of *possible* combinations of all of these. There is no *actual* combination at all. Is the subject of the loss to be a merely possible combination? Which one? This alternative does not yield an actual subject of harm either (Marquis 1989, 201).

Only after the sperm and egg cells fuse to form a new being—a fetus—is there something on the scene to be deprived of a future of value. However, recall from the previous chapter that for the first two weeks of pregnancy, it is still possible for *twinning* to occur. Then, plausibly, there's no determinate individual on the scene for the first two weeks of pregnancy either. So Marquis's argument might not show that abortion in those *very early stages* is wrong. Pro-lifers who take abortion to be wrong from conception might not get enough mileage out of Marquis's argument.

> Can we reply to Marquis's reply by saying that *the possible fetus* that would have been formed (if contraception had not been used) is deprived of a future of value? Are there such beings as possible fetuses? (For more on these questions, see Roberts 2010.)

Objection 2:

The next objection against premise 1 is the *equality objection*. This objection alleges that if depriving a being of a future of value is wrong, then depriving a being of more of a future of value is more wrong. Since a younger person typically has more of a future of value than does an older person—younger people usually have more life left to live—killing the younger person would typically deprive them of more future of value, and so it would be worse than killing the older person. But, the objection goes, *killing a younger person is not worse than killing an older person.* So depriving a being of a future of value is not wrong.

Reply:

There are two points to consider in light of the equality objection. The first is that, *maybe, killing a younger person is actually worse than killing an older person.* This might not be so apparent when they are close enough in age and opportunities, for example, killing someone who is thirty years old versus killing someone twenty years old. But, the reply goes, where the age difference is greater it is apparent: many would admit that killing a one-year-old infant is worse than killing a hundred-year-old person who is on their deathbed. Or, at least, what the objection requires—that killing the one-year-old is as bad as killing the hundred-year-old—is not obviously true.

The second (which is put forward by Marquis) is that to deny that the wrongness of taking away a future of value means *that it is more wrong to take away more of a future of value.* For instance, some might think that killing, say, a ten-year-old is worse than killing a one-year-old. The "more future of value, more wrong" principle would get the wrong result in this case. Marquis does not claim that depriving a being of a future of value is the only ingredient to the wrongness of killing. He allows that causing physical pain, or causing family or friends emotional distress, or preference interference can also *contribute* to the wrongness of killing: killing us would be wrong for depriving us of a future of value; it would be more wrong if it deprived us of a future of value *and* caused us physical pain or interfered with our preferences; and it would be even more wrong still if it did all this and caused our family and friends emotional distress. Enough of these other ingredients could increase the wrongness of killing someone older so that it is not less wrong than killing someone younger.

Marquis (2007) considers the ingredient of *admirability*:

> one might hold, as does Feldman (1992, p. 184), that in addition to the wrongness of killing that has its basis in the future life of which the victim is deprived, killing an individual is also made wrong by the admirability of an individual's past behaviour. Now the amount of admirability will presumably vary directly with age, whereas the amount of deprivation will vary inversely with age. This tends to equalize the wrongness of murder. (145)

In addition, an older person might have more family and friends than a newborn would. Killing the younger person would deprive her of more of a future of value, but killing the older person would cause more emotional distress to family and friends—because he has more family and friends. Also, an older person has life plans, projects, and goals, and a newborn does not, and so killing the older person might interfere with more of their preferences than would killing the newborn. The ingredients in each case could balance each other out so that neither case of killing is worse than the other.

> Imagine a case where admiralty is held fixed. Perhaps someone older does not have greater admirability (they are a mean person) or more family and friends (they're a hermit) than someone younger, so their admiralty is perfectly equal. Do you think that killing the younger person would be worse? If so, does that support the objection or the reply?

2.2. Objection to Premise 2

Let's now turn to an objection to (P2), which says that abortion deprives a being of a future of value. The premise assumes that fetuses are beings with futures of value: in the usual course of things they develop into people like us, with experiences and opportunities like ours. The objection is that fetuses are not beings with a future of value. They do not in the usual course of things develop into people like us. The objection contends that the being that has a future of value is something other than the fetus. We, who have a future of value, were never fetuses. There are various ways of spelling this out. Here are two ways:

> **Way 1:** *We are either immaterial souls (or soul-body combinations)—not mere bodies.* Souls and bodies are different things. Fetuses are early stages of bodies. Souls are immaterial parts. So souls and fetuses are different things. Our souls connect to our bodies at some stage. Prior to this stage, only the body (fetus) exists. That thing on its own is not us, since we are souls (or soul-body combinations). So the fetus on its own does not have a future of value. If that's right, then killing a fetus that is not yet connected to a soul doesn't deprive that fetus of a future of value. Killing the fetus will only deprive something of a life of value *once the soul has connected to the fetus.* If the soul does not attach to the fetus until a later stage of the pregnancy, then many abortions will not be wrong—at least not for depriving the soul of a future of value. (This parallels an objection to the sanctity of life argument which we considered in Chapter 1.)
>
> **Way 2:** *We are streams of consciousness.* A **stream of consciousness** is a person's thoughts, feelings, and experiences, perceived as a continuous flow. Streams of consciousness and bodies are different things. Fetuses are bodies in an early stage. So streams of consciousness and fetuses are different things. But the stream of consciousness appears in a body—realized in the brain—at some stage. Once the stream is there, killing the body ends the stream and deprives it of a future of value. If the stream is not present in the fetus, then killing the fetus does not end the stream and deprive it of a future of value. If the stream only emerges in the fetus's brain at a late stage of pregnancy, then killing the fetus at an earlier stage does not detach the stream and deprive it of a future of value. Killing the fetus at the later stage would deprive the stream of a future of value, but if that stage is late enough, most abortions will not be wrong—at least not for depriving the stream of a future of value.

If Way 1 or Way 2 is right, (P2) is false and the future of value argument fails. So *what is the being that has a future of value?* Is it the fetus only? A soul (or soul-body combination)? A stream of consciousness? In answering this question, it helps to consider what we are. Are we merely bodies that began as fetuses? Souls (or soul-body combinations)? Streams of consciousness?

> Can you think of other ways fetuses might not be the beings with a future of value?

> Some people believe in life after death—in heaven, resurrection, or reincarnation. If there is life after death, does killing someone deprive them of a future of value since they go on? Can someone who believes in life after death still accept Marquis's theory of the wrongness of killing?

3. Conclusion

The future of value argument contends that killing a fetus is wrong even if it is not a person. This is because even if it lacks personhood, it still has a future of value like ours. In our next and final chapter on the (im)permissibility of abortion, we turn to a famous pro-choice argument that contends that abortion is not impermissible even if we grant that the fetus is a person with a right to life and a future of value like ours. Get ready to ask: Would you kill the violinist?

Further Reading

The future of value argument is put forward by Marquis (1989; 2007). Objections are leveled by Cudd (1990), McInerney (1990), Norcross (1990), Sinnott-Armstrong (1997), Korcz (2002), Card (2006), Strong (2008), and Reitan (2015). Some replies from Marquis can be found in Marquis (1994; 2009). Different accounts of the wrongness of killing, with different implications for abortion, can be found in McMahan (2002) and Tännsjö (2015).

Chapter 4
The Famous Violinist Argument

1. Introduction

In the last two chapters, we discussed pro-life arguments that take the fetus to have a right to life or a future of value like ours. We now turn to an influential pro-choice argument—the *famous violinist argument*, presented by Judith Thomson (1971). Thomson thinks that these pro-life arguments go wrong. For the sake of argument, she grants that the fetus is a person and does have a right to life. She doesn't necessarily believe this; instead she relies on premises that even a pro-lifer would accept. (You may remember from the introduction that good arguments involve plausible premises; Thomson's tactic—which is a good one for you to adopt when constructing your own arguments—is to use premises that even her opponents will find plausible.) She wants to show that *even if fetuses do have a right to life, that would not mean that abortion is **wrong**.* In a nutshell, her argument suggests that even if the fetus has a right to life, that right does not mean that it is wrong to kill it, because *that right does not entail a right to another person's body*. Again, we will first present the argument, and then we will consider some objections and replies.

2. The Argument

Thomson's (1971) paper is full of little stories. These are called **thought experiments**. Thought experiments are *imaginary cases*; they are often *designed to lead the person considering them to accept a particular judgment with the aim of proving a philosophical point*. We'll discuss a few of the ones Thomson presents. The first, and the source of the title of this chapter, is a story about a famous violinist:

> You wake up in the morning and find yourself back to back in bed with an unconscious violinist. A famous unconscious violinist. He has been found to have a fatal kidney ailment, and the Society of Music Lovers has canvassed all the available medical records and found that you alone have the right blood type to help. They have therefore kidnapped you, and last night the violinist's circulatory system was plugged into yours, so that your kidneys can be used to extract poisons from his blood as well as your own. The director of the hospital now tells you, "Look, we're sorry the Society of Music Lovers did this to you—we would never have

permitted it if we had known. But still, they did it, and the violinist is now plugged into you. To unplug you would be to kill him. But never mind, it's only for nine months. By then he will have recovered from his ailment, and can safely be unplugged from you." (48–49)

Thomson next asks: *Are you morally obligated to stay connected to the violinist?*

> Let's pause here and let you answer the question. Do you think you're morally obligated to stay connected to the violinist for nine months?

Thomson says that you *are not* morally obligated to stay connected. This means that it is permissible for you to unplug yourself. She points out that you would not be convinced even if the hospital director points out that all people have a right to life, that the violinist is a person, and thus, that the violinist has a right to life. After all, you already know that the violinist is a person and has a right to life. You also would not be convinced that you are morally obligated to stay plugged in if the hospital director pointed out to you that if you unplug yourself, you will kill the violinist. Again, you already know that unplugging yourself will kill the violinist. The entire point is that you are not morally obligated to stay connected, *even though the violinist has a right to life and even though you will kill the violinist by unplugging yourself.*

So here's the claim that the thought experiment is meant to support: "the right to life consists not in the right not to be killed, but rather in the *right not to be killed unjustly*" (Thomson 1971, 57). The violinist's right to life does not entail that it is wrong for you to disconnect precisely because the violinist has no right to use your body for nine months. The right does entail that under ordinary circumstances, it is wrong for you to shoot the violinist, or hit the violinist with your car. Of course, you *can* stay plugged in if you want, and it would even be admirable if you did. But in general, no one, including the violinist, has a right to use your body.

With the lesson from the famous violinist in mind, it's time to start constructing our pro-choice argument. For our first premise, we'll start with the judgment about the case itself:

(P1) Unplugging from (and thus killing) the violinist is not wrong.

Nothing we've said thus far directly relates to fetuses. But you've probably noticed some similarities between the predicament the violinist is in and the situation that fetuses face. Like the violinist, fetuses require being "plugged into" someone's body for nine months in order to survive. Both, Thomson is willing to concede, have a right to life. Similarly, like you (the person keeping the violinist alive), the person keeping the fetus alive faces a huge imposition. Staying plugged in requires sacrificing your bodily autonomy for an extended amount of time. Importantly, neither the violinist nor the fetus is entitled to the body of the person sustaining their life—according to Thomson, that is. These considerations bring us to our second premise:

> (P2) Unplugging from (and thus killing) the violinist is *relevantly similar* to "unplugging" from (and thus killing) a fetus. (So if unplugging from, and thus killing, the violinist is not wrong, "unplugging" from, and thus killing, a fetus is not wrong.)

Putting (P1) and (P2) together, we get our conclusion:

> (C) "Unplugging" from (and thus killing) a fetus is not wrong.

Before moving to objections, there is an interesting thing to note about this argument. It is what's called an *analogical argument*. In an analogical argument, we *start with some observed similarities between two things, and we infer a further unobserved similarity.* For instance, domestic cats and lions have many similarities. They are both members of the cat family, have claws and teeth, sleep most of the day, and occasionally kill things. Here's something we know about domestic cats: they love catnip. Should we also then infer that lions like catnip because they're similar to domestic cats? Here's another way to put the question: does the fact that cats and lions are similar support the conclusion that lions also like catnip?

> Venture a guess (if you don't already know the answer)! Do lions like catnip?

It turns out that lions (and most other big cats) do like catnip. This is because all cats share an underlying biological trait connected to catnip: they are attracted to nepetalactone, an oil that catnip contains. Notice that the similarity between cats and lions supports the conclusion that lions also like catnip. So we can say the following analogical argument is a good one:

> (i) Domestic cats like catnip.
> (ii) Domestic cats are relevantly similar to lions. (So if domestic cats like catnip, then lions do.)
> (iii) Therefore, lions like catnip.

If we inquired about whether humans—who are less similar to cats than lions are—like catnip, the analogy between humans and cats wouldn't be strong enough to support the conclusion that humans like catnip. (As it turns out, catnip has the opposite effect in cats than it does in humans; while it is a stimulant for cats, it is actually a sedative for humans and is often an ingredient in nighttime teas.) So the following analogical argument is not a good one:

(i)   Domestic cats like catnip.

(ii)   Domestic cats are relevantly similar to humans. (So if domestic cats like catnip, humans do.)

(iii) Therefore, humans like catnip.

The argument is not good because (ii) is false since domestic cats and humans are not similar. Here's our first lesson about arguments from analogy: *the more similar the two cases are, the more strongly they support the conclusion about the unobserved similarity.*

> Do you like catnip?

Bringing this back to the violinist and fetus cases, the argument will work better the more similar the cases are. As we'll see, one of the objections to the argument centers on whether the violinist and fetus cases are similar enough to support the conclusion.

But here's an important thing to note about arguments from analogy. They can sometimes lead us astray. We've already discussed the similarities between domestic cats and lions. Domestic cats purr. Should we conclude that lions also purr?

> Venture a guess (if you don't already know the answer)! Do lions purr?

It turns out that lions do not purr. Lions and cats are not analogous when it comes to purring. Most big cats (except cheetahs) cannot purr because of the structure of their skulls. (On the plus side, this is the structure that enables them to roar.) Smaller cats have different skull structures and can purr, but they can't roar. So it turns out this analogical argument isn't good:

(i)   Domestic cats purr.

(ii)   Domestic cats are relevantly similar to lions. (So if domestic cats purr, so do lions.)

(iii) Therefore, lions purr.

Like (ii) in the human argument, (ii) in this argument is false. But how can this be when domestic cats and lions are similar? The crucial point is that they are not *relevantly* similar when it comes to purring, though they are when it comes to catnip. Here's the important lesson: *arguments from analogy work best when the observed similarities between the two cases are relevant to explaining the unobserved similarity.*

Bringing this back to the violinist and fetus cases, the argument from analogy is going to work best if the observed similarities between the two are relevant to explaining the unobserved similarity—the conclusion about the permissibility of "unplugging" and thus killing. As we'll see, another objection to this argument is whether the observed similarities are relevant to explaining the unobserved similarity.

> Before reading ahead, do you think that the violinist and fetus cases are *relevantly similar*? What are some potential dissimilarities?

3. Objections and Replies

There are two primary ways in which philosophers have objected to Thomson's argument. The first way centers on (P1) and claims that contrary to what Thomson says, it is wrong to unplug yourself from the violinist. The second way centers on (P2). Even if it's not wrong to unplug yourself from the violinist, it is wrong to "unplug" yourself from the fetus because the cases are not relevantly similar. We'll consider each of these ways in turn.

3.1. Objections to Premise 1

Not everyone agrees that it is not wrong to unplug yourself from the violinist. To borrow an example from John Martin Fischer (1991), suppose you are staying in an extremely remote cabin when a stranger stumbles upon you. He will die from exposure unless you let him enter your cabin, but unfortunately, because of weather and your remote location, a rescue party will not arrive for nine months. Accordingly, you must choose between feeding and sheltering him in your cabin for nine months or preventing him from entering, thus allowing him to die.

Fischer believes that it is wrong to kick the stranger out of your shelter, thus condemning him to die from the elements. After all, the stranger is innocent and has not violated any of his duties—he was kidnapped before finding him-

> Do you agree that it is wrong to kick the stranger out of your shelter?

self at your doorstep. Further, though allowing him to stay is of great inconvenience to you, dying is of even greater inconvenience to him! Sometimes life presents you with situations in which you must make a sacrifice for someone else's greater good. Sure, you have a right to your property, but that right is outweighed by the stranger's dire need.

Fischer's thought experiment is intended to be analogous to Thomson's violinist case. This means that we can construct the following argument from it:

(P1) It is wrong to evict the stranger.

(P2) The stranger is relevantly similar to the violinist. (So if it is wrong to evict the stranger, it is wrong to unplug the violinist.)

(C)   Therefore, it is wrong to unplug the violinist.

If this is right, then we can add Thomson's claim that the violinist and fetus cases are analogous, thus arriving at an opposite conclusion to the one at which she arrived:

(P3)   The violinist is relevantly similar to a fetus. (If unplugging the violinist is wrong, so is unplugging the fetus.)

(C2)   Therefore, it is wrong to unplug a fetus.

Reply:

Thomson (1971) anticipates this type of argument and makes the fetus-mother analogue explicit:

> Grant that the fetus is a person from the moment of conception. . . . Every person has a right to life. So the fetus has a right to life. No doubt the mother has a right to decide what shall happen in and to her body; everyone would grant that. But surely a person's right to life is stronger and more stringent than the mother's right to decide what happens in and to her body, and so outweighs it. So the fetus may not be killed; an abortion may not be performed. (48)

In response, *she doubles down on her claim that the right to life does not entitle one to use of another person's body, even if that use is minimal.* She writes:

> In some views having a right to life includes having a right to be given at least the bare minimum one needs for continued life. But suppose that what in fact IS the bare minimum a man needs for continued life is something he has no right at all to be given? If I am sick unto death, and the only thing that will save my life is the touch of Henry Fonda's cool hand on my fevered brow. Then all the same, I have no right to be given the touch of Henry Fonda's cool hand on my fevered brow. It would be frightfully nice of him to fly in from the West Coast to provide it. It would be less nice, though no doubt well meant, if my friends flew out to the West Coast and brought Henry Fonda back with them. But I have no right at all against anybody that he should do this for me. (55)

It seems that Thomson is really committed to the claim that the right to life does not entail the right to using another person's body, no matter how minimal that use is. And perhaps there is something about this that resonates with you. Why should anyone be entitled to *your* body? Plausibly, the right to life only entails the right to not have others unjustly interfere with your life. It doesn't entail that others have to sacrifice their bodies to sustain your life.

Reply to the reply:

Forget the talk of rights. Doesn't it just *seem* obvious that if there is some small thing that you can do to save someone's life you ought to do it? If you're sick unto death, and all I have to do is touch your fevered brow to save you, isn't it wrong for me to refuse to do so? We'll talk more about this in Chapter 11 on charity, but it seems pretty plausible that if you can save someone's life by sacrificing something much less significant than a life, it would be wrong not to.

Reply to the reply to the reply:

Even if it is true that it would be wrong to not sacrifice something of much less significance than a life in order to save someone, sacrificing one's body for nine months of pregnancy, followed by birth, is not "something of much less significance than a life." Some pregnancies are incredibly taxing on the mother's body and even require months of bed rest—all while being in extreme discomfort. Giving birth is excruciatingly painful and can last for days. It's pretty plausible that the physical pain of giving birth is equivalent to some forms of torture, and most people do not believe that you would be **morally required** to sustain a day of torture to save someone. Furthermore, being pregnant and giving birth permanently changes one's body, sometimes in extremely significant ways. So, even if it is true that we can be obligated to sacrifice to save someone's life, the imposition on bodily autonomy in the case of pregnancy is so great that it very well could be permissible to decline saving someone.

3.2. Objections to Premise 2

Objection 1:

The violinist and fetus cases are not relevantly similar. Unplugging the violinist spares you far more difficulty than aborting the fetus does. *Being plugged into the violinist is much harder than the typical pregnancy.* Being plugged in means that you are bedridden alongside a violinist—which means that for nine months you cannot travel (cannot go to work, family occasions, or entertainment) and that you have no privacy (no conversational or physical intimacy with your friends or family). Pregnancy is usually not so demanding until the very end—the pregnant woman typically is still mobile and still has privacy. Since one stands to lose more from being plugged into the violinist than from pregnancy, unplugging from the violinist is permissible whereas abortion is not (see Hursthouse 1987, 202–3).

Reply 1:

Even if being attached to the violinist is usually more demanding than pregnancy, some pregnancies are as demanding—or even more demanding. Some pregnancies do keep the mother bedridden and/or gravely ill. The violinist analogy would apply to, and show that abortion is permissible in, these cases. However, this reply may concede too much to the objection. Depending on how many pregnancies are in fact like this, the violinist analogy may not apply to many cases of abortion.

Reply 2:

The objection underestimates the demands of even the typical pregnancy and birth. Pregnancy can affect the mother in every aspect of her life. Here are some typical negative effects:

> **Physical**: nausea; vomiting; headaches; backaches; bleeding gums; nosebleeds; frequent urination; constipation; indigestion; cramps; heartburn; weight gain; irreparable damage to one's body; excruciating pain; potential death
>
> **Emotional**: mood swings; anxiety; tiredness; forgetfulness; stress; impatience; irritability; weepiness; depression; changes to libido; cravings for foods; postpartum depression (which can include radical changes to one's desire to parent the child)

> What other burdens might go along with pregnancy and birth? It's also worth considering: how many of these burdens can be avoided with abortion? Are there additional burdens that an abortion might introduce?

Objection 2:

The second objection suggests that there is another difference between aborting the fetus and unplugging the violinist: the difference between **killing** and **letting die**. Killing is actively taking a life, whereas letting someone die is more passive. We let people die when we don't intervene to prevent their death. For example, suppose you could give up your own food to feed a starving child but choose not to. You've let the child die. This seems less bad than stealing food from the child so they starve. So it seems that *killing is worse than letting someone die.*

Now, consider this distinction in the abortion and violinist cases. Though Thomson says that unplugging the violinist is equivalent to killing, it really looks a lot more like letting the violinist die: he can no longer use your kidneys and will soon thereafter die. In contrast, in abortion the fetus is usually not left to die, but killed: typically, the procedure kills it before it is removed from the body.

The violinist case would be more analogous if you didn't merely unplug the violinist, but had to kill the violinist in order to unplug him. Suppose that the only way of extracting yourself was by actively killing the violinist. Perhaps instead of just unplugging, you would have to strangle him in order to unplug yourself. Would this be **morally permissible**? Once we modify the case to preserve the analogy, it's not as obvious that killing the violinist is permitted. And if it's not permissible to kill the violinist in the modified case, the modified case could even turn out to show that abortion is wrong—not that it is permissible (see Finnis 1973, 139–40).

Reply 1:

Thomson does not say that killing the fetus is permissible. What she says is that abortion by *disconnecting* is not wrong. If there were a way to remove the fetus from the womb so that the fetus didn't die, Thomson thinks we should definitely do that. (Unfortunately, medical technology does not yet allow us to do that until about twenty-four weeks.) Similarly, if there were a way to unplug without the violinist dying, we should do that. As Thomson (1971) puts it:

> I am not arguing for the right to secure the death of the unborn child. It is easy to confuse these two things in that up to a certain point in the life of the fetus it is not able to survive outside the mother's body; hence removing it from her body guarantees its death. But they are importantly different. I have argued that you are not morally required to spend nine months in bed, sustaining the life of that violinist, but to say this is by no means to say that if, when you unplug yourself, there is a miracle and he survives, you then have a right to turn round and slit his throat. You may detach yourself even if this costs him his life; you have no right to be guaranteed his death, by some other means, if unplugging yourself does not kill him. (66)

Reply 2:

There is no morally relevant difference between killing and letting die. If letting the violinist die is not wrong, then neither is killing the violinist. Since letting the violinist die is not wrong, killing the violinist is not wrong. The idea that there is no moral difference between killing and letting die is supported by the following scenarios (from Rachels 1975):

> **Scenario 1**: Smith will inherit a fortune if his six-year-old cousin dies. Smith sneaks into the bathroom when the child is in the bath, and drowns him. Smith cleans the scene so that it looks like an accident. He inherits the fortune.
> **Scenario 2**: Jones will inherit a fortune if his six-year-old cousin dies. Jones sneaks into the bathroom, planning to drown the child in the bath. As Jones enters, the child slips and hits his head. Jones stands ready to hold his head under the water if need be. But, there is no need. Jones inherits the fortune.

Smith's acting is not worse than Jones's refraining to act; both are equally bad. Killing and letting die have the same moral status. If a case of killing is wrong (as in Scenario 1), then a similar case of letting die is wrong (as in Scenario 2). And if a case of letting die is not wrong (as in the original violinist case), then a case of killing is not wrong (as in the case where you strangle the violinist). By analogy, killing the fetus is not wrong (compare Thomson 1973, 158–59).

Reply to Reply 2:

While some cases (such as Scenario 1 and Scenario 2) support the idea that there is no moral difference between killing and letting die, other cases support the idea that there is a difference (from Foot 2002, 81–82):

> **Scenario 3**: We are hurrying in our jeep to save five people who are all in immediate danger of dying. We hear of a single person who is in danger elsewhere. If we go and save him, we won't reach the other five and they will die. Regretfully, we let the one die and go save the five.
> **Scenario 4**: We are hurrying in our jeep on a narrow, rocky path to save five people. This is the only route we can take to save them. A man is injured on the path, and the only way to save the five is to drive over him. If we stop, we can save him, but we won't reach the other five in time and they will die. We drive over the guy in the path, killing him, and save the other five.

Scenario 3 is a case of letting die and Scenario 4 is a case of killing. Scenarios 3 and 4 look morally different: many of us would say that what we do in Scenario 3 is permissible, but what we do in Scenario 4 is not. So Scenarios 1 and 2, on the one hand, and Scenarios 3 and 4, on the other, pull us in opposite directions. In the end, we have three options:

> **Option 1:** Killing and letting die are morally different, and something has gone wrong in our verdicts about Scenarios 1 and 2.
> **Option 2:** Killing and letting die are morally the same, and something has gone wrong in our verdicts about Scenarios 3 and 4.
> **Option 3:** Killing and letting die are sometimes morally different and sometimes morally the same.

Which option is right? Whether this objection works depends on the answer to this question. If Option 1 is right, then the difference between the abortion and violinist cases weakens Thomson's argument. If Option 2 is right, then the difference is not morally relevant and does not weaken the argument. If Option 3 is right, then killing the violinist is probably morally worse than letting the violinist die. After all, our initial impression about these cases (like our impression about Scenarios 3 and 4) is that killing the violinist is morally worse than letting him die. Analogously, there would be a moral difference between killing a fetus and letting it die, such that abortion is usually wrong. However, we will soon consider an analogy that may show that killing a fetus is not wrong.

Objection 3:

The third objection is that the violinist differs from the fetus in that the violinist has become connected to you by no voluntary act of your own, whereas the fetus typically becomes attached to the mother by a voluntary act of hers (consensual sex). The famous violinist argument shows that abortion is permissible where the fetus becomes attached to the mother without consensual sex; thus, *the analogy shows that abortion is permissible where the pregnancy is the result of rape*. But the moral does not extend beyond such cases to pregnancies resulting from consensual sex.

Reply:

Thomson's reply to the objection is that if the argument shows that abortion is permissible where the pregnancy results from rape, then it shows that abortion is permissible in other cases too. Otherwise we would be saying that fetuses conceived from rape have different rights from other fetuses. On the assumption that the fetus is a person—which Thomson is granting for the sake of argument—we would be saying that people have different rights depending on whether or not they were conceived out of rape. But *people do not have different rights depending on how they were conceived*; as Thomson (1971) puts it: "Surely the question of whether you have a right to life at all, or how much of it you have, shouldn't turn on the question of whether or not you are a product of a rape" (49). The moral that the right of the fetus to life does not entail a right to use the mother's body must similarly hold for all fetuses, however conceived.

The critic might reply that the difference in the permissibility of abortion in cases of rape versus cases of consensual sex is not due to differences in the rights of the respective fetuses. Rather, the difference is due to the fact that, in having consensual sex, the mother voluntarily does something she understands can result in pregnancy, and thus she undertakes the responsibilities associated with pregnancy should pregnancy occur. This means that *she acquires duties towards the fetus* that she would not have in the case of pregnancy resulting from non-consensual sex. This difference in duties explains why abortion of a fetus that results from consensual sex is wrong. In other words, how the fetus is conceived does not determine whether it has a right to life, but it does determine whether the mother has a duty to allow the fetus the use of her body.

In response, Thomson (1971) presents three new thought experiments to try to show that *even where the pregnancy results from consensual sex where the mother understands the potential for pregnancy, abortion is permissible*. Here's the first story:

> If the room is stuffy, and I therefore open a window to air it, and a burglar climbs in, it would be absurd to say, "Ah, now he can stay, she's given him a right to the use of her house—for she is partially responsible for his presence there, having voluntarily done what enabled him to get in, in full knowledge that there are such things as burglars, and that

> burglars burgle." It would be still more absurd to say this if I had had bars
> installed outside my windows, precisely to prevent burglars from getting
> in, and a burglar got in only because of a defect in the bars. (58–59)

In opening the window, the homeowner voluntarily does something that she
understands can result in a burglar entering, just as in having consensual sex the
mother does something she understands can result in a fetus. But just as it is not
wrong for the homeowner to evict the burglar even where the homeowner is partly
responsible for him being there, so too it is not wrong for the mother to "evict" the
fetus—that is, *abortion is not wrong—even where the mother is partly responsible for
the conception of the fetus.*

The analogy is problematic because there are big differences between the burglar case and the abortion case:

- **The fetus is innocent**; the burglar is not.
- **Abortion kills the fetus**; evicting the burglar does not kill him.

Since the cases are so dissimilar, it may still be the case that while evicting the
burglar is permissible, abortion is not.

Thomson immediately presents another scenario which avoids the first difference. In this scenario the trespasser is not a burglar, but an innocent person who
blunders into the house—say, a very little boy who has lost his way. But the verdict is the same: the little boy has no
right to stay, even if the homeowner is
partly responsible in leaving her window open: "It remains equally absurd
[to say that the trespasser has the right
to stay] if we imagine it is not a burglar who climbs in, but an innocent
person who blunders or falls in" (1971,
59). Even so, the second difference
between the innocent blunderer and
the fetus remains.

> Recall the cabin example from Fischer
> (1991). Imagine that this little boy stum-
> bles into your remote mountain cabin.
> Would it be wrong to kick him out if that
> would certainly lead to his death–say,
> from hypothermia in the snow? Is this
> case more or less analogous to an abor-
> tion than is Thomson's burglar case?

Thomson (1971) next presents a scenario where all the differences are removed:
(i) the trespasser is innocent, and (ii) eviction does kill the trespasser. The story
is about magical seeds that float around until they embed themselves into furniture, where they become people—something like Thumbelina. Here's how it
goes:

> People-seeds drift about in the air like pollen, and if you open your win-
> dows, one may drift in and take root in your carpets or upholstery. You
> don't want children, so you fix up your windows with fine mesh screens,
> the very best you can buy. As can happen, however, and on very, very rare

occasions does happen, one of the screens is defective, and a seed drifts in and takes root. Does the person-plant who now develops have a right to the use of your house? Surely not—despite the fact that you voluntarily opened your windows, you knowingly kept carpets and upholstered furniture, and you knew that screens were sometimes defective. (59)

The analogy: Just as removing the person-plant is not wrong, so too removing the fetus is not wrong—even where this kills the subject. But should we think that uprooting the plant is not wrong? Thomson takes it as obvious. But the critic will propose that we have been misled: the analogy trades on our thinking about person-plants as similar to ordinary plants. Thomson's description of person-plants is quite non-personal: seeds drift in, take root. Uprooting an ordinary plant is not wrong. Indeed, a plant is so insignificant in the actual world that it's hard to imagine it as the sort of thing that is a person with a right to life. But a person-plant is not at all similar to an ordinary plant. It is a person with the right to life. Just imagine little Thumbelina crying as you try ripping her from the sofa. Is it now so obvious that uprooting the person-plant is permissible? If not, we need some argument for the conclusion that it is permissible, so that we can then draw the same moral for the fetus by analogy (compare Maitzen 2003, 386).

> By opening the window, the homeowner enables the people-seeds to enter, but she does not do anything more that risks causing them to enter. But now imagine she installs a fan that she knows runs a risk of sucking in people-seeds, despite its filter (compare Fischer 2013, 292). She turns the fan on, and a seed is indeed sucked in. Would it now be wrong for her to uproot it? Is this case more similar to the case of pregnancy resulting from consensual sex?

You might think that we've gone from one extreme to another: Thomson depicts the plant too impersonally, but the critic depicts it too personally. Indeed, if we start thinking of fetuses as if they were Thumbelinas, then we're more likely to come to a pro-life conclusion. The pro-choicer will object that fetuses are nothing like Thumbelinas. But recall that Thomson has granted for the sake of argument that fetuses are persons. Fetuses would then be quite like Thumbelinas. She contends that the moral question of abortion does not hinge on the question of fetal personhood. But if the question of fetal personhood does matter, then we are back to the debate of Chapter 2.

4. Conclusion

Whether the famous violinist argument works depends on whether it's permissible to unplug from the violinist and whether unplugging from the violinist is relevantly similar to abortion. Furthermore, we have seen that, even if the violinist analogy does not apply to all cases of abortion, it might still apply to some cases and show that those abortions are permissible. We leave the question of just how broadly Thomson's defense of abortion applies to the reader.

Further Reading

The famous violinist argument is put forward in Thomson (1971). Objections are leveled by Finnis (1973), Hursthouse (1987), Wilcox (1989), Fischer (1991, 2013), Kaczor (2015), Maitzen (2003), Watt (2016), and Schouten (2017). Thomson (1973, 1995a, 1995b) responds against a few critics. Replies to various objections can also be found in Boonin (2003).

Section 2

Animal Ethics

Chapter 5
The Contractarian Argument

---

1. Introduction

In the next three chapters we turn to the debate over **animal ethics**: Is farming and experimenting on animals morally wrong? Is killing and eating animals wrong? In this chapter we cover what we call the **contractarian argument**. Originally presented by Peter Carruthers (1992), the contractarian argument tries to show that our use of animals is not wrong. As usual, we will first present the argument, and then we will consider some objections and replies. In the next chapter we'll cover the most influential arguments against our use of animals.

2. The Argument

The contractarian argument defends our use of animals—for example, farming animals, experimenting on animals—on the basis of a normative moral theory. **Normative moral theories** are general principles about right and **wrong** actions. In Chapter 1 we assigned actions that are always or usually right, such as giving to charity, caring for children, and keeping promises, to a Good List, and assigned actions that are always or usually wrong, such as killing parents, torturing puppies, and telling lies to the Bad List.

We might think that it is a cosmic coincidence that all the actions on the Good List are right, and that all the actions on the Bad List are wrong. We might think that there is nothing more to be said about why these actions are right or wrong respectively. But we might not. We might instead propose that there is some feature common to the actions on the Good List and that makes them all right, and that there is some feature common to the actions on the Bad List and that makes them all wrong. Normative moral theories are proposals about

- what features of all right actions make them right; and
- what features of all wrong actions make them wrong.

Recall the big question we considered in Chapter 3: What makes cases of wrongful killing wrong? We worked through various proposals, including Don Marquis's idea that killing is wrong because it deprives the victim of a future of value. Normative moral theories are more general than those principles, because

> Why think that there is some common ingredient in right actions that makes them all right? Why think that there is some common ingredient in wrong actions that makes them wrong?

normative moral theories tell us not only what features make killing wrong, but also what features make *all* wrong actions wrong.

The contractarian argument is based on a normative moral theory known as **contractualism**. Contractualism is basically the view that morality is the set of rules that would be agreed upon by rational agents. Carruthers (1992) first defends contractualism against rival normative moral theories, and then he shows how contractualism applies to our use of animals. Putting this together, the argument can be presented in two stages as follows:

Stage 1:

(P1) Either cultural relativism, or the divine command theory, or utilitarianism, or . . . or contractualism is true.

(P2) Neither cultural relativism, nor the divine command theory, nor utilitarianism, nor . . . is true.

(C1) Therefore, contractualism is true. (From (P1) and (P2).)

Stage 2:

(P3) If contractualism is true, then an action is wrong **if and only if** rational agents in a hypothetical contract would forbid the action.

(P4) Rational agents in a hypothetical contract would not forbid using animals.

(C2) Therefore, if contractualism is true, then our use of animals is not wrong. (From (P3) and (P4).)

Then, from the conclusions of each stage we reach the ultimate conclusion:

(C3) Therefore, our use of animals is not wrong. (From (C1) and (C2).)

We'll consider each stage of this argument in order. The first stage will take us on a little tour of normative moral theories.

3. Stage 1

Carruthers supports the first stage by an **argument from elimination** (see Chapter 2). In other words, he eliminates *rival* normative moral theories, including cultural relativism, the divine command theory, and utilitarianism. Assuming that

(P1) of Stage 1 includes quite an exhaustive list of moral theories, we can turn to the defense of (P2) and consider the normative moral theories that rival contractualism. In each case, the theory is first outlined and applied to the morality of using animals; then support for the theory, and objections against it, are presented. If we can eliminate each, then (P2) is secured.

> Before reading ahead, what do you think might be the common ingredient in all right actions that makes them right? What do you think might be the common ingredient in all wrong actions that makes them wrong?

3.1. Cultural Relativism

Cultural relativism has morality depend on the say-so of a culture or society. Thus, an action is morally

- **obligatory** for an agent to perform if and only if *the rules of their culture require the action.*
- **wrong** for an agent to perform if and only if *the rules of their culture forbid the action.*
- **permissible** for an agent to perform if and only if *the rules of their culture neither forbid nor require the action.*

Application: On cultural relativism, the morality of using animals depends on the rules of the culture. If the rules of society require or permit using animals, then doing so would be obligatory or permissible; if the rules of society forbid using animals, then doing so would be wrong. Thus, eating animals in German culture (which permits eating animals) would be permissible, whereas eating animals in Jain culture (which forbids eating animals) would be wrong.

For the Theory: Cultural relativism is usually supported on the basis of:

- **Cultural differences:** For example, some cultures allow polygamy and others do not; some allow drinking alcohol and others do not; some allow cremation and other do not. From this it is supposed to follow that what is permissible or wrong differs between cultures, as cultural relativism says.
- **Tolerance:** Non-relativists have often taken their own culture's moral rules to be superior and have tried to impose them on other cultures with disastrous effects. From this it is supposed to follow that cultural relativism is superior.

However, this support is not compelling. As for cultural differences, *different rules do not mean that what is permissible really differs between cultures.* Perhaps some cultures just get morality wrong and have bad rules. Compare: when people disagree about non-moral matters (e.g., about whether the Earth is round) we do not think that all the parties can be correct. As for tolerance, the *cultural relativist must actually tolerate intolerance.* If the rules of a culture (e.g., Nazi culture) demand intolerance, then the relativist will recognize the intolerant behavior as **morally permissible** for those within that culture.

Against the Theory: There are at least two direct objections against the theory:

1. **Complex identities:** People often belong to different cultures which conflict in their rules. For example, a Jain might also be a German. Jain culture forbids eating animals, whereas German culture permits eating animals. Cultural relativism would seem to imply that eating animals is at once both permissible and wrong for the person—which is impossible.
2. **Counterintuitive consequences:** If the rules of a culture permit genocide or slavery, then genocide or slavery is morally permissible for that culture. Ironically, the theory that promised tolerance can also count extreme intolerance as permissible. For example, Nazi culture permitted genocide; American culture permitted slavery. But genocide and slavery could never be and were never moral. So cultural relativism must be false.

If cultural relativism fails, are there any normative moral theories that might do better by not having morality depend on society's say-so? On to our next theory.

> Cultural relativism can avoid the problem of complex identities by stipulating that the rules of one culture count more than the rules of another. How might the cultural relativist go about deciding which culture's rules are to count more?

3.2. Divine Command Theory

The **divine command theory** has morality depend on the say-so of God. Thus, an action is morally

- **obligatory** if and only if *God commands the action.*
- **wrong** if and only if *God forbids the action.*

Application: The divine command theory has the morality of using animals depend on the commands of God. If God commands or permits using animals, then doing so is obligatory or permissible; if God forbids using animals, then doing so is wrong. God might also command, permit, or forbid some uses of animals but not others. Some religious traditions have ideas about what God has commanded about animals. We could then figure out the morality of using animals by determining, first, which religious tradition—if any—is the true one, and, second, what it teaches about using animals. This would be a pretty big undertaking.

For the Theory: Divine command theory is usually supported on the basis of:

- **Divine sovereignty:** Religions teach that *God is the source of everything*. If God is the source of everything, then God must be the source of morality too, and so what is right or wrong will depend on God, as divine command theory says.
- **Moral revelations:** Religions teach that *God does command us to do some actions* and forbid us from doing other actions. These are often actions we recognize as right (e.g., giving charity) and wrong (e.g., stealing). Thus, in many cases, divine command theory seems to deliver verdicts that fit well with our moral intuitions.

However, this support is not compelling. As for divine sovereignty, *when religions teach that God is the source of everything they most obviously have in mind worldly objects*. But they do not obviously have in mind philosophical things like moral principles. For example, the book of Genesis tells us that God created heaven and Earth, man and the animals, but it does not teach us about God creating morality. As for moral revelations, *God's commands might inform us about what is right or wrong, or they might motivate us to do what is right and not do what is wrong*—but in neither case does God's command *make* the actions right or wrong. Even if God's commands do make some actions right or wrong, that could be derivative—we have an obligation to obey God, but that obligation is not created by God's commands.

Against the Theory: Carruthers levels two objections directly against the divine command theory:

- **Atheist objection:** Most atheists will reject the divine command theory. They believe that some actions are right or wrong—even while they do not believe in God. So they won't take morality to depend on the say-so of God. Of course, religious believers will not reject the divine command theory on such grounds!

- **Euthyphro objection:** The objection is that if morality depends on God's say-so, then God *could have* made, for example, torturing children for fun **morally obligatory** just by commanding it. But this is absurd. Furthermore, if there are no moral principles to guide God's commands; God could *with as much reason* have commanded torturing children for fun as he could have commanded giving to charity. This *makes anything God commands arbitrary.*

If the divine command theory fails, are there any normative moral theories that might do better by not having morality depend on God's say-so? On to our next theory.

> We might avoid the Euthyphro objection by rewording the divine command theory like this: an action is obligatory/wrong if it is commanded/forbidden by a *loving* God, who could not have commanded torturing children for fun. Is this a promising suggestion? Do you see any problems for it?

3.3. Utilitarianism

Carruthers devotes more attention to utilitarianism, and so will we. **Utilitarianism** has the morality of an action depend on happiness: right acts maximize happiness over unhappiness; wrong acts don't. But utilitarians disagree on what happiness is or exactly how we should maximize it. On **hedonistic utilitarianism** what matters is the pleasure and pain an action produces. Thus, an action is morally

- **obligatory** if and only if *it produces a greater balance of pleasure over pain than any alternative action does.*
- **wrong** if and only if *it produces less pleasure over pain than an alternative action does.*

On **preference utilitarianism** what matters is how well an action fulfills desires (it is good for an action to fulfill both a large number of desires and also to fulfill especially strong desires). Thus, an action is

- **obligatory** if and only if *it fulfills desires better than any alternative action does.*
- **wrong** if and only if *it does not fulfill desires better and an alternative action does.*

Hedonistic utilitarianism tells us that murder and stealing are wrong because they don't produce the highest balance of pleasure over pain. While murder and stealing might make murderers and thieves happy, they cause too much suffering to the victims. Preference utilitarianism tells us that murder and stealing are wrong because they don't fulfill the most desires; they might fulfill the desires of murderers and thieves, but this is outweighed by the unfulfilled desires of their victims. The two versions look close: After all, don't we desire pleasure and the absence of pain? But insofar as we might desire things apart from pleasure or pain (for example, knowledge or wisdom) the theories come apart.

Application: Both versions of utilitarianism are *impartial*: what matters are the consequences for *everyone* affected by the actions, whatever their race, gender, or even species—so long as they can feel pleasure and pain or have desires. Thus, utilitarianism takes the pleasures, pain, or desires of humans as well as animals into account. Utilitarianism means the morality of using animals depends on the pleasure and pain produced or desires fulfilled—both in the humans using the animals and in the animals being used. If using animals produces a greater balance of pleasure over pain or desires fulfilled (depending on the version of utilitarianism) than any alternative action, then doing so is permissible; if using animals produces less pleasure over pain or has fewer desires fulfilled than an alternative action then, doing so is wrong. While we cannot determine precisely how much pleasure and pain is produced or how many desires are fulfilled by, for example, farming animals for food, the pleasure and fulfillment we derive from farming and eating animals will be easily outweighed by the pain they experience and their thwarted desires, especially in the horrific confinement and torture of factory farms. See Chapters 6 and 7 for just a couple grizzly details.

For the Theory: Utilitarianism is often supported on the basis of:

- **Impartiality:** Utilitarianism says we ought to take into account the happiness of all affected by our actions. This can explain certain important features of morality, for instance, why racist and sexist behaviors are wrong—we shouldn't merely consider how our actions affect people of our same race or sex. It can also explain why acting on the basis of unfair biases is wrong; we shouldn't give the job to some unqualified person just because they are our friend.

- **Importance of happiness:** Whether we think of happiness as consisting in pleasure or in desire satisfaction, it's obviously morally important. We want happiness for ourselves and those we love, and we often care about other things because of how they impact happiness. Further, the morality of actions often depends on how they impact happiness: for instance, if something will hurt you, that's a reason not to do it. So it might seem intuitive to say that all morality is ultimately about maximizing the balance of happiness in the world.

- **Simplicity:** Many people think that simpler theories are more likely to be true than complicated ones, all else being equal. Sometimes this is expressed by the principle known as Occam's Razor: "do not multiply entities beyond necessity." Utilitarianism is very simple: it posits just one fundamental good (happiness) and one fundamentally bad thing (unhappiness), and it tells us to respond to these values in a straightforward way (maximizing the balance of good over bad).

Against the Theory: Utilitarianism faces a number of objections, including:

- **The over-demandingness objection:** Since utilitarianism emphasizes pleasure or desire, you might have thought it a fun theory—obligating as much sex and drugs as possible. But since the pleasure and desire of everyone affected is to be taken into account, utilitarianism turns out to be quite demanding. After all, by devoting most of your possessions and most of your time to charities, you'd plausibly be producing more pleasure and fulfilling more desires overall, even if not your own. If utilitarianism is true, it turns out to be wrong, for example, to spend any money or time at the movies rather than at a soup kitchen. Since this is implausibly demanding, utilitarianism is false.

- **The medical sacrifice:** If a doctor could secretly kill a healthy patient and transplant his organs into five dying patients, then he would be obligated to do so based on utilitarianism—since it would produce the most pleasure over pain or fulfill the most desires by saving five people at the loss of only one. Since killing the healthy patient would not be obligatory or even permissible, utilitarianism is false.

- **The unjust punishment objection:** On utilitarianism, an apparently unjust action could be morally permissible or even obligatory, so long as it has the right consequences. Suppose a mob is convinced that an innocent man committed a murder. If the man is released, the mob will riot and many more innocent people will be killed. The judge knows that the actual murderer has already died of natural causes. Further, the judge knows that if she frames and executes the innocent man, no one will ever find out that the man was really innocent. Should she execute the man? This seems clearly unjust, yet utilitarianism seems to require that she do so, since more lives will be saved (and therefore more happiness will be produced) on balance.

If utilitarianism fails, are there any normative moral theories that might do better by not having morality depending on the consequences of our action? On to our next theory.

3.4. Kantian Ethics

The next theory we consider is the normative moral theory of Immanuel Kant. To be sure, Carruthers considers **Kantian ethics** as a version of contractualism and does not cover it much. Traditionally, Kantian ethics is considered separately from contractualism, and for the sake of completeness we cover it here. But Kantian ethics is complicated, and so we simplify it a bit.

Kantian ethics has the morality of an action depend on whether the action is **universalizable**: *whether we could consistently will that everyone perform that kind of action*; that the action becomes, as it were, a universal law, one that applies to everyone, everywhere, at all times. Kant ([1785] 1997) illustrates how the idea determines that promise breaking is wrong. Anyone about to make a false promise, for example, to return a loan, must imagine what would happen if everyone followed the following rule or "maxim":

> When I believe myself to be in need of money, I will borrow money and promise to repay it, although I know I shall never do so.

But when he thinks through this scenario, he cannot consistently desire that everyone follows the maxim, or that the maxim becomes a universal law. Because

> the universality of a law that everyone, when he believes himself to be in need, could promise whatever he pleases with the intention of not keeping it would make the promise and the end one might have in it itself impossible, since no one would believe what was promised him but would laugh at all such expressions as vain pretenses. (32)

If everyone always made a false promise, then no one would trust any promises. If no one would trust any promises, then there would be no point in making false promises. So a maxim allowing false promises would undermine itself if universalized. Since making false promises is not universalizable, Kant concludes that making a false promise is wrong.

> Kant similarly argues that lying and suicide are wrong. Can you consistently desire that everyone lie? Can you consistently will that everyone commit suicide?

More generally, on Kant's ethics, an action is

- **obligatory** if and only if *the action is universalizable*.
- **wrong** if and only if *the action is not universalizable*.

Kant ([1785] 1997) elsewhere states his moral theory not in terms of universalizability but in terms of respect for humanity: "So act that you use humanity, whether in your own person or in the person of any other, always at the same time as an end, never merely as a means" (37). Then an action is right if it treats people as ends in themselves, and wrong when it treats people as mere means to an end. How the points about universalizability and the points about respect fit together are obscure, though Kant promises that they come to the same thing.

Application: Kantian ethics will have the morality of using animals depend on whether using animals is universalizable. If using animals is universalizable, then it's permissible; if it's not universalizable then it's wrong. Can we consistently will that everyone farms animals for food? Can we consistently will that everyone experiments on animals? We don't end up in the same kind of absurdity about making false promises. Using animals would then seem to be permissible. Framing Kantian ethics in terms of respect has the same result. That way of going about things is explicitly about treating *humanity* as an end in itself rather than a mere means, but says nothing about treating animals as a means. Kant (1798/2010) himself concludes that "one may deal and dispose [with animals] at one's discretion" (239). His only concern for animals is that cruelty toward animals might eventually lead to cruelty toward people.

To be sure, Kantian ethics is tricky, and Kant might not have been infallible about the application of his own views. Christine Korsgaard (2018) uses Kantian ethics to come to conclusions on animal ethics that are opposite from Kant's. For Kant, humans are special because they are rational agents: they can critically evaluate different courses of action and decide what to do. But Korsgaard claims that the type of agency possessed by animals also entitles them to respectful treatment as ends in themselves, even though their agency is different from ours.

For the Theory: Kantianism might be supported by appealing to factors such as the following:

- **The importance of universalizability:** When discussing the right thing to do, we sometimes say things like "What if everybody else did that?" or "How would you like it if other people did the same thing?" Maybe this suggests that we think ethical behavior should be universalizable: refusing to follow the rules you want other people to follow seems to treat yourself as special or better than them in a morally bad way. Similarly, we usually think showing respect for others is important, and treating them as mere tools for your own purposes is wrong.
- **Avoiding sacrifice:** Kantianism may be able to avoid some of the problems faced by utilitarianism. Consider the medical sacrifice case. Secretly killing a patient to harvest their organs does not seem

universalizable: if all doctors did that, people wouldn't go to the doctor. Further, harvesting the patient's organs seems to treat them as a mere means to saving others. So Kantianism gets the intuitively correct result in this case.

- **The nature of agency:** Kantians sometimes argue roughly like this (the argument is very complicated, so this will be a simplification): when you pursue an end, you have to think the end is worthy of pursuing. But the only reason it would be worth pursuing is that you value it, so the fact that you value it must make it valuable. But you have to think that your ability to do this doesn't rest on something else—you must, as a rational agent, have *intrinsic* value which allows you to bestow derivative value on things. As Korsgaard (1997) puts the point: if the value of the particular ends we pursue "does not rest in themselves, but rather in the fact that they are important to us, then in pursuing them, we are in effect taking ourselves to be important" (xxii). And if you do, you must recognize that all other agents have that value, too, and it would be unreasonable to treat them as if they didn't. So for your actions to make sense, you must think that all agents have intrinsic value and deserve to be treated as ends in themselves.

Against the Theory: But Kantianism also faces objections, including:

- **Lying:** We saw above that Kantianism rules out "false promising." This seems plausible in most cases. But the same reasoning seems to show that *all* lying is wrong, which seems less plausible. Suppose a murderer comes to your door asking where the person he wants to murder is. You can save this person, but only by lying about their location so they can get away. Should you lie? Most people say yes, but Kant explicitly says that you cannot. (After all, if people always lied to murderers, the murderer wouldn't believe you.) This seems implausible. More broadly, Kantianism is not as sensitive to the consequences of actions as utilitarianism. It seems to imply not only that it would be wrong to sacrifice an innocent person in the medical sacrifice, but also that it would be wrong even if it was the only way to, for example, prevent everyone else in the world from being tortured to death. Is that plausible?

- **Specifying maxims:** One problem for universalizability is that there are multiple ways of describing the same action, some of which are universalizable and some of which aren't. Can I become a philosophy professor? If we say that, in doing so, I'm following the maxim "Become a philosophy professor," it seems that the answer is no: there aren't enough philosophy jobs for everyone, and besides, if no one became farmers, doctors, and so on, society would collapse and there wouldn't even be philosophy professors. On the other hand, if we describe the maxim in some other way, such as "Choose a vocation which allows you to utilize your talents," it might be universalizable. But what makes one better than the other? Couldn't I, say, describe lying to save a life in some other way that makes it universalizable?

- **The meaning of 'mere':** Kantianism doesn't say you can never use someone as a means. That would be implausible. For instance, you use your professors as a means to getting knowledge, and that's okay. It says you can never use someone as a *mere* means. The difference is supposed to be that use as a mere means is incompatible with showing proper respect for someone's status as an end in themselves whose autonomously chosen goals have importance. But it's harder to say what this means in practice. For instance, Kant himself believed you wrongfully treat yourself as a mere means if you engage in any sexual activity outside of heterosexual marriage ([1797] 1996, 61–64). But it's hard even to say exactly what Kant's argument for this is, much less to be convinced by it.

> What verdicts would each of the above normative moral theories give about the other debates covered in this book: abortion, global poverty, punishment, disability, the environment?

3.5. Contractualism

With all these normative moral theories eliminated, left standing is Carruthers's favorite: contractualism, the view that *morality is what would be agreed upon by rational agents who decide what rules we should follow.* As rational agents, they would have the intellectual abilities to deliberate over rival systems of rules, and, on some versions of contractualism, they would have other knowledge too—of things like human psychology, sociology, and economics.

John Rawls (1999) illustrates how the rules are decided by having these agents deliberate behind a **veil of ignorance**: they are ignorant of their own place in the world (whether they are rich or poor, male or female, etc.), and thus ignorant of how the rules will end up bearing on them in particular. These agents also deliberate on the basis of **self-interest**: they settle on rules they take to be the best for them. But the veil of ignorance protects from unfair rules, since the agents are ignorant of what, for example, gender or race they have. For instance, they will not settle on a rule that persecutes people on the basis of gender, because no rational, self-interested agent, ignorant of what gender they will have in the world, would adopt a sexist rule. If, say, the rule allows discrimination against women, what if *you* turn out to be a woman and are discriminated against? And thus, on contractualism, persecuting a person on the basis of gender will turn out to be wrong. Of course, the story isn't literally true: there are no perfectly rational agents and there is no veil of ignorance. But morality is still determined by what such hypothetical agents in such idealized circumstances *would* decide.

Not all contractualists make use of the veil of ignorance, however. T. M. Scanlon (1998) instead posits rational agents who know their place in the world. But their decision is governed by two other conditions that protect against unfair rules. First, the agents must come to **free agreement**: their priority must be to agree on rules for society in a free and unforced way. Second, they must agree to rules that no rational agent could **reasonably reject**: a rule that there is a good basis for a rational agent to reject will not be included. So, again, they will not settle on a rule that persecutes people on the basis of gender or race because those persecuted would reasonably reject such a rule. Thus, again, sexism will turn out to be wrong.

Whether we spell out the details according to Rawls or Scanlon, on contractualism, an action is morally

- **obligatory** if and only if *rational agents in a hypothetical contract would require the action.*
- **wrong** if and only if *rational agents in a hypothetical contract would forbid the action.*

Carruthers has more to say in favor of contractualism than the elimination of rival theories. He advertises contractualism as securing various plausible rules and delivering the right verdicts in uncontroversial cases. Rational agents would not frame rules allowing such things as the medical sacrifice (as could be allowed by utilitarianism) or intolerance (as could be allowed by moral relativism) or torturing children (as could be allowed by divine command theory).

> Do you agree that contractualism does better than the rival moral theories? Do you think rational agents could ever agree to immoral rules?

However, contractualism is also supposed to deliver the verdict that our use of animals—whether in farming, food, and medical experiments—is not wrong. Next we turn to this step of the argument.

4. Stage 2

With contractualism in place, Carruthers argues that contractualism implies that our use of animals is not wrong. In this section, beings with **moral standing** are beings that we have moral obligations toward. So Carruthers argues that humans have moral standing, but animals do not. We can use them for farming and experiments because they don't have moral standing. Recall Stage 2 of the argument:

(P3) If contractualism is true, then an action is wrong if and only if rational agents in a hypothetical contract would forbid the action.

(P4) Rational agents in a hypothetical contract would not forbid using animals.

(C2) *Therefore, if contractualism is true, then our use of animals is not wrong.*

(P3) is true from the definition of contractualism. So the big question now is about (P4): Why would rational agents not forbid using animals? Why would they permit farming, eating, and experimenting on animals? How can we say that "humans are in, and animals are out" of their contract? Let's consider the contractualisms of Rawls and Scanlon in order.

For Rawls, morality is determined by the decisions of rational agents acting out of self-interest behind the veil of ignorance. Since the agents are behind the veil, they won't know whether they are male or female, Black or white, and so forth. Even from a self-interested perspective, they will decide on rules that respect both males and females, Black people and white people, and so on. They won't know which rational agents they are, but they will know that they are rational agents—and thus they will know that they are not animals. As self-interested, they won't agree to applying the same rules to non-rational agents such as animals.

> Since it is rational agents who are to choose the system of rules, and choose self-interestedly, it is only rational agents who will have their position protected under the rules. There seems no reason why rights should be assigned to non-rational agents. Animals will therefore have no moral standing under Rawlsian contractualism, insofar as they do not count as rational agents. (Carruthers 1992, 98–99)

Thus, on Rawls's contractualism, (P4) is true, and *rational agents in a hypothetical contract would not forbid using animals.* Farming animals for food and experimenting on animals turns out not to be wrong.

For Scanlon, morality is determined by rules the rational agents could not freely and reasonably reject. As Carruthers (1992) reminds us, "The only idealisations made are that choices and objections will always be rational, and that all concerned will share the aim of reaching such an agreement" (104). Rational humans like us could reasonably reject any rules that do not respect other rational agents, whether male or female, Black or white, and so on. In contrast, they could reasonably reject rules respecting non-rational agents such as animals. After all, *there is much disagreement about how animals should be treated*, and many of the rational agents would have, for example, religious views that permit using animals. Remember, on Scanlon's view, we are talking about real agents, much like ourselves—just rational ones. Agents like this could reasonably reject rules that entail having obligations to animals. Thus, Scanlon's contractualism also supports premise 5.

Both versions of contractualism give moral standing to humans but not animals: *our use of animals is not wrong.*

> What, if anything, would contractualism say about the morality of abortion? What would it say about other debates we cover, like global poverty or the death penalty?

5. Objections and Replies

Recall the whole argument. Stitched together it runs as follows:

- (P1) Either cultural relativism, or the divine command theory, or utilitarianism, or . . . or contractualism is true.
- (P2) Neither cultural relativism nor the divine command theory nor utilitarianism nor . . . is true.
- (C1) Therefore, contractualism is true.
- (P3) If contractualism is true, then an action is wrong if and only if rational agents in a hypothetical contract would forbid the action.
- (P4) Rational agents in a hypothetical contract would not forbid using animals.
- (C2) Therefore, if contractualism is true, then our use of animals is not wrong.
- (C3) Therefore, our use of animals is not wrong.

With so many moving parts, there'll be much to question about the argument. As usual, we turn to objections to this argument and replies to those objections.

> Before reading ahead, think about Carruthers's argument. Do any of its premises seem false or questionable? What is the best way to object to it?

Objection 1:

Against (P1), even if all the rival theories considered can be decisively refuted, the theories considered are not exhaustive. There remain other theories that Carruthers does not consider. For example, the argument for contractualism has overlooked

- **natural law theory**, on which an action is right if and only if it accords with natural laws given by reason (see Besong 2018);
- **virtue ethics**, on which an action is right if and only if a virtuous person would perform it (see Hursthouse 2001);
- **care ethics**, on which an action is right if and only if a caring person would perform it (see Slote 2004); and
- **moral pluralism**, on which there are several different, equally fundamental moral principles, and an action is right if and only if it strikes the right balance between them (see Ross 2002).

Or for a more radical alternative, take

- **moral particularism**, on which there are no neat and universal moral principles about what makes a right action right and what makes a wrong action wrong (Dancy 2004).

Moral particularists argue that when it comes to any moral ingredient that is supposed to make wrong actions wrong, we can discover cases where the ingredient does not make the action wrong or even makes the action right. For example, that an action promotes pleasure usually counts in favor of performing an action, but we can imagine a case where it counts against the action:

> A government is considering reintroducing hanging, drawing, and quartering in public for terrorist murders. If reactions to public hangings in the past are anything to go by a lot of people may enjoy the spectacle Does that constitute a reason in favor of reintroduction? . . . It would be perfectly possible to take just the opposite view. The fact that spectators might get a sadistic thrill from the brutal spectacle could be thought to constitute an objection to reintroduction. (McNaughton 1988, 193)

Do you think this example supports moral particularism? Can we make sense of the example in a way that does not support particularism?

Reply:

There's only so much time in a day. Carruthers's book is long enough. But there's much to say against the alternative theories he overlooks too. For example, we will cover virtue ethics at length and consider objections against it in Chapter 12. We discuss some problems for Singer's utilitarianism in Chapter 6 (see especially objection 3 there).

Objection 2:

Against (P2), Carruthers's elimination of rival normative moral theories isn't decisive. Proponents of these theories have replies to the stock objections. For example, against the medical sacrifice objection, the utilitarian could move to a more specific kind of utilitarianism. For example, **rule utilitarianism** says that an action is right if and only if it conforms to a *rule* that would produce the most pleasure or preference satisfaction. A rule that permits killing a healthy patient will not produce the most pleasure or desire fulfillment, since society would become terrified about routine medical checkups. The medical sacrifice would thus turn out to be wrong. Carruthers's argument is hostage to complicated controversies about moral theories, and the other moral theories might not be as quickly eliminated as Carruthers advertises.

Reply:

This is no special problem with Carruthers's argument: *many arguments in applied ethics rely on a controversial moral theory.* For example, Singer's argument (in Chapter 6) draws on principles from utilitarianism, and Slote's argument (in Chapter 12) relies on virtue ethics. Carruthers makes his normative moral theory explicit and provides an argument for it. Nonetheless, those who are not convinced by the truth of contractualism will have an easy way to avoid Carruthers's conclusion.

> Do all the arguments we cover in this book rely on normative moral theories, even if implicitly? Is it an advantage or a disadvantage for an argument to rely on such a theory?

Objection 3:

Even if animals aren't parties in the contract because they lack rationality, the contracting agents might have *preferences on behalf of animals.* They might represent them and make a successful case for their moral standing, similar to the way that lawyers in a courtroom represent their clients. Thus, contrary to (P4), rational agents in a hypothetical contract might forbid using animals.

Reply 1:

The rational agents would not all agree to give animals moral standing. Even if some of them would advocate for animals, not everyone behind the veil would share this priority. For this reason, it is not obvious that rules that protect animals would be included in their final agreement.

Reply 2:

Let us grant to the objector that the agents behind the veil did agree to include rules that protected animals. Because these rules are only included due to the human advocates, they would give the animals only *indirect* moral standing. This would mean that we have a duty to respect animals only because we have a duty to animal lovers and animal owners. Thus, we wouldn't have a direct duty to animals themselves, and our use of animals would only be wrong insofar as animal lovers and animal owners disapprove of it.

Objection 4:

Many people adore their pets. Even if acting out of self-interest, the rational agents, not knowing whether they will adore their pets, would want pets taken care of, and thus, contrary to (P4), they would give pets moral standing.

Reply 1:

Not everyone adores pets. Pets are not universal. Further, even if rational agents would agree to give pets moral standing (which is disputable), this still wouldn't secure the **rights** of most animals. Most animals we farm and experiment on are not pets. Thus, our farming and experimentation on non-pets would not be wrong.

Reply 2:

Whatever attachment some do have to pets, this attachment is very different from the attachment they have to their non-rational relatives and infants. Suppose your cat and your infant child were both drowning and you could only save one. Almost all rational agents would save the child. In fact, many would say it is irrational and immoral to let the infant drown. Or, consider a similar case where you have to pick one to experiment on or to farm. Almost all rational agents would pick the cat. Thus, those behind the contract would not secure pets the same rights as non-rational humans.

Objection 5:

If contractualism is true, and this implies that using animals is not wrong, then dousing a kitten in kerosene and igniting it for sadistic fun is not wrong. But dousing a kitten in kerosene and setting it on fire is wrong. So either contractualism is false for implying otherwise (contrary to (C1), which means either (P1) or (P2) is false) or contractualism must be developed in a way that gives moral standing to non-rational agents, so that harming non-rational humans as well as animals will be wrong (contrary to (P4)).

Reply 1:

On contractualism, kittens have no moral standing, but cat lovers do insofar as they are rational agents. Then, igniting a kitten would be wrong because doing so would emotionally harm the cat lovers, and harming cat lovers would be wrong: our duties to cat lovers give us an indirect duty to the kitten. Thus, on contractualism, igniting the kitten would turn out to be wrong, albeit indirectly.

Reply to the reply:

The reply shows that igniting the kitten is wrong because cat lovers would be emotionally harmed. But the reply does not cover cases where no rational agent cares about an animal, and so no rational agent would be harmed by torturing the animal. Torturing such an animal still seems wrong. Suppose that Astrid, an eccentric billionaire, blasts off into space. The ship is aimed for a distant star, and there is no way to change course. Furthermore, she has no communication equipment. Accordingly, she knows she will never interact with anyone else ever again, and no one has any way of finding out what she's doing up there. She brought along a cat she found, but eventually she gets tired of it and decides to skin it alive before throwing it out the airlock (Carruthers 2011, 394–95)

What Astrid does is wrong, even if no one ever loved or knew about the cat. But on contractualism, harming such a cat would not be wrong. Thus, contractualism is false.

Reply 2:

Torturing the cat is *extremely cruel*. For society to flourish, it is important that people develop and exercise **virtues** (such as kindness) and avoid **vices** (such as cruelty). Other parties to the contract could object to Astrid's behavior because of the cruelty it displays. But this wouldn't be objecting *for the sake of the cat*. Instead, they would be objecting because of the effects that developing and promoting cruelty could have *for other humans* (cf. Carruthers 2011, 396).

Reply to reply 2:

It's actually not clear that this account produces the judgment Carruthers wants in Astrid's case. We stipulated that Astrid has no way of ever interacting with anyone on Earth again. We can suppose that she'll never have any contact with any other astronauts or aliens either. In that case, why would other parties to the contract care whether she is cruel or develops other vicious character traits? There is no chance of her cruelty affecting any other human being (see Swanson 2011, 11–12).

> Is Carruthers's reply plausible? Do you agree that, even though mistreating animals reflects poorly on one's character, we don't have any duties to animals?

Objection 6:

Not all humans have the same capacity for rationality. For example, infants, people with mental disabilities, and people who are senile are not rational. As we have seen, contractualism does not give moral standing to non-rational agents. Thus, just as contractualism permits our using animals, it permits our using infants and people who are senile or who have mental disabilities. But farming these people for food and experimenting on them would be wrong. So either contractualism is false for implying otherwise (contrary to (C1), which means that either (P1) or (P2) must be false) or contractualism must be developed in a way that gives moral standing to non-rational agents, so that harming non-rational humans as well as animals will be wrong (contrary to (P4); see Rowlands 2009, chap. 6).

Reply 1:

On Scanlon's version, morality is determined by rules that we could not reasonably reject. We are deeply and reasonably attached to infants and people who are senile or who have mental disabilities. In contrast, many of us do not have such an attachment to animals. Thus, any principle that gives moral standing to non-rational humans cannot be reasonably rejected, but any rule giving moral standing to animals can be reasonably rejected. This verdict fits with our commonsense intuitions: farming and experimenting on non-rational humans is wrong, but doing so to animals is not wrong.

Reply 2:

On Rawls's version, morality is determined by self-interested rational agents in a hypothetical agreement behind the veil of ignorance. Behind this veil, they don't know what kind of human they might be; they might turn out to be senile, for example. Thus, they have a self-interested reason to give all humans, including senile humans, moral standing. But the agents behind the veil do know that they won't turn out to be animals, and so they have no self-interested reason to give animals moral standing. Again, this fits with our commonsense intuitions.

> Do you think that you could have been a dog? Why should we think you could have been a member of another gender or race, but not another species?

Reply to the reply:

The second reply simply assumes that the rational agents behind the veil know that they will turn out to be humans and not animals. Either the rational agents know that they will turn out to be rational or they don't know this. If they do know that they will turn out to be rational, then they can know that they will not be senile humans or animals—and so will not give moral standing to either. If they don't know that they will turn out to be rational, they cannot know whether they will be senile humans or animals—and so will give moral standing to both. Thus, the moral standing of non-rational humans as well as animals falls or stands together. Either way contractualism cannot ensure that animals and non-rational humans have different moral standing (cf. Rowlands 2009, 159).

Reply to the reply to the reply:

If the rational agents cannot rule out that they will be animals, then they cannot rule out that they will be, for example, sticks or stones or applied ethics textbooks either. Thus, contractualism would give moral standing to sticks and stones and textbooks. But these do not have moral standing. Thus, the rational agents must be able to rule out that they will be sticks or stones or textbooks—or animals!

Reply to the reply to the reply to the reply:

Even if the agents behind the veil cannot rule out being sticks or stones or textbooks, that does not mean that sticks and stones or textbooks are given moral standing. After all, the agents will know that inanimate objects have no preferences. Thus, the agents would not care about what happens to sticks, stones, or textbooks—even if they turned out to be such things. So even if the agents end up being inanimate objects without preferences, then how the rules treat them won't matter. Behind the veil, the agents only need to consider the possibilities where they have desires and preferences. But non-rational humans as well as animals have desires and preferences, and contractualism will give both together moral standing (see Rowlands 2009, 160).

> Reply 1 has been left standing. Can it be answered in the same way as reply 2? Does the answer work for either reply?

Reply to the reply to the reply to the reply to the reply:

The veil is supposed to make the rational agents behind it ignorant of morally irrelevant features they will turn out to have, like their race or gender. But whether species is morally relevant is controversial. Many people think that species membership is morally relevant, and this could explain why, if an infant and a cat are drowning and you can only save one, you should save the infant. Thus, species is morally relevant, so agents would know their species behind the veil of ignorance, and out of self-interest, would give moral standing to non-rational humans, but not to animals (see Carruthers 2011, 393; 1992, 101–3).

Reply to the reply to the reply to the reply to the reply to the reply:

If the species of the agents behind the veil is morally relevant, then something makes species morally relevant prior to the decision behind the veil. But, on contractualism, the decision behind the veil determines morality, and so no feature, including species, can be morally relevant prior to that decision. Thus, on contractualism, the species is not morally relevant—not any more relevant than what their races or genders will turn out to be.

> Is there any other reason (not presupposing the moral relevance of species) to think that the agents behind the veil would have knowledge of their species, but not other facts about themselves like their race or gender?

6. Conclusion

The contractarian argument is in many ways attractive: there's much to be said for contractualism. But there are also problems with contractualism and with Carruthers's claim that it denies moral status to animals. We leave readers to decide how plausible this argument is. But whether we should believe the conclusion also depends on how plausible arguments in the opposite direction are. In the next chapter, we turn to arguments for the conclusion that our use of animals is morally wrong.

Further Reading

The contractarian argument is put forward by Carruthers (1992, 2011). Objections to the contractarian argument are put forward by Regan (2004, chap. 5.4) and Rowlands (2009, chap. 6). Contractualism in general is defended by Rawls (1999) and Scanlon (1998). For a thorough treatment of various normative moral theories, see Copp (2007). For other arguments for the conclusion that using animals is not wrong, see Hsiao (2015, 2017).

Chapter 6
Animal Welfare and Animal Rights

1. Introduction

In the previous chapter, we presented and evaluated arguments for the permissibility of farming and experimenting on animals. In this chapter, we turn to arguments against farming and experimenting on animals. There are two views that answer that our widespread treatment of animals is **wrong**: the *animal welfare view* and the *animal rights view*. The animal welfare view is most famously defended by Peter Singer (2002) and the animal rights view is most famously defended by Tom Regan (2004). We first turn to Singer's argument and then to Regan's argument—along with objections and replies.

2. Singer's Argument

Singer begins with the wrongness of racism and sexism: we should not discriminate against humans on the basis of their race or sex. Singer tries to discover *why* exactly racism and sexism are wrong. What he discovers turns out to have wider application: it applies equally to animals. Just as racism and sexism are wrong, discrimination against animals turns out to be wrong too. Prejudice against animals is called **speciesism**.

If some prejudices are wrong and others are not, then there must be a relevant difference between them. More generally, *there cannot be a moral difference without there being some other relevant difference which explains the moral difference.* For example, if Smith acts wrongly when he kills someone, then Jones similarly acts wrong when he kills someone similar in the same circumstances. Smith acts wrongly and Jones acts rightly only if there's a big difference in the killings, for example, Jones kills in self-defense but Smith does not. So if racism is wrong but speciesism is not wrong, then there must be some relevant difference between the prejudices. Singer argues that there are no relevant differences between the prejudices. Let's consider the most salient differences: species membership and intelligence.

Could racism and sexism be wrong because all races and sexes are members of the species *homo sapiens*, while speciesism is not wrong because animals are of different species? Singer objects. Species membership is not a relevant difference for two reasons:

1. *Species is just another biological distinction like race and sex.* Thus, if species membership justifies discrimination, then it justifies racism and sexism too. After all, why should biological difference matter in the one case but not the others? But racism and sexism are wrong. So species membership does not justify discrimination.

2. If species membership justifies discrimination, then it would not be wrong to discriminate against an extraterrestrial species like E.T. But *it would be wrong to discriminate against E.T.* We can see as much even though E.T. does not actually exist. So species membership does not justify discrimination.

Speciesists might answer that species membership per se does not justify discrimination between humans and animals. Rather what comes along with species membership does: intelligence. Humans are much smarter than animals, though we are not smarter than E.T. We can reason, imagine, and invent; animals cannot do so at all or nearly as well.

Now we have actually turned to the other salient difference between humans and animals. Could racism and sexism be wrong because all races and sexes have the same intelligence, while speciesism is not wrong because other species have lesser intelligence? Singer (2002) objects, quoting Thomas Jefferson: "Because Sir Isaac Newton was superior to others in understanding, he was not therefore lord of the property or persons of others" (6). Intelligence differences do not support speciesism for two reasons:

1. If intelligence differences support speciesism, then intelligence differences support discrimination against less intelligent humans too: we could divide humans by intelligence and favor the intellectual elite. However, *discrimination against less intelligent humans is wrong.* So intelligence differences do not support speciesism.

2. If intelligence differences support speciesism, the intelligence differences support discrimination against humans who are no more intelligent than animals, for example, infants or senile people: we could farm infants or senile people for food or scientific experimentation. However, *farming and experimenting on infants or the senile is wrong.* So differences in intelligence do not support speciesism.

The last objection is an instance of the **argument from marginal cases**: the speciesist proposes that some difference between humans and animals supports discrimination against animals. But those differences exist among some humans to the same degree. The consistent speciesist must then either support discrimination against those humans or—what seems more reasonable—give up the proposed relevance of the difference between humans and animals.

The argument from marginal cases similarly shows that differences in reasoning, language, creativity, and moral agency between humans and animals do not support speciesism. Singer further points out that if such differences were relevant, then the wrongness of racism and sexism would be *hostage to scientific discoveries*: for example, if it *were* discovered that Indian people are generally more intelligent

> Can you think of any difference between humans and animals, apart from species membership, that supports speciesism and avoids the argument from marginal cases?

than Japanese people, then the difference would support racist discrimination between Indians and Japanese. But even if the intelligence difference did exist, such racism would still be wrong. So such differences are not relevant. Singer (2002) cites the African American feminist Sojourner Truth (1797–1883):

> They talk about this thing in the head; what do they call it? ["Intellect," whispered someone nearby.] That's it. What's that got to do with women's rights or Negroes' rights? If my cup won't hold but a pint and yours holds a quart, wouldn't you be mean not to let me have my little half-measure full? (6)

What makes racism and sexism wrong is not that all races and sexes belong to the same species or have the same intelligence, whereas animals do not. What makes racism and sexism wrong? Singer (2002, chap. 1) puts forward his own answer in terms of the Principle of Equal Consideration of Interests. Here's a slightly paraphrased version of the **principle of equal consideration of interests (PEC)**: we should give equal weight to the like interests of all those affected by our actions.

An *interest* is something that affects your **well-being**. According to PEC, if our action increases the well-being of a subject, then that counts in favor of performing the action; if our action decreases the well-being of a subject, then that counts against performing the action. And how much it counts in either direction does not depend on the subject's race or gender. PEC entails that we should not give more weight in our moral deliberations to the interests of one race or sex over another—all count equally. PEC thus entails that racism and sexism are wrong.

PEC makes sense of the wrongness of racism and sexism, better than do other proposals based on our shared humanity or intelligence. As we have seen, proposals about our common species, reasoning, language, creativity, or moral agency give wrong verdicts for E.T., Newton, infants, or the senile. In contrast, PEC makes sense of why racism and sexism are wrong and does not give wrong verdicts for any of these cases. PEC tells us that the interests of infants and people who are senile count and count equally.

But neither is there anything in PEC that distinguishes between humans and animals; it applies to any creature with interests. There is always an interest in experiencing pleasure and not suffering pain. Since animals can experience pleasure and pain, they too have an interest in experiencing pleasure and not experiencing pain.

Most of us take it as obvious that some animals can feel pleasure and pain: for example, petting a cat makes it happy and that stabbing a dog hurts it. There are at least two kinds of evidence that animals have such psychological states: *behavioral and physiological evidence*. For example, the behavioral evidence for pain includes withdrawing from something causing bodily damage and crying out after such damage; if we witness another person on fire, writhing and screaming, we can tell they are in pain. Similarly, if Bambi gets burned in a forest fire, her distressed behavior tells us that she is in pain. The physiological evidence of feeling pain includes specific brain activity. If we discover such activity in Bambi's brain, we can tell that she is in pain too.

Mammals generally display a lot of the relevant behavior and physiology for pain. Birds and fish display some such behavior and physiology too. The reasoning we use here might be the analogical kind of reasoning we outlined in Chapter 4: animals are similar to us in behavior and physiology; we feel pleasure and pain; therefore, animals also feel pleasure and pain.

> Which animals, if any, do you think have psychological states, like beliefs, desires, emotions, or sensations? Why do you think this?

Just as we should give equal consideration to the interests of all races and sexes, so too should we give equal consideration to the interests of all species. Just as racism and sexism are wrong, speciesism is wrong. PEC does *not* mean that we should treat animals exactly the same way we treat people; it does *not* call for giving mice the right to vote or admitting horses to college. PEC tells us to consider animal interests equally. Since their interests and the ways they realize those interests are different, the treatment animals require is different. Humans have an interest in college but horses do not precisely because humans can learn and benefit from college classes, whereas horses cannot.

But animals can feel pain and have an interest in not feeling pain. That an action would hurt an animal thus counts against performing the action. It need not count *decisively* though: the action might still be in the overall interest of the animal (e.g., a vaccination) or other subjects (e.g., kicking a rabid dog away). When all the relevant interests are weighed, PEC might require causing the animal pain. However, *Singer argues that our treatment of animals, especially in farming and experimentation, systematically violates PEC.* These widespread practices require radical revision: we should stop virtually all farming of and experimentation on animals.

Virtually all. Some farming and experimentation might take the interests of all affected into proper consideration. For example, some family farming might not cause much suffering to animals while bringing enough benefit to the people who farm and eat them (see Chapter 7). But most **factory farming** is horrific (see Singer 2002, chap. 3; DeGrazia 2002, chap. 5). For example, little piglets start off their lives being castrated and having their tails chopped off—*without anesthetic*. This abusive treatment continues throughout the course of their lives. And things are hardly any better for the fifty billion cows, sheep, and chickens who are factory farmed each year. Chickens' nerve-filled beaks are seared off with a hot blade at an early age to prevent feather pecking. Then, they are packed together in tiny cages, often with less floor space than a sheet of letter-sized paper. Both chickens and cows are often injected with substantial amounts of growth hormones and other chemicals, many of which are believed to cause cancer and other serious health problems.

Similarly, some animal experimentation might be lifesaving and bring enough benefit to doctors and patients. But *much experimentation is unnecessary* (see Singer 2002, chap. 2; DeGrazia 2002, chap. 7). For example, Harvard experimenters repeatedly electrocuted dogs in small compartments to discover whether the dogs—who would at first yelp, shriek, urinate, defecate, and smash themselves against the compartments—would eventually give up hope and stop trying to escape. To be sure, that experiment was conducted in the 1950s, and recent laws forbid such torture. But whether we are now giving animals *equal* consideration depends on whether we would be prepared to submit an infant or senile human—on the intellectual or emotional level of the animals—to experiments. Probably not.

Putting this all together, Singer's argument can be summarized as follows:

(P1)   Because of PEC, we should give equal weight to the like interests of all those affected by our actions.

(P2)   Farming and experimenting on animals typically does not give equal weight to the interests of animals affected by our actions.

(C)   Therefore, we should not typically farm or experiment on animals.

Premise 1 is supported by the argument for PEC laid out earlier: PEC best explains why racism and sexism are wrong. Premise 2 is supported by the facts of farming and experimentation.

3. Objections to Singer and Replies

Objection 1:

The argument from marginal cases ignores an important difference between humans and animals: humans have souls, while animals don't. In Chapter 2, we discussed the possibility that ensoulment provided a morally relevant difference between early- and late-term fetuses. Similarly, it provides a relevant difference between humans and animals.

Reply 1:

As we discussed earlier, it's controversial whether humans have souls. If they don't, this objection fails.

Reply 2:

Why think animals don't have souls? (No, that's not in the Bible.) Swinburne's reason (in Chapter 2) for doubting whether early fetuses have souls was that there's no reason to suppose ensoulment occurs before an individual is conscious. But animals are conscious. If a soul is supposed to explain the existence of your consciousness and mental life, it seems reasonable to think animals have souls, since they are also conscious and have mental lives. Further, unless you're certain that they don't have souls, it makes sense to err on the side of caution and not hurt them unless you have a good reason.

Objection 2:

According to the argument from marginal cases, if differences matter between humans and animals, then relevant differences should matter between humans too, such that consistent speciesists should support discrimination against those humans or give up the relevance of the difference. The objection bites the bullet. For example, take R. G. Frey (1987):

> I do not regard all human life as of equal value; I do not accept that a very severely mentally enfeebled human or an elderly human fully in the grip of senile dementia or an infant with only half a brain has a life whose value is equal to that of normal, adult humans. (58)

Speciesists can and should discriminate between humans and animals just as they can and should discriminate between humans.

Reply 1:

This is implausible. Are you really willing to give up on the idea that all humans are equally valuable in order to avoid the implication that humans and animals are equally valuable?

Reply 2:

Even if some humans are of less value than others, this does not mean that abusing them is not wrong. Even if the "severely mentally-enfeebled" or senile are of less value than other humans, torturing them is still wrong. Similarly, *even if animals are of less value than humans, farming and experimenting on them is still wrong.*

Objection 3:

The suffering inflicted by farming and experimentation can be avoided without completely abandoning farming and experimentation. Factory farming causes immense suffering. But we could farm animals while taking their interests into account and not causing them such suffering: we could *replace factory farms with family farms where animals are respected and happy.*

Reply:

Singer's argument still stands against factory farming and animal experimentation. Since most farming and experimentation does in fact inflict so much suffering on animals, *the arguments show that most such practices are wrong.* Further, killing animals also plausibly harms them; after all, killing humans harms them. So even if family farming does not cause as much suffering to animals as does factory farming, it plausibly still harms them in killing them. (But whether killing animals is wrong, even without causing suffering, is controversial, as we will see in the next chapter.)

Objection 4:

PEC states that we should give equal weight to the interests of all those affected by our actions. While this initially sounds plausible, it has counterintuitive implications in some cases. Consider this case from T. M. Scanlon (1998):

> Suppose that Jones has suffered an accident in the transmitter room of a television station. Electrical equipment has fallen on his arm, and we cannot rescue him without turning off the transmitter for fifteen minutes. A World Cup match is in progress, watched by many people, and it will not be over for an hour. Jones's injury will not get any worse if we wait, but his hand has been mashed and he is receiving extremely painful electrical shocks. Should we rescue him now or wait until the match is over? Does the right thing to do depend on how many people are watching—whether it is one million or five million or a hundred million? (235)

If enough people are watching, PEC will recommend that we let Jones continue to be electrocuted until the match is over. Each of the viewers has a comparatively trivial interest in watching the match uninterrupted. However, if we give just a little weight to each viewer's interests, those interests add up.

Yet Scanlon, and many others, think we should save Jones regardless of how many people are watching the match. They think Jones has a **right** to be saved, even if weighing all interests equally recommends not saving him. This fits better with the kind of rights-based view discussed by Regan in the next section of this chapter.

Reply:

Perhaps we shouldn't trust the intuition that we should save Jones no matter how many people are watching. Our intuitions about very big numbers are unreliable, so we are probably just underestimating how important the small pleasures of millions and millions of people are. We will talk more about this in Chapter 8, when we discuss the so-called repugnant conclusion. See Section 5 there for some arguments that we likely underestimate how good providing a large number of people with a small benefit each can be.

Objection 5:

Yet another worry is that PEC doesn't care about the *kind* of interests involved: it demands that we give equal weight even to the bad interests of bad people (cf. Regan 1997, 106). Perhaps we can modify Scanlon's World Cup example to help illustrate this. Suppose that Roman-style gladiatorial combat had survived until the present day. Two slaves are about to fight to the death. The match will be broadcast to billions of eager fans around the world. If the fans are eager enough, and there are enough of them, their interest in seeing the combat might outweigh the slaves' interest in avoiding it. Shouldn't we still stop the combat in this case?

Reply 1:

Indulging sadistic desires like this will actually reduce overall happiness in the long run by encouraging people to mistreat one another. Airing the match might bring about some short-term happiness, but it sends the wrong message about what sort of values are acceptable, encourages people to become more cruel, and so on. Treating all interests equally means that the interests which will be set back by these bad effects outweigh the short-term promotion of interests caused by proceeding with the match.

Reply 2:

We could modify PEC to exclude sadistic interests like this: it would still treat every individual equally—sadistic desires would be discounted whether they are yours or mine—but it would avoid the implication that we should let the match proceed. Perhaps we could even claim that indulging sadism is not really good for you—not really in your interest. Then we might avoid the implication without even changing PEC.

Are objections 4 and 5 convincing arguments against PEC? Do you find the responses available to proponents of PEC convincing? Are there other responses they could make?

Now we turn to Regan's argument for animal rights. The argument has a similar conclusion to Singer's, but it does not depend on PEC, and so avoids the above objections.

4. Regan's Argument

Tom Regan's argument also focuses on the sentience of animals and condemns the widespread mistreatment of animals, especially in farming and experimentation. Since much of this has already been described, Regan's argument can be presented more briefly.

The argument differs most significantly from Singer insofar as it invokes its own technical terminology, especially: subjects-of-a-life and inherent value. Being a **subject-of-a-life** *means having psychological states, such as beliefs, desires, emotions, or sensations.* The psychological life of subjects-of-a-life could go well or badly for them: they could be happy or suffer. Humans are subjects-of-a-life. Regan argues that many animals are too—especially mammals and birds, though he is a little less sure about fish.

Having **inherent value** means *having value that does not depend on*:

- **the interests of others:** subjects have inherent value whether or not they are useful to or valued by others;
- **efforts:** they have it whether or not they have behaved well or badly;
- **well-being:** they have it whether or not they are, for example, happy or miserable.

Having inherent value also brings along *moral rights*. Recall from Chapter 2 that rights are what allow us to make legitimate demands on others: *they create obligations to do or not do certain things on our behalf.* Just as inherent value does not depend on others, so too the moral rights they bring along do not depend on others. Moral rights differ in this respect from legal rights. Legal rights are conferred by the state, depend on the state, and can differ from state to state: for example, people in the United States have a legal right to bear arms, while people in the United Kingdom do not. Moral rights are not conferred by the state, do not depend on the state, and thus do not differ between states: for example, people in the United States have as much moral right to life as do people in the United Kingdom.

Why think that there is such a thing as inherent value? Regan answers that inherent value is needed to make sense of why human beings should not be harmed, no matter their use to others: since human beings have inherent value, they have moral rights that do not depend on their use to others. In other words, it's needed to help explain why human beings have rights that protect them even when harming them would bring greater benefit to others. We will talk more about this in the next chapter, when we discuss whether individuals are "replaceable" (i.e., whether you can make up for killing one individual by creating another, equally happy one). The inherent value view suggests that individuals are not replaceable, but are instead owed a special kind of respect.

Why think inherent value comes along with being the subject-of-a-life? One answer parallels the arguments for the PEC discussed by Singer. If the basis for having inherent value is, say, intelligence, then why don't more intelligent people have more inherent value? Or if you say humans have inherent value while animals don't because humans are more intelligent, what about humans who aren't as smart as some animals? Since all (or virtually all) humans are subjects-of-a-life, Regan's view can explain why everyone has equal inherent value. However, if animals are also subjects-of-a-life, presumably they have inherent value, too, and have rights for the same reason we do.

Regan's argument can be framed as follows:

(P1) Animals are subjects-of-a-life.

(P2) Anything that is subject-of-a-life has inherent value.

(P3) We typically should not harm anything with inherent value.

(P4) Therefore, we typically should not harm animals. (From (P1) to (P3).)

(P5) Killing, farming, and experimenting harms animals.

(C1) Therefore, we typically should not kill, farm, or experiment on animals. (From (P4) to (P5).)

Premise 1 is supported by the evidence about animals' psychology. Premises 2 and 3 make sense of why all and any human beings should not be harmed. Premise 5 is supported by the facts of farming and experimenting on animals, which we outlined in our treatment of Singer.

> Before reading ahead, what are the main differences between Singer's version of the argument and Regan's? Do you prefer Singer's version or Regan's? Why?

5. An Objection to Regan

Objection 1:

Inherent value is mysterious. The Mona Lisa and diamonds are valuable, in part, because they are valued by people: being valued confers value. But Regan is clear that inherent value doesn't depend on being valued by other people. Something can be inherently valuable even if no one cares about it at all, but it is hard to understand what this would mean, or what the source of this value would be, if it is not the result of other people's values (cf. Rowlands 2009, 86–89).

Regan does propose that being the subject-of-a-life gives rise to inherent value. But how it does so is also mysterious. What is the glue connecting subjects-of-a-life and their inherent value? For example, we understand how sex gives rise to pregnancy: there's a physical process of conception. We also understand how squareness is connected to rectangularity: squareness entails rectangularity by definition. But we have no such understanding in the case at hand.

Reply:

First, there is a mystery in the connection between moral features and natural features quite generally. Inflicting unnecessary pain is wrong, but what connects unnecessary pain with wrongness? Saving a drowning child is obligatory, but what connects saving the child and obligatoriness? These are puzzling questions for metaethics. But they do not generally press us to give up on the connections. Inherent value is in the same boat, and we should no sooner give up on it.

Second, *Regan's argument can be changed so as not to depend on inherent value at all.* Consider the following modification:

(P1) Animals are subjects-of-a-life.

(P2) We typically should not harm anything that is a subject-of-a-life.

(P3) Therefore, we typically should not harm animals. (From (P1) to (P2).)

(P4) Killing, farming, and experimenting harms animals.

(C) Therefore, we typically should not kill, farm, or experiment on animals. (From (P3) to P4).)

Removing the premise about inherent value makes the argument simpler, and (P2) is still plausible: we shouldn't harm sensitive psychological subjects, exceptional cases aside. Thus, the notion of inherent value isn't crucial to Regan's argument, and it may be more plausible without it (cf. Rowlands 2009, 93–97).

> Is Regan's argument better with or without the notion of inherent value? Why?

6. General Objections

Some objections apply to the arguments of both Singer and Regan. We present and respond to these here.

Objection 1:

Since animals harm other animals, there's nothing wrong with humans harming animals too. Singer calls this the *Benjamin Franklin objection* after Benjamin Franklin—naturally enough—who told his prospective dinner: "If you eat one another, I don't see why we may not eat you" (Singer 2011, 60).

Reply:

That animals harm each other is no moral justification for us harming them. Animals are not generally moral models for humans: lions kill and eat humans, otters rape baby seals and eat them, female praying mantises eat their mates, raccoons and monkeys steal stuff. These are no reasons for us to kill, rape, cannibalize, or steal. There are also big differences between animals and humans that render a moral analogy between animals and humans weak: for example, animals need to eat other animals to survive, whereas humans do not; humans have moral responsibility, whereas animals do not—so animals cannot be morally blameworthy for eating other animals, whereas we can.

Objection 2:

Steven Davis (2003) argues that if we want to cause the least harm to animals, we should actually eat certain animals (like cattle). This is because *combines, tractors, and other farming equipment used to grow crops actually kill a lot of animals* like mice, gophers, rabbits, and pheasants. Davis calculates that the number of animals killed by growing crops is greater than the number of animals killed by rearing cattle in that same area (including the cattle).

Reply:

Davis's argument overlooks a crucial fact: that an area of land used for crops would feed about ten times as many people as would the same land used for grass-fed cattle (see Singer 2011, 122). Thus, when the quantity of food produced is considered, far fewer animals are killed producing the same quantity of food for vegans than for others.

Objection 3:

Animals should be prevented from killing humans: for example, *if you could prevent a lion from eating a child, you should*—even if it comes to shooting the lion. But if we should consider animal interests or if animals have rights, then they should also be prevented from killing other animals: for example, *if you could prevent a lion from eating a gazelle, you should*—even if it comes to shooting the lion. More generally, the interests or rights of prey mean that we should try to develop contraceptives to prevent the reproduction of predators (and, if need be, their prospective prey too). But this is implausible. So the interests of animals should not be considered and animals do not have rights.

Reply:

Put this issue on hold for now: we'll return to the question of whether we should intervene in the natural world in Chapter 10. As we'll see, animal rights advocates respond to this question differently. Many deny that they're committed to saying we should intervene in nature. Perhaps, say, the animal world is like its own society, and what happens between predators and prey isn't any of our business. On the other hand, when animals threaten humans, that becomes our business. On this view, we should not unnecessarily harm or exploit animals, but otherwise we should leave them be.

However, a different view grants that, in principle, it would be good to intervene in the natural world to reduce suffering. We probably shouldn't do that very much now: ecosystems are exceptionally complicated, and in most cases we don't have the technology or knowledge to make sure that we won't just make things worse. However, if we someday develop the ability to greatly improve the well-being of wild animals, we should do so. We'll consider arguments for this later.

7. Conclusion

Singer and Regan each argue against farming and experimenting on animals. But their arguments face objections. Some of the objections are easily answered, but some are tricky. We leave the reader to decide whether Singer and Regan can convincingly answer all the objections. In the following chapter, we turn from the question of the morality of farming and experimenting to the question of the morality of killing animals—which, as we will see, draws on some new considerations.

Further Reading

Singer's argument is put forward most famously in Singer (2002), and Regan's argument in Regan (2004). Objections against Singer are also presented in Regan (1997), and objections against Regan are presented in Frey (1987); Cohen and Regan (2001) contains a debate between Regan and an opponent of animal rights. For alternative arguments, see Gruen (2014) and Korsgaard (2018). Other neat treatments are Rowlands (2009) and DeGrazia (2002). Comprehensive collections are Armstrong and Botzler (2008) and Sunstein and Nussbaum (2004).

Chapter 7
Humane Farming

1. Introduction

When we discussed farming earlier, we mostly had in mind **factory farming**. Factory farms try to produce meat as cheaply as possible on an industrial scale. This means caring little for the **well-being** of the farmed animals. Factory-farmed animals are often kept in extremely cramped and unclean conditions, unable for their entire lives to engage in natural behaviors, move freely, or even see the sun. They are often subjected to extremely painful medical procedures (such as castration, without anesthetics) and they often develop serious health problems due to overcrowding, stress, inability to rest, bad air quality in the warehouses where they are kept, or the growth hormones and medications they are administered. They also frequently experience cruelty at the hands of workers (Fischer 2019, chap. 2). Their lives often end in painful slaughter. For instance, chickens are crowded onto conveyor belts, shackled upside down, and electrocuted into unconsciousness. They then have their throats slit and are dipped in scalding water to remove their feathers. Sometimes the process doesn't work correctly, and they remain alive and conscious while being boiled (Fischer 2019, 13).

If animals have moral status, this is gravely wrong. Both Peter Singer's animal welfare view and Tom Regan's animal rights view agree. Recall Singer's **principle of equal consideration (PEC)**: *we should give equal weight to the like interests of all those affected by our actions.* PEC entails that factory farming is **wrong**, since the intense suffering of billions of factory-farmed animals outweighs the much weaker interest humans have in cheap meat. Regan's animal rights view entails that it is wrong, since treating billions of **subjects-of-a-life** in this way violates their rights. Since the vast majority of animal products in our society come from factory farming, these views condemn our current farming practices. Indeed, some philosophers even conclude that factory farming may be the *worst problem in the world*, since it causes so much suffering to so many individuals (cf. Huemer 2019, 51–53).

But farming doesn't have to be like this. Some farms give animals fairly nice lives before killing them as painlessly as possible. At minimum, farms *could* do that. Could **humane farming** be permissible? Here, the animal welfare and animal rights perspectives often part ways. Singer (2011, chap. 5) defends the **replaceability argument** for the permissibility of such farming. Others—especially those defending the animal rights perspective—criticize it. First, we will treat

Singer's argument. We'll then turn to a related but simpler argument, the "logic of the larder," including the "diner's defense."

In this chapter, we focus on the morality of *farming practices that kill animals.* Therefore, our discussion will most obviously apply to humanely farming animals for meat and fur, and less obviously to farming for, say, eggs or dairy. But the distinction here is not always clear. For instance, egg producers generally kill male chicks, since they are not useful for their industry. We will also focus specifically on the morality of these practices in modern industrial societies, where most people can easily get adequate nutrition without killing animals.

2. The Replaceability Argument

Recall from Chapter 5 that **utilitarianism** tells us to maximize the balance of either pleasure over pain (for **hedonistic utilitarians**) or satisfied desires over frustrated desires (for **preference utilitarians**). Singer is a utilitarian. And his PEC is supported by utilitarianism: utilitarianism tells us to maximize the satisfaction of interests, no matter whose they are, and this requires treating everyone's interests equally, including those of animals. So to understand what Singer's view entails about the morality of killing animals, we can consider what utilitarianism says about the morality of killing more broadly.

For a utilitarian, killing a person is ordinarily wrong for two reasons (cf. Singer 2011, chap. 4):

1. it **reduces** the amount of pleasure or desire satisfaction, and
2. it **increases** the amount of pain or desire frustration.

Consider the perspective of a hedonistic utilitarian first. Generally, if a person lives, they will have various pleasant experiences in the future. Killing them prevents these experiences, and so decreases the pleasure in the world. Further, killing a person also traumatizes family and friends and terrifies others besides. In this way, killing usually causes bad experiences, increasing the amount of pain in the world. Hedonistic utilitarianism delivers the verdict: killing is (generally) wrong.

A preference utilitarian can say similar things (being scared is unpleasant, but it also frustrates a desire, since people generally don't want to be scared). But for preference utilitarians, death can be bad in an additional way. Generally, people have various **future-directed desires**, that is, *desires about how the future goes.* One of these may be a desire to continue living. Others are not explicitly about living, but require that you continue living. For instance, in the future, you may want to get married, try out a certain restaurant, finish a project you're working on, or see your grandchildren graduate from college.

These sorts of future-directed desires are often among the strongest desires you have. And all of these will be frustrated if someone kills you right now. A preference utilitarian sees this as very bad.

> Which do you find more plausible: hedonistic utilitarianism or preference utilitarianism? Why?

But there's a difference. To see the difference, imagine a mad scientist creates a fully formed adult person. This new person wants to continue living more than anything in the world. They experience a little pleasure and, after five seconds, the scientist painlessly kills them. For a hedonistic utilitarian, it seems that this situation is better than one where the scientist doesn't create the person. The person got to experience a little pleasure and no pain. In contrast, for a preference utilitarian, creating the person is probably worse than the alternative. The person's strongest desire was frustrated, and *having a desire frustrated is worse than having no desire at all*.

> Do you think it is better or worse for the scientist to create the happy person for only five seconds? Does this fit with your answer to the previous question?

How do these differences apply to animals? Start with the point about *causing* bad things. From the hedonistic perspective, it may not be wrong to painlessly kill a farm animal without further bad effects. Animals don't realize they're being farmed for food, so they won't be scared of their impending slaughter. It's hard to know whether animals miss their friends who get slaughtered. At worst, you could slaughter them together, so they don't have time to mourn.

But the situation may be more complicated from the preference utilitarian perspective. Do animals care about the future? Do they understand that there is such a thing as the future at all? Singer (2011) here introduces a distinction between

- **self-conscious** beings who are aware of themselves as distinct individuals with pasts and futures (76); and
- **merely conscious beings**, who lack such awareness.

Singer (2011) thinks that self-consciousness is necessary for having future-directed desires. If I don't have a concept of myself as a distinct individual moving through time into the future, how can I form any preferences about what happens in the future? He writes that

> the merely conscious being does not have a preference for continued life. Perhaps while having a pleasurable experience it has a preference for that experience to continue, or while having a painful experience it has a preference for that experience to end, but it will not have any preferences for the long-term future. (86)

Merely conscious beings have preferences about what is currently happening to them. They might like it if they're eating grass out in the sunshine. If they're kept in dirty, cramped conditions or subjected to painful medical procedures, they may want that to stop. If animals are merely conscious, then factory farming them is extremely wrong because it violates these preferences. But *they don't have preferences about the future* which can be frustrated by a painless death, so that kind of fact can't count against killing them. They don't have plans about what they want to do tomorrow, or desires about how their life goes overall. Singer (2011) writes:

> For preference utilitarians, taking the life of a person will normally be worse than taking the life of some other being, because persons are highly future-oriented in their preferences. To kill a person is therefore, normally, to violate not just one but a wide range of the most central and significant preferences a being can have. Very often, it will make non-sense of everything that the victim has been trying to do in the past days, months or even years. In contrast, beings that cannot see themselves as entities with a future do not have any preferences about their own future existence. This is not to deny that such beings might struggle against a situation in which their lives are in danger, as a fish struggles to get free of the barbed hook in its mouth; but this indicates no more than a preference for the cessation of a state of affairs that causes pain or fear. The behaviour of a fish on a hook suggests a reason for not killing fish by that method but does not in itself suggest a preference utilitarian reason against killing fish by a method that brings about death instantly, without first causing pain or distress. Struggles against danger and pain do not suggest that fish are capable of preferring their own future existence to non-existence. (80)

> Do you think animals are merely conscious or self-conscious? Why?

But is it really true that non-human animals are merely conscious? Singer's answer here is somewhat ambivalent. He thinks that certain cognitively sophisticated animals, such as great apes, clearly *are* self-conscious. He is less sure about other animals. He notes that many dog and cat owners think of their pets as self-conscious, and suggests that "if dogs and cats qualify as persons, the mammals we use for food," such as pigs, who are about as smart as dogs, "cannot be far behind." Chickens seem able to recognize particular other chickens, and "at a more anecdotal level, many people who keep free range hens and lock them up at night describe them as eager to get outside in the mornings—an attitude that suggests anticipating the future." He notes that "of the animals that regularly appear on our plates, fish may seem the least likely" to be self-conscious, but that even they "vary widely in their abilities" (2011, 102). If we're unsure whether an animal is self-conscious, Singer thinks it makes sense to avoid killing it without a good reason, just to be on the safe side. At the same time, he grants that even many non-human animals who have future-directed desires may be *less* oriented toward the future than humans, so that this kind of reason not to kill them is less weighty.

Obviously, this raises difficult scientific questions we can't address here. But suppose we can know that some animals *are* merely conscious. Remember, there was another reason utilitarians might object to killing: apart from increasing the amount of badness, it might decrease the amount of goodness by preventing the individual killed from experiencing future pleasure or desire satisfaction. But this is where the "replaceability" in the replaceability argument comes in. When farmers kill an animal, generally this frees up resources for them to raise a *new* animal in its place. As long as the new animal will be just as happy as the old one, killing a merely conscious being and replacing it with a new one does not decrease the amount of pleasure or desire satisfaction in the world as compared to simply letting the original animal live but not creating a new animal. *Merely conscious beings can be replaced without loss by new, equally happy beings in a way that self-conscious beings cannot.* Killing a self-conscious being and replacing them with a new, equally happy self-conscious being is, on preference utilitarianism, not like this, since killing them contains an additional bad thing (frustrating their future-directed desires) that letting them live while not creating a new person does not. But merely conscious beings lack future-directed desires. As Singer (2011) puts it:

> When we come to animals that, as far as we can tell, lack self-awareness, the best direct reason against killing points to the loss of a pleasant or enjoyable life. . . . Even when the animal killed would have lived pleas- antly, it is at least arguable that no wrong is done if the animal killed will, as a result of the killing, be replaced by another animal living an equally pleasant life. . . . Thus, it is possible to regard merely conscious animals as interchangeable with one another in a way that beings with a sense of their own future are not. This means that in some circumstances—when animals lead pleasant lives, are killed painlessly, their deaths do not cause suffering to other animals and the killing of one animal makes possible its replacement by another that would not otherwise have lived—the killing of animals without self-awareness is not wrong.
>
> Is it possible, along these lines, to justify raising any animals for their meat, not in factory farm conditions but roaming freely around a farm- yard? Suppose that we could be confident that chickens, for example, are not aware of themselves as existing over time (and as we have seen, this assumption is questionable). Assume also that the birds can be killed painlessly, and the survivors do not appear to be affected by the death of one of their numbers. Assume, finally, that for economic reasons we could not rear the birds if we did not eat them. Then the replaceability

argument appears to justify killing the birds, because depriving them of the pleasures of their existence can be offset against the pleasures of chickens who do not yet exist and will exist only if existing chickens are killed. (20)

We can state the argument as follows:

(P1) If painlessly killing an individual is wrong, it is because doing so either (i) *reduces* the amount of pleasure or desire satisfaction, or (ii) *increases* the amount of pain or desire frustration.

(P2) Painlessly killing a merely conscious being does not reduce the amount of pleasure or desire satisfaction, as long as it allows you to replace it with another, equally well-off being, and you do so.

(P3) Painlessly killing a merely conscious being does not increase the amount of pain or desire frustration.

(C) Therefore, painlessly killing a merely conscious being is not wrong, as long as it allows you to replace it with another, equally well-off being, and you do so.

> Before reading ahead, do you think the replaceability argument is plausible? If not, which premise would you object to and why?

3. Objections

Objection 1:

Proponents of the animal rights view are likely to reject (P1) on the grounds that *animals have a right to life*. If an individual has a right to life, this may not mean that it is *always* wrong to kill them. For instance, if killing an innocent person was the only way to stop a nuclear bomb from destroying New York City, perhaps their right to life will be overridden. But the mere fact that we are able to replace you with another, equally happy individual doesn't justify violating your right to life. Echoing an influential criticism of utilitarianism, Tom Regan (2017, 110–11) suggests that utilitarianism fails to recognize that *individuals are valuable*. Instead, it views happiness itself as valuable, with individuals valuable only insofar as they serve as receptacles for happiness—this is the **value receptacles objection to utilitarianism**. He says that, on utilitarianism, we are like cups that hold a valuable liquid: we are important for what we contain, but not in ourselves. Once you have poured the soda into a glass, you can get rid of the can. And if you can get just as much happiness by creating a new individual, it's fine if that requires getting rid of the old one. But Regan suggests that what has fundamental value is *us*, not our experiences: we have **inherent value**. And Regan thinks *this value is possessed, not just by human beings, but by all subjects of lives, including animals.*

Notice that this response also accords with some of the material in Chapter 3. Recall that Marquis agrees with utilitarians that killing is wrong partly because it deprives an individual of a **future of value**. But unlike utilitarians, Marquis doesn't think that depriving an individual of a valuable future is wrong just because it decreases the amount of happiness in the world. If he did, he would have to say that **abortion** is okay, as long as you immediately got pregnant again, so that the overall number of valuable futures was unchanged. And he would have to say that abortion and contraception—or even just abstinence—are morally equivalent after all, since they all have the same effect (one less person with a valuable future). His claim was instead that abortion is wrong because it takes a valuable future away *from the particular individual who is aborted*—it violates their right against losing this future.

> Do you think the value of humans and non-human animals comes from the beings themselves or from their experiences? Is your answer the same for both humans and non-humans?

Reply 1:

Whether we attribute value to *ourselves* or to our *experiences* doesn't make any difference here. If I have a really expensive cup, I don't care if it breaks, if that results in my getting another, equally expensive cup. Similarly, even if individuals have value, the amount of value isn't changed if one is destroyed but replaced by another individual of the same sort.

Reply to the reply:

This illustrates that the *kind* of value Regan thinks individuals have is different from the kind of value liquids or cups have—or, for that matter, the kind of value utilitarians think happiness has (cf. Pettit 1989). Utilitarians think happiness should be *promoted*: that is, we should bring about as much of it as we can. But Regan thinks people and animals should be *respected*. I don't respect you just by maximizing the number of **subjects-of-a-life**. Instead, respecting you means, among other things, not hurting you without a very good reason. The fact that you have the kind of value which deserves respect is what generates your **rights**, including your right to life. And the same is true for animals.

> At first blush, the utilitarian idea that we should maximize happiness is plausible. However, this seems to imply that the value of humans is (in some way) similar to the value of cups. Do you think this means that we shouldn't maximize happiness?

Reply 2:

This response requires rejecting utilitarianism. But, of course, many people find utilitarianism plausible. Whether it works will depend on what we think about moral theories more broadly (see Chapter 5).

Objection 2:

Expanding on the previous objection, the proponent of the animal rights view might assert that the replaceability argument really illustrates a fundamental absurdity with utilitarianism itself. Consider that *many human beings appear to be merely conscious*, in Singer's sense: for instance, infants and people with certain severe intellectual disabilities. Most of us wouldn't want to say that these individuals are replaceable. Yet Singer's view seems to imply that it would be okay to kill them, provided it allows you to replace them with another, equally happy person.

Reply 1:

Usually, other people have attachments to these human beings. Killing them is wrong because it hurts these other people who care about them.

Reply to reply:

Suppose others didn't have these attachments, though. It's still wrong to kill unloved orphan infants, even if you replace them with other, equally happy infants.

Reply to reply to reply:

Singer (2011) actually accepts that his argument implies that *such humans are replaceable*. He is even sympathetic to the thought that, if you have an unhealthy baby, it might be good to kill it and replace it by having a new, healthier baby (160–67). This might maximize overall well-being if the new baby will enjoy their life more and be less burdensome to others. Obviously, this seems extremely implausible to many people, but Singer thinks this is due to a cultural bias. Infanticide has been considered acceptable in many places, and he thinks "our present absolute protection of the lives of infants is a distinctively Christian attitude rather than a universal ethical value" (153).

Reply 2:

Perhaps humans and animals are morally different. (See the "utilitarianism for animals, Kantianism for people" reply in the next section, below.)

4. The Logic of the Larder

Here's a somewhat different way of defending humane farming. The nineteenth-century English writer Leslie Stephen once wrote that

> of all the arguments for Vegetarianism none is so weak as the argu-
> ment from humanity. The pig has a stronger interest than anyone in the
> demand for bacon. If all the world were Jewish, there would be no pigs
> at all. (As cited in Singer 2011, 105)

Stephen's thought seems to be that farming animals for meat *is actually good for them, since those animals wouldn't even exist* if not for humans breeding them. This type of argument is often called the **logic of the larder** (a larder is a kind of food cupboard). Unlike Singer's argument, this argument does not *depend on* utilitarianism. Everyone thinks it's good to do things that are good for others, right? But we'd better pay attention to exactly what the argument is claiming.

A first attempt at stating the argument might look like this:

(P1) If an individual wouldn't exist without a practice, the practice doesn't wrong them.

(P2) Animals farmed for meat wouldn't exist without the practice of farming them for meat.

(C)   Therefore, farming animals for meat doesn't wrong them.

Do (P1) and (P2) seem plausible? If not, which one(s) would you deny and why?

An immediate problem for this argument is that (P1) is questionable. After all, some lives might not be worth living. If your life will be very bad, you might be better off not existing at all. For instance, if I know any children I have will suffer from a terrible genetic condition which will kill them after a short life of miserable suffering, perhaps I shouldn't have kids. This might be a reason against factory farming, since it's plausible that factory-farmed animals have lives which are not worth living. Remember, though, that we're talking about humane farming. And a pleasant life on a nice farm does seem better than nothing, even if the life is a short one. So perhaps we could reframe the argument like this:

(P1*) If a practice benefits an individual, it doesn't wrong them.

(P2*) Humanely farming animals for meat benefits them (since they wouldn't exist otherwise, and they have lives worth living).

(C*) Therefore, humanely farming animals for meat doesn't wrong them.

However, like (P1), (P1*) seems questionable. Sometimes an action benefits someone, but *I should instead take a different action which benefits them more*. Suppose I see you drowning. I could throw you the life preserver which is next to me. Instead, I sing you a beautiful hymn to comfort you as you die. My singing benefits you compared to my doing nothing. But it's still wrong for me to sing *instead of* throwing you the life preserver. Perhaps an advocate for the animals could say the same here. Since humane farming involves breeding the animals, and they have good lives, it does benefit them compared to doing nothing. But there's another option which is *even better* for the animals involved, namely, breeding them but *not killing them*, instead letting them live out their natural lives. Maybe we should do that instead.

The defender of the logic of the larder might point here to a disanalogy with the life preserver case. When I see you drowning, it is *wrong* for me to do nothing. Singing you a comforting song is wrong because it is not *good enough*, but doing nothing is even worse. However, it might seem plausible that we aren't obligated to breed animals at all. If so, then in giving them short, happy lives, we are already doing more for them than we had to. It might be *nice* to give them long, happy lives instead, but how can we be required to do so, when we are already going above and beyond the call of duty? We might reframe the argument again, to look like this:

(P1**) If practice X is better for an individual than practice Y, and practice Y doesn't wrong them, practice X doesn't wrong them.

(P2**) Humanely farming animals for meat is better for them than not breeding them at all, and not breeding them at all doesn't wrong them.

(C**) Therefore, humanely farming animals for meat doesn't wrong them.

However, (P1**) also seems questionable. Consider the following case from the philosopher Derek Parfit. I have three choices:

Choice A: at some great cost to myself, I can save a stranger's right arm;
Choice B: I do nothing; or
Choice C: at the same great cost to myself, I can save both the arms of this stranger. (Parfit, 1982, p. 131)

If the cost is great enough, Parfit thinks it might seem permissible to choose B. It's certainly nice to help the stranger, but I am allowed to prioritize my own well-being instead. However, Parfit thinks that if I help the stranger, it is wrong to choose A. I should instead choose C. *I can permissibly refuse to bear the cost at all. But if I'm going to bear the cost, I have no reason not to save both the person's arms, rather than just one.* If B doesn't wrong the stranger, A is better for the stranger than B, and A does wrong them, it looks like (P1**) is false.

Perhaps the defender of the logic of the larder can respond again. In Parfit's case, choosing A is wrong because there's another option, C, which does more good for the stranger but doesn't cost me anything more. However, breeding animals like pigs without killing them for meat would be much costlier, on balance, than giving them short, happy lives and then killing them for meat. Indeed, it might not be economically sustainable in the long run, since the farmers would lose their main source of income. So perhaps we could again reformulate the argument, to something like:

(P1***) If practice X is better for an individual than practice Y, and practice Y doesn't wrong them, and any practice which is better for them than practice X is very costly to the people acting, then practice X doesn't wrong them.

(P2***) Humanely farming animals for meat is better for them than not breeding them at all, and not breeding them at all doesn't wrong them, and the only option which is better for them than humanely farming them for meat (breeding them without slaughtering them) is very costly to the people acting.

(C***) Therefore, humanely farming animals for meat doesn't wrong them.

We could keep tweaking the argument, but it's already getting pretty complicated. It might be good to instead pause and ask whether we're even on the right track.

> What do you think about the logic of the larder argument so far? It initially seems odd to think that we're really doing animals a favor by farming them for meat. But is the reasoning in the argument strong enough to overcome that sense?

5. An Objection

Objection:

Proponents of the animal rights view may be unimpressed with this argument. Here's a reason they might deny (P1***). You might think there's no obligation to bring individuals into existence. If I don't create you, you don't exist, and non-existent people don't have rights. However, you might think that *if I do create you, then you have various rights, among them the right not to be killed.* In this way, creating a person might be similar to making a promise. Maybe I don't have to promise to give you ten dollars. But if I *do*, you have a right to my giving you ten dollars. It wouldn't be enough to only give you five dollars and say that I must not have done anything wrong, since (before making the promise) I didn't have to give you anything. Similarly, maybe I don't have to create you, but if I do, you have rights that go above and beyond just my ensuring that your life is better than nothing.

Robert Nozick (1974, 38) defends this view by asking us to imagine a world where people limit themselves to having a certain number of children due to overpopulation. In this world, a couple asks whether they can have an extra child, provided they prevent the child from using too many resources by eating him when he turns three. Surely not! But what would be wrong with that? The alternative is that the child never even exists, and living for just a few years seems better than not living at all. The answer seems to be that, while the couple has no obligation to create the child, once the child exists he possesses certain rights, such as the right not to be eaten, even if he only exists because the couple was planning to eat him.

> What did you think of the logic of the larder argument after the last section? What do you think of it now?

Reply:

In response to his argument, Nozick imagines that someone might endorse a view he terms "utilitarianism for animals, Kantianism for people." On this view, *(i) you should maximize the good (i.e., happiness or desire satisfaction) for people and animals insofar as you can without violating rights, and (ii) only human beings have rights.* Unlike Carruthers's version of **contractarianism** (Chapter 5), this view has an easy time ruling out factory farming and cruelty to animals. Since these actions generally harm animals more than they help people, they fail to maximize the good, and refraining from them doesn't violate anyone's rights. At the same time, it might allow us to endorse the logic of the larder argument without endorsing the claim that the couple in Nozick's **thought experiment** acts permissibly. Since human beings have a right against being killed, the couple acts wrongly in killing their child, even though they treated him well up to that point. But since animals don't have rights, all we need to worry about in our treatment of them is whether we are maximizing the good. And killing an animal may not decrease the overall good (at least if they are merely conscious, and we replace them with another happy animal).

Reply to the reply:

Whether "utilitarianism for animals, Kantianism for people" is plausible depends on whether there is a convincing explanation of why all human beings have rights when all animals do not. It will therefore depend on what we thought about the arguments of the previous two chapters. For instance, if Regan is correct that individuals have rights because they are subjects-of-a-life, and the animals we eat are subjects-of-a-life, then "utilitarianism for animals, Kantianism for people" is undermined, since animals possess the basis for rights just like we do.

6. The Diner's Defense

Here is a further modification of the logic of the larder argument called the **diner's defense**. It was developed by the philosopher Abelard Podgorski (2020). Podgorski doesn't himself claim that it justifies humane farming, but he does at least think it shows that consuming humanely raised meat doesn't harm animals, and so undermines a major reason you might have for thinking that doing so is wrong.

The argument is called the diner's defense because it specifically focuses on the actions of the *consumer, not the farmer*. So far, we have mostly talked about humane farming in general terms, as though the morality of what *everyone involved* does depends on the morality of killing animals. But, of course, it's quite possible that you have never personally killed a farm animal, even if you have purchased lots of meat. Initially, we might think that this doesn't seem like an important point. After all, if it's wrong for you to kill someone, it's also wrong for you to hire someone else to kill them. And we might think buying meat is the same: I'm essentially paying the farmer to kill the animal and give me their meat.

However, Podgorski thinks this isn't quite right. If I hire someone to kill my spouse, it's obvious who I harm—namely, my spouse. The hitman wouldn't have killed them if not for me. Similarly, when the farmer kills an animal, it's obvious who the farmer harms—the animal, who is deprived of a potentially valuable future. The animal wouldn't have died if the farmer hadn't killed it. *But when I buy meat, who am I hurting?* Not the animal that the meat came from. That animal is already dead. Either someone else will buy the meat, or it will go to waste. Nor am I hurting the animals who are currently being farmed for meat. Even if the farmer starts selling less meat, it wouldn't make any economic sense for her to keep these animals alive at her own expense.

Instead, if I make any difference, it will be this: *by contributing to the demand for meat, I might cause the farmer to raise more animals in the future.* Of course, if the animals will have very bad lives—like the animals on factory farms—it seems bad to cause more of them to come into existence. But we are talking about animals who live in reasonably nice conditions. Am I hurting them by causing them to be created? Of course, the farmer will eventually kill them, and it would be better for them if she didn't, since they would get to live long, happy lives instead of short, happy lives. So, again, maybe the farmer hurts them. But *if I don't buy meat, this won't mean they get long, happy lives. Instead it means they get no lives at all*, since the farmer won't breed them. So, instead of hurting them, I seem to be *benefiting* them, by getting them some joy instead of none.

So Podgorski thinks it is too quick to say that humane farming is wrong because it hurts animals. What the farmer does in killing the animal might harm it, but, given what the farmer does, the only animals affected by my purchase of humanely raised meat are actually better off. We might go further to say that this not only undermines a reason for objecting to humane farming, but actually shows that humane farming is permissible. If we do this, we might endorse an argument like this:

(P1) If an action is better for everyone affected than any other action I can perform, it isn't wrong.

(P2) Buying humanely raised meat is better for everyone affected than any other action I can perform.

(C) Therefore, buying humanely raised meat isn't wrong.

If we are utilitarians, we might go further still and claim that all this even shows that buying humane meat is *obligatory*. After all, everything else being equal, causing beings who will live happy lives to come into existence produces more good than not doing so.

> What do you think of the diner's defense? Is it an improvement over the original logic of the larder argument? Why or why not?

7. Objections

Objection 1:

Unlike the replaceability argument and the ordinary logic of the larder argument, the diner's defense acknowledges that a wrong is being done to the animals who are humanely farmed for meat. But it fails to acknowledge that it's often wrong for you to participate in, and particularly to benefit from, a practice that wrongs someone, even if your individual participation doesn't, itself, cause any harm. For instance, suppose you sit down for a sumptuous meal at my house, and I inform you that the food was prepared by the children I have enslaved in my kitchen. Would you eat the food? What if I told you that you might as well, since it's already been made, and your protest isn't going to convince me to free the children anyway?

Similarly, buying humane meat makes you *complicit*—or *guilty by association*—*in the wrongful killing of the animals.* You are willingly benefiting from the wrong-doing of the farmer; you are exploiting the animals, treating them as mere means to your own ends. As Christine Korsgaard (2018) writes:

> The question is not about just numbers and consequences. It is about you and a particular animal, an individual creature with a life of her own, a creature for whom things can be good or bad. It is about how you are related to that particular creature when you eat her, or use products that have been extracted from her in ways that are incompatible with her good. You are treating her as a mere means to your own ends, and that is wrong. (223)

Similarly, Regan (2004) writes:

> Farms animals raised for human consumption are today treated as renewable resources, and this is a verdict we reach whether these animals are raised in close confinement or "humanely." . . . To treat farm animals as renewable resources is to fail to treat them with the respect they are due as possessors of inherent value. . . . Since . . . the current practice of raising farm animals for human consumption fails to treat these animals with respect, those who support this practice by buying meat exceed their rights. Their purchase makes them a party to the perpetuation of an unjust practice. (345–46)

Reply:

Perhaps it's *sometimes* wrong to benefit from an unjust practice in this way. But is it *always* wrong? Most of the territory of the United States was unjustly seized from Native Americans. Does this mean everyone of European descent is now required to move out of the country? Many people are concerned about the working conditions in Amazon warehouses. Is it wrong for me to use a product purchased from Amazon? Indeed, nearly every product you use is in *some* way the result of an injustice: either it is made from a resource that was stolen from another group in the past, or the workers who produced it are not treated well, or it was shipped in an environmentally irresponsible way, and so on. To avoid any involvement in injustice, we'd have to find some inhospitable area and live as hermits. But surely we aren't obligated to do that.

> According to this reply, all of us benefit from injustice merely by participating in civilization. Can you think of ways you benefit from injustice? What do you think you should do when that happens?

Reply to the reply:

Maybe it isn't feasible to avoid all involvement with injustice. But you should still avoid it when you can, especially when it isn't too costly. If the alternative to turning down my slave-produced meal is starving to death, you could justify eating it. But that doesn't mean you should eat it just because it looks tasty. And eating humanely raised meat is like the second case. You don't *need* to eat it. You just like the taste of meat.

Reply to the reply to the reply:

This assumes that the only reason for eating humanely raised meat is taste. But the point of the diner's defense is that there's at least one more reason: namely, it's actually *good* when consumers buy humanely raised meat, since it allows more animals to live (short but) happy lives. Eating meat actually *promotes animal flourishing.* Maybe it's too bad that promoting animal flourishing requires complicity in an unjust practice. But we should care more about increasing the number of happy individuals than about keeping our hands clean.

Reply to the reply to the reply to the reply:

We can bring back a familiar argument: *you wouldn't accept this if we were talking about human beings.* Suppose people began humanely raising human babies before slaughtering them and selling their delicious meat. You could say all the same things in defense of this practice (buying the meat actually benefits the children, etc.) as are said in defense of humanely farming animals. But obviously that justification fails in the baby case. So it fails for animals too.

Reply to the reply to the reply to the reply to the reply:

We can counter with a familiar response: perhaps "utilitarianism for animals, Kantianism for people" is true. Then we can't reason our way from the fact that it would be wrong to humanely farm children to the claim that it would be wrong to humanely farm animals.

> What do you think of the "utilitarianism for animals, Kantianism for people" view? Does it seem plausible to you? Can you think of any objections to it?

Objection 2:

The philosophers Tyler John and Jeff Sebo (2020) give a utilitarian argument against humane farming; if it succeeds, it will defeat not only the diner's defense but also the replaceability and standard logic of the larder arguments. They agree that, in a perfectly ideal situation, utilitarianism might allow, or even support, humane farming. But they claim that *in practice* utilitarians should oppose it—individuals shouldn't buy meat from humane farms, and societies shouldn't accept them.

To see why this is, consider that *consciously trying* to do something is often not the best way to do it; instead it can be **self-defeating**. Consider going to sleep: laying in bed trying hard to fall asleep might keep you from going to sleep. You're more likely to fall asleep if, instead of consciously trying, you do some other, unstimulating activity and fall asleep naturally. Or consider the twin goals of "avoiding inconvenience" and "not shooting yourself." Gun enthusiasts say that you should always treat a gun as if it is loaded. In some sense, it would be better if you could treat the gun as if it was loaded *only* when it really was. Then you would be safe *and* could avoid some inconvenience. But "treat the gun as if it's loaded only when you think it is" is a bad rule. You might make a mistake and shoot yourself, and that would be much worse than any inconvenience. Or, finally, consider trying to make yourself happy. If you consciously focus only on trying to make yourself happy all the time, you may wind up very unhappy. For instance, other people will realize you are selfish and avoid you. Promoting your own happiness requires focusing on things besides your own happiness.

Similarly, utilitarians might agree that consciously trying to maximize happiness isn't the best way to do it. If my friend calls me crying and asking for support after their breakup, my pulling up a spreadsheet to try to figure out whether I could better encourage happiness by doing something else won't promote happiness. In most everyday situations, instead of consciously following utilitarianism, I should just follow ordinary moral rules that are easy to apply, that aren't so demanding that I get demoralized, that help me build good habits, and that don't make me seem like a callous robot to other people. These will be rules like "don't kill," "keep your promises," "help your friends in need," and the like. If I do this, unless my situation is unusual (e.g., I'm transporting someone to the hospital who is about to die), I won't try to calculate anything when my friend calls. I will simply support them without thinking, and this will be better, *from the perspective of utilitarianism*, than consciously trying to follow utilitarianism.

> Some people think it's a big problem for an ethical theory if consciously trying to follow it is self-defeating. Does that seem right? Why or why not?

John and Sebo think humane farming is like this. Maybe, in the abstract, "eat humane meat, but only humane meat" sounds like a good principle. But consciously trying to follow it is worse than following a simpler rule like "be a vegan." They give two reasons for thinking this:

1. They suggest that *eating humane meat makes it difficult for individuals to really see animals as morally valuable*. For instance, they cite research showing that study participants who have just eaten

beef tend to say that cows are less morally significant than those who have just eaten nuts (Loughnan, Haslam, and Bastian 2010). People apparently find it difficult to reconcile the idea that animals are morally important with the fact that they eat them, and they resolve the dissonance by deciding animals aren't important after all. Further, in a society where humane farming is allowed and accepted, many people will infer from this that it must be morally okay—and, since it's psychologically difficult to reconcile this with the claim that animals are morally important, they'll decide animals aren't. Of course, if people don't recognize the moral importance of animals, this will make it harder to combat wrongs against them, like factory farming.

2. John and Sebo suggest that, in practice, individuals and societies that try to follow "eat humane meat, but only humane meat" are *liable to wind up eating a lot of non-humane meat*. For instance, they cite research (Rothgerber 2015) according to which "conscientious omnivores" are more likely than vegans to violate their diets and consume factory-farmed products, and feel less guilty when they do. Sebo and John think giving up meat cold turkey will make it psychologically easier to refuse factory-farmed products when you are tempted by them (say, at a nice restaurant or a social gathering) than if you already eat meat sometimes. Further, at a societal level, they think it would be difficult to allow humane farms, but only humane farms. Factory farms exist because their methods are more profitable. But these same economic factors will continue to push in their direction for as long as people eat meat (unless lab-grown meat allows us to remove animals from meat production altogether). Further, enforcing animal welfare standards on humane farms might be difficult. Animals can't go to the police if they're mistreated. Today, many "humane" farms allow various inhumane conditions, even if they still tend to be better than factory farms (Reese 2018), and the problem of regulating them would be even worse in a society which tried to substitute humane farming for factory farming on a large scale.

> Is John and Sebo's argument against humane farming convincing? How would we figure out whether it works?

For reasons like these, John and Sebo conclude that, *even if humane farming makes sense in principle, we would do better in practice to cultivate the idea that animals are friends, not food.*

8. Conclusion

This chapter discussed whether it's permissible to humanely farm animals for meat. Singer's replaceability argument and Podgorski's diner's defense try to show that the answer may be yes, even if we think animals are morally important. But we've seen that they also face criticisms, and it's possible that proponents of humane farming may ultimately need to rely on the "utilitarianism for animals, Kantianism for people" view. Perhaps surprisingly, some of the issues raised in this chapter will actually come up again in the next chapter, when we discuss our obligation to future generations of human beings.

Further Reading

For an influential treatment of the ethics of killing in general, see McMahan (2002). For a defense of humane farming on somewhat different grounds, see Cuneo (2015). For more on the ethics of benefiting from or being complicit in wrongful practices, see Driver (2015), Hooley and Nobis (2015), McPherson (2015), and Fischer (2019, chap. 6). For a classic statement of the idea that utilitarianism fails to respect the "separateness" of different individuals, see Rawls (1999, sec. 30); for a response, see Yetter Chappell (2015). For whether consuming meat might be justified by benefiting other animals as a form of "moral offsetting," see Chan and Crummett (2019).

Section 3

Environmental Ethics

Chapter 8
Future Generations

1. Introduction

We'll now discuss **environmental ethics**. This branch of ethics *deals with our interaction with the natural environment*—for example, it deals with pollution, the use of natural resources, the destruction of habitats, and our interactions with wild animals. One set of questions in environmental ethics concerns the impact of our actions on *currently existing people*. On the one hand, exploiting the environment can increase our quality of life: many of the things that make our lives comfortable and prosperous require using up natural resources, creating pollution, and so on. On the other hand, these activities can also harm currently existing people: for instance, every year tens of thousands of Americans die from diseases caused by pollution, and those most affected are racial minorities and the poor (Neuhauser 2019).

Balancing the considerations at play for currently existing people seems hard enough. But how we should interact with the environment might also depend on other factors, such as how our actions affect *future generations, wild animals, and the environment itself.* These are the considerations we will focus on in the coming chapters.

In this chapter we'll look at how our treatment of the environment should be affected by the interests of **future generations**. Many people worry about "the planet we're leaving for our children." If we pollute too much, use too many resources, fail to address global warming, and so on, then, even if this makes *our* lives easier, it may make the lives of future people worse. However, thinking about our obligations to future people raises certain puzzles. These puzzles arise because our actions will affect not only how well-off future people are, but also *which* future people will exist, and *how many* there will be. (Surprisingly, many of the same issues will arise as in our discussion of humane farming in Chapter 7.) Of course, environmental policy is not the only area that raises questions about our obligations to future generations, but it's an important one.

In what ways do your everyday activities and consumption affect the environment? What potential effects for future generations might they have?

Most of this chapter will be the **non-identity problem** developed by the philosopher Derek Parfit (1984, chap. 16). After describing it, we will discuss three ways one might respond to it. As we'll see, each of these has certain drawbacks, and philosophers do not agree about which way is best. You'll need to decide that for yourself. At the end, we will discuss another issue that Parfit raised: the so-called **repugnant conclusion**.

2. The Non-Identity Problem

Consider the following scenarios:

- **Resource depletion:** We can institute a policy allowing people to use natural resources at an unsustainable rate. If we do, then we will have a *slightly* higher quality of life. However, people several generations from now—in the future, after everyone who is currently alive has died—will have a *much* lower quality of life for a very long time.

- **Waste dump:** We can relax regulations on toxic waste dumps. If we do, people now will save a little money. However, over time, some of the waste dumps are likely to start slowly leaking contaminants. Several generations from now, some people will have serious health problems due to the waste.

- **Global climate change:** We can continue emitting CO_2 at some particular, fairly high level. If we do, people in the near future will be a little wealthier. However, several generations from now people will have to deal with serious problems due to climate change.

These are realistic cases: it seems plausible that we face decisions relevantly like these, and that people have faced decisions like them in the past. And people often think that we should take the "environmentally friendly" course of action in these cases (conserving resources, regulating waste dumps, and cutting down on CO_2), at least if the cost to us of doing so is much less than the cost to future people of our not doing so. But Parfit's reasoning causes some philosophers to question this. Surprisingly, *it may turn out that doing the environmentally unfriendly thing in each of these cases doesn't actually make anyone worse off.* And we might suppose that, if an act doesn't make anyone worse off, it isn't **wrong**.

For it to be true that these actions don't make anyone worse off, two things must be true. First, it must be true that, despite the problems we introduce into the lives of future people, their lives are still worth living. Of course, this might be false—for instance, if the waste causes *severe* health problems, or if we let global climate change get so bad that civilization collapses. But it seems plausible that there will be cases where the future people have lives which are better than nothing, even if their lives are very hard.

Second, the people who will be born if we do the environmentally unfriendly thing must be *different people* than those who will be born if we do not. Think about all the stuff that had to happen for you, *specifically*, to be born. Of course, your parents had to meet each other and have a child, but there's more to it. Millions and millions of sperm were competing to fertilize the egg when you were conceived. If your parents had conceived *even a second earlier or later*, or under just *slightly different conditions*, then in all likelihood a different sperm would have won the race and a person with different DNA than yours would have been born.

Now consider that something as major as which environmental policy we implement will impact lives in all sorts of ways: it will affect where people work, how they commute, what they buy at the store, among many other things. This will cause some of them to encounter and marry different people, conceive children at different times and under different conditions, and so on. And these changes will lead to more and more differences over time, in a "butterfly effect." So when we consider whether to implement an environmental policy, it may be that the following is true: the future people who exist if we (say) conserve resources will be much better off than the future people who exist if we do not. However, these will all be *different people* than those who would have been born without the policy. This is the sense in which depleting resources might not make anyone worse off: each course of action leaves every future person as well-off as they can be, since their lives are better than non-existence and, if we had taken a different course of action, they wouldn't even exist. The people in the resource-depleted future, looking back at our actions, might be tempted to wish that we had conserved resources because they might imagine that *they* would have had better lives if we did. But they really wouldn't have existed at all. The people who existed would have been better off than they are, but they wouldn't be the same people. Since the people in the resource-depleted future only exist if we deplete resources, and since their lives are worth living, perhaps they should be *glad* that we depleted resources.

On this basis, we can construct the following argument for what might otherwise look like selfish, shortsighted environmental policies:

(P1) If an action is better for everyone affected than any other action I can perform, it doesn't wrong anyone.

(P2) Doing the environmentally unfriendly thing in Resource depletion, Waste dump, and Global climate change doesn't make anyone worse off than they would have been if we had done something else, as long as it causes different people to exist in the future and these people have lives worth living.

(P3) Therefore, doing the environmentally unfriendly thing in Resource depletion, Waste dump, and Global climate change doesn't wrong anyone, as long as it causes different people to exist in the future, and these people have lives worth living.

The argument is about whether doing the environmentally unfriendly thing wrongs anyone. If an action doesn't wrong anyone, does it follow that it's *not wrong, period?* Many people think so: they think that there are no "victimless crimes." If this is true, then we can go on to argue:

(P4) If an action doesn't wrong anyone, it isn't wrong.

(C)   Therefore, doing the environmentally unfriendly thing in Resource depletion, Waste dump, and Global climate change isn't wrong, as long as it causes different people to exist in the future, and these people have lives worth living.

> (P1) and (P4) here entail the truth of (P1) in the **diner's defense** argument presented in Chapter 7. (That premise said: "If an action is better for everyone affected than any other action I can perform, it isn't wrong.") Did you agree with the diner's defense argument? Do you agree with the argument above? If you agree with one argument but not the other, why are your judgments about them different?

At this point, we have three options, more or less. First, we might just **bite the bullet** and accept the above argument: we might decide that many apparently selfish and shortsighted environmental policies are *not wrong after all.* Second, we might say that these policies *wrong the people who exist in the future, even though their lives are worth living, and even though they would not have existed if we did not implement the policies.* Third, we might say that these policies are *wrong, even though they don't wrong anyone.* They would be victimless crimes, or what philosophers call **impersonal wrongs**. As we will see, each of these options has some drawbacks, so there is no consensus among philosophers about which is best.

3. Biting the Bullet

Some philosophers (e.g., Boonin 2014) think we should just accept the argument given above: they would agree that we can do the environmentally unfriendly thing in resource depletion and the other cases. In defense of this, they might cite the plausibility of (P1) and (P4), as well as the problems with other approaches we discuss in the next two sections.

Objection:

Parfit himself thinks this is just too intuitively implausible and doesn't take it very seriously. We may be able to think of other cases that make this view seem even stranger. Consider the following example, adapted from one given by the philosopher Gregory Kavka (1982, 100–103):

> **Slave Child:** Slavery has been legalized. A slaver offers to buy a couple a yacht if they agree to have a child and give the child to him as a slave. The couple knows that if they make the agreement, there will not be any way to back out (the slaver will track them down and take the child). They also know that life as a slave will not be very good, but will at least be better than nothing. Finally, they know that if they refuse to make the agreement, any child they have will be different from the child they would have had if they'd made the agreement, because conception would happen under different circumstances. (Perhaps the slaver will book them a cabin in which to conceive the child, but only if they agree.)

This view seems to imply that it's permissible for the couple to accept the slaver's offer and sell their child into slavery. After all, the child won't exist if they refuse the offer, and existing is better for the child than nothing. But this seems implausible. Specifically, it seems quite natural to think that they wrong their child by making the agreement, even though making the agreement is necessary for the child to exist, and even though the child has a life (barely) worth living. Perhaps this case gives us some reason to reconsider whether (P1) is true then. We discuss that in the next section.

4. Wronging Future People

A second option is to say that we do wrong the particular future people who live in the resource-depleted world, even though their lives are worth living and they wouldn't have existed otherwise. Perhaps they have some sort of right which we violate. Maybe they have a right to a life which is *good enough*, not just a right to one which is better than nothing. Or perhaps they have a right to a life which is *as good as ours*, or to their *own fair share* of the Earth's natural resources, and it is unfair of us to use up so much before they arrive on the scene.

> Which premise does this second option reject?

Of course, this route is controversial too. Parfit (1984, 364–66) raises two main worries about the claim that we wrong the future people.

Objection 1:

First, note that whatever the alleged right is—the right to a good enough life, the right to an equal share of resources, and the like—it is not possible for us to ensure that the people in the resource-depleted world have that right fulfilled. Suppose the alleged right is the right to a good enough life. If we deplete resources, these future people exist but their right is not fulfilled; if we don't deplete resources, they don't exist at all. There is no course of action where they actually get a good enough life.

Many philosophers believe that **ought implies can**. That means that you are only *obligated* to do something if you *can* do it. For example, some philosophers think you are obligated to donate money in order to help people in poverty (see Chapter 11). But no one thinks you are obligated to instantly, single-handedly end world poverty. Why are you obligated to do the first but not the second, when the second would do so much more good? Presumably, part of the answer is that you *can't* do the second, and it doesn't make sense to say you have to do something that you can't do. Or suppose I promise to help you move, but I don't show up on moving day because my car breaks down and I can't reach your apartment. I don't act wrongly, since I couldn't fulfill the promise I made earlier.

If ought implies can, then it can't be the case that we have an obligation to give the particular future people in the resource-depleted world a good enough life, since we *can't* give them a good enough life—we can only create *different* people with good enough lives. The person who thinks we violate their rights, then, can't say that we violate their right to a good enough life. They instead need to say that what's wrong is not that we fail to satisfy their right to good enough lives, but instead that we create them, knowing that their right to a good enough life will not be satisfied. Doing so violates their right against being brought into existence under conditions where another right of theirs—the right to a good enough life—cannot be satisfied.

Perhaps there is some plausibility to the claim that people have a right like this. Suppose I have a child, knowing that I have no way to feed them, and they immediately, painfully starve to death. Clearly, I have wronged them. But if ought implies can, what I did wrong was *not* failing to feed them. After all, I couldn't feed them, so it can't be the case that I ought to have fed them. Instead, the problem is that I had the child knowing that I wouldn't be able to feed them. And this is part of a broader phenomenon where it seems wrong to create situations where someone will have a right which I cannot fulfill. For instance, suppose I promised to help you move *knowing* that my car would break down and I wouldn't be able to fulfill my promise. It can't be that I should have kept my promise, since I couldn't have. But it was wrong for me to make the promise in the first place: I knew I was giving you a right to have me help you move when I wouldn't be able to do so.

But this brings us to the core of Parfit's response. Usually, when we have rights, we also have the ability to *waive* rights—to voluntarily give them up. For instance, if I have a house, I have a right against having you walk in and sleep on my couch. But I can waive this right—I can invite you to come in and sleep on my couch, and if I do, there is nothing wrong with your doing so. Or suppose you promised to help me move, and then I realize that I don't need your help. I can tell you that you don't need to come, and then you're no longer obligated to do so.

Further, note that there are times when you are not able to waive a right, but where I know that *you would if you could*. For instance, suppose you have been knocked unconscious in an accident, and the only way I can save your life is to use your car to drive you to the hospital. Since you are unconscious, you are not able to waive your right against my using your car. But surely you *would* waive your right and let me use your car, if you could. This seems like enough for it to be true that I don't violate your rights by using your car.

Parfit thinks that if the future people have a right against being created when their right to a good enough life cannot be satisfied, they would nonetheless waive this right, if they could. After all, the only alternative is their not being born at all, and their lives are still worth living. Since the people in the resource-depleted world would—if they could—happily waive any right they have against our depleting resources, Parfit thinks it is implausible to say that we wrong them by depleting resources.

> In the 1980s, the Reagan administration declined to enact and enforce environmental regulations that would have limited things like air pollution and hazardous waste. Plausibly, if those things had been regulated earlier, then people today would be slightly better off. Possibly, the effects of these regulations may have affected whether or not you were born. Suppose you have the right to a less polluted world. Do you now waive that right in light of the fact that you may not exist in the less polluted world?

Objection 2:

Parfit also raises a second worry for this view: in some cases, it may not be clear that people have the relevant rights at all. So far, you may have been imagining that the people in the future have very difficult lives which are only *barely* worth living. But this might not be true. Suppose we deplete resources, but technological advances mean the people still have lives that are as good as ours. However, if we'd conserved resources and made the technological advances, the (different) people who would have lived in the future would have had *much, much better* lives. If the costs to us of conserving resources would have been fairly small, this might still seem wrong. However, in this case, it seems hard to say exactly which right of the future people we're supposed to have violated. It doesn't seem like it's their right to good enough lives, or to lives as good as ours, or to their fair share of resources. After all, their lives are just as good as ours! Perhaps we could say that they have a right to a life that's as good as we can give them. But we *did* give *them* the best life that we could: conserving resources would mean different people were born. Of course, we will not violate any right of the future people against our depleting resources if they have no such right to begin with.

> Suppose that, if your parents had waited longer to have a child, they could have saved more money and that child (who would have existed instead of you) would have had a better life than you do. Have your parents wronged you by not waiting longer to have a child?

5. Impersonal Wrongs

Here is a final option, and the one that Parfit himself seems to prefer: perhaps implementing the environmentally unfriendly policies is a kind of victimless crime.

It's true that no particular person is made worse off, since the people in the resource-depleted world would be replaced by other people if we did the environmentally unfriendly thing. But it still seems plausible to say that, in some sense, the *overall situation* is worse if we do the environmentally unfriendly thing: there is less happiness in the future if we do it. Perhaps depleting resources is wrong, not because it makes any particular person worse off than they would otherwise be, but because it makes *the world worse than it would otherwise be.*

> Which premise does this final option reject?

Utilitarianism, the view that we should maximize happiness (see Chapter 5), seems to have this result. The world will contain more happiness if we conserve resources for future generations. Since what utilitarianism cares about is the amount of happiness, regardless of who experiences the happiness, the fact that different people will get the happiness is not important. In Chapter 7, we saw that Tom Regan criticized utilitarianism for not recognizing the value of individuals. He claimed that, on the utilitarian view, we are like cheap cups which contain a valuable liquid. Just as it doesn't matter whether a cup breaks so long as no liquid is spilled, so, too, it doesn't matter what happens to particular individuals, so long as the amount of happiness is maximized. But where Regan saw this as a *flaw* in utilitarianism, here it may be an *advantage*, if it helps us give a more plausible answer concerning our obligations to future people.

Unsurprisingly, however, this view also faces certain objections.

Objection 1:

One worry is that, intuitively, *it might not seem that we are required to bring about as much future happiness as we can.* Typically, we think that *if* we have children, we are required to give them good lives. But we don't think that the fact that the child would have a good life, if we had one, means that we *have* to have the child. The view that actions are only *wrong if they wrong someone* could explain this. If I have a child but give them a bad life, I have wronged someone (that child). But if I don't have a child at all, no actual person is wronged by what I have done. (You might be tempted to feel sorry for the possible child who missed out on a good life. But this child is *merely* possible: they don't really exist if I don't have them. Presumably I can't wrong a child who never exists, any more than I could wrong Santa Claus or Sherlock Holmes.)

However, if it is impersonally wrong for me to take a course of action which results in there being less future happiness than there could otherwise be, it seems that I'd be obligated to have a child if they'd be happy, unless they would have such negative impacts on the happiness of other people that the positive impact of creating them was canceled out. However, we don't ordinarily think we're under such obligations. Does someone act wrongly just because they don't have a child when they could (cf. Hare 2013, 79–80)?

To see how counterintuitive this can be, we might return to the slave child example from Section 3. Ordinarily, people think that (i) it wouldn't be wrong for the couple not to have a child at all, but (ii) it would be wrong for them to have a child whom they sell into slavery. But the "impersonal wronging" solution to the non-identity problem says that what the couple does is wrong because it did not maximize the amount of value in the world. However, if the slave child has a life that has (even barely) more happiness than suffering in it, it might seem plausible that their life makes the world better than it would be if the couple had no child at all (see Sections 5 and 6). If this is right, it turns out that, while the couple acted wrongly (since they could have had a different child who was happier, since they didn't sell the child into slavery), it would have been *even worse if they'd had no child at all*, since they would have failed to produce even the value in the slave child's life. But that's counterintuitive!

Objection 2:

This discussion also helps illustrate a major difference between different ethical theories. Some, like utilitarianism, focus on the *value of the world*. Others, like Kantianism or contractualism, focus on *our obligations to particular individuals*. These latter views are concerned with whether we behave in ways that the other parties to the social contract could agree to, or whether we treat other agents as ends in themselves, or whether we show appropriate respect for **subjects-of-a-life**, and so on. But views like these may rule out the possibility of impersonal wronging. The world is not a party to the social contract, or an agent, or the subject-of-a-life, so, on these views, it is hard to see how we could have any obligation to improve the value of the world by bringing about one group of people rather than a different, less happy group of people.

If we agree with this, we could reason in one of two ways. If we are convinced that the impersonal wronging solution to the non-identity problem is correct, we might argue:

(P1) If contractualism (or Kantianism, etc.) is correct, then the impersonal wronging solution to the non-identity problem is not correct.

(P2) But the impersonal wronging solution to the non-identity is correct.

(C) Therefore, contractualism (or Kantianism, etc.) is not correct.

On the other hand, if we were convinced by earlier chapters that one of these views is correct, we might instead reason like this:

(P1) If contractualism (or Kantianism, etc.) is correct, then the impersonal wronging solution to the non-identity problem is not correct.

(P2) Contractualism (or Kantianism, etc.) is correct.

(C) Therefore, the impersonal wronging solution to the non-identity problem is not correct.

Which of these arguments we find persuasive, if either, will depend on which ethical theory we think is most plausible, and whether we think either of the other solutions to the non-identity problem might work.

6. The Repugnant Conclusion

The impersonal wronging solution to the non-identity problem suggested that it might be wrong to take a course of action which makes the world less valuable, even if this action is not worse for any particular person. This naturally raises the question of what things make the world more or less valuable. One question that arises in the context of environmental ethics is, *Is it better to have fewer people with a higher quality of life or more people with a lower quality of life?*

Many environmentalists worry about **overpopulation**, the world having too many people for the environment to support. (This will also play a big role in Chapter 13). They think it would be better if there were fewer human beings, or they are worried about there being too many human beings in the future. Some efforts to combat overpopulation focus on poorer nations, where people tend to have more children. But the population in wealthier nations may be more of a concern, since people in wealthier nations create much more pollution and use many more resources; for instance, a person in the developed world produces hundreds of times as much CO_2 as a person in Malawi (Scheinman 2019). As a result, some people in developed nations decide to have fewer children or not to have children at all. Some people who are concerned about overpopulation are worried about the environment itself: about the fact that human beings destroy natural resources and so on. But others are worried about the impact on human life: they are worried that if there are too many people, people's lives will be worse. There will be too much pollution and not enough resources. Maybe they're motivated by the belief that it's better to have fewer people with a higher quality of life than more people with a lower quality of life.

But this belief may be threatened by the so-called *repugnant conclusion* (Parfit 1984, chap. 17). The repugnant conclusion says that for any world full of happy people, a world full of people whose lives were just barely worth living would be better, provided that the latter world contained enough people (Huemer 2008, 899).

Parfit himself found this conclusion repugnant (hence the name). So do many other people. *Could it really be true that the world would be better if everyone had a life only barely worth living, as long as there were enough people around?* On the other hand, it seems to follow from a fairly natural way of thinking about the value of the world. You might think the greater the balance of happiness over suffering, the better. But this implies that having a *lot* of people, each with a *little* happiness, would be better than having *fewer* people, each with a *lot* of happiness, as long as there were enough people in the first group. For instance, suppose someone with twenty net units of happiness (i.e., the amount of happiness they have, minus the amount of suffering they have) has a really great life, while someone with just one net unit of happiness has a life only barely worth living. Then a world with a billion people, each with twenty units, would not be as good as a world with twenty-one billion people, each with one unit.

If the repugnant conclusion is true, this would not immediately show that people are wrong to worry about overpopulation. If we add more people, maybe everyone will just have lives that *aren't worth living*. For instance, maybe there will be widespread war, famine, and such. Or maybe the people we add will have nice lives but will subtract *more* net happiness from the lives of others than they experience themselves. For instance, maybe if we add more people in wealthier countries, these people will have happy lives, but their lives will subtract even more net happiness from the lives of people in poorer countries (which may be less equipped to deal with climate change, resource shortages, etc.).

What the repugnant conclusion would show is *not* that it would be good for the population to be as large as possible. What it would show is that *it would be best if the population was at the level where adding any further people would subtract more net happiness from the world than it added, even if being at this level means that people, on average, have much worse lives than they would if there were fewer people.* Where this level is in practice—whether reaching it requires increasing the population, or decreasing it, or keeping it stable—is a further question. We won't try to investigate this question here. Instead, we will ask, is the claim in italics true, even in principle?

As mentioned, Parfit himself found the repugnant conclusion repugnant and rejected it. However, he also discovered what seems to be a compelling argument for the repugnant conclusion (1984, chap. 19). He considered this a **paradox**: an argument which seems persuasive, but which leads to a very implausible conclusion. Specifically, he termed it the **"mere addition paradox"** because one of its main assumptions is that "merely adding" people to the world who have lives worth living will not make the world worse.

In explaining the mere addition paradox, we'll rely on a formulation of it from the philosopher Michael Huemer (2008, 901–6). We will also simplify Huemer's statement of it slightly. But this presentation is true to Parfit's original reasoning. The paradox can be formulated by appealing to three assumptions, each of which seems plausible on its own. The first assumption:

> **Mere addition principle:** Suppose that all the same people who exist in world X also exist in world Y, and world Y also has some additional people who don't exist in world X. Everyone who exists in world X is better off in world Y. And the people who only exist in world Y have lives worth living. If this is true, then world Y is better than world X.

This principle is quite intuitive. To get from world X to world Y, first, we make everyone who exists happier on balance. Surely that makes the world better! Next, we add some more people, and all of them have lives worth living. Surely, that at least won't make the world worse. So it seems that world Y is better than world X. Another way to think about it is to note that world Y seems better than world X from the perspective of every single person (cf. Huemer 2008, 903–4). All the people who exist in both worlds should prefer world Y, since they are better off in it. And the people who only exist in world Y should prefer world Y, since they only exist in world Y, and their lives are worth living.

The second assumption:

> **Non-anti-egalitarianism:** If all the same people exist in world Y and world Z, but world Z has more happiness, a higher average happiness, *and* a more equal distribution of happiness, then world Z is better than world Y.

This principle also is quite plausible. Earlier, we talked about whether it would be good to add more people to the world if it meant that the total amount of happiness would increase, though the average amount of happiness each person got would decrease. But we can avoid that question for now. Surely adding more total happiness to the world *and* increasing the average amount of happiness will make the world better. And surely distributing happiness more equally among people at least won't make the world *worse*. Many people think it would be *better* if the happiness were distributed equally; some others think it doesn't matter either way. But few people think it's best if happiness is concentrated among just a few people, without others getting a share (cf. Huemer 2008, 904). For instance, we don't think it would be good to take money from poor people and give it to rich people, even when it will benefit the poor people much more. This is why the principle has the odd name of "non-anti-egalitarianism"; it's saying we are at least *not against equality*.

The third assumption:

> **Transitivity:** If Y is better than X, and Z is better than Y, then Z is better than X.

Transitivity seems intuitively plausible: if you improve world X to make world Y, and improve world Y to make world Z, presumably you won't end up worse than where you started! Further, there are arguments for it which aim to show that if we assign values in a way that is not transitive, we will make clearly irrational decisions. One of these is the so-called **money-pump argument** (cf. Huemer 2008, 904). It tries to show that if we have preferences which are intransitive and act in accordance with them, we will give up things we care about for no reason.

Here's the money-pump argument. Suppose you prefer apple pie to blueberry pie, blueberry pie to cherry pie, but prefer apple pie to cherry pie. Your preferences are not transitive: even though you prefer blueberry to apple, and cherry to blueberry, you don't prefer cherry to apple. Now, suppose you have a slice of apple pie. I offer to trade you your slice of apple pie for (i) my slice of blueberry pie and (ii) some other thing you care about only slightly—let's say a penny. Since you like blueberry more than apple, you decide it's worth it and make the trade. Now I offer you another trade: I'll give you a piece of cherry pie in exchange for the piece of blueberry pie you just got and another penny. Since you like cherry pie more than blueberry pie, you make the trade. Now I offer you yet another trade: I will give you back your original piece of apple pie in exchange for the cherry pie and another penny. This is where transitivity comes in: since you like apple pie more than cherry pie, you make this trade too. But now you have the same piece of pie you started with and have lost three cents. And of course, I can keep doing this until, presumably, I have taken all the money you have, and you are left with that same piece of apple pie. But surely you prefer having the slice of apple pie and your money to having the slice of apple pie and no money. *So, by following intransitive preferences, you can be inevitably led to make a series of trades that leaves you much worse off.* Many people think this is clearly irrational, and so they think rational preferences must be transitive.

Each of these three assumptions—the mere addition principle, non-anti-egalitarianism, and transitivity—seems highly plausible. But it turns out that if we accept all three, we are committed to the repugnant conclusion. It is easiest to see why with the following example and the visual in Figure 5.

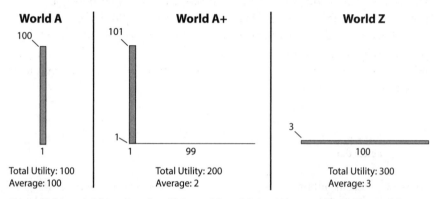

Figure 5. Mere Addition Paradox. (Adapted from Michael Huemer, "In Defense of Repugnance," Mind 117 (2008): 903.)

Suppose we start with world A. Let's say it has one person in it, who is at 100 units of happiness (a very good life). Now we move to world A+. To get to world A+, we make the person who existed in world A *slightly* happier—now they have 101 units of happiness. We also add 99 additional people. Each of them has a life which is worth living, but only by a *very very slight* amount: each of them has only 1 unit of happiness. By the mere addition principle, world A+ is better than world A. The only differences are that (i) the person who existed in world A is a little better off in A+, and (ii) there are some additional people whose lives are worth living, if only barely.

Now we move from world A+ to world Z. To get there, first we evenly distribute the happiness that already existed among everyone. If you do the math, you'll see that world A+ contained 200 units of happiness, which, divided equally among all one hundred people, means that each person gets 2 units. Next, we make everybody just a little bit happier, bumping them up to 3 units of happiness each—a life which is still only barely worth living, even though it's better than the mere 1 unit most people had in world A+. Compared to world A+, world Z contains *more happiness* (300 units vs. 200 units), has a *higher average happiness* (3 unit vs. 2 units), and the happiness is distributed *more equally* (the distribution is perfectly equal, as opposed to concentrated almost entirely among a tiny portion of the population). So, by non-anti-egalitarianism, world Z is better than world A+.

The mere addition principle implies that world A+ is better than world A. Non-anti-egalitarianism implies that world Z is better than world A+. Now we can finish the argument: transitivity implies that, since A+ is better than A and Z is better than A+, Z is better than A. But of course, the comparison between world A and world Z is between a world with a small number of very happy people and a larger number of only barely happy people. And there is nothing special about the particular numbers we chose: by the same reasoning, we can show that any world with a certain number of people, all of whom are very happy, is worse than a world with way more people, all of whom have lives only barely worth living, as long as the second world has enough people. For instance, to return to our earlier example, we could show that a world with one billion people each at twenty units of happiness is worse than a world with twenty-one billion people each at only one unit. So the repugnant conclusion is true if each of the three assumptions above is true. Are they? Or is there some way around them?

7. Avoiding Repugnance?

To avoid the repugnant conclusion, we must reject at least one of the three assumptions that generate the mere addition paradox. One natural alternative might be to say that the value of the world depends not on the *total amount* of happiness in the world, but on the *average amount* which individuals possess (Parfit 1984, sec. 143). Thanos in *Avengers: Infinity War* appears to like this alternative. He goes as far as to believe that the higher average level of happiness that would result from halving the population is valuable enough to justify killing off half of the population.

The average amount view requires rejecting the mere addition principle. If we add people to the world whose lives are worth living but who are less happy than the average, this brings the average happiness down and, according to this view, makes the world worse. This seems surprising, especially if each person's life would be very good, considered on its own. Suppose we live in a world where everyone is *very* well-off: everyone has 100 units of happiness, which, we can suppose, is a whole, whole lot. I have a child, but he's prone to get stuffy noses, so he only has 99.9 units of happiness. He brings down the average very, very slightly. But his fantastic life doesn't thereby make the world worse, does it?

Things seem even worse if we flip the situation and consider a world where people have incredibly *bad* lives. Parfit (1984, 422) asks us to consider a situation where we all live in complete misery, but if we have children, they will be *slightly* less miserable than we are. Having children who live in abject misery, but slightly less misery than we do, would raise average **well-being** in this scenario (from "extremely bad" to "very slightly less bad"). The average view therefore implies that what would make the world best in this scenario is having as many children as possible, even though they will be tortured horribly throughout their lives. That doesn't seem right! For reasons like these, Parfit rejects the average view, even though he also rejects the repugnant conclusion.

But if we want to avoid the repugnant conclusion *and* reject the average view, what view should we hold instead? Philosophers have developed many sophisticated answers to this question. But other philosophers are unhappy with these answers, claiming that they also have implausible implications (Huemer 2008, 911–16). They suggest that maybe we should accept the repugnant conclusion after all.

Consider: we didn't have an *argument* against the repugnant conclusion. It just didn't seem right. But sometimes we realize that things would seem a certain way to us, whether or not they actually were that way. For instance, if something looks red to me, that's usually a reason to think it's red. But suppose I'm wearing red-tinted glasses that make everything look red, regardless of what color it is. Then the fact that something looks red is no longer a reason to think it really is: it would look red no matter what.

The philosopher Michael Huemer (2008, 907–11) argues that, for a similar reason, perhaps we should distrust our anti-repugnant conclusion judgment. It may be the result of certain mistakes or biases that make the repugnant conclusion seem false for reasons having nothing to do with whether it's really false. For instance, he suggests that it may be because *we are bad at imagining large numbers*. Suppose someone told you that you would live happily for a *million* years, and you believed them. You'd be excited! But would you be any more excited if they told you it would be for a *billion* years? Probably not (Huemer 2008, 208). How can that be, when a billion years of happiness is obviously so much better than a mere million? The answer is probably something like, both a million years and a billion years are way too long for you to imagine. In either case, if you try, what you're really imagining is just "a really long time." You may know, intellectually, that a billion years is better, but it might not *feel* much better when you imagine it. In the same way, perhaps your intuition about the repugnant conclusion doesn't really take into account all the extra people in the more heavily populated world. Can you really imagine the difference between a billion people and twenty-one billion people, or do you just imagine "a really big group of people" in either case?

Relatedly, Huemer suggests that our intuition may be affected by a kind of *self-centered bias*. Maybe, when we compare worlds A and Z, what we are really thinking about is which world we would rather live in. Of course, you might prefer to live in world A, since you will be much better off there. But what you were supposed to be considering is which world is better overall, and if you just think about which one you would be better off in, you won't take into account that there are so many additional people with lives worth living in world Z. Further, Huemer thinks we may be *underrating low-quality lives*. What do you imagine when you think of a life that's "barely worth living"? Perhaps you are thinking of a life without anything good in it at all, without joys or comforts or loving relationships, where every moment is a struggle for existence. But lives that are barely worth living are still worth living, and perhaps what you're really imagining is a life that *isn't* worth living. Of course we wouldn't want everyone to have lives that aren't worth living. But that isn't what the repugnant conclusion is about.

So Huemer claims that we should *accept the repugnant conclusion after all.* On the one hand, we have what seem like good arguments for it. On the other hand, we can explain why it would seem wrong to us whether or not it was, and views which avoid it (like the average view) have other problems. Fortunately, he claims that even if the conclusion is repugnant "in theory," it need not be repugnant "in practice" (2008, 928–30). Remember, it doesn't say that we should make as many people as possible, bringing about a world where "each of our descendants occupies a single, cramped room and there is just enough gruel to keep them from hunger" (928). It says that it would be best if the population were at the level where adding more people would detract more happiness, on balance, than it produces. It is hard to say where that level is, but Huemer thinks we'd probably reach it before everyone had to eat gruel.

Bringing this back to environmental ethics, many people worry about over-population since as the world becomes more and more populated, people may live less good lives due to scarcity of resources, increased conflict, and the like. But if the repugnant conclusion is correct, a heavily populated world *might* actually be better than a non-overpopulated one, provided that the happiness of the additional less happy people outweighs the loss of happiness to the other people. Again, however, this doesn't *immediately* follow from the repugnant conclusion: it depends on whether the happiness of the additional people really did outweigh the loss in happiness to others. How much we should worry about overpopulation might then become a partly empirical question.

> Is Huemer's position persuasive? If it isn't, can you think of a way of evaluating worlds that would allow us to avoid both the repugnant conclusion and the problems faced by the average view?

8. Conclusion

In this chapter, we've discussed our obligations to future generations of human beings and the impact these might have on how we should treat the environment. Of course, how we treat the environment also affects wild animals, as well as the environment itself. We'll discuss these in the next two chapters.

Further Reading

Parfit (1984) helped set the agenda in population ethics; since its publication, it has become a huge area of philosophical interest. Boonin (2014) surveys much of the recent literature on the non-identity problem; for a shorter introduction, see Roberts (2019). For an argument relating questions about non-identity to the questions about whether we should intervene in nature discussed later in this book, see Korsgaard (2018). For an interesting treatment that focuses more on an individual's decision about whether to have children, see Weinberg (2016). For an overview of the repugnant conclusion, see Arrhenius and Tännsjö (2017); for an edited volume on it, see Ryberg and Tännsjö (2004). For an argument that a satisfactory population ethics is (given certain assumptions) actually impossible, see Arrhenius (2000).

Chapter 9
Environmentalism

1. Introduction

In the previous chapter, we discussed obligations to **future generations**. In the next chapter, we discuss obligations to wild animals. But many people think it is morally important how we treat certain aspects of the environment itself, apart from how this treatment affects individual people or animals. They might think it matters, for its own sake, that we *preserve ecosystems* (say, by avoiding habitat destruction and preventing the introduction of invasive species), that we *preserve biodiversity* (say, by keeping endangered species from going extinct), or that we *preserve natural beauty* (as found in, say, the Grand Canyon, or waterfalls, or redwood forests). One famous take on this position comes from writer Aldo Leopold in his famous 1989 book, *A Sand County Almanac*: "A thing is right when it tends to preserve the integrity, stability, and beauty of the biotic community. It is wrong when it tends otherwise" (224). (A "biotic community" is a bit like an ecosystem.) Leopold called this view the **land ethic**. Something like this seems to be central to much contemporary **environmentalism**.

In one broad sense, environmentalism is just the view that *you should care about the environment*. In this sense, you could be an environmentalist even if you think nature has no intrinsic value. Perhaps you think we should preserve the environment only because doing so will promote the interests of people and animals. But in this chapter, we'll use 'environmentalism' in a more specific way, for the philosophical view that we should care about the environment (ecosystems, biodiversity, natural beauty, etc.) *for its own sake*, apart from how doing so impacts people or animals. In the terminology of Chapter 8, destroying the environment might be an impersonal wrong: something which is wrong despite not wronging any particular individual. This view is held by Leopold and by many other philosophers who write on environmental ethics.

It's important to understand this distinction. Concern for people and animals is obviously *related* to concern for the environment. People and animals live in ecosystems, we like to look at natural beauty, and so on. But they're not the same. In fact, sometimes they may conflict: concern for the environment itself might require that you do things which are *worse* for the people and animals affected. For instance, suppose every person and animal except for you has died in a great cataclysm. You would like some firewood, so that you are not so cold. You can get it by chopping down one of the last redwood trees in existence. (Redwoods are those huge trees that grow in California and that are featured on Endor in *Star Wars: Episode VI: Return of the Jedi*.) Should you cut down that redwood (Attfield 1983, 155–56)?

Many people would at least *hesitate* to cut down the tree. One possible explanation for this is that the tree *itself* has interests we need to consider. Perhaps trees have rights against being killed, just as people do. Even if we agree with this, it's not clear that it completely accounts for the judgment. You probably wouldn't worry nearly as much about cutting down an ordinary tree for firewood. What really seems to drive the intuitions are concerns about biodiversity and natural beauty: this is the *last* redwood, and redwoods are particularly impressive. Cutting it down might be better for the only conscious being affected: you. But perhaps you have reasons not to do it, anyway.

> Perhaps you think it's obvious that you would (and maybe even should) cut down the redwood in that situation. But we can still ask whether there is at least a reason not to. Did you hesitate before answering? Or feel a twinge of sadness at the thought of cutting down the last redwood? If you said yes, do you think that shows there is a reason to not cut down the last redwood (even if it's outweighed by the importance of your survival)?

Or consider another example from the philosopher Elizabeth Anderson (2004):

> Rabbits in Australia are . . . driving various species of plants to extinction. Environmentalists advocate sacrificing the rabbits for the sake of the plants. This is perverse from both an animal rights and animal welfare perspective: The animals have moral considerability, but the plants have no competing claims to consider. (279)

Of course, if these plants are driven to extinction, perhaps that would affect the ecosystem in ways that ultimately hurt other animals (for instance, members of some other species that feeds on them). But suppose this isn't the case. In that situation, if we are just concerned about the **well-being** of animals, we might leave the rabbits alone. However, many environmentalists would still support attempting to preserve biodiversity and natural ecosystems, even though it means killing members of the invasive animal species.

So the question at issue in this chapter is not whether you should care about these features at all. If you care about people and animals, then you will care about the environment insofar as the environment affects people and animals. The question is instead: Do you care about the environment *only because of how the environment affects conscious beings, or do you instead care about ecosystems, biodiversity, and/or natural beauty for their own sake?* The proponent of the land ethic supports the latter view. Recognizing this distinction may be particularly important for understanding the discussion in the next chapter. As we'll see, some philosophers think caring about wild animals may require radically changing the environment in which they live.

2. Arguments in Favor

2.1. Arguments from Wonder

There are at least two main types of arguments to which environmentalists might appeal. We might call the first the **argument from wonder**. In defending their view, environmentalists sometimes appeal to the positive **emotions** we feel when interacting with nature. Consider the following passage from Anderson (2004):

> When I take my seven-year-old daughter to the Huron River in Michigan, or to the Atlantic Ocean in midcoast Maine, we spend endless hours together by the water, looking for shells, crawfish, crabs, fish, seaweed, and other living things. She speaks to me, wide-eyed, of how there must be a "kabillion" grains of sand on the beach. Her fine observational skills lead her to one discovery after another: minute, perfectly formed snail shells in unexpected locations, metallic green beetles and flies, an extraordinarily dense tangle of red worms under a rock in a tidal pool (we wonder how they can survive in the sharp sand, unlike slugs). She asks, and sometimes correctly answers, questions about how one creature is related to another: Do seagulls eat snails? What lives among the seaweed? Are those freshwater crawfish just little lobsters? Comparing the flora and fauna at the different locations, she grasps, at some level, that the living things she knows are part of one vast interconnected system. Our responses to the natural world around us on such occasions are wonder and awe. (292–93)

We might wonder what our feeling certain emotions has to do with anything. This is a philosophy book; aren't we supposed to be focusing on *reason*, not just feelings? But it seems plausible that an emotion can be rational or irrational, depending on whether it is directed toward something that is appropriate, given the emotion it is. For instance, it seems rational to be afraid of a tiger charging at me, but not to be afraid of a paperclip. This is because fear is appropriate when it is directed toward something dangerous, and (presumably) only one of those things is dangerous (cf. Anderson 2004, 292).

Can you think of times in your life when you've had an appropriate emotional reaction? How about an inappropriate one? What do these cases tell you about whether emotions can inform your judgments about various situations or claims?

Or consider a specifically moral example. Suppose you read a detailed, true story about someone lighting a cat on fire for fun. If you're an ordinary, decent person, you'll likely feel some strong emotions in response, such as *outrage and revulsion* toward the perpetrator and *sympathy* for the cat. But if we think that our emotional reactions to things usually make sense, we might take the fact that ordinary, decent people have these reactions as evidence that the person's action really is revolting and outrageous, and that the cat does deserve our sympathy. And we might in turn take this to show that what the person has done really is morally bad, and that the cat really does have a kind of value which demands that we not treat it cruelly (cf. Anderson 2004, 292).

If all this is correct, then we can ask whether our responses of awe and wonder to nature are appropriate, and, if they are, whether they tell us anything morally important. Anderson (2004) thinks that, when we reflect on them, we see that they are appropriate after all, and that this shows us that nature is an appropriate object of our curiosity, care, and respect:

> The proper object of awe is the sublime, that which is so grand that it gives us intimations of the infinite. The proper object of wonder is the wonderful, that which commands our contemplation and quest for understanding. Nature is both sublime and wonderful, so these responses are rational, too. They make us want to study nature, and also to preserve and protect it, in its full integrity and complexity. (293)

Though Leopold isn't really explicit about it, something like the argument from wonder may have been his own justification for the land ethic (cf. Callicott 1998). Large parts of *A Sand County Almanac* are spent on things like lovingly describing the ecology around Leopold's farm. One of the authors of the book you are currently reading was assigned *A Sand County Almanac* as a college freshman and, quite frankly, couldn't figure out what the point of any of that was. But maybe Leopold's hope was that, by revealing the intricacy and interconnectedness of nature, he could instill a sense of wonder and awe in the reader too.

2.2. Arguments from Cases

Here is a second environmentalist argument. We might call it an **inference to the best explanation (IBE)**. IBE is a type of argument that counts a theory or principle's explanatory power as evidence for the truth of that theory or principle. The idea would be that environmentalism can give a plausible explanation of our judgments about certain cases. On the basis of its explanatory power, we should accept environmentalism. Recall our earlier redwood example. There, many people think you have reason not to chop down the redwood, but it is hard to explain this without attributing some kind of intrinsic value to biodiversity and natural beauty. Or consider the fact that, as Holmes Rolston III (1985) notes, hundreds of elk starve in Yellowstone National Park each year, and the Park Service is not alarmed, but the starving of an equal number of grizzly bears [an endangered species], which would involve about the same suffering in psychological experience, would be of great concern. (722)

If you should save the life of a grizzly bear over that of an elk, what explains this? Presumably it's not because the interests of the grizzly bear matter more. If you could give either animal an equally fun toy, you wouldn't be obligated to give it to the grizzly bear. And presumably it isn't because the grizzly bear's rights are stronger. Why would that be? It must be because saving the grizzly bear is more important from the perspective of maintaining biodiversity and functioning ecosystems. After all, presumably you'd make the same judgment in the case of members of other endangered species (panda bears, black rhinos, etc.).

> We've now considered two arguments that you should care about the environment for its own sake: the argument from wonder and the **argument from cases**. This time, it's your turn: take a stab at putting these arguments in premise-conclusion form.
>
> Once you've done so, examine your arguments. Does the conclusion follow from the premises? Do the premises seem true? If not, are there ways you can modify the arguments to make them better?

3. Objections

Objection 1:

Look again at Leopold's statement of the land ethic: "A thing is right when it tends to preserve the integrity, stability, and beauty of the biotic community. It is wrong when it tends otherwise." Notice that, as stated, this *doesn't accord any intrinsic importance to any of the individual people or animals who actually make up an ecosystem*; what matters is just the "integrity, stability, and beauty" of the ecosystem itself. As Elizabeth Anderson (2004) notes, "The environmentalist's object of concern is typically an aggregate or system: a species, an ecosystem, the biosphere. Organisms, from this perspective, are fungible, valued for their role in perpetuating the larger unit, but individually dispensable" (278).

We saw in Chapter 6 that Tom Regan criticizes **utilitarianism** for allegedly failing to recognize the intrinsic value of individuals. He claimed that utilitarianism treats individuals as valuable only insofar as they serve as containers for happiness. But this view seems not to be concerned with individuals *or* happiness, except insofar as they play a role in the ecosystem. What matters is only the *collective*.

People sometimes seem to think this way when it comes to wild animals. They are concerned when they hear about, say, a member of an endangered species dying. But they aren't concerned at all when other wild animals die, even when they die in very painful ways, such as through predation, disease, or starvation. It seems as though these people want for there to *be* animals and for there to be lots of different kinds of them. But they don't particularly care if individual animals suffer and die, as long as there are enough others of the same kind. But does this make sense morally speaking? If individual animals have intrinsic value, or if their well-being matters (see Chapter 6), shouldn't we care about *them* and not just the collective?

Think of the implications of caring only about the collective. Your pet dog doesn't really seem important to the ecosystem. In fact, producing food for him is probably slightly bad for it. Should you therefore kill him? Or think of the implications of this view for the treatment of *human beings*. Regan (2004) notes that

> if . . . the situation we faced was either to kill a rare wildflower or a (plentiful) human being, and if the wildflower . . . would contribute more to the "integrity, stability, and beauty of the biotic community" than the human, then presumably we would not be doing wrong if we killed the human and saved the wildflower. (362)

But Regan thinks this implication is unacceptable. He goes so far as to name the view in question **"environmental fascism."** Just as political fascism cares only about a nation or race and cares about individuals only insofar as they affect the collective, environmental fascism cares only about the ecosystem as a whole and not about the individual humans and other animals who live in it.

Reply:

For the land ethic to be plausible, it will have to acknowledge that *ecosystems, taken as a whole, are not the only thing that matters morally*. Perhaps we could say that the fact that something "tends to preserve the integrity, stability, and beauty of the biotic community" *counts in favor* of doing it, while the fact that an action tends otherwise *counts against* doing it, but that these considerations can be outweighed by other factors. This might allow us to explain why we should kill the wildflower instead of the human: although its importance to the biotic community counts in favor of saving the wildflower, there are other, more important reasons to save the human. At the same time, perhaps this also explains why (say) I shouldn't cut down the redwood: although it would be nice to have firewood, this reason isn't important enough to outweigh the loss to the biotic community.

Of course, if we adopt this view, it doesn't tell us exactly how we should weigh considerations having to do with particular people and animals against those having to do with the environment. This will come up again in the next chapter.

Objection 2:

We might think, though, that traditional ethics can't agree even with the idea that we have moral reasons to care about the biotic community as a whole *in addition to* the reasons we have to care about the interests or rights of individuals. Think about the moral theories discussed in Chapter 5. Utilitarians are concerned about happiness or desire satisfaction. Kantians are concerned about rational agents. Contractualists are concerned about parties to the moral contract. But ecosystems and species don't experience anything, aren't rational agents, and aren't parties to contracts. So it seems that these moral theories will say that environmental considerations matter *only* when they affect conscious beings. If we accept one of these moral theories, then, it seems that we'll need to reject even modest versions of the land ethic.

Reply 1:

Leopold himself might say this shows a limitation in these ethical theories. Philosophers often discuss the idea that our "moral circle"—the group of things we think are worthy of moral concern—has *expanded* over time. We have come to realize that we should care about everyone, not just people of our own tribe, nation, race, and so on. Leopold (1989) notes that, in the *Odyssey*, when Odysseus finally reached his home, "he hanged all on one rope a dozen slave-girls of his household whom he suspected of misbehavior during his absence" (201). He viewed them as mere property. But now we realize that his actions were wrong. (Of course, maybe some people back then realized they were wrong too—certainly they *should have* realized it. But the text seems to expect that the audience won't have a problem with it.) If you were convinced by the arguments from Peter Singer or Tom Regan in Chapter 6, you will think that we often treat animals as mere property when we should be showing moral concern for them.

In the same way, Leopold (1989) suggests that we must develop a new ethics to account for our obligations to the environment itself:

> There is as yet no ethic dealing with man's relation to land and to the animals and plants which grow upon it. Land, like Odysseus' slave-girls, is still property. The land-relation is still strictly economic, entailing privileges but not obligations. The extension of ethics to [the environment] is, if I read the evidence correctly, an evolutionary possibility and an ecological necessity. . . . Individual thinkers since the days of Ezekiel and Isaiah have asserted that the despoliation of land is not only inexpedient but wrong. Society, however, has not yet affirmed their belief. I regard the present conservation movement as the embryo of such an affirmation. (201)

Reply 2:

Perhaps traditional moral theories can do more to accommodate environmentalism than initially seems to be the case. For instance, utilitarianism is a form of

consequentialism. Consequentialism says that the morality of an action is determined by its consequences. Utilitarianism says that the only ultimately valuable thing is happiness. We can think of utilitarianism as consequentialism *combined with* the view that we should evaluate consequences in terms of the amount of happiness present. However, if other things are also valuable, they also could matter for evaluating consequences. A **pluralistic consequentialist** accepts consequentialism but says multiple different things have value. (The utilitarian thinks only one thing—happiness—does.) A pluralistic consequentialist could say that both happiness and the environment have value, so we should take both into account morally.

Here is a different, non-consequentialist approach. A central set of ethical questions is about *right and wrong*—what are you **morally required** to do, what are you **morally permitted** to do, and what are you **morally forbidden** from doing? These are very important questions, and they are what the moral theories we discussed focus on.

However, there are further distinctions we can draw in ethics. Focus on the actions which you are morally permitted to do, but not required to do. Some of these are *neutral*, like wiggling your toes. Others are *good*, like calling your parents on the weekend or sharing your candy with your little brother. You don't *have* to do these things, but it would certainly be nice if you did. On the other hand, some are *bad*, like grabbing the last seat on a bus before an old lady can get it or refusing to share your candy with your little brother. These aren't so bad that you're forbidden from doing them, but they're still jerk moves. You have some moral reasons to do the good things and avoid the bad things, even though you are permitted to do all of them.

In a similar way, the contractualist T. M. Scanlon suggests that we must distinguish between what he calls **narrow morality** and **broad morality**. Narrow morality involves judgments of what is right and wrong or, as Scanlon describes it, of "what we owe to each other" (1998, 6–7). Broad morality, on the other hand, involves further ethical questions which are not answered just by figuring out what is right and wrong. For instance, he notes that "idleness" and "wastefulness" might be morally criticized even when they aren't wrong—even when we don't owe anybody our being thrifty and productive (6). Scanlon's version of **contractualism** is meant specifically to describe narrow morality. But it leaves open the possibility that actions might be good or bad in other ways.

The point here is that Scanlon (1998) is open to the idea that *we might have reasons to care about the environment for its own sake*. It's just that these will belong only to *broad* morality:

> It does not seem that all the reasons we have are grounded in the moral
> claims or the well-being of individuals, either ourselves or others. Many
> people, for example, believe that we have reason not to flood the Grand

Canyon, or to destroy the rain forests, or to act in a way that threatens the survival of a species (our own or some other), simply because these things are valuable and ought to be preserved and respected, and not just because acting in these ways would be contrary to the claims or interests of individuals. Whether they are correct in thinking this is not, however, a question to be settled by an account of the morality of right and wrong; it belongs to morality in the wider sense and to the broader subjects of reasons and value. (219)

Leopold takes a stricter stance than Scanlon here. Leopold thinks unnecessarily harming the environment is *wrong*, whereas all Scanlon will say is that, though we are *permitted* to do it, we have some reasons not to.

> Whose position makes more sense here, Leopold's or Scanlon's? Do the arguments for the land ethic which we discussed in Section 2 support one view over the other?

4. Conclusion

In this chapter, we discussed the idea that how we treat the environment matters morally for its own sake, and how this idea might fit with or conflict with the idea that we have obligations to the particular humans and animals who depend on the environment. This conflict will come back with a vengeance in the next chapter, which will discuss what we should do if preserving nature turns out to be radically incompatible with doing what's best for wild animals.

Further Reading

Leopold (1989) is an extremely influential text. For Regan's charge of environmental fascism and his own take on environmentalism, see Regan (2004). For helpful overviews of environmental ethics, see Brennan and Lo (2015) and Cochrane (n.d.). The founding text of "deep ecology" (an approach not discussed in this chapter, but which has certain similarities with Leopold's land ethic) is Næss (1973). Zimmerman et al. (1998) contains many helpful readings. Baxter (1974) advances the view that only human interests should be taken into account in environmental policy; it thus contradicts both the environmentalist position discussed here and the interventionist position discussed in the next chapter. For a broader statement of Anderson's understanding of the connection between emotions and reasons, see Anderson (1993).

Chapter 10
Wild Animals

1. Introduction

There are *lots* of wild animals: probably trillions of land-based vertebrates and even more vertebrates living in the oceans (fish, dolphins, etc.). If we include *invertebrates* (insects, mites, crabs, etc.), then the number goes up further still. There might be *quintillions* of these (Tomasik 2019). People usually don't think much about the welfare of wild animals except insofar as, for environmentalist reasons, they worry about members of endangered species (Chapter 9). But perhaps they should. Since there are so many of them, maybe the welfare of wild animals is the most important thing in the world.

But if wild animals are morally important, what does that mean in *practical* terms? We might think it would support the things environmentalists want: preserving habitats, maintaining ecosystems, and the like. After all, the habitats are where the animals live. Perhaps the way to help wild animals would be to ensure that nature can keep doing its own thing.

One problem is that nature's "own thing" often seems *horrific*. The biologist Richard Dawkins (1995) writes:

> The total amount of suffering per year in the natural world is beyond all decent contemplation. During the minute it takes me to compose this sentence, thousands of animals are being eaten alive; others are running for their lives, whimpering with fear; others are being slowly devoured from within by rasping parasites; thousands of all kinds are dying of starvation, thirst and disease. It must be so. If there is ever a time of plenty, this very fact will automatically lead to an increase in population until the natural state of starvation and misery is restored. (131–32)

Dawkins is famous for his writings defending atheism. But similar observations have been made by many religious people. In his poem "In Memoriam," the Christian poet Alfred Lord Tennyson famously wrote that humanity

> . . . trusted God was love indeed
> And love Creation's final law–
> Tho' Nature, red in tooth and claw
> With ravine, shriek'd against his creed.

The idea is that nature, "red [with blood] in tooth and claw," stands in defiance of God's loving plan for the world by painfully destroying its inhabitants. Or consider the famous passage from the book of Isaiah (11:6–7: KJV) which predicts the end of predation when God's kingdom is finally realized on Earth:

> The wolf also shall dwell with the lamb, and the leopard shall lie down with the kid; and the calf and the young lion and the fatling together; and a little child shall lead them. And the cow and the bear shall feed; their young ones shall lie down together: and the lion shall eat straw like the ox.

Why would the end of predation be portrayed positively—as something that comes when God's kingdom is realized—unless Isaiah thinks predation is bad?

If the natural way of things leads to horrific suffering and death among wild animals, and we care about wild animals, maybe we should *intervene* in nature to help wild animals. Sometimes this seems uncontroversial. Suppose you find some baby ducks whose mother has died. If you leave them, they'll starve. But you also know there are people at a wildlife rescue who will be happy to take care of them. Letting those people know, thereby saving the baby ducks from the natural way of things, seems good.

But what if we could combat suffering and death among wild animals on a larger scale, perhaps through the use of new technologies? What if we could, say, eliminate or reduce disease or predation or famine among wild animals, and we could do so without causing other, worse problems? Would that be good? Some philosophers think this is a realistic possibility, and that if we develop such technologies, it will be good to use them. They defend **interventionism**, the idea that *(if we can) we should intervene in the natural world on a large scale to help the animals in it avoid suffering and death.* Much of this chapter is about that view. We'll close by considering the "logic of the logger" argument. Surprisingly, it suggests that the best way to help wild animals is to *destroy* nature.

Have you ever found an injured wild animal—perhaps a rabbit or bird—and tried to help it? Or have you ever stopped your dog or cat from murdering a smaller wild animal? If so, you've *intervened*. There are many other animals similarly situated to the ones you may have tried to help. If it were easy to help them, too, do you think that would be a good thing to do?

---

2. Interventionism

Some interventions on behalf of wild animals are already possible. For instance, sometimes we can combat disease among them with medicine or vaccines. For instance, rabies has been eliminated or reduced in some wild animal populations by leaving out bait containing an oral vaccine. So far, medical interventions like this have mostly been motivated either by *human interests* (we don't want wild animals spreading rabies to us) or by *environmentalist concerns* (we don't want some species wiped out by a disease). However, in principle, it seems we might be able to use these interventions with the aim of promoting the interests of the *animals themselves* (Animal Ethics 2020). Of course, we might research ways to do this more effectively, if we decide it's worthwhile. Organizations like Animal Ethics and the Wild Animal Initiative are currently doing research like this.

It may also be, though, that new technologies will allow much deeper intervention in nature. Scientists are already investigating using **gene drives** to promote human interests. Gene drives are, essentially, *attempts to genetically re-engineer wild animal populations.* Many of these attempts have focused on ways to prevent mosquitoes from spreading malaria and other diseases. Scientists would develop a gene that had some desired effect, insert it into some specimens, and then release them into the wild, allowing them to breed with other animals. It's possible to ensure that, when an individual with the engineered gene breeds with an individual without it, all of their offspring inherit the gene (as opposed to the ordinary 50 percent), making the gene spread through the population exponentially faster than a natural mutation. They might keep introducing specimens with the mutation again and again to make sure the gene spreads even more effectively. What happens after the gene spreads throughout a population depends on what it was engineered to do. For instance, if it decreases fertility among mosquitoes, it might ultimately drive a mosquito population to extinction. Or it might quickly kill mosquitoes after they're infected with malaria or other viruses. This would prevent the mosquitoes from spreading these diseases, since any mosquitoes which could spread them would die (Scudellari 2019).

This is new technology. But who knows how it could develop in the future? Perhaps we could use gene drives to render predators infertile, causing them to become extinct. Or perhaps we could even genetically re-engineer them to become vegetarians. If you know a little about ecology, you may be worried at this point: without predation keeping their population in check, won't prey species breed beyond what the environment will support? Removing predation doesn't sound that great, if it means the animals just starve to death instead. But perhaps we could also use gene drives on members of prey species to reduce their fertility. We might make sure that they have *only as many offspring as the environment will support* (McMahan 2016, 273–76).

Further, even if gene drives don't pan out, perhaps there are other technological solutions. Scientists are already investigating ways of chemically castrating wild animals as a way of controlling stray dog and cat and wild deer populations; perhaps these methods could be used more extensively (McMahan 2016, 275). Dawkins writes that "if there is ever a time of plenty, this very fact will automatically lead to an increase in population until the natural state of starvation and misery is restored." But what if we could keep the wild animal population in check through humane means instead?

Deer in America and kangaroos in Australia are overpopulated (though admittedly, the overpopulation is partially caused by humans killing off natural predators). Left unchecked, these species grow until their habitats can't support them, leading to mass starvation. In order to prevent their destruction of their habitats, these states encourage **culling**, or the "humane" killing of them through things like hunting.

Given overpopulation, do you think the best option is (a) letting animals multiply until they destroy their habitat and starve, (b) culling them, or (c) using technology to do things like chemically castrate them?

It sure sounds difficult. But *if* we reach a point where we can pull it off, the case for doing so seems fairly simple. The philosopher Jeff McMahan (2016) writes:

> The case in favor of intervening against predation is quite simple. It is that predation causes vast suffering among its innumerable victims, and to deprive those victims of the good experiences they might have had were they not killed. Suffering is intrinsically bad for those who experience it and there seems always to be a reason, though not necessarily a decisive one, to prevent it. . . . The elimination of predation could . . . make the difference between an indefinitely extended future in which millions of animals die prematurely and in agony every day and an alternative future in which different animals would live longer and die in ways other than in terror and agony in the jaws of a predator. (273)

McMahan's argument is straightforward. Suffering is **intrinsically bad**—bad in and of itself, because of how it feels. But natural suffering feels the same as suffering caused by humans; McMahan writes that "if animal suffering is bad when we cause it, it should also be bad when it results from other causes, including the action of other animals" (273). We have reason to prevent intrinsically bad states of affairs. Further, predation causes animals to die younger than they otherwise might have, and so it is bad because its victims are deprived of valuable futures (see Chapter 3). So if we can replace a natural order full of predation with one that gets by without it, and can do so without giving up anything nearly as important as preventing all this suffering and death, we should do so. We might frame the argument in something like this way:

(P1) The suffering and death caused by predation are bad.

(P2) If it is in our power to prevent something bad from happening, without sacrificing anything nearly as important, it is wrong not to do so.

(P3) If we someday develop the technology to end predation
      without causing other, worse problems for animals, then it
      will be in our power to prevent the suffering and death caused
      by predation and to do so without sacrificing anything nearly
      as important.

(C)   Therefore, if we someday develop the technology to end
      predation without incurring unreasonable costs to ourselves or
      causing other, worse problems for animals, it would be wrong
      not to use this technology to end predation.

If we eliminate predation and famine, perhaps we could go even further. David
Pearce (2007) argues that we might someday be able to replace pain with various
gradients of bliss. Here's the idea. Currently, pain and pleasure serve an important biological function: things that promote the fitness of the organism tend to
cause pleasure, incentivizing the organism to do them, while things that hinder
the fitness of the organism tend to cause suffering, incentivizing the organism to
not do them. But suppose we made all these experiences feel better by the same
amount: the experiences that used to be painful now feel good, but the experiences
that used to feel good now feel *really* good. Perhaps organisms would be equally
attracted to survival-promoting activities (since they would still feel better), but
without horrible suffering when they failed in pursuing them.

But we should pause to see whether even these more modest ideas are good
ones.

3. Objections

Objection 1:
This is ridiculous.

Reply:
Why?

Reply to the reply:
It's just intuitively ridiculous.

Reply to the reply to the reply:
That's not very convincing.

Reply to the reply to the reply to the reply:
But it's not just me. We mentioned in Chapter 6 that some authors object to
the animal rights and animal welfare positions by pointing out that they might

imply that we should intervene to help animals in the natural world. These authors regard this result as intuitively ridiculous. Defenders of the animal rights and animal welfare positions often agree: they try to show that their view doesn't imply this (McMahan 2016, 271–72). If both critics and defenders of the animal welfare and animal rights views think this is ridiculous, it probably is.

Reply to the reply to the reply to the reply to the reply:

Is this really that intuitively crazy, though? Consider the following **thought experiment** (cf. Bostrom and Ord 2006; Pearce 2015, 162):

> **Pandora's box:** On your planet, animals live free from predation, parasites, famine, and the like. They have only as many offspring as the environment can support and die when they reach old age. The world has always been like this. You have a box. If you open it, predation, parasites, and famine will be introduced into the natural world. The amount of flourishing will vastly decrease, and the amount of suffering will vastly increase. The natural world will become like the one on Earth.

It seems clear that *you shouldn't open the box* in this situation. But this is an odd judgment if you think the interventionist proposal is ridiculous. Why would it be (i) obviously wrong to *introduce* suffering to the natural world but (ii) obviously ridiculous to *remove* it?

Here's what's probably happening. Human beings have a cognitive bias known as **status quo bias**, an "irrational . . . preference for an option because it preserves the status quo" (Bostrom and Ord 2006, 658). For instance, if you randomly give students either a mug or a chocolate bar and let them trade whichever they got for the other one, they are overwhelmingly likely to keep what they got, *whichever one it was* (Bostrom and Ord, 2006, 658–62).

It seems plausible that the anti-intervention intuition is really a case of status quo bias. People like things to stay the way they are, and intervening to reduce suffering in the natural world would be a really big change, so it seems like a bad idea. But if there wasn't suffering in the natural world, adding it would be a really big change, so that adding it would seem like a bad idea. But we shouldn't trust an intuition that stems from an irrational cognitive bias. So *we shouldn't trust the intuition that intervention is ridiculous.*

> Can you think of other examples of status quo bias? Have you ever exhibited this bias in your own life?

Reply to the reply to the reply to the reply to the reply to the reply:

What the Pandora's Box thought experiment shows is really that wild animal suffering is bad *when it's caused by human beings.* If you open the box, you cause all the suffering that results. But wild animal suffering on Earth is mostly not caused by human beings. Therefore it isn't bad.

Reply to the . . . etc.:

Why would that be true, though—why would wild animal suffering be bad only when caused by human beings? We agreed before that suffering is *intrinsically* bad. It was bad, in and of itself, because of how it *felt*. But suffering feels just as bad whether or not it's caused by human beings. So suffering *is* bad whether or not it's caused by human beings. Maybe the whole state of affairs is in some way worse when humans cause suffering: there's a moral **wrong** involved then, in addition to the badness of the pain. But the pain itself is bad either way.

Even apart from that, does it really seem right that wild animal suffering is bad only when caused by humans? We don't think suffering among *people*, or *pets*, is okay as long as caused by (say) a disease. They aren't wild animals, but why would being a wild animal change this? Recall the baby ducks from this chapter's introduction. Isn't part of the reason to help them that their suffering and death would be a bad thing, even though it's caused by nature?

Objection 2:

Even if the idea of intervening in nature isn't ridiculous in *principle*, it's ridiculous in *practice*. The technologies you would need are sci-fi nonsense, and there's no point in talking about them.

Reply:

This isn't an objection. The argument said *if* we develop the right technology, we'd be obligated to use it. You're just saying we won't develop it.

Reply to the reply:

Okay, but it's an objection to *talking about* the argument. If we develop magic spells that cure world hunger, I guess we should cast those too. But we won't. And we won't develop this technology either.

> Here's your chance to think critically. Which premise do you think this objection addresses? If you don't think it addresses any particular objection, what should you think of the objection?

Reply to the reply to the reply:

What makes you think that? Today, we have all kinds of technologies that would have seemed impossible to people even a few decades ago. And as explained above, the technologies needed to effectively intervene in nature are really just better versions of technologies, like genetic engineering, that already exist. It's hard to know, but it's plausible that we might develop the needed technology at some point. As McMahan (2016) writes:

Ecological science, like other sciences, is not stagnant. What may now seem forever impossible may yield to the advance of science in a surprisingly short time—as happened when Rutherford, the first scientist to split the atom, announced in 1933 that anyone who claimed that atomic fission could be a source of power was talking "moonshine." Unless we use Rutherford's discovery or others like it to destroy ourselves first, we will likely be able eventually to eliminate predation while preserving the stability and harmony of ecosystems. (274)

Reply to the reply to the reply to the reply:

Maybe we'll develop the technology some day. But it's pointless to talk about until then.

Reply to the reply to the reply to the reply to the reply:

Talking about it now is important, for at least two reasons. *First*, if we decide that using this technology to reduce wild animal suffering would be a good idea, that might *spur us to develop the technology more quickly.* Developing it might seem much more important. And because so many wild animals are suffering, developing it as soon as possible is important. A delay of, say, just one year might mean that trillions of animals suffer and die unnecessarily.

Second, if such technology is developed, future people might *not* use it to reduce wild animal suffering. Maybe they'll initially think such an idea is ridiculous, like many people do now. (If intervention would be expensive, some people might be motivated to promote the idea that intervention is ridiculous too.) Perhaps they'll figure out what they should do eventually, but the amount of unnecessary suffering in the meantime could be incalculable. It would be better to establish a consensus in favor of intervention ahead of time, so that *the right thing would be done as soon as possible.*

Objection 3:

The environmentalist considerations from Chapter 9 show that this proposal is a bad idea. (P3) overlooks the fact that, in ending predation, we'd be sacrificing something as important as the suffering and death of animals: namely, the value of ecosystems and of biodiversity. The proposal requires radically altering natural ecosystems, and it would hurt biodiversity. On one version of the proposal, we'd drive predatory species extinct. On another, we'd genetically re-engineer them so their descendants were vegetarians. But this is just another way of driving them extinct. Siberian tigers transformed into plant eaters would not be Siberian tigers. They'd be something else. And the loss of Siberian tigers would be terrible.

Reply:

We wouldn't need to get rid of all of them. Perhaps we could create some special sanctuaries for them. Of course, sanctuaries aren't *necessarily* nice—we all saw

Tiger King—but we could make these nice. Scientists are even working on ways of growing meat in laboratories. We could feed this to them, and they could maintain their carnivorous ways without having to hurt any other animals.

Reply to the reply:

That's not good enough. Keeping some Siberian tigers in sanctuaries isn't the same as letting them live free. They specifically need to be able to hunt and kill as part of natural ecosystems.

Reply to the reply to the reply:

Is that really what makes them valuable? Humans usually live in civilizations now instead of hunting and killing as part of natural ecosystems, but we don't think that *in itself* is a great tragedy.

Reply to the reply to the reply to the reply:

Yes, that's at least part of what makes them valuable. Maybe it's different for humans.

> Suppose we were able to make extremely realistic deer robots made out of lab-grown meat. Think of *Westworld*—these robot deer would be virtually indistinguishable from real deer. Would allowing Siberian tigers to hunt these preserve their tigerhood?

Reply to the reply to the reply to the reply to the reply:

It's not obvious why that would be, but let's grant it. Even if tigers continued to exist, moving them out of natural ecosystems would harm the value of the environment. But there are still going to *be* ecosystems under this proposal: the ecosystems will just be different. And there is still going to *be* biodiversity under this proposal: the species will just be different. If some get transferred out of wild ecosystems, we can engineer new ones and put those in the ecosystems. The new ones might be even cooler and more majestic. And what's so bad about that? Ecosystems have been changing, and species have been coming in and out of existence, for as long as life has existed on Earth. If you say a new ecosystem can't make up for the loss of an old one, or a new species can't make up for the loss of an old one, you have to say that the world has been constantly getting worse over time (cf. McMahan 2016, 276–77). And besides, if ecosystems inevitably change anyway, isn't it true that we might as well intervene to make sure that they change for the better—in ways that lead to less suffering and more flourishing?

> In *Jurassic Park*, scientists bring back an old ecosystem. This is slightly different from the concern raised in the previous reply, which discusses bringing new ecosystems into existence.
>
> Based on what that reply says about new ecosystems, what do you think it would say about bringing back old ones? What would the relevant considerations be? What would the opposing side say?

Reply to the reply to the reply to the reply to the reply to the reply:
In Chapter 7, we discussed whether you could make up for killing an individual by creating a new, equally happy individual. Some people, like Regan, thought you couldn't: individuals demand respect of a sort that's incompatible with treating them as "replaceable" in that way. Species are like that too. Maybe destroying one species (or preserving it but removing it from its natural environment) and replacing it with another, cooler species doesn't make things "worse," exactly. But it does fail to show appropriate respect for the value of the species.

Reply to the reply to the reply to the reply to the reply to the reply to the reply 1:
Species and natural environments don't have value of *that* sort. Maybe there's value in biodiversity, and so on. But it's not the sort of value that makes it wrong to remove one species while introducing a new one.

Reply to the reply to the reply to the reply to the reply to the reply to the reply 2:
Even if ecosystems *do* have that kind of value, preventing large amounts of terrible suffering and death is more important. Suppose driving a species from an ecosystem was the only way to prevent its preying on human beings, and you knew this wouldn't have any other bad effects (McMahan 2016, 277–78). That seems okay: preventing suffering and death seems more important than preserving the predatory species in its natural habitat. Of course, we're talking about humans, rather than animals, here; how important you think that is may depend on what you make of the arguments given in earlier chapters. But at the same time, driving the species away would be justified even to save a small number of humans, whereas predation affects *vast numbers* of animals. Even if the suffering and death of a prey animal is much less important, the fact that there is so much more suffering and death involved may make up for this.

Objection 4:
This would be playing God.

> Which premise does this objection address?

Reply:
What does this mean? Maybe something like: we'd be interfering with God's design or doing things only God is allowed to do. But we interfere with nature all the time to prevent death and suffering—for instance, when we take medicine. Don't most people think God *approves* of that?

We change nature in other ways too. We build dams and drain swamps. We eradicated smallpox. We even change plant and animal species. Some people worry about "genetically modified" crops being sold in grocery stores. But the crops you were already buying were selectively bred by human beings over time to be tastier, to be easier to grow, and so on. The corn, apples, and other fruits and vegetables that you've been eating look nothing like their ancestors from thousands of years ago. Similar things are true of various domesticated animals, such as dogs. Selectively breeding plants and animals is not really different than genetically engineering them: genetically engineering them is just quicker. Of course, doing things like this might well be wrong *in some particular case*. But does anybody think they're wrong *in principle*, when we have a good reason for them (such as preventing tremendous suffering)?

Reply to the reply:

Don't take the term "playing God" so literally. The point is that this is **anthropocentric**—or *arrogantly human-centered*—to try to do this. You're imposing your subjective human values on a natural world that couldn't care less about them. Consider the following, fairly rude, comment McMahan (2016) received from a prominent ecologist:

> It is clear you have either never taken a course in ecology and evolution, or forgot the message. There is this strange thing called a food web—in which organisms are primary producers, eat primary producers, eat the eaters of primary producers—and so on. That is called life. It has NO ethical or moral values. Those are HUMAN values. A wolf or lion kills another animal—the pain and suffering are not ecological issues—the life of the wolf or lion is the issue. If the wolf or lion dies of starvation— then the prey potentially become overpopulated—like the deer in Princeton. Your values are not the values of nature. (287)

Reply to the reply to the reply:

One worry the quoted person has concerns overpopulation of prey animals, which was already discussed in Section 2. Beyond that, frankly, it's not clear what point this person was making. First of all, perhaps it's true that the suffering and death of prey animals "are not ecological issues," in the sense of harming the ecosystem or something. But then again, the suffering and death of ecologists are not ecological issues either, and we still think we should prevent those when we can. The arguments of the last few chapters help show that the health of ecosystems is not the *only* thing that matters morally.

Second, the suggestion that these are mere "human" values seems to suggest that there aren't right and wrong answers in morality. But most philosophers

---

Suppose a coyote tries to eat your dog. Do you think that the coyote's attempt to eat your dog is a moral action on the part of the coyote? Do you think the answer to that first question affects whether you should try to help your dog?

think that there *are* right and wrong answers in morality. In that case, talking about "merely" human values doesn't make any more sense than talking about "human math" or "human physics." Maybe the point of the statement "Your values are not the values of nature" is just that natural ecosystems, as a matter of fact, don't work to minimize unnecessary suffering. But this is hardly an *objection to* the proposal. In fact, it's the *reason for* the proposal: the claim is that, *since ecosystems don't minimize unnecessary suffering, we need to intervene to make them.*

Third, suppose our opposition to suffering and death is a mere subjective preference. Presumably, it's one we share with the other animals: they don't like suffering and death either. So it's not really clear how we're "imposing" our values on them. It looks like we're promoting values they share.

Reply to the reply to the reply to the reply:

That's too simple. Of course the *prey* animals don't like being eaten. But the *predatory* animals like eating them. It's not our job to pick winners and losers, just because, from our human perspective, we happen to sympathize more with one group. It's a bit like invading another country because we don't like how they do things. First, we shouldn't be so sure that our way of doing things is better, but second, even if it is, other societies aren't any of our business. Appropriate respect for animals means letting them do their own thing without human interference. Consider Tom Regan's (2004) statements that

> the total amount of suffering animals cause one another in the wild is not the concern of morally enlightened wildlife management. Being neither accountants nor managers of felicity in nature, wildlife managers should be principally concerned with letting animals be, keeping human predators out of their affairs, allowing these "other nations" to carve out their own destiny. (357)

And

> our ruling obligation with regard to wild animals is to let them be, an obligation grounded in a recognition of their general competence to get on with the business of living, a competence that we find among members of predator and prey species. . . . As a general rule, they do not need help from us in the struggle for survival, and we do not fail to discharge our duty when we choose not to lend our assistance. (xxxvii)

Reply to the reply to the reply to the reply to the reply:

A minute ago, the interventionist was accused of imposing human values on nature. But this seems as anthropomorphic as anything. Unlike human beings living in other societies, animals don't have the ability to consider different ways their communities might be structured and to choose one way rather than another. *Ecosystems are determined by nature*, not by the autonomous choices of their inhabitants. So it's hard to see how changing them could violate animals' autonomy in the way that intervening in another society might.

Further, animals don't comprise a *shared* community. If anything, there seem to be multiple communities among them, some of which survive by destroying others. As McMahan (2016) writes:

> The limitation of this argument . . . is that it fails to apply in situations in which there are two or more distinct communities, or collective "selves," living within the same political boundaries and one seeks to rule, expel, enslave, or exterminate another. When, as in Rwanda in 1994, one group is engaged in genocide, nonintervention is not a matter of "allowing these 'other nations' to carve out their own destiny." . . . But conditions in which the members of one human group systematically exploit and kill the members of another are the analogues in human affairs of predation among animals, though the analogy is imperfect because the situation of prey in the wild is generally even more hopeless in the absence of intervention. Prey are seldom able to defend themselves and there is certainly no prospect, as there is in conflicts involving human beings, that predators and prey will, on their own, eventually achieve a modus vivendi [i.e., a way of life] that will enable them to live together peacefully in the manner prophesied by Isaiah. (286)

Reply to the reply to the reply to the reply to the reply to the reply:

Look, even if this all sounds good in principle, in practice, *ecosystems are too complicated for us to manage them like this*. This isn't just the earlier point about how complicated the technology would have to be, though that also matters. The point is that *we* wouldn't be smart enough to use that technology to rearrange an entire ecosystem in a productive way, even if we had it. Ecosystems are delicately balanced, and our track record trying to affect them isn't good. For instance, in the 1930s, the United States was having big problems with soil erosion, because farmers cleared away lots of plants that ordinarily prevented it. The government promoted kudzu, an invasive vine from Japan. Planting it was supposed to keep the soil in place. If you've spent much time in the American South, you may have seen kudzu: it's this vine that grows all over everything, choking out and killing other plants. It turns out that the same properties which were supposed to make kudzu effective against erosion (fast-growing, hardy, etc.) also make it hard to keep in check after you've planted it. But if we can't even predict what planting a single species of vine will do, why think we can predict what totally changing ecosystems like this would do?

Aldo Leopold (1989) makes the point like this:

> A land ethic changes the role of *Homo sapiens* from conqueror of the land-community to plain member and citizen of it. . . . In human history, we have learned (I hope) that the conqueror role is eventually self-defeating. Why? Because it is implicit in such a role that the conqueror knows, *ex cathedra*, just what makes the community clock tick, and just what and who is valuable, and what and who is worthless, in community life. It always turns out that he knows neither, and this is why his conquests eventually defeat themselves. . . . The ordinary citizen today assumes that science knows what makes the community clock tick; the scientist is equally sure that he does not. He knows that the biotic mechanism is so complex that its workings may never be fully understood. (204)

So this is the sense in which the proposal involves playing God: *it involves arrogantly thinking we know more than we do.*

Reply to the reply to the reply to the reply to the reply to the reply to the reply: If it's true that we will never know enough to intervene without doing more harm, then of course we shouldn't intervene. And of course it's possible that we never will. But why be so sure? Think about human societies, which are complex in some of the same ways ecosystems are. Of course, there's still a lot we can't understand about them. But we've clearly made progress in our understanding: for instance, economics, as we understand it, didn't even exist a few hundred years ago. If we seriously devote effort to better understanding the natural world, if computers continue to improve our ability to collect and process information, and so on, who knows what sort of understanding we might gain?

Besides that, it's important to keep in mind that it's not like the status quo is great. We established above that whatever "delicate balance" is present in ecosystems isn't aimed at maximizing the **well-being** of creatures. *When the status quo involves so much suffering and death, how much worse could we really make things?*

4. The Logic of the Logger

The idea that the status quo for wild animals isn't that great may suggest another route to solving the problem of animal suffering. Is it possible that wild animals have bad lives on balance? If so, would it be best if we just put them out of their misery? We might attempt to selectively euthanize individuals or species with lives that are on-balance bad, though that sounds complicated. On the other hand, if wild animals *as a group* have net negative well-being, we might just destroy whole habitats, thereby reducing the number of wild animals. This avoids our earlier worries about feasibility: people are perfectly capable of paving over wild spaces, and they often want to do so. Some researchers estimate that human activity has reduced the size of wild animal populations by about 45 or 50 percent over the past few decades (Tomasik 2017). People often think this is extremely bad. But if it has prevented quadrillions of animals from living lives worse than death, perhaps it's actually extremely good.

In Chapters 7 and 8, we mentioned the idea that some lives are bad enough that it would be better for the individuals who live them not to be born. If the lives of wild animals tend to be like this, it might be good to prevent their lives and even to end them when we can. Far from the intuitive idea that we can help wild animals by preserving their habitats, the most effective way to help them might be mercy killing. Obviously this position is extremely unpopular, but some authors, such as the animal activist Brian Tomasik (2017), have advocated it. The philosophers Tyler John and Jeff Sebo (2020), whom we discussed in connection with the **logic of the larder argument**, name this the **"logic of the logger argument"** (the idea being that loggers might use it to justify their actions).

In one version, the logic of the logger argument might be framed as a surprising twist on McMahan's argument for ending predation. It could go like this:

(P1) The suffering of wild animals is bad.

(P2) If it is in our power to prevent something bad from happening, without sacrificing anything nearly as important, it is wrong not to do so.

(P3) There is far more suffering than flourishing among wild animals.

(P4) If there is far more suffering than flourishing among wild animals, then it is in our power to prevent the suffering of wild animals by reducing the number of wild animals, without sacrificing anything nearly as important. (Of course, we will sacrifice any flourishing those animals would have experienced. But this is not as important as preventing their suffering, if they suffer far more than they flourish.)

(C)   Therefore, it is wrong not to reduce the number of wild animals.

Of course, while there's lots of suffering among wild animals, sometimes they do fun animal stuff, like flying around or having sex. So why should we accept (P3), which claims that their lives are mostly bad? One possible reason is that many animals r-select rather than K-select. Animals which **K-select** (like human beings, dogs, cats, etc.) have few offspring and take good care of them, so many of their offspring survive. Animals which **r-select** (like mice, insects, most fish, etc.) have as many offspring as possible, and only a fraction survive. So most r-selected animals quickly die off without getting to do any cool animal stuff. The problem is that, since members of r-selected species have vastly more offspring, the vast majority of wild animals are members of r-selected species (Crummett 2017, 83–84). For instance, some people estimate that there are *quintillions* of insects: hundreds of millions or billions of insects per every human being.

This raises further questions.

> **First:** How many wild animals are conscious? If insects, for instance, experience pain, there might be much more suffering in the natural world than if they don't (Crummett 2017, 79). This seems like a hard question, so we'll probably have to take things on a case-by-case basis. In the case of insects, we don't really know for sure whether they're conscious (74–78). We also have to think about fish, among others. And the members of some r-selected species, like mice, are obviously conscious.
>
> **Second:** How do their experiences compare with those of members of more cognitively sophisticated species? You might think that if insects (say) have conscious experiences, their conscious experiences probably aren't as vivid as those of more sophisticated animals. Maybe the happiness of one bald eagle flying around makes up for the suffering of many ants. On the other hand, if there are billions of times as many members of r-selected species, their numbers might more than make up for that (78–80).
>
> **Third:** If many members of r-selected species don't suffer as much, a related question is how to add up the experiences of different individuals. For instance, are a bunch of very minor instances of pain as bad as a single, very bad experience, as long as there are enough of them (80–83)? This raises some of the same questions as are involved in evaluating the repugnant conclusion. (See Chapter 8)

As these remarks suggest, figuring out whether (P3) is true *seems pretty complicated*. We'll return to this in the objections below.

Note that this argument isn't saying you should go around randomly killing wild animals. It's unclear what effect that would have on the overall number of wild animals (e.g., other animals might eat the food that animal would have eaten). The idea is instead to *cut wild animal populations off at the source*, so to speak, by destroying the environments which support the large plant populations necessary for large animal populations to exist.

5. Objections

Objection 1:

This would increase the suffering of animals in the short term, as they die due to losing their habitats.

Reply:

The long-term reduction in suffering will *outweigh* any short-term increase.

Objection 2:

The environmentalist objection has more force here. In Section 3, one response to the idea that the value of ecosystems, biodiversity, and so on should keep us from intervening was that intervening wouldn't really hurt these things: ecosystems would be *changed* by eliminating predation, but they would still exist and be diverse. However, this obviously isn't true for just outright destroying nature.

Reply:

This seems right. But preventing large amounts of intense suffering is more important than preserving nature.

Objection 3

If we did this, it would hurt us human beings, who rely on the environment in various ways.

Reply 1:

Maybe it would if we totally destroyed nature. But causing some damage to the natural world is often beneficial for human beings: that's how we get civilization. Perhaps what this shows is just that we shouldn't feel bad about eliminating habitats, up to the point where it would seriously harm us. Maybe we'll eventually develop ways of surviving while depending even less on nature too.

Reply 2:

Maybe we have to take one for the team. Given how many wild animals there are, their interests, added together, are probably much more important than human interests. So *preventing their suffering might be worth some cost to human beings.* Perhaps it's even worth driving the human race extinct. Yew-Kwang Ng, a prominent economist, helped found the discipline of "welfare biology," which aims to improve the situation of wild animals. He says that

> if the net suffering of animals is larger than the net welfare of humans (as I suspect to be the case) and this unfortunate situation cannot be changed forever, from an overall perspective (all sentients including animals and humans), the destruction of the whole world is a better option. (Quoted in Carpendale 2015, 201)

However, Ng goes on to add that he *doesn't* favor destroying the world, since he thinks it isn't true that the situation can never be changed: with new technologies,

"I believe that, in the long term, we will be able to help animals to reduce their suffering; we will also be able to increase our welfare dramatically" (quoted in Carpendale 2015, 201).

> Some people might be skeptical that animal interests can outweigh human interests in the way that Ng suggests. But suppose your mother has a painful hangnail, and an evil person is about to torture a puppy to death. If you prevent only one of these bad things, which would you prevent? What does this say about the way we should weigh human and animal interests against each other?

Objection 4:

At the very least, *we don't know enough to say whether or not this is a good idea.* Consider four things:

1. Maybe wild animals have net positive lives on balance after all. If this is true and we go around killing them, we might be doing something very bad.
2. In line with the proposal from Section 2, even if the lives of wild animals are currently bad on balance, we may be able to change this in the future. In that case, destroying habitats might prevent many future individuals with happy lives from coming into existence.
3. There's the possible cost to humans mentioned above. It's one thing to sacrifice human interests in the name of weightier animal interests, but it's different when you're unsure whether you're even acting in the interests of the animals.
4. We have to consider what impact pursuing a policy of deliberate environmental destruction might have on our attitudes and character traits—and how those in turn might affect animals in the future. Tyler John and Jeff Sebo argued that considerations like this helped undermine "logic of the larder" arguments (see Chapter 7); they suggest that similar considerations may also help undermine the logic of the logger, though they admit to being less sure (John and Sebo 2020, sec. 4).

In light of all this, *it's better to play things safe for the time being.* Perhaps we'll eventually learn enough to figure out whether destroying habitats is a good idea. But we don't know that now. So really what the proponent of the logic of the logger should be advocating at this point in time is more research into these questions, along with taking other steps to help animals, like combating **factory farming**.

Something like this is what Yew-Kwang Ng advocates. Consider this exchange from an interview with the researcher Max Carpendale (2015):

MC: What practical steps do you think we should take to reduce wild animal suffering in the short term?

Y-KN: I do not advocate large-scale help to wild animals in the short term. We should first concentrate on two things: doing more research and try to improve the conditions of farm animals. This short-term preference on reducing suffering for farm animals first is based on several considerations: (1) We know more about the suffering of farm animals than wild animals now; (2) we can reduce the suffering of farm animals at relatively low costs (including the danger of disrupting the ecological balance) to ourselves; (3) people are generally more susceptible to the feasibility and moral obligation of reducing suffering of farm animals. However, this short-term strategy should not preclude doing more research on the welfare of wild animals now and our obligation to help them in the future.

MC: Is the best way to help wild animal suffering to spread concern about wild animal suffering?

Y-KN: This is one way. Another is to study to learn much more about wild animal suffering. I want to echo . . . [the philosopher Oscar] Horta, . . . "Promoting debate on this issue, doing research on it and questioning speciesism appear to be the most important ways in which we all can work today in order to reduce the immense amount of suffering and death that exists in the world." (200–201)

Reply:

Maybe there's some truth to this; it depends on what the data supports. We should do more research: the stakes are extremely high, and getting even a slightly more accurate picture of things could be incredibly useful. But notice that waiting around until more research is done isn't really "playing things safe." If we leave habitats intact, and it turns out that wild animals have bad lives on balance, this could mean that *countless animals suffer and die unnecessarily because of our waiting.* And the same is true of holding off on other sorts of interventions.

At the very least, if we say we're going to delay things so we can do more research, it's important that we actually do more research: we shouldn't just use that as a cop-out and then not do anything. We certainly aren't devoting the resources to research right now that we would if we took the suffering of wild animals seriously.

> Suppose that your middle-aged cat can't walk well anymore and clearly won't recover. If she's suffering, you would euthanize her to spare her that suffering. But you can't tell if she's suffering—no one really can.
>
> What is the appropriate course of action to take? If research might shed some light on her condition, should you support that research? What do the argument, objection, and reply suggest you should do?

6. Conclusion

In this chapter, we discussed whether it would be good to intervene in the natural world on behalf of wild animals, if we gain the technology and ability to do so. This concludes the discussion of our treatment of animals and the natural world—which began all the way back in Chapter 5. In the next few chapters, we'll turn to a very different topic: charitable giving and our obligations to the global poor.

Further Reading

A historically important piece on wild animal suffering is Clark (1979). The most influential recent piece on wild animal suffering is McMahan (2016). For a criticism of McMahan, see Korsgaard (2018). For a criticism of Korsgaard, see Paez (2020). For an importantly different approach, see Hale (2016). For more on the theological significance of wild animal suffering, see Creegan (2013). An important paper in the history of welfare biology is Ng (1995). Wild animal suffering has only recently become a major topic in philosophy, so much discussion has occurred on blogs and websites rather than in formal academic venues: two good resources are Brian Tomasik's reducing-suffering.org and David Pearce's hedweb.com. For discussions of how responsibilities to domestic animals and responsibilities to wild animals might differ, see Anderson (2004) and Donaldson and Kymlicka (2011).

Section 4

Charitable Giving

Chapter 11
The Obligatory View

1. Introduction

Now, we turn to questions of global injustice and poverty. Specifically, we will look at the question, Are we morally obligated to help the poor? There are three main answers to this question:

1. **Obligatory view**: Helping the poor is a moral requirement.
2. **Wrong view**: Helping the poor is immoral.
3. **Supererogatory view**: Helping the poor is a nice thing to do, but you are not morally required to help the poor.

In this chapter, we consider arguments for the obligatory view. Peter Singer (1972, 2009) developed an influential argument for the view that we are obligated to donate to charity and to donate much more than most of us imagine—the shallow pond argument. We will present two versions of Singer's argument, and after each we will consider some objections and replies.

> Singer gives about 40 percent of his income to charity. How much do you give? Do you think you should give more? If so, why don't you?

2. An Analogy

Hundreds of millions of people live in extreme poverty. The very poor, especially the poor living in the Global South, lack adequate food, shelter, clean water, and medical care. So despite working extremely hard to feed themselves and their families, many are still hungry, malnourished, and sick. Life expectancy is low, and infant mortality is high: about five million children under five years old die every year from starvation and easily preventable diseases (World Health Organization 2020). You have probably seen the harrowing pictures of infants—bony, swollen bellies, covered in flies. Yet hundreds of millions of people live in wealth, and millions among them are extremely wealthy. They live in luxury: dining at fancy restaurants, drinking glacier water, driving Lamborghinis, and vacationing everywhere—or anywhere far enough away from the starving babies covered in flies. According to Oxfam, in 2018 the top 26 wealthiest people had as much wealth as the bottom half of the world's population; if we include other factors like debt, then a "more modest" estimate is that the top 147 richest people had as much as the bottom half of the world's population in 2018.

This is an obscenely unjust distribution of wealth. Shouldn't the extremely wealthy donate more to the extremely poor? The donation of just a few dollars can save a life, by providing things like childhood vaccines or mosquito nets. How many lives could be spared at the cost of that extra Porsche, Bugatti, or Lamborghini? How many lives could be spared by selling that extra vacation home?

But hold on: What about you? Even if you are not extremely wealthy, you too could donate more to the extremely poor. Even if you don't have a fleet of Lamborghinis, you might drive a car that is fancier than you need. Even if you don't vacation everywhere, you might take trips to the beach—or go to the movies, or buy new shoes, or a Frappuccino, and so on. *Or should you forgo the little luxuries in your own life to save those who are starving and suffering?*

Peter Singer argues that you should. Indeed, you should donate so long as you are not sacrificing anything nearly as morally important as the lives you are saving. That means that you should donate until you have just what is necessary for a minimally decent life yourself. Singer thinks that not doing so is *seriously* morally wrong.

Singer (2009) presents little stories—**thought experiments**—to draw us to this startling conclusion. He first tells us this story about a child drowning in a shallow pond:

> On your way to work, you pass a small pond. On hot days, children sometimes play in the pond, which is only about knee-deep. . . . As you get closer, you see a very young child, just a toddler, who is flailing about in the pond, unable to stay upright or walk out of the pond. You look for the parents or babysitter, but there is no one else around. The child is unable to keep his head above the water for more than a few seconds at a time. If you don't wade in and pull him out, he seems likely to drown. Wading in is easy and safe, but you will ruin the new shoes you bought only a few days ago, and get your suit wet and muddy. . . . What should you do? (3)

Of course, you should save the drowning child. Not saving the child would be morally monstrous. Even if your whole wardrobe would be ruined and you'd lose your wages for the day—it doesn't matter. Most would agree that wading into the pond to save the child is still morally obligatory.

By donating to the right charities, you can make a huge difference in the lives of people in poorer nations without sacrificing anything nearly as important. For instance, by donating to an effective anti-malaria charity like the Against Malaria Foundation, you can prevent a case of malaria for only $11, and can save the life of a child who would otherwise die from malaria for between $1,000 and $2,500 (Hillebrandt 2015; GiveWell 2019). *So should you not save the child dying from poverty just as you should save the drowning child?* Are you not as much a moral monster for not donating online as you would be for not jumping into the pond? Singer (2011) thinks so:

> By donating a relatively small amount of money, you save a child's life. Maybe it takes more than the amount needed to buy a pair of shoes—but we all spend money on things we don't really need, whether on drinks, meals out, clothing, movies, concerts, vacations, new cars, or house renovations. Is it possible that by choosing to spend your money on such things rather than contributing to an aid agency, you are leaving a child to die, a child you could have saved? (5)

Recall Judith Thomson's famous violinist from Chapter 4. In that case too, saving another person demands sacrifice on your part. Yet Thomson denies that you have any obligation to save the violinist. Is there a difference between the drowning child and the famous violinist that can explain why we're obligated to save the child but not the violinist?

Singer eventually frames the argument in a more complicated form, as we will see. But we can first see the argument as a simple analogy from the pond scenario—the **shallow pond argument**:

(P1) Children dying from poverty every day are like the drowning child.

(P2) You should do what you can to save the drowning child, even if it requires considerable sacrifice.

(C) Therefore, you should do what you can to save the children dying of poverty every day, even if it requires considerable sacrifice.

(P2) is plausible; most everyone will agree that not saving the child in the pond is seriously morally wrong. (P1) is also plausible; the deaths of the children, whether from poverty or from drowning, are equally tragic and are preventable with some sacrifices. How then can we avoid the conclusion that we should sacrifice to save the children and that not doing so is seriously morally wrong?

Do you think the **argument from analogy** works? Before reading ahead, how would you object to it?

3. Objections and Replies

Many objections target (P2), *and argue that there is a relevant difference between the imaginary child drowning in the pond and actual children dying from poverty*—recall from Chapter 4 how analogical arguments can be criticized. The differences are supposed to mean that while we would be obligated to sacrifice significantly to save the child in the pond, we are not similarly obligated to sacrifice significantly to save children dying from poverty.

Objection 1:

One difference between the child in the pond and the actual children is *physical distance from those in need.* The child drowning is right in front of you, whereas the children dying from poverty are a world away.

Reply 1:

There are *children in need who are not physically distant from us.* Many of us, especially in large cities or developing countries, pass by homeless children, but without making any effort to help them.

Reply 2:

Physical distance is not morally relevant. Imagine you were watching a live video of a child drowning on the other side of the planet. By pushing a button you can alert a lifeguard who will save the child, but pushing the button costs you $1,000. Still, you should push the button. Letting the child drown is morally wrong, even though the child is physically distant from you (cf. Kamm 2000).

Objection 2:

The child drowning is *easily identifiable*: you're saving *this* particular child. In contrast, the child your donation will save is not easily identifiable: your money goes into a charity account that is eventually redistributed among many children dying from poverty that you will never see. You cannot tell which particular child your donation saves.

Reply:

Identifiability is not morally relevant. Suppose two children are drowning far away from each other, and pushing the $1,000 button will alert a lifeguard who can only save one and will choose which to save at random. You should still press the button, even though you cannot tell which child will be saved.

Objection 3:

Another difference between the drowning child scenario and the children dying from poverty is the *confidence we have in the outcomes.* You are certain that your sacrifice will indeed save the drowning child—you yourself will be physically pulling the child out of the water. In contrast, you are not certain whether your donations to dying children will save their lives: perhaps the charitable organization is corrupt or unreliable, or perhaps the child will soon die either way.

Reply:

Peter Unger (1996, 134) tells us another story in response to this objection. Suppose an elderly man, Bob, has invested heavily in a Bugatti, a fancy car. The car is a source of joy and meaning for him, as well as economic security in retirement. His car breaks down on a pair of railroad tracks. While he's waiting for the mechanic, he sees a runaway trolley car barreling toward a child who is playing on another track and hasn't noticed the train. He can save the child, but only by flipping a switch so that, instead of hitting the child, the trolley will instead go down the track his Bugatti is on, destroying the car.

The death of the child is not certain; the child might notice the train and run away. Nevertheless, Bob's risking the child's life is seriously morally wrong, no matter the value of the car. Similarly, *despite the uncertainty over the outcome, our not donating to save the dying children is seriously morally wrong.*

Objection 4:

You are the only person present to save the child drowning in the pond, whereas you are not the only person present to save the children dying from poverty. Many other people are aware of the children dying of poverty, and they could just as easily donate to save them.

Reply:

The number of people present is not morally relevant. Suppose you are not the only person present who can save the drowning child. There's a crowd around the pond, but nobody else cares; they're just watching the child drown. Even though there are other people present who can save the child, your not jumping in is still seriously morally wrong. The presence of others then makes no moral difference. Indeed, suppose there are ten drowning children, and nobody else cares. Then you should jump in time and time again to save each child, even while nobody else does anything. You are obligated to do more than "your fair share."

Objection 5:

Jumping in the pond will save a drowning child's life, whereas donating to charity does not often have such a drastic effect. Donating improves the *quality* of lives, but it is less likely to *save* lives.

Reply:

There are two replies to the objection. *First,* donations *do* save lives. *Second, we are obligated to improve the quality of lives too.* Singer (2009) illustrates this with the following story:

> You are driving your vintage sedan down a country lane when you are stopped by a hiker who has seriously injured his leg. He asks you to take him to the nearest hospital. If you refuse, there is a good chance that he will lose his leg. On the other hand, if you agree to take him to hospital, he is likely to bleed onto the seats, which you have recently, and expensively, restored in soft white leather. (14–15; adapted from Unger 1996, 24–25)

Picking up the hiker does not save his life, and it would cost thousands of dollars to restore the leather seats. Nevertheless, you have an obligation to pick up the hiker; leaving him to lose his leg would be seriously wrong. Similarly, not donating to improve the quality of lives is seriously wrong, even when this does not save lives.

> Are there other differences between saving the drowning child and saving the child dying from poverty? Are they morally relevant? In other words, do they show that we are obligated to save the child in the pond but not donate to charity?

4. The Principled Argument

While the analogical argument is usefully simple, Singer goes on to give a more complex argument. *He uses the drowning child scenario to support a general principle about when we should sacrifice to save others.* Then he applies this principle to the case of children dying from poverty to show that we should sacrifice to save them too. Singer (2009, 15) presents the argument as follows:

(P1) Suffering and death from lack of food, shelter, and medical care are bad.

(P2) If it is in your power to prevent something bad from happening, without sacrificing anything nearly as important, it is wrong not to do so.

(P3) By donating to aid agencies, you can prevent suffering and death from lack of food, shelter, and medical care, without sacrificing anything nearly as important.

(C) Therefore, if you do not donate to aid agencies, you are doing something wrong.

(P1) and (P3) are plausible. (P1) is obviously true, and (P3) is supported by the fact that there are many organizations—Oxfam, GiveWell, and the Against Malaria Foundation—that effectively save children dying from poverty.

(P2) is a general principle about saving and sacrifice, and it is trickier. However, the principle is supported by the scenario of the child drowning in the pond. The principle makes sense of why not saving the child would be wrong: the death of the child is bad, and the sacrifice of your shoes is not nearly as important a sacrifice, and so the principle tells you that you should save the child. The principle recognizes limits to sacrifice too: if jumping into the pond would *somehow* mean sacrificing your own child, then there would be no obligation to save the drowning child—since your child is as important as the drowning child. For the most part, though, we can donate without sacrificing anything nearly as important as the children we save, and thus it is wrong not to donate a lot.

> Before reading ahead, think about this second argument. Do any of its premises seem false or questionable? What is the best way to object to it?

5. Objections and Replies

The previous objections against the analogical argument can be leveled against the **principled argument** too. The objections state that the differences should limit the principle of (P2): for example, that the principle applies where there is no physical distance between you and the bad thing you could prevent. Then we can apply the objections by again illustrating cases where, say, you are physically distant, but still obligated to help. However, further objections remain.

Objection 1:

Saving the child is not merely good, but obligatory. You would be blameworthy if you passed on by. If the analogy works, then you would similarly be blameworthy for not donating to charity. (P2) states that preventing bad things, like poverty, is obligatory, and this means that the failure to donate to charity would make us blameworthy. But are you really blameworthy if you don't donate? The objection is that this is *counterintuitive: we just don't feel the same way about saving the drowning child and saving children dying from poverty.*

Reply:

Counterintuitiveness does not count for much if *we can easily enough explain why we have mistaken intuitions.* For example, people used to find sexism and racism intuitive, and the view that all sexes and races are equal was counterintuitive. They found themselves with different feelings about their own group when compared to other groups. But this counterintuitiveness does not count in favor of their views, since we can make sense of both why they had those feelings and why they were mistaken. After all, there are sociological and psychological explanations of such mistaken moral intuitions—for evolutionary reasons, we tend to favor our own group over other groups.

Thus, our feelings are shaped by social norms and psychology. We are raised early on to think that helping those nearby is obligatory, but that helping those far away is not; hence, we quite naturally feel an obligation to saving the drowning child, but not to donate to charity. Further, the face of a drowning child elicits our sympathy more than anonymous reports of children dying from poverty a world away. Sociological and psychological factors make sense of our intuitions about donating to poverty, even though those intuitions are misleading.

> On some views, we have special obligations to those close to us. We should do more to help our own family or close friends than we should to help a stranger. Does this seem true to you? What implications would it have for Singer's argument?

Objection 2:

Against (P3), charity may not do that much good after all. Most of the money probably just gets wasted or paid out to executives. Further, *charity causes long-term economic damage by fostering dependency.* When we donate, the poor survive on charity instead of sustainable economic development. For example, sending food to a poor area and distributing it for free might sound like a good idea. But this risks undermining local farmers who need to sell their food to make a livelihood. In the long run, this will prevent people from building up the local infrastructure needed to be prosperous.

Reply:

We can donate in better ways. There are now organizations—such as GiveWell and the Life You Can Save—that rank the long-term effectiveness of charities. They make sure that the money is really used in ways that are effective, and effective in the long term. For instance, poor health causes short-term suffering, but it also harms economic development by preventing people from working and fully using their talents. Combating diseases (such as malaria, via donations to the Against Malaria Foundation) helps people in both the short and long terms.

> Visit givewell.org or thelifeyoucansave.org. Did you donate anything there? If so, to whom and why? If not, why not?

Objection 3:

Against (P2), *we earn our money*; it belongs to us. The children dying from poverty do not earn our money; it does not belong to them. Thus, we have a right to spend our money as we please, and children dying from poverty have no right to it. We are permitted to spend our money on whatever luxuries we want, and have no obligation to donate it.

Reply:

The objection applies to the case of the drowning child as much as to that of the child dying from poverty; in both cases, saving the child costs you your money—either directly or by ruining your expensive shoes. But the right to your shoes does not undermine your obligation to save the drowning child. Similarly, then, the right to your money does not undermine your obligation to save the child dying from poverty.

Furthermore, *we might be implicated in the poverty of others*—so that they have a claim on us, and so that we do not have a right to the money we earned. We might earn the money we do because of injustice against the poor, unwitting though it be. We are all aware of how rich and powerful countries have committed wrongs against poor countries in order to better exploit their natural resources and cheap labor. Most of us in rich nations probably benefit from these injustices in one way or another. Of course, it may not make sense to *blame* us for this: we didn't ask politicians and corporate leaders to commit these injustices. But at the same time, if we are wealthier than these other people due to unjust systems, it hardly seems reasonable to claim that we earned our money fair and square and are entitled to keep all of it.

Objection 4:

The principled argument implies that we have to donate to charity until doing so would cause us to sacrifice something almost as important as a child's life. However, this conclusion is quite extreme: much more extreme than the conclusion that you ought to save a child drowning in front of you. In fact, it is more like a scenario where you encounter dozens of children drowning in ponds every day, and saving each one requires a serious sacrifice on your part. At a certain point, you might think, you can stop saving children and take just a few hours for yourself, especially if others know about the children and can save them as well (cf. Timmerman 2015).

Reply 1:

You might think it is actually selfish and wrong to take a few hours to yourself. Can you really sit down and watch a TV show when children around you are dying? Further, at a certain point, given the progress that is being made helping those in need and preventing global poverty, you will stop encountering drowning children (as the analogy goes).

Reply 2:

If the case resonates with you, you might think that Singer's principle in (P2) is too extreme. However, even if we need a weaker principle, we still may have an obligation to donate quite a lot—in the same way the person encountering ponds should save many children, even if they need not spend every second of their time saving children. (And Timmerman agrees.) So accepting objection 4 is still consistent with an extreme version of the obligatory view—just maybe one slightly less extreme than Singer presents.

> Suppose you encounter a pond with a hundred children drowning and a large group of people watching. You wade in and spend many hours saving fifty of the children. Is it then okay for you to leave and go about your day? Why or why not? What implications does your answer have for Singer's argument?

Objection 5:

Garrett Cullity (2004, 132ff.) argues that the reason we care about saving the lives of the world's poor is so that they can pursue meaningful relationships, goals, and life projects. However, the pond argument requires that we sacrifice our own meaningful relationships, goals, and life projects to devote our lives to saving those in need. The meaningful pursuits of some are thus given priority over the meaningful pursuits of others, which is arbitrary.

For example, by donating so much to the poor, a rich person might sacrifice the quality of her child's education in order to secure the quality of a poor child's education. But the poor child is not of greater value than the rich child, and her education is not more important than the rich child's. Cullity concludes that we need not give as much as Singer requires; we don't have to give to the point where we are sacrificing our own special relationships, goals, or life projects.

> Suppose you see the child drowning, but you know if you save him, you will be late for work and lose your job, ruining the career you've worked for over many years. Do you still have an obligation to save the child?

Reply 1:

The first reply is that the objection does not apply to someone whose most important life project is helping the poor. For example, helping the poor might be the primary life project of social workers, pro-bono lawyers, pious nuns, communal rabbis—and even some brave politicians. By devoting more of their resources to the poor, they are giving their own lives more meaning too. Perhaps we should try to be more like them. They probably have some of the most meaningful lives anyway.

Reply 2:

Another reply is that the objection wrongly assumes that we'd be redistributing what makes life meaningful in an arbitrary or unfair way. The redistribution could be both fair and non-arbitrary. After all, Singer is not saying that you need to make yourself *worse off* than the people you're trying to help. Rather, he says you should give until you would need to sacrifice something comparable to the bad things you're preventing. And completely impoverishing yourself wouldn't be a good idea anyway, since it would reduce your ability to help in the long term.

Think about it like an equation. Suppose having more resources does provide more meaning in life. There is one rich person with 100 units of meaning, and dozens of poor people with only 10 units. If the rich person relinquishes 50 units, then all the poor people will have 50 units. Now there is more meaning overall, and it is more fairly distributed. This would require the rich sacrifice some, but not all, of their meaningful life projects and special relationships. To return to the example, the rich person would sacrifice the quality of her child's education for the quality of the poor child's education because her child and the poor child are of *equal* value—not because the poor child is of more value. And the rich person needn't be giving up on her child's education altogether. She'd just be sending her kid to a regular school alongside the poor kid.

> How would the fairer redistribution of wealth proposed differ from the imposition of communism? Would it be better or worse than communism?

Reply 3:

Even if Cullity is right, we probably should still give much more than we do (and Cullity agrees). Lots of the money we spend isn't really on stuff that makes our lives more meaningful. Like Timmerman's objection, what this really supports is a view like Singer's, just a little less extreme.

Objection 6:

Susan Wolf (1982) discusses *moral saints*—those whose *only* goal in life is to be maximally morally good. Every action they take is as morally good as possible, and they care about nothing but morality. Wolf asks: is this really the kind of person we should want to become? She thinks the answer is no, and argues that moral saints are unattractive for several reasons. They

- don't have time to appreciate things like sports, music, or literature;
- lack the ability to "enjoy the enjoyable things in life," like sitting and watching a beautiful sunset or drinking a hot cup of coffee;
- are so "very, very nice" to the point that they are bland, and don't have a good sense of humor; and

- don't have time to develop non-moral talents, like athletic ability, musical or artistic talent, or culinary skill. They have no non-moral virtues.

This is not the kind of person most of us want to become. Wolf concludes that there is more to life than morality. Morality is important, but there is good reason to think that the best kind of person is not a moral saint.

However, Singer's argument assumes that morality is all that matters. His argument entails that we should make big sacrifices—including developing our own talents, playing sports, appreciating art, enjoying coffee, or watching sunsets—in order to do our moral duty. In other words, Singer requires that we become moral saints. But if there is more to a good life than morality, we might be able to use our money to pursue non-moral goods, contra Singer.

Reply 1:

Suppose you are on a hike to go see a beautiful sunset, and you encounter a child drowning in a pond next to the trail. If you save the child, you will completely miss the sunset. It seems terrible to abandon the child in favor of seeing the sunset, but Wolf's argument suggests that making this kind of decision is sometimes okay. This story supports the idea that maybe we actually should prioritize morality, at least when it conflicts with Wolf's conception of being the best kind of person. Saving lives is more important than music or basketball games or sunsets.

Reply 2:

As we mentioned before, Singer isn't really saying you need to impoverish yourself and spend every waking moment working to combat global poverty. Not only does your own well-being matter, but you'd also probably get burned out and be less effective in the long run if you tried to do that. So you can have friends, passion projects, hobbies, and the like (although it would be better if you found cheap hobbies). Plus, the knowledge that you are helping others in such a major way can be an important source of meaning and satisfaction in your life. When we take all this into account, Singer's path doesn't sound so bad.

> Some of the objections we've just considered also apply to the first analogical argument. Which ones apply? Which premise of the first argument do they challenge?

6. Conclusion

The arguments we've considered have drastic consequences: if we lived up to the obligation—giving until we're sacrificing something as important as the lives we are saving—most of us would be living very differently. We would spend very little on ourselves—mostly buying only necessities and donating the rest to charity. Even if we *half* lived up to the obligation, our lives would be very different. Do we have such an obligation? To determine this, we should evaluate Singer's argument—as well as arguments for the opposing views. In the next chapter we turn to arguments that giving lots of money to charity is supererogatory. Then, we will look at an argument for the conclusion that donating to charity is morally wrong.

Further Reading

The obligatory view of charitable giving is defended by Singer (1972, 2009, 2011, 2016) and Unger (1996); a less extreme version of the obligatory view is defended by Cullity (2004). We especially recommend Singer (2009) for an accessible argument for the obligatory view. Objections to the obligatory view are given by Wenar (2010), Wisor (2011), Barry and Overland (2013), and Timmerman (2015). Other relevant works on this topic include Illingworth, Pogge, and Wenar (2010), Sonderholm (2012), Gabriel (2017), and MacAskill (2016).

Chapter 12
The Supererogatory View

1. Introduction

In the last chapter, we examined Peter Singer's argument for the view that donating a lot to charity is **obligatory**. We now turn to a more moderate view: that donating a lot to charity is good, but doing so goes above and beyond what is obligatory. There is a fancy word for actions that are good but not obligatory: **supererogatory**. These are the sort of things moral heroes do: like jumping on a grenade to save your comrades or running into a burning building to save a puppy. The **supererogatory view** about charity is that *donating a lot to charity is good, but not obligatory.*

Here's a fancy word for actions that are bad but not wrong: suberogatory. Can you think of any actions that are suberogatory?

We turn to the arguments for the supererogatory view, along with objections and replies. But a preliminary before we begin: some of the arguments conclude that *donating something to charity might be obligatory, but donating as much as Singer demands is not.* Thus, while some charity is obligatory, the conclusions are much more moderate than Singer's. The arguments still conclude that donating a lot is supererogatory.

2. Positive and Negative Rights

Some of the arguments begin by distinguishing between the different kinds of rights (see Pojman and Fieser 2012, 38; Arthur 2016). First, rights differ in their *valence*:

- **Negative rights:** rights not to be interfered with; for example, the right not to be killed, robbed, or abused.
- **Positive rights:** rights to receive something; for example, the right to be fed, clothed, or housed.

Our having a negative right not to be harmed means that harming us is normally wrong. Our having a positive right to be fed means that feeding us is normally morally obligatory. (Recall from Chapter 2 that most people think rights aren't *absolute*. For example, I normally have a right against you pushing me around.

But if you push me to save me from being hit by a bus, my right is *overridden* by other considerations.)

> Is there anything more to, for example, a right not to be harmed than the wrongness of harming someone? Why talk about rights rather than about what actions are obligatory or wrong?

Next, rights differ in their fundamentality. This includes the following:

- **Natural rights:** rights we have in virtue of the kind of being that we are; for example, the right to life.
- **Voluntaristic rights:** rights arising from someone voluntarily assuming an obligation to you, such as through promises, agreements, or contracts; for example, the right to a contractor's labor.

(There may be rights that don't fall into either category, but we can ignore those for now.) Our having the natural right to *life* means that, in virtue of the kind of beings we are, *killing us is wrong*. Our having the voluntaristic right to a contractor's labor means that, in virtue of the contract we signed, *the contractor is obligated to repair the kitchen*.

There is a view about rights that leads quickly to the supererogatory view about charity, that is, *all positive rights are voluntaristic rights*. This view is initially plausible. After all, just because something would be of benefit does not mean that there is a right to it. For example, many would benefit from having sex with us—we flatter ourselves. But they have no right to sex with us. Even if abstinence would cause them so much distress that they would harm others, they have no right to sex (see Arthur 2016). That all positive rights are voluntaristic rights makes sense of this; while it would be wrong for us to go out of our way to harm others, they have no right to something positive from us, even if it would greatly benefit them. This view also makes sense of why blind people have no right to our eyes, and those with kidney failure have no right to our kidneys.

Here's how the view about rights leads to the supererogatory view about charity:

(P1) If the global poor have a right to someone's charity, it is a positive right.

(P2) The global poor have a positive right to someone's doing something only if that person voluntarily assumes an obligation to do it (since all positive rights are voluntaristic rights).

(P3) But the vast majority of people in wealthy nations have not voluntarily assumed an obligation to help the global poor (say, by promising to make charitable donations).

(C)   Therefore, the global poor do not have a right to charity from the vast majority of people in wealthy nations.

(P1) seems obviously true: the right to charity is a right to have someone else do something for you. We discussed the reasoning underlying (P2) above. And (P3) again seems uncontroversial: it seems obvious that most people have not voluntarily assumed any kind of general obligation to help the global poor.

> Before reading ahead, think about this argument. Do any of its premises seem false or questionable? What is the best way to object to it?

This argument concludes that helping the poor is not obligatory. However, proponents of this argument also *assume that donating a lot is a good thing*, and this assumption is quite plausible. The argument *combined* with this assumption gives the two ingredients for the supererogatory view: donating a lot is good but not obligatory. We will turn to challenges against the assumption in the next chapter. Assuming it is nevertheless good, donating is supererogatory.

> Some religions teach that donating a lot to charity is obligatory. Is it plausible that by being a member of a religious group, one may have actually promised to donate, even to random strangers? How does this bear on the argument above?

3. Objections and Replies

Objection 1:

Contrary to (P2), the poor *do* have a positive right to our charity. The poor have a right to *restitution*. The rich have robbed the poor through colonialism and other forms of exploitation, past and present. The rich are now obligated to restore the wealth of the poor. Compare: if we steal your television, we are now obligated to restore it or pay you for it (see Nussbaum 2006, chap. 4).

Reply:

While rich nations have robbed the poor, rich *individuals* generally have not. It is hard to see how, as *individuals*, we impose a particular economic or social structure on the world's poor. Maybe some nations have, but why should this confer on each of us an obligation to give more to charity?

It might mean certain things for us: that we should refrain from buying from companies that violate human rights and maybe try to buy fair-trade goods. But it is hard to see how we are individually responsible for the world's unjust social and economic structures.

> Is there collective responsibility—responsibility held by a group that doesn't reduce to the responsibility of the individuals in the group? If so, might we have a collective responsibility to help the poor because as a group we impose unfair structures on them?

Reply to the reply:

The reply misses the point. The claim isn't that you, personally, are responsible for the injustices against poor nations. It's more like *you're in possession of stolen goods, so you have an obligation to give them back.* Even if you didn't steal them yourself, you still should return them to their rightful owner. One way to return the goods that the rich nations have robbed from the poor nations is by giving to charity.

> Suppose your friend sells you a nice TV for cheap, then you find out your friend stole it from your neighbor. Do you have an obligation to give the TV back to your neighbor? What does your answer imply about our obligations to give to charity? Do you think the TV case is similar to the global poverty case?

Objection 2:

Contrary to (P1), people do have natural, positive rights. Consider a crying baby, abandoned on the side of the road. The baby has the right to be taken care of, even if we haven't promised to do so. Or, recall Singer's pond scenario. The supererogatory view seems to assume that we do not have an obligation to save the child drowning in Singer's pond scenario. But it seems as if we do have an obligation to save the child. So the supererogatory view is wrong.

Reply 1:

In many cases similar to Singer's, the child might have a *voluntaristic* right to be saved: for example, because the child is a member of our community and we have all implicitly promised to help one another, or we have to help the poor because we joined a particular religious group. In these cases, we have some kind of contractual obligation to save the child.

Reply 2:

Otherwise, we have no obligation to save the child.

This reply is really hard to swallow; you might think that any argument that has this consequence must go wrong somewhere. So now, we will look at another argument, that concludes that while we ought to save the drowning child, donating a lot of money to charity is still supererogatory.

4. Slote's Argument

Michael Slote (2004; 2007, chap. 2) draws upon a **normative moral theory** to argue both that Singer's argument fails and that his conclusion is false: Slote thinks that donating *some* money to charity is obligatory, but donating as much as Singer thinks is supererogatory. In Chapter 5 we introduced various normative moral theories covered by Peter Carruthers—theories that tell us what ingredients *make* all right actions right and all wrong actions wrong. The normative moral theory Slote invokes is different. Slote relies on a version of **virtue ethics**.

The theories already introduced focus on things like consequences, as per **utilitarianism**; social norms, as per *moral relativism*; divine commands, as per the **divine command theory**; what treats others as ends in themselves or could be willed as a universal law, as per **Kantianism**; or what we could all agree to in a fair contracting situation, as per *contractualism*. In contrast, virtue ethics focuses on *the person* in determining whether an action is wrong. The big question is whether or not a virtuous person would perfect the action in question. In general, virtue ethics states that an action is morally:

- **obligatory** if and only if *a virtuous person would perform the action*;
- **permissible** if and only if *a virtuous person might perform the action*; and
- **wrong** if and only if *a virtuous person would not perform the action*.

A virtuous person is—naturally enough—a person with virtues. **Virtues** are positive character traits that dispose people to act in similar ways across various circumstances. Examples of virtues include honesty, courage, and wisdom. **Vices**—like dishonesty, cowardliness, and foolishness—are the opposite of virtues. A virtuous person is thus a person disposed to tell the truth (honesty), to bravely fight in a just war (courage), and not put a tomato in a fruit salad (wisdom). A vicious person would lie (dishonesty), hide (cowardice), and make an awful salad (foolishness).

Suppose we are evaluating the morality of *peeing on strangers*. Is peeing on strangers the kind of thing a virtuous person would do? Besides honesty, courage, and wisdom, another virtue is

> Explain how virtue ethics might apply to murder, stealing, coveting, caring for one's children, and keeping a promise. What verdict would virtue ethics have for each of these actions? Are they obligatory, permissible, or wrong?

friendliness. A friendly person would not pee on strangers. Thus, according to virtue ethics, peeing on strangers is morally wrong.

Slote (2007) invokes a special version of virtue ethics known as the **ethics of care**. The ethics of care claims to be based on the moral perspectives of women. Carol Gilligan (1982) discovered that in moral evaluations:

- men tended to focus on *justice* (e.g., protecting individual rights, appealing to abstract principles) and
- women tended to focus on *care* (e.g., protecting relationships, appealing to particulars in each case).

Being caring means feeling for, sharing in, and being motivated by the pain and happiness of others. Caring is a particular virtue that the ethics of care focuses on. Thus, the ethics of care states that an action is morally:

- **obligatory** if and only if *a caring person would perform the action*;
- **permissible** if and only if *a caring person might perform the action*; and
- **wrong** if and only if *a caring person would not perform the action*.

The ethics of care is a version of virtue ethics, and Slote's own theory is a version of the ethics of care. Slote focuses on a particular aspect of care: empathy. Empathy is *imagining yourself in someone else's shoes and experiencing their resulting feelings.* Suppose you see a homeless man looking for food in a dumpster. If you are empathetic, you will imagine yourself in his position and take on his feelings of sadness and desperation.

> What is the difference between *empathy* and *sympathy*? What would it be like to feel sympathy for the homeless man, and how would this differ from feeling empathy?

Slote argues that morality arises from this kind of feeling. On his view, an action is morally:

- **obligatory** if and only if *an empathetic person would perform the action*;
- **permissible** if and only if *an empathetic person might perform the action*; and
- **wrong** if and only if *an empathetic person would never perform the action*.

Furthermore, on Slote's view an action is:

- **supererogatory** if and only if *only* those with an unusually high degree of empathy would perform the action.

Most people have some degree of empathy; for example, most of us would feel distressed if we saw someone torturing a child. But just how empathetic is the *empathetic person* in the definitions? Slote often refers to "normal or fully developed" empathy, "normally or fully empathetic caring motivation," and "normally flowing human empathy" (2004, 148). So the empathetic person Slote has in mind presumably has as much empathy as the *normal* empathetic person has—whatever *that* means. Many of us may not acquire sufficient empathy until we intentionally cultivate it or are trained and taught about morality and about the needs of others.

The definition of supererogatoriness takes an unusually high degree of empathy to be more empathy than most of us could develop—even with a lot of practice and education. Those who devote their lives to caring for others, like Florence Nightingale or Mother Teresa, might develop an unusually high degree of empathy, but most of us do not.

> Before reading ahead, what do you think the ethics of care view implies about Singer's drowning child argument? What parts would Slote agree with, and what parts would he disagree with?

Slote puts these definitions to work in order to undermine Singer's argument and to rebut his conclusion: the understanding of obligatoriness is used to show that Singer's argument fails to support his conclusion, and the understanding of supererogatory is used to show that his conclusion is actually false—and that donating a lot to the poor is not obligatory but supererogatory.

Recall Singer's **shallow pond argument** from Chapter 11:

(P1) Children dying from poverty every day are like the drowning child.

(P2) You should do what you can to save the drowning child, even if it requires considerable sacrifice.

(C)   Therefore, you should do what you can to save the children dying of poverty every day, even if it requires considerable sacrifice.

The ethics of care fits with (P2). An empathetic person, discovering the drowning child, would feel the child's fear and pain and save the child. So, on the ethics of care, saving the drowning child is obligatory.

However, the ethics of care does not fit with (P1). The children dying from poverty every day are *not* like the child drowning in the pond. While the empathetic person would save the child in the drowning pond, the normal empathetic person would *not* feel as intensely for children dying from poverty. They might well make a donation (and donating this amount would therefore be obligatory), but they probably wouldn't be willing to donate most of their money. And for this reason, children dying from poverty around the world are *not* like the child in the pond. A highly empathetic person like Mother Teresa, who was both educated about the world's poverty and had a special care for others, might sacrifice to save those far away. But a normal empathetic person would not. Since empathetic people wouldn't save those far away, giving lots of money to charity to save those far away isn't obligatory. Thus, Singer's first premise is false, and his conclusion does not follow.

The ethics of care not only undermines a premise in the pond argument but also shows that the conclusion is false. Slote (2004) explains how:

> Turning away from someone we see (even if only at an extreme distance) seems *worse* than ignoring someone whom one knows about only by description; and assuming, for example, that one has the means instantly to deliver help either to someone whose danger or need one sees through long-distance vision or to someone whose danger or need one merely knows about, most of us, I think, would consider it inhumane to turn away from the person whose plight one saw and then (coldly) decide to give the aid to someone one merely knew about. What is inhumane here arguably has something to do with empathy, with a failure of empathic response to someone whose need one sees. (150)

We can set his reasoning above as follows:

(P1)   An action is obligatory if and only if an empathetic person would perform the action.

(P2)   A normal empathetic person would not donate a lot to the poor.

(C)   Therefore, donating a lot to the poor is not obligatory.

(P1) is the definition of an obligatory action from the ethics of care. Slote supports the ethics of care by showing that it captures our moral intuitions better than rival theories. For example, Slote (2004) argues that the ethics of care gives a better verdict than utilitarianism in the **case of the miners**:

> 50 miners are trapped in a mine as a result of a cave-in. You have only $1,000. You can either use that money to save the 50 trapped miners, or let them die, but install safety devices that will almost certainly save more than 50 lives in the future. (151)

Utilitarianism tells us that saving the miners is *wrong* because an alternative action would save more future people. But that seems to be the wrong verdict. In contrast, the ethics of care tells us that saving the miners is *obligatory*, since normal

Do you agree with Slote that it would be wrong to let the miners die, even though the safety devices would save many more future lives?

empathetic people would save them. That seems to be the right verdict. (P1) makes sense of why acting out of empathy is sometimes more important than acting for the best consequences.

(P2) is a true psychological claim. A normal empathetic person would not necessarily donate as Singer demands. This is for two reasons. First, Singer's argument suggests that our obligations to give to charity are much stronger than most of us would have ever thought; it doesn't seem like one must give as Singer requires in order to be an empathetic person. Second, an empathetic person feels more empathy for those physically or relationally closer than for those physically or relationally far away. For example, they would care about the drowning child, or their own family, or their own community more than strangers far away. Thus, if moral obligations are based on empathy, then even if saving the drowning child is obligatory, donating to help strangers far away is not.

This argument thus far tells us that donating a lot to the poor is not obligatory. But this isn't enough to establish that donating is supererogatory—after all, donating could be merely permissible, or even wrong, as Hardin argues in the next chapter. Slote (2004) explains how the ethics of care implies that donating a lot to the poor is supererogatory:

> Our general account will yield the conclusion that we are not morally obligated to sacrifice most of our time and money to help needy others, because a failure to do so doesn't evince an absence of normally or fully developed human empathy. In that case, if it would take someone with an unusually high degree of empathy and empathic concern—a degree of empathy and empathic concern beyond what most people can be led to develop—to be willing to make such a sacrifice, then such sacrifice will be morally supererogatory—morally praiseworthy and/or good but not (pace Singer) obligatory. (153)

The reasoning can be presented as follows:

(P1) An action is supererogatory if and only if *only* those with an unusually high degree of empathy would perform the action.

(P2) Only those with an unusually high degree of empathy would donate a lot to the poor.

(C)   Therefore, donating a lot to the poor is supererogatory.

Once again, (P1) is the definition from the ethics of care. Once again, the definition can be supported by our moral intuitions about cases. For example, jumping into a burning building to save a stranger would be supererogatory and only those with an unusually high degree of empathy would do so. And, once again, (P2) is a plausible psychological claim.

The argument supports the supererogatory view because it concludes that, while we are obligated to save the drowning child, donating a lot to the poor is supererogatory. While some charity, for example, to those close to us, is morally required, a lot more charitable giving, for example, to those far away, is not.

Before reading ahead, evaluate Slote's arguments. Do any of his premises seem false or questionable? What is the best way to object to his arguments?

---

5. Objections and Replies

Objection 1:

Contrary to (P2) of each of the above arguments, normal empathetic people *do* feel for those suffering far away—at least once they learn about their plight. These feelings are not reserved for those with unusual degrees of empathy.

Reply:

This is true, and for this reason, donating *some* money is obligatory. But even while normal people often feel for those far away—especially after some moral education—they do not feel enough empathy to cause them to donate *most* of their income to those far away. The premise stands: normal empathetic people would not donate a lot to the poor; only unusually empathetic people do. After all, evidently most people do not donate as much as Singer requires; only rare moral heroes do.

Objection 2:

A worry for (P1) of the above arguments is that some people rarely or never feel empathy. They might simply not be emotional—like Spock from *Star Trek*—or they might have a disorder that prevents them from feeling empathy. Nonetheless, they might have a strong desire to do the right thing. Can we still act morally even if we can't feel empathy?

Reply:

Slote's view doesn't require we have empathy in order to do the right thing; it simply requires that we act as an empathetic person would. As long as we can imagine or learn what an empathetic person would do and act in that way, we can act rightly. Further, psychological studies show that almost anyone can develop empathy, with proper moral education.

Objection 3:

Contrary to (P1) of each of the above arguments, what empathetic people do is not necessarily obligatory. For example, some people would have empathy for a poor bank robber and, on that basis, help him rob the bank. (P1) would mean that robbing the bank would be obligatory. But robbing the bank would be wrong. So acting as an empathetic person would isn't enough to make an action moral.

Reply:

While empathetic people might feel some empathy for the bank robber, they would not normally have *enough* empathy to help him rob the bank. This might be because they also empathize with the customers of the bank, who would suffer from the robber, or because their empathy is tempered by other virtues, such as justice. Since normal empathetic people would not rob the bank, (P1) would not mean that robbing the bank is obligatory.

> What if an unusually empathetic person felt a special empathy for the bank robber? Would this make robbing the bank supererogatory? Would that count against the ethics of care?

Objection 4:

In (P1) of the first argument, the definition of an obligatory action, appeals to "an empathetic person." In (P1) of the second argument, the definition of a supererogatory action appeals to "an unusually empathetic person." But these appeals are *vague*: What exactly counts as a normally empathetic person or unusually empathetic person? What are the thresholds? While the ethics of care does give a verdict on the case at hand, the ethics of care will not give clear verdicts for other moral dilemmas. Consider Thomson's case of the famous violinist from Chapter 4 on abortion. Would an empathetic person stay connected to the violinist, saving his life but sacrificing nine months of her own? Would an unusually empathetic person stay connected? The answer to these questions isn't at all clear. Thus, we should reject the ethics of care, along with the premises of the above arguments based on it.

More generally, virtue ethics is often criticized because what a *virtuous* person would do is not clear. Would a virtuous person have an abortion? Would a virtuous person eat meat? The answer to these questions isn't obvious, so some argue that appealing to virtues won't help us make progress in moral philosophy.

Reply:

A moral theory could still be true even if it does not give an easy verdict for the most complex moral dilemmas. In the same way, proofs are a good tool for finding mathematical truths, even if we can't use them to prove or disprove all theorems. So even if the ethics of care and virtue ethics more generally do not give determinate answers for all moral dilemmas, this does not mean that they are false theories. Indeed, rival moral theories do not give easy verdicts for complex moral dilemmas either. For example, as we saw in Chapter 5, the divine command theory requires knowing what God commands in order to know what is right or wrong. But what God commands might not always be easy to determine. And utilitarianism requires knowing the consequences of alternative actions in order to know what is right or wrong. But the consequences of our actions might not always be easy to determine. Sometimes ethics is just hard.

Objection 5:

Normal people tend to be more empathetic to people who are *similar* to them. If we tend to care about those similar to us, the empathetic person might care more about those of their same race or gender, and give those people special treatment. Psychological studies support this (including Johnson et al. 2002, and Trawalter et al. 2012). (P1) states that what a normal empathetic person would do is obligatory. Thus, it would justify preference for one's own race or gender, which would seem to make racism and sexism obligatory. Since racism and sexism are wrong, (P1) is false (cf. Singer 2011, chap. 3).

Reply 1:

The first reply maintains that a preference for those of one's own race or gender may not be morally objectionable, as long as it doesn't involve indifference or hatred to people of other races or genders. Jorge Garcia (1996) argues that preference for one's own race or gender is not necessarily racism or sexism. He understands racism as "a form of racially focused ill-will . . . disregard, [or] disrespect" (9). In contrast, "discrimination *on the basis* of race . . . need not be immoral. It is discrimination *against* people because of their racial assignment that cannot but be immoral" (14). Thus, it might not be wrong to have more empathy for, and thus preference for, your own race or gender—as long as this doesn't result in hating or discriminating against people of other groups.

> Do you think Garcia's view of racism is plausible? Can you think of an example of how you might show a preference for your own race or gender without discriminating against other races or genders?

Reply 2:

The second reply, preferred by Slote, is that normal empathetic people would not have a preference for their own race and gender. First, the psychological evidence is inconclusive, and Slote thinks there is room to question whether normal people even have this preference. And even if they do, fully empathetic people, especially those with the proper moral training, would not give social groups similar to theirs special treatment.

Objection 6:

Even if Slote is correct that a fully empathetic person wouldn't be racially biased, we can imagine *other sorts of biases* they might have. Suppose (to modify an example given by Alastair Norcross [2000, 140–41]) that a new birth defect causes children to be born with ugly, scaly green skin and an inability to emotionally bond with other people. Rather than cute and sympathetic, their appearance is repulsive to us. When they are in distress, they express this in ways that seem grating and bizarre. Perhaps they even release a pheromone (a smelly biology thing you secrete) which causes people to be emotionally cold to them. For these and other reasons, seeing them in distress does not arouse our empathy any more than does, say, seeing a fly caught in a spider web. We know in the abstract that they can suffer, but this arouses only the kind of empathy we feel for faraway children we can't see.

Do you think it is plausible that a fully empathetic person wouldn't show special treatment to those of their race or gender? Do you think a *fully* empathetic person might give more money to charity than Slote thinks, even to those far away?

Slote's view seems to imply that our obligations to these children would be much weaker than our obligations to other children. For instance, if such a lizard-child was drowning in front of me but saving them would require that I sacrifice a lot of money, it seems that, on Slote's view, I would be morally permitted to let them drown. But this cannot be right. Surely these children shouldn't be allowed to die just because of their appearance and odd behavior. But then, neither should faraway children be allowed to die just because we can't see them.

That shows us something important about empathy. It is morally useful because it causes us to care about others. However, empathy doesn't *determine* what is right; rather, it can *show* us what is right, and make us care about what is right, by drawing our attention to the interests of others. But sometimes it is misleading: our **emotions** might respond to morally irrelevant things, like how someone looks. Whether we can see someone is probably just another morally irrelevant feature to which our emotions respond: we shouldn't think that our obligation to save the child in front of us is stronger than our obligation to save the distant child, even though the former is more emotionally engaging.

Reply:

As far as we know, Slote doesn't respond to exactly this kind of case. At least initially, it does seem that his view implies that we'd have weaker obligations to the green-skinned children. Perhaps he could simply **bite the bullet** here: his view has attractive implications in many *other* cases, and the green-skinned children case is very weird and unrealistic, anyway.

Can you think of a way Slote might flesh out his view to avoid saying that our obligations to the green-skinned children are weaker? What would this imply for our obligations to distant children?

6. Conclusion

We have now examined two views of global poverty: the shallow pond argument that concludes giving to the poor is obligatory, and the arguments in this chapter that conclude giving to the poor is supererogatory. We will now turn to the arguments for *charity skepticism*, which conclude that giving to the poor is morally wrong, or at least that we should seriously rethink our approach to charitable giving.

Further Reading

The supererogatory view is defended by Slote (2004, 2007, 2010), Pojman (1992, chap. 10), O'Neil (1986, 1987), and Kagan (1989). Objections to the supererogatory view are made by Singer (1972, 2009, 2011) and Nussbaum (2006). For more on the view that all natural rights are negative rights, see Nozick (1974) and Arthur (2016). For more on the ethics of care, see Gilligan (1982), Noddings (1982), and Held (2006). For an overview of virtue ethics, see Hursthouse (1999) and Timmons (2013, chap. 10).

Chapter 13
Charity Skepticism

1. Introduction

We've examined arguments for the **obligatory view**, that we have an obligation to give to charity, and for the **supererogatory view**, that giving to charity goes above and beyond our moral duties. Now, we will turn to arguments that are less positive about charitable giving. The first claims that, due to overpopulation, charitable giving to save the lives of people in developing countries is actually **wrong** because it will just cause more suffering in the long run. As we'll see, this argument faces serious problems. But we'll then discuss a different line of criticism: the so-called **institutional critique** of charitable giving, as presented by the philosopher Amia Srinivasan. This claims not that charitable giving is bad, but that it's a mistake to think of helping the global poor primarily as a matter of charitable giving. It suggests that we should focus more on trying to bring about better *institutions* which would make charitable giving unnecessary.

2. The Wrong View

Peter Singer (2010) notes that "when speaking to audiences about global poverty, I'm often challenged along the following lines: 'Saving the lives of poor people now will only mean that more will die when the population eventually crashes because our planet has long passed its carrying capacity'" (120–21). He traces this view back to the famous "eighteenth-century English economist and clergyman Thomas Malthus, who famously claimed that population would always outstrip food supplies" (121).

A more recent statement of the argument comes from the American ecologist Garrett Hardin. Like many of the arguments we've considered, Hardin presents various *analogies* to support his conclusion that *giving to charity is morally wrong*. He tells a story about people on a small lifeboat. Others are drowning around the lifeboat. Those on the lifeboat can bring them aboard. But the lifeboat is near capacity, and risks sinking. As Hardin (1974a) puts it:

> [Those drowning] swim for awhile in the water outside, hoping to be admitted onto a rich lifeboat, or in some other way benefit from the 'goodies' on board. *What should the passengers on the rich lifeboat do?* This is the central problem of "the ethics of the lifeboat." (561; emphasis ours)

Those on the lifeboat have three options:

1. **Let some aboard.** But this is *unwise*, since the more they let aboard the more likely the lifeboat will sink, as well as *unjust*, since a fair selection process seems impossible.
2. **Let all aboard.** But this is *unwise*, since then the lifeboat will sink and everyone will drown.
3. **Let none aboard.** This is the only option that is *both wise and fair.* Hard choices are sometimes needed for the greater good.

Hardin reasons that those on the lifeboat should not let those drowning aboard. But (he thinks) the world's rich are like those on the lifeboat, and the world's poor are like those drowning. *Just as saving the drowning puts everyone at risk, so too trying to save the poor puts everyone at risk.* Donating to the poor puts everyone at risk because it leads to overpopulation—which stretches our resources and leaves everyone in dire need. Thus, Hardin concludes, the rich should not help the poor—donating to the poor is morally wrong.

> Do you agree with Hardin that letting none aboard is the best choice? What would you do if you were on a lifeboat in this situation?

Is Hardin right about overpopulation? Consider some recent population statistics. The world's population is steadily growing—according to World Atlas, by 2100, about 4 billion people are expected to be added to the world's current population of 7.5 billion. Further, the population of many nations, especially poor nations, is quickly increasing. For example, in many African countries, such as South Sudan, Niger, and the Democratic Republic of the Congo, the population is expected to double or even triple by 2050. For this reason, Hardin (1974a) advocates that we cut off aid to poor countries, enabling the rapid population growth to be balanced by a rise in death rates:

> A demographic cycle of this sort obviously involves great suffering in the restrictive phase, but such a cycle is normal to any independent country with inadequate population control. The third-century theologian Tertullian . . . expressed what must have been the recognition of many wise men when he wrote: "The scourge of pestilence, famine, wars and earthquakes have come to be regarded as a blessing to overcrowded nations, since they serve to prune away the luxuriant growth of the human race." (564)

Hardin illustrates how donating exacerbates the predicament of the poor, along with everyone else, by a *ratchet effect*: a famine strikes a poor nation and many are on the brink of death. But we intervene and save them. They survive, and have more children. Famine strikes again. Rinse, wash, and repeat. Eventually, however, our donations run dry—we do not have the resources to support an ever increasing population. Finally, famine strikes and an even larger population suffers and dies. We try to help, but we end up hurting more: "Such [are] the implications of the well meant sharing of food in a world of irresponsible production" (Hardin 1974a, 565).

The **lifeboat argument** can be framed as a simple analogy:

(P1) Saving those drowning around the lifeboat is similar to donating to the poor.

(P2) Saving those drowning around them in the lifeboat is wrong.

(C)   Therefore, donating to the poor is wrong.

> What do you think of Hardin's analogy? Does it seem plausible? Misguided? Cruel?

Hardin further illustrates how sharing resources makes things worse with the **tragedy of the commons**. A rational herdsman won't allow his flocks to ruin his own field; he will take care of the field, limiting flock usage to preserve the field. However, things look different if he is grazing his flocks on public pasture open to all herdsmen. Since he doesn't own the field, he cares much less about whether the field is preserved—and anyway, even if *he* limits the number of sheep he grazes, other people probably won't, so that the field will be ruined anyway. Accordingly, it's in each person's self-interest to put as many sheep as possible on the common, even if this means that the common will inevitably be destroyed, leaving everyone worse off.

Generally, *people abuse public resources for personal gain*: parks are vandalized, oceans are littered, and no one cleans the shared fridge in the office lounge. We spend the money of others very differently than we spend our own. The resources of our planet are a commons, and by sharing them freely, we risk ruining the resources for everyone. We can try to get people to agree to only take their fair share, but this is difficult to enforce. And as soon as one person breaks this rule, all others will be incentivized to break it as well, and the commons is destroyed.

Hardin claims that international aid works the same way: well-run nations will just wind up subsidizing poorly run nations. This will take resources from the well-run nations while also incentivizing reckless behavior, making things worse for everyone.

Hardin applies his reasoning to an ongoing controversy: *immigration*. He argues that wealthy nations should not let in too many immigrants. While opening the borders helps immigrants

> Can you think of other examples of the tragedy of the commons? Have you ever experienced something like it?
>
> Another question: the tragedy of the commons assumes people are selfish. However, we often act altruistically and are not only concerned with personal benefit. Do you think Hardin's arguments are too pessimistic about human nature? (Cf. Susan Jane Buck Cox 1985.)

in the short run, the consequences are dire in the long run—because resources are stretched too thin. Even if the rich benefit from the cheap labor of immigrants in the short term, they do not in the long term, or, at least, their future generations do not: compare the **well-being** of Native Americans in North Dakota against the well-being of those who immigrated to North Dakota.

3. Objections and Replies

Objection 1:

Against (P2), those in the lifeboats should save those drowning. It doesn't matter if it is costly or puts them at a great risk. They can't just let those people drown; that would be awful.

Reply:

The idea that sometimes we should let some people die in order to save more lives can be hard to swallow, but there are other cases that support this idea. In Chapter 4, we considered a case where you are rushing badly injured people to the hospital, and as you drive there, you pass another person on the side of the road who is severely injured and in need of help. However, if you stop to help this person, those you are taking to the hospital will die. It seems okay to let the person by the side of the road die, because doing so will save more lives overall. More generally, when time or resources are scarce, sometimes it is right to let some die in order to save the most lives in the end.

An analogy from wartime may help the reader see this point (see Singer 2011, 205). Suppose that in wartime, there are a large number of soldiers in need of serious medical attention and only a small number of doctors. In order to cope with the casualties, the medics adopt a **triage policy**, dividing injured soldiers into three groups: Those who will probably

1. survive without medical assistance;
2. survive with medical assistance but otherwise probably will die; or
3. die with or without medical assistance.

Devoting their resources as efficiently as possible, the doctors focus their attention on the middle category. After all, those in the second group depend critically on the doctors, whereas those in the first group will probably survive anyway, and those in the last group will probably die anyway.

According to Hardin, our predicament is similar to the wartime doctors: *limited resources and many in need.* Consigning some people to death may sound cruel and heartless. But we can all agree that in certain tragic emergency situations, it's the best thing to do. For Hardin, we are in exactly such an emergency situation:

there are too few resources for everyone, or, if there aren't, there will be soon. Returning to the lifeboat analogy, those who will die without our aid are like those drowning outside the boat. Since space is limited, we should let many die in order to save others—this is the best way to save as many as we can overall.

Objection 2:

Even if we grant all that, Hardin's argument only works if we really are in a situation analogous to the lifeboat or triage cases: if there really aren't enough resources for everyone. But is that true? Many of our resources are renewable and thus potentially unlimited; for example, a properly managed grazing commons can be exploited without end if managed properly (cf. Lutts 1984, 291).

Our resources appear limited because they are often wasted. According to the Food and Agriculture Organization of the United Nations, one third of the food produced for human consumption is wasted—about 1.3 billion tons of food per year. People starve not because the world doesn't produce enough food, but because of economic and logistical reasons. Further, much of the food that's produced is used in ways which aren't very efficient at feeding people. Large quantities of grain are turned into biofuel to run our vehicles (Singer 2010, 121). And the demand for meat and other animal products means that plants are fed to animals rather than being eaten directly by human beings. If you learned about "trophic levels" in biology class, you will know that nutritional value is lost during that process: you could feed more people if you gave the people the plant food directly. As Singer (2010) notes:

> According to the United Nations Food and Agriculture Organization, 756 million tons of grain were fed to animals in 2007. Just to give you a sense of how much grain that is, imagine it equally divided among the 1.4 billion people living in extreme poverty. It would give each of them more than half a ton of grain, or about 3 pounds per day, which gives you twice as many calories as you need. Add to that most of the world's 225-million-ton soybean crop, which is also fed to animals, and you can see how much of the food we grow is not eaten directly by humans. When we use animals to convert crops into meat, eggs, or milk, the animals use most of the food value to keep warm and develop bones and other parts we can't eat. . . . The world is not running out of food. The problem is that we—the relatively affluent—have found a way to consume four or five times as much food as would be possible, if we were to eat the crops we grow directly. (122)

Singer jokingly suggests that, rather than mass starvation, our main threat is "mass vegetarianism" (2010, 123). Of course, as we saw in earlier chapters, there may be good ethical reasons to be vegetarians anyway.

More broadly, even though the population of the world has increased in recent decades, *the number and rate of actual people dying from poverty is decreasing.* According to the World Bank, in 1990, 1.85 billion lived in extreme poverty (on less than $1.90 a day); in 2013, only 767 million lived in extreme poverty. That's a difference of 1.1 billion people. If our predicament is like a lifeboat, then there is a helicopter lifting us out of the lifeboats—creating much more space to bring others aboard.

You might worry that this will lead to more suffering later on, as the population continues to increase. However, the rate of population increase peaked in the 1980s. *The population is eventually expected to level out or even decrease:* according to the US Census Bureau, worldwide births have remained relatively constant since 2011 (~135 million per year) and deaths are expected to increase (56 million in 2011, but around 80 million deaths predicted per year by 2040).

Further, the decrease in poverty and the decrease in the population growth rate are likely connected: when nations become wealthier, people have fewer children. Where there are very high infant mortality rates and no social safety nets, people try to have many children—for instance, so they have some family to care for them when they are old. Donations that improve health, reduce childhood mortality, and lead to economic growth can mitigate the need to have many children. Furthermore, when people—especially women—become more educated, they have fewer children. Donations to education can thus reduce population growth too (Singer 2010, 123–24). The conflict Hardin imagines between saving the global poor and reducing population growth therefore doesn't even arise.

Reply:

There's no getting around it: these facts seem pretty damning for Hardin's argument. Perhaps the most someone could say in response is that, while helping the global poor is not in tension with fighting overpopulation, it would still be good to fight *further* overpopulation, perhaps by increasing the access women in poor countries have to birth control. If you think it's good for women to have access to birth control in general, this would be a good thing anyway. Singer (2010) actually agrees: he says that "if you think that stopping population growth is an overriding priority, you should donate to organizations like Population Services International, or the International Planned Parenthood Federation, asking that your gift be earmarked for family-planning projects" (124).

> Think back to the discussion of the **repugnant conclusion** in Chapter 8. Does that argument change how you think about overpopulation? If so, how?

Objection 3:

As we mentioned in Chapter 8, the main threat to the environment actually comes from the global *rich*. While people in poorer nations have more children, people in richer nations have a *much* bigger environmental impact. (Singer notes that since wealthier people eat more meat, they [indirectly] consume much more food; and we mentioned in the earlier chapter that a person in the developed West produces hundreds of times as much CO_2 as a person in Malawi.)

Accordingly, if you're willing to let people die in order to reduce the strain on the environment, it seems that you should start *here*, not in the developing world. For instance, the view seems to entail that, if I see a French child drowning, I perhaps should just let them drown so they don't grow up to use disproportionately many resources. *That's* not right. But if we accept Hardin's reasoning, it seems we are committed to accepting something like that, unless we unjustifiably think the lives of people in wealthy nations are much more important than the lives of people in poor ones. So something must be wrong with Hardin's reasoning.

Reply 1:

Someone who accepts Hardin's reasoning here may just have to **bite the bullet** and say we shouldn't save people who live in wealthy nations, either.

Reply 2:

Based partly on statements Hardin made elsewhere and partly on some of the groups with which he cooperated, the Southern Poverty Law Center (n.d.) argues that Hardin was actually a white nationalist who "used the specter of environmental destruction and ethnic conflict to promote policies that can be fairly described as fascist." On this view, the reason he was concerned with reducing population in the (largely non-white) developing world and not in the (largely white) developed world is that "his concern with overpopulation was primarily a cover for his racist ideology," one aimed at preventing non-whites from immigrating to the United States and at preventing non-whites from greatly outnumbering whites. In other words, he actually *did* think the lives of some people were much more important than the lives of others. Hardin died in 2003, so he didn't have a chance to respond to this report; you can find the SPLC report online.

Racism and fascism are heinous. If they explain why Hardin wasn't bothered by this objection, so much the worse for him. So we're not putting forward reply 2 here as a serious way of defending Hardin's view. However, it may be useful as an opportunity to reflect on *whether there is value in considering arguments offered with bad motivations.*

You are likely familiar with attempts to remove offensive material and immoral authors from classroom syllabi. Hardin's argument is for a conclusion that seems seriously wrong, it rests on a false empirical basis, and (according to the Southern Poverty Law Center) it was secretly motivated by his personal racism. Was there still value for you in engaging with the argument, or would it have been better for the authors to omit these sections? How would you have handled this topic, if you were the author of this book? Do Hardin's actual motivations matter at all for understanding or evaluating the argument, or is it better to focus just on the reasoning he offers without caring about why he offers it?

4. The Institutional Critique

Is there a better argument against the approach to charitable giving that we discussed in Chapters 11 and 12? We'll now discuss the *institutional critique of charitable giving*. The form of the critique we'll discuss focuses specifically on a movement known as **effective altruism**. Effective altruism encourages people to *do the most good possible*. In principle, it can apply to any area of one's life—from whether to buy fair-trade coffee to whether to eat vegan to whether to take a trip that will produce a lot of CO_2—but, in principle, effective altruists often focus largely on charitable donations. This is because they're impressed by arguments like Singer's from Chapter 11 which point out how much good a single individual can do with a modest charitable donation.

Effective altruists often encourage people not only to donate as much money as they can, but also to *make* as much money as they can, so that they can donate more. Sometimes this takes the form of so-called **earning to give**: someone who wishes to do good might be encouraged not to try to do good *directly* (say, by being a doctor or an aid worker) but instead to take a high-paying job so that they'll have more money to donate. Effective altruists also encourage people to donate wherever their donation will do the *most* good. For instance, if you were choosing whether to donate to help homeless people in your own community or to purchase malaria bednets for people in the developing world, effective altruists would recommend that you do the latter, since it will probably do the most good overall. In the attempt to determine which charities are most effective, they rely on reason, evidence, and independent charity evaluators. (That's why, in Chapter 11, we mentioned all those statistics about how much good various donations do, and talked about charity evaluators like GiveWell.) This emphasis on using evidence to do the most good is why they are known as *effective* altruists—they want to be effective at helping people.

> Based on that description, does effective altruism sound like a reasonable movement to you? What things do you agree with or disagree with in their approach?

Accepting Singer's argument from Chapter 11 doesn't *immediately* commit you to effective altruism. However, it's easy to see how it might naturally lead to effective altruism. In fact, Singer is a major promoter of effective altruism, and in many ways is one of its intellectual founders.

Unlike Hardin's argument, the institutional critique of effective altruism doesn't *condemn* charitable giving. (Amia Srinivasan [2015], whose version of the institutional critique we'll consider, even mentions that reading a book by Will MacAskill, a major effective altruist, caused her to set up a recurring donation to GiveDirectly, an organization which gives money to poor households in Uganda and Kenya.) However, it condemns the effective altruist approach championed by Singer for focusing too much on charitable giving rather than institutional reform. As we'll see, this could be framed as an in-principle problem for effective altruism, or it might instead be framed as a kind of practical problem: maybe effective altruism is fine in the abstract, but in practice it tends to distract us from important things.

To understand the institutional critique, consider the huge impact that political and economic institutions have on those who live under them. Think about the United States a hundred years ago. *First*, people were generally much poorer than they are now. *Second*, there were many specific economic injustices that have since been eliminated or at least improved: children worked in factories, workers faced unsafe conditions and grueling hours more broadly, there was no minimum wage, elderly people routinely lived in poverty, there was no social safety net for the unemployed, and so on.

What changed?

> **First**, people have a lot more money generally. But this wasn't because nice individuals in some wealthier country sent money to people in the United States. It's because a lot of *economic growth* happened. This economic growth was enabled by certain institutions: for instance, ones which allowed businesses to survive without needing to pay bribes to corrupt government officials, or which prevented the outbreak of civil war or other major forms of instability. (It was also, sadly, made possible partly through American *imperialism*, which helps illustrate the need for *global* institutions.)
>
> **Second**, there were lots of policy changes to help address those specific injustices we mentioned: labor laws mandating safer working conditions and outlawing child labor, social security and other programs, among others. The United States has plenty of problems, but things really have gotten better in many ways, and this has been largely because of institutions, or institutional changes. (And we haven't even talked about other monumental institutional changes, like the end of segregation.)

We mentioned above that the amount of extreme poverty in the world has greatly decreased in the past few decades. This has been driven largely by a decline in the amount of extreme poverty in East Asia. But this decline was not due to nice individuals in the West sending donations. It was because *governments in these countries pursued policies which allowed for economic development*—often against the wishes of Western governments (Chang 2006). On the other hand, not nearly as much progress has been made in, for instance, sub-Saharan Africa. It seems plausible to think that this is largely because, when the European

---

Think of all the different institutions that have affected your life: the government, schools, hospitals, religious organizations, and so forth. How does their impact compare with the impact of various individuals who have affected you?

colonial powers left Africa after exploiting it for decades, they left behind weak or dysfunctional political and economic institutions in many places.

But if institutional factors have such a big impact on poverty, it may seem odd that Singer and other effective altruists focus so much on charitable giving and so little on working for institutional reform. Admittedly, the examples given above were about *domestic* institutions: a country's own internal political and economic system. Perhaps there is relatively little you can do to directly affect the internal institutions of other countries, and that might seem like meddling, anyway. But in an increasingly globalized world, international institutions, as well as your own country's institutions, can have a big effect on the global poor too. For instance, within your own country, you might support international institutions that better protect developing nations from exploitation and imperialism at the hands of wealthy countries, or promote equitable trade and other economic relationships between your own country and others, or work to ensure that your own country's policies about building institutions in other countries are good ones. You might also try to ensure that the large sums of money given as foreign aid are used in ways that do the most good (see Singer 2010, chap. 7).

All this helps set the stage for the institutional critique. While Srinivasan (2015) makes a number of points, we'll focus on two main components of her argument:

1. **Ignorance point:** effective altruism encourages us to ignore important facts about institutions.
2. **Uncertainty point:** because it's so hard to tell whether efforts to improve institutions will succeed, effective altruism, with its focus on evidence-based approaches to doing the most good, is biased against such efforts.

These two factors, Srinivasan alleges, result in effective altruism discouraging people from working for institutional reform: the first discourages them from realizing that institutional reform is even necessary, while the second encourages them to invest their efforts in things that are easier to measure, even if they realize various institutional reforms would be nice. We'll discuss these in turn.

After saying that MacAskill's 2015 book on effective altruism, *Doing Good Better*, "doesn't dwell much on the horrors of global inequality, and sidesteps any diagnosis of its causes. The word 'oppression' appears just once," Srinivasan (2015) adds that

> effective altruism, so far at least, has been a conservative movement, calling us back to where we already are: the world as it is, our institutions as they are. MacAskill does not address the deep sources of global misery—international trade and finance, debt, nationalism, imperialism, racial and gender-based subordination, war, environmental degradation,

> corruption, exploitation of labour—or the forces that ensure its repro-
> duction. Effective altruism doesn't try to understand how power works,
> except to better align itself with it. In this sense it leaves everything just
> as it is. (para. 14)

This is a version of the *ignorance* point. Srinivasan thinks effective altruism's focus on charitable giving encourages people to *seek out the most effective way to work within the system—say, by "earning to give"—without examining the system itself*. "Effective altruism doesn't try to understand how power works, except to better align itself with it." Confronted with an opportunity to take a high-paying job, for instance, an effective altruist might be excited by the opportunity to do a lot of good, but without thinking so much about the broader unjust system that produces extremely high-paying jobs, on the one hand, and extreme poverty, on the other.

Second, Srinivasan thinks that, because of effective altruism's focus on "evidence-based" charitable giving, it tends to be *biased against efforts at institutional change*, since the effects of these are often extremely difficult to quantify in advance. She notes that, having performed a cost-benefit analysis (see the next section), MacAskill concludes that it might make sense for a PPE major from Oxford to enter politics with the goal of becoming a member of parliament. However, she says:

> It's not clear that anyone with less conventional political ambitions
> would get the same pass. What's the expected marginal value of becom-
> ing an anti-capitalist revolutionary? To answer that you'd need to put a
> value and probability measure on achieving an unrecognisably different
> world—even, perhaps, on our becoming unrecognisably different sorts of
> people. It's hard enough to quantify the value of a philanthropic inter-
> vention: how would we go about quantifying the consequences of radi-
> cally reorganising society? (para. 10)

The political scientist Emily Clough (2015) echoes a similar point, saying:

> Effective altruists are committed to evidence-based selection of charities,
> but . . . they have prioritized certainty, narrowing the scope of impact
> they consider in identifying top charities.
> 　This choice has built political and institutional blind spots into the
> way the effective altruism movement redistributes money. (paras. 7–8)

(We'll see what she thinks these "blind spots" are in the objections section.) In light of these, we might state Srinivasan's overall argument like this:

(P1)　Effective altruism discourages efforts at institutional reform.

(P2)　Institutional reform is really the best way to help people in need.

(P3)   If effective altruism discourages efforts at the best way to help people in need, it's a problematic approach.

(C)   So effective altruism is a problematic approach.

We've left this argument a little vague. (For example: in saying effective altruism is a "problematic approach," are we saying it's *wrong*, or just that, while it might be right in principle, trying to follow it can be misleading in practice?) This is because, as we'll see, there are different ways of fleshing out the argument depending on how we respond to certain objections. Considering these objections will help us get clearer on exactly what the argument could be.

5. Objections

Objection 1:

The institutional critique simply *misses the point*. Effective altruism is about what individuals can do. Perhaps it would be best if institutions changed to better serve the global poor. However, I can't realistically affect whether or not these institutions change: even if I devote my life to activism, the odds that I will make any difference are vanishingly small. If millions and millions of people devote their lives to similar activism, something might change, but then they probably won't need me. On the other hand, if those other people *don't* devote their lives to such activism, my doing it won't do any good. In light of this, (P3) of the institutional critique is false: whether institutional reform would be the best thing is irrelevant, since institutional reform is beyond my power. I should instead focus on what I can control: namely, whether particular individuals in poor countries suffer and die or instead flourish because of my charitable donations.

The idea that effective altruism focuses on the individual precisely because you are an individual and can decide on your own actions is echoed by Jeff McMahan (2016):

> I am neither a community nor a state. I can determine only what I will do, not what my community or state will do. I can, of course, decide to concentrate my individual efforts on changing my state's institutions, or indeed on trying to change global economic institutions, though the probability of my making a difference to the lives of badly impoverished people may be substantially lower if I adopt this course than if I undertake more direct action, unmediated by the state. (4)

Reply 1:

We saw in Chapter 5 that some moral theories claim the morality of an action depends not on the consequences of that particular action, but instead on what would happen if people in general behaved in that way. Kantianism is a good example. Another example can be seen in the distinction between act and rule consequentialism.

Recall that **consequentialism** is the view that the morality of an action is determined by its consequences. There are two kinds of consequentialism. According to **act consequentialism**, the right action is one that *produces better consequences than its alternatives*. According to **rule consequentialism**, the right action is the one that *accords with the rules that would produce the best consequences if people generally followed them*. For instance, suppose I borrow five dollars from my acquaintance and promise to pay him back. However, as I'm going to pay him back, I realize that I could instead give the five dollars to a highly effective charity, so the money goes to someone who needs it much more than him. I'm moving and we weren't going to stay in touch anyway, so it doesn't matter if this hurts our relationship. Further, while he'll probably be upset with me, I think the harm this causes will be a little less than the extra good done by the charitable donation. Accordingly, breaking my promise and giving the money to charity will produce slightly more good.

If that's true, *act* consequentialism says I should break the promise. On the other hand, *rule* consequentialism asks me to consider what would happen if people generally followed rules allowing them to break or keep promises. These rules might look something like this:

> **Rule 1:** Break a promise whenever it will do even slightly more good.
> **Rule 2:** Keep promises, unless you're in some sort of emergency situation where breaking the promise is exceptionally important.

It seems plausible to think that generally following rule 2 would produce better consequences than following rule 1. Rule 1 would make it very difficult to trust that other people will keep their promises, and the institution of promising would break down as a result. Further, people trying to follow rule 1 might make lots of mistakes due to limited information or motivated reasoning, and in those cases breaking the promise would do more harm anyway.

One appeal of rule consequentialism is that it seems to fit better with our ordinary intuitions. For instance, the idea that I should pay my friend back in the case above seems intuitively right. Or consider the medical sacrifice case in Chapter 5. There, we considered whether it would be right for a doctor to secretly kill a healthy patient in order to transplant his organs into five other people who would die without them. Act consequentialism seems to suggest that this would be **morally obligatory**, as long as no one will find out, and so on. But rule consequentialism asks us to consider what would happen if doctors generally behaved that way. People would lose faith in the medical system—to say the least—and the results would be bad overall. Accordingly, rule consequentialism says it's wrong to kill the patient—again, the intuitively correct result.

Importantly, rule consequentialism also seems to give better judgments in many cases of **collective action**, such as in cases where a large group of people needs to take an action in order for it to succeed. Consider fighting global warming. If left unchecked, climate change will be a big problem. However, you might suppose that nothing you can do to fight this large-scale problem (whether that means reducing your personal carbon emissions or fighting for political action) is really going to make a difference. If everybody thinks like that, though, then the problem won't be addressed. Accordingly, rule consequentialism might help make better sense of why individuals should fight climate change.

The objection seems to fit most naturally with act consequentialism: it focuses on the consequences of your particular action, given what everybody else is doing. However, if we accept rule consequentialism (or some other theory that makes the morality of actions depend on what happens if people behave that way generally, such as Kantianism), things look different. Think of all the positive institutional changes that have happened in the United States over the past century.

Imagine that everyone who fought for those changes had figured that their contribution probably wouldn't make any difference and had instead focused on charitable giving. That might have done some good, but the world would probably be worse overall. So perhaps rule consequentialism recommends that you "do your part" to bring about institutional change, even if, as a single individual, you aren't likely to make a difference.

> What seems more plausible to you, act or rule consequentialism? Is it weird to think (as rule consequentialism implies) that the morality of an action can depend on what would happen if everyone did that thing, when you know everyone *won't* do it? If you're instead sympathetic to one of the other moral theories we've discussed, how might it address collective actions?

Reply 2:

Even if act consequentialism is true, we still might have good reason to focus on institutional factors. There are two reasons for this. First, *sometimes working for institutional change might make sense even in act consequentialist terms.* Perhaps your chance of making any difference is tiny. However, if you *do* make a difference— if your involvement is the "tipping point" that brings about a big institutional change—that would be a *really big* difference. Accordingly, it might make sense, in terms of a cost-benefit analysis, to fight for institutional change, at least in some cases. (See the discussion of cost-benefit analysis below.)

Second, even if you aren't working directly for institutional change, *understanding the institutional context in which you're working can be important*, since that can affect the consequences of your actions. (This builds on Srinivasan's ignorance point, but goes in a different direction than her own argument.) For instance, Clough (2015) argues that effective altruists have not properly taken into account the ways in which charitable work can reduce pressure on governments to provide services, sometimes making the very poor even worse off:

> It seems that once effective altruists have—for good reasons—ruled out governments as eligible recipients of effective aid, their attention to the state drops off entirely. . . .
>
> Yet any scholar of the political economy of development would be skeptical of the assumption that the welfare state in poor countries would remain unaffected by a sizeable influx of resources into a parallel set of institutions. . . .
>
> In the worst case, the presence of NGOs induces exit from the state sector. When relatively efficient, well-functioning NGOs enter a health or education market, for example, citizens in that market who are paying attention are likely to switch from government services to NGO services. The result is a disengagement of the most mobilized, discerning poor citizens from the state. These are the citizens most likely to have played a previous role in monitoring the quality of state services and advocating for improvements. Once they exit, the pressure on the government to maintain and improve services eases, and the quality of government provision is likely to fall.
>
> This dynamic, sometimes called skimming, has unfortunate consequences for those most in need of services. Even when NGOs intend to target the poorest and most marginalized, their services tend to be utilized by the slightly less poor, who are particularly good at seeking out the best services. These are the people who represent the most high-value citizens from the perspective of pro-poor state development—they share the general interests of the most marginalized, but they have more political voice and thus provide local public goods by advocating for better services from the government. When they exit the state system, it has distributional consequences for those who receive state services—those who are already the worst-off are left behind in the state system, service quality drops, and their interests are harmed. (paras. 9–12)

Clough's criticism is controversial, and effective altruists have responded (Hillebrandt 2015). But it at least illustrates the importance of understanding institutions when doing charitable work. McMahan himself (2016) admits that he finds such criticisms "quite forceful" and that effective altruists "certainly must not ignore the . . . serious empirical claims" of people like Clough (6).

Reply to the reply:

This isn't an objection to effective altruism. Effective altruism says you should do the most good. You're saying that, in order to do the most good, effective altruists should learn more about institutions and take more seriously the idea that they should work to change them. Maybe so. But if that's true, effective altruists should agree with you. That wouldn't make effective altruism wrong; at most, it might be an objection to how some effective altruists have implemented it.

Reply to the reply to the reply:

Sure. This isn't exactly an objection to the basic idea of effective altruism, that we should do the most good. But we saw in Chapter 7 that sometimes intentionally trying to pursue a goal is not the best way to pursue it. (Trying really hard to fall asleep is not the best way to fall asleep.) In a similar way, if following effective altruist principles tends to make people insensitive to important institutional factors, it might be that, *even if the effective altruist goal is good, intentionally trying to be an effective altruist is not the best way to pursue that goal.*

Objection 2:

The uncertainty point fails because there is a perfectly good way of deciding how to do the most good in the face of uncertainty: namely, doing a so-called **cost-benefit analysis** or **expected utility calculation**. This is a mathematical method for weighing the risks and rewards of a course of action.

Specifically, a cost-benefit analysis (CBA) takes the likelihood of incurring a cost and multiplies that by the badness of the cost. That then gets added to the likelihood of incurring a benefit multiplied by the goodness of that benefit. This often gets represented in an equation where costs and benefits are represented by 'C' and 'B', respectively, and 'Pr(e)' is read as the probability of some event occurring (like the cost or benefit occurring):

$$CBA = [Pr(C) \times C] + [Pr(B) \times B]$$

A positive CBA means there's an expected benefit; a negative CBA means there's an expected cost. (If it's zero, then there's no expected cost or benefit.) For instance, suppose you're offered a bet where a fair coin is flipped. If it lands heads, you get two dollars, and if it lands tails, you lose one dollar. The CBA would be as follows:

$$\$0.50 = [0.5 \times \$2] + [0.5 \times \$\text{-}1]$$

In other words, the "expected value" of taking the bet is $0.50 (that is, fifty cents). Roughly what this means is that on average and in the long run you should expect to make about fifty cents per bet. Since fifty cents is more than zero cents, it makes sense (pardon the pun) to take the bet.

When you are uncertain about the effects of your actions, an effective altruist will tell you to *do the thing that does the most expected good.* Return to Srinivasan's example of the anti-capitalist revolutionary. To determine whether it makes sense to become one, we'll need to figure the possible costs (execution by capitalists, accidentally creating a Stalinist dystopia, etc.), how bad they are, and how likely they are, as well as the possible benefits (bringing about a more just economic system), how good they are, and how likely they are. We then need to do the CBA and compare the expected value of being a revolutionary anti-capitalist to the expected value of everything else we might do instead. Easy!

Reply 1:

Srinivasan herself is doubtful that we can actually do this when it comes to complicated decisions like being an anti-capitalist revolutionary. Where are you going to get the numbers from? She even worries about this approach's "susceptibility to being used to tell us exactly what we want to hear"—in other words, *you might just make up whatever numbers you want to justify things you want to do for other reasons.*

Reply 2:

Perhaps Srinivasan's skepticism is unjustified, and we really can come up with at least very rough values for CBAs. Or suppose effective altruists agree with Srinivasan and try to make their decisions some other way. It might still be that the emphasis on being "effective," on doing the most good and backing that up with evidence, tends to bias us in favor of things whose effects are easier to quantify and away from things (like fighting for institutional change) whose effects are harder to quantify. Again, this wouldn't necessarily mean that effective altruism is *wrong*, but it might call into question how useful it is as a method for making decisions.

> Do you agree with the arguments that effective altruist principles aren't particularly useful for making decisions? How might an effective altruist respond?

Objection 3:

Charitable giving and working for institutional change aren't mutually exclusive. Admittedly, if you become an activist, you might have less disposable income than if you'd done something more lucrative. But you'll still have some, and that money could help other people. (Even if you're skeptical of traditional charities, you could give the money to political organizations fighting for institutional change.) So you should give *that* away. Further, it's okay for some people to focus on one thing and others to focus on another, depending on their different skills, interests, and the like. McMahan (2016) notes:

> It is obviously better . . . if people do both [directly helping others and trying to bring about institutional change]. Yet there has to be a certain division of moral labor, with some people taking direct action to address the plight of the most impoverished people, while others devote their efforts to bringing about institutional changes through political action. To suppose that the only acceptable option is to work to reform global

economic institutions and that it is self-indulgent to make incremental contributions to the amelioration of poverty through individual action is rather like condemning a doctor who treats the victims of a war for failing to devote his efforts instead to eliminating the root causes of war. (4)

So even if we grant everything Srinivasan says, *that doesn't mean it's bad if some people focus mostly on charitable giving, and it doesn't mean that even people fighting for institutional reform shouldn't also give to charity.*

Reply:

At least in principle, it seems that a proponent of the institutional critique could agree with this. Remember, the critique is not *against* charitable giving. Instead it criticizes what it regards as an *excessive focus* on charitable giving, to the exclusion of institutional reform, among some people inspired by Singer's arguments. It's compatible with this that people should still give to charity.

6. Conclusion

Over the past few chapters, we have discussed the view that charitable giving is morally obligatory, the view that it's supererogatory, the view that it's wrong, and the view that, while it might be okay, institutional reform should really be our focus. Next, we'll turn to a quite different topic: the morality of punishment.

Further Reading

The lifeboat argument is defended by Malthus (1798), Hardin (1968, 1974a, 1974b), and Lutts (1984). Objections to the lifeboat argument are given by Nell (1975), Buck Cox (1985), Ryberg (1997), Brzozowski (2003), Singer (2011, 205–9), and Okyere-Manu (2016). For the carefulness charity requires, see Corbett and Fikkert (2012) and Lupton (2012). For debate over altruism and human nature, see Nagel (1970), Sober and Wilson (1998), and Miller (2018). For further discussion of the institutional critique, see Nussbaum (1997), Herzog (2016), Weathers (2016), and Berkey (2018).

Section 5

Punishment

Chapter 14
Justifying Punishment, Part 1

1. Introduction

Many people—perhaps even you—have been grounded, given detention, and ordered to pay fines for speeding. Others experience more severe treatment: spankings, expulsion, and imprisonment. All of these can count as **punishments**, and many people assume that such punishments are sometimes justified. In the next three chapters, we'll investigate whether this assumption is correct, and especially *whether punishment by the government is justified.*

Many philosophers have argued for the conclusion that punishment is justified, but they've done so with radically different arguments. Collectively, these are what are often called **theories of punishment,** and most theories fall into one of two genres: **retributivist justifications** and **consequentialist justifications**. In this chapter, we'll set the stage by defining punishment and introducing the **problem of punishment**, which challenges proponents of punishment to explain why the practice is justified. We'll then present and evaluate retributivist justifications. The next chapter, Chapter 15, presents and evaluates consequentialist justifications and **theoretical abolition**, the position that says that punishment is never justified because none of the theories of punishment successfully explain why punishment is justified. Finally, there are those who think that punishment can be justified, in theory, but that our particular current practices are not justified due to practical problems such as systemic racism. We'll call this position **practical abolition** and investigate it in Chapter 16.

> Think of a time you were punished. Was the punishment justified? Why or why not?

2. What Is Punishment?

Before diving in, we must first get clear on what punishment—and more specifically, punishment by a government, or **state**—is. Most philosophers agree that punishment in general involves an infliction of harm in response to acting wrongly. To be more precise, they offer an **analysis** of what it means for one person, X, to punish another person, Y. An analysis of a concept *specifies what does and does not fall under a concept by giving the most central components of that concept.* For instance, an analysis of what it is for X to punish Y will give us the central components of punishment so that we can figure out whether particular cases count as instances of X punishing Y. (We'll talk more about a similar issue in Chapter 17, when we try to get clear on the concept of disability.) The phrase **if and only if** indicates when one thing is an analysis of another thing. Here's the analysis that we'll work with, inspired by Boonin (2008):

X punishes Y if and only if

(i)   X harms Y,

(ii)   the harm is intentional,

(iii)   the harm is inflicted *because* of a (perceived) wrong act committed by Y, and

(iv)   X intends to communicate condemnation of Y's wrong act.

> Imagine your parents are forcing you to stay home to protect you (and the community) from a new coronavirus outbreak. Would that count as punishment?

This general analysis of punishment captures all types of punishments, such as parental, school, and state punishment. When we move on from this introduction, we're going to focus specifically on punishment by the state. State punishment falls under the umbrella category of punishment. Thus, the two—punishment and state punishment—stand respectively in what's called a **genus-species relationship**. This relationship is the same one that captures the relationship between punishment and parental punishment, tiger and Bengal tiger, or coronavirus and COVID-19. In other words, state punishment is a specific type of punishment.

Because state punishment is a specific type of punishment, giving an analysis of state punishment is easy. We just need to add another component to the four we already have:

(v)   X is acting on behalf of the state in their official capacity as an agent of the state.

This fifth component includes things like a prison warden overseeing the imprisonment of someone who has been convicted of a crime and sentenced to a prison term. It does not include the warden forcing a prisoner to do something that the state has not approved as punishment. For instance, the warden in *The Shawshank Redemption* who forces inmate Andy Dufresne to do his taxes is not acting on behalf of the state in his official capacity.

Putting it all together, we get the following:

X (a state) punishes Y if and only if

(i)   X harms Y,

(ii)   the harm is intentional,

(iii) the harm is inflicted *because of* a (perceived) wrong act committed by Y,

(iv) X intends to communicate condemnation of Y's wrong act, and

(v) X is acting on behalf of the state in their official capacity as an agent of the state.

We've now analyzed both punishment in general and state punishment specifically. This means we're now prepared to look more closely at whether state punishment is justified. But it's awkward to say 'state punishment', so for the rest of this book, whenever we say 'punishment', we mean specifically 'state punishment' unless otherwise specified.

> In light of how we added another component to define state punishment, how would you define parental punishment?

3. The Problem of Punishment

There's a lot of recent debate about whether punishments for recreational marijuana use are justified. There's a lot more historical debate over whether the death penalty is ever justified. Yet a less popular—but more fundamental—debate is over whether *any* punishment is ever justified. After all, if it turns out punishment is never justified, then the answers to the debates about recreational marijuana use and the death penalty are obvious. And if punishments are sometimes justified, the debate should shed light on *when* this is so, which will also have implications for recreational marijuana use, the death penalty, and the like.

Punishments harm people, and harming people is *usually* wrong. Harming people might always be **prima facie wrong**—*prima facie* is Latin for "at first glance." But sometimes, harming people is not **all-things-considered wrong**. Something is all-things-considered wrong when it is overall wrong once all the relevant factors are taken into account. For example, shoving you might always be *prima facie* wrong. Shoving tends to be wrong and is wrong at first glance. But shoving you might not be all-things-considered wrong if it's the only way I can save you from a pouncing tiger. Importantly, in order for shoving you to be all-things-considered permissible, I have to provide a justification for why I shoved you, since shoving you is *prima facie* wrong. Similarly, the debate about punishment is over whether the harm of punishment is all-things-considered permissible, even though harm is *prima facie* wrong. And since harm is *prima facie* wrong, the defender of punishment must provide a justification that explains why that harm is permissible all things considered.

Here's how we might put things more formally:

(P1) Punishment involves harming someone, which is *prima facie* wrong.

(P2) If a practice involves a *prima facie* wrong, then for that practice to be permissible, there needs to be a justification for why that practice is not all-things-considered wrong.

(C) There needs to be a justification for why punishment is not all-things-considered wrong.

Notice that both (P1) and (P2) are true in virtue of what it means to punish and what it means to be a *prima facie* wrong. In addition, the argument is valid. That means that the conclusion is true, and punishment requires justification.

Here's another way to think about why the practice of punishment requires justification. Punishment inherently requires treating two groups of people differently: we inflict harm upon those who have (or are perceived to have) committed a wrong, and we do not inflict harm upon those who have not (or are perceived not to have) committed any wrongs. Sometimes, harming people based on what group they belong to is wrong. For instance, it would be bad for a professor to divide students into those who like cats and those who don't, then grade the first group according to their performance in class and automatically fail those in the second group. But other times, it is permissible. For instance, if a professor divides students into those who plagiarize and those who do not, it is permissible to fail the former group and not the latter. These two examples suggest that if we are to justify harming members of one group but not another, there has to be something about the features that divide the two groups that make the harm permissible in one case but not the other.

> Have you ever been harmed because you were a member of a group? What feature made you a member of that group? Was the harm that you suffered justified?

In the case of punishment, the supposed difference between the two groups is that the members of one group have performed acts that are wrong and the members of the other group have not. Thus, if the practice of punishment is justified, that justification needs to have something to do with the distinguishing feature: having performed an act that is wrong.

With all this in mind, we can now state the **problem of punishment**. Punishment inherently involves harming a group of people—those who (are perceived to) have performed a wrong action. How can performing a wrong action justify being harmed by the state? Now we'll turn to our first genre of solutions, retributivist justifications. (For more on the problem, see Boonin 2008, especially chap. 1.)

4. Retributivist Justifications

The two most popular types of solutions to the problem of punishment are retributivist theories and consequentialist theories. We'll look closely at retributivist theories in the remainder of this chapter, then turn to consequentialist theories in the next. Many different theories fall under the category of 'retributivist'. What unites them is the claim that punishment is justified *because of* the wrongdoing. It's often said that retributivist theories are "backward looking" because the past wrongdoing serves as the justification for punishment. This means that punishment is justified even if the punishment serves no further purpose, such as deterrence of future crimes, rehabilitation, or catharsis on the part of victims. But what distinguishes these views from each other are significant differences regarding the exact way in which wrongdoing justifies punishment. This in turn generates differences when it comes to things like society's obligation to punish wrongdoers and what counts as an appropriate punishment. In this section, we'll explore some of these different retributivist theories, as well as the worries associated with them.

4.1. Desert-Based Justifications

Now that we've examined *what* retributivism is, we'll turn to particular retributivist theories and look at their arguments for *why* punishment is justified as a response to wrongdoing. Our first argument is based on **desert**. The word 'desert' is derived from the same root of "deserve." (Thus, though it is pronounced like "dessert," it is spelled with only one 's'.) And roughly, someone's desert is what they *deserve*. For example, a student who works hard and turns in good work deserves a high grade; the high grade is the desert that the hardworking student should receive. Similarly, a student who plagiarizes their assignments deserves a failing grade; the failing grade is the desert that the plagiarizing student should receive.

Notice that even though the hardworking student deserves a high grade and the plagiarizing student deserves a failing one, they may not actually receive what they deserve. For instance, the professor may not have enough evidence to pursue an academic dishonesty case against the plagiarizing student, and so that student might still receive a passing grade. However, the important point is that the professor would be justified in giving these students their desert (the high or failing grades) *precisely because* that is what they deserve.

> Have you ever received a grade that you didn't believe you deserved (either because it was too high or low)? Was that just?

Desert plays an important role in some retributivist justifications of punishment. Roughly, the idea is that punishing wrongdoers is justified because punishment amounts to giving them what they deserve (see, e.g., Moore 1993, 15; Mundle 1954, 221). But *how* exactly do desert-based retributivists argue for this claim? They tend to offer an **argument from cases**. An argument from cases uses carefully selected cases designed to bring out a particular **intuition**, or an "intellectual seeming" regarding, for example, a judgment about a case or the truth of a claim or principle. (A "seeming" is what it sounds like—how things seem to be.) For instance, Michael Moore (1993, 25) asks readers to imagine an offender who does a serious wrong in a culpable way—for example, Dostoevsky's Russian nobleman in *The Brothers Karamazov*, who turns loose his dogs to tear apart a young boy before the eyes of the boy's mother. John Kleinig (1973, 67) appeals to the example of the unrepentant Nazi war criminal, an example that many others make use of as well (see, e.g., Primoratz 1989). These cases feature extremely morally bad wrongdoers and are used to support intuition that extremely morally bad wrongdoers deserve to suffer punishment.

> Do you share the intuition that the Russian nobleman and unrepentant Nazi deserve to suffer punishment?

Of course, the claim that extremely morally bad wrongdoers deserve punishment is not enough to justify the majority of punishments. After all, the vast majority of offenders do not rise to the level of the Russian nobleman or the unrepentant Nazi. So these cases must support the closely related claim that all wrongdoers deserve to suffer punishment (perhaps in proportion to the severity of their wrongdoing). Putting this all together, the argument from cases starts looking like this:

> (P1)   Extremely morally bad wrongdoers (e.g., the Russian nobleman and unrepentant Nazi) deserve punishment.
>
> (P2)   If extremely morally bad wrongdoers deserve punishment, then all wrongdoers deserve punishment.
>
> (C)   All wrongdoers deserve punishment.

Now that the argument is on the table, let's turn to some worries one might have about this argument.

Objection 1:

Consider (P2) and the fact that this argument moves from *extreme* cases of wrongdoing to *all* cases of wrongdoing. "All cases" of wrongdoing include some minor wrongdoing, such as stealing a candy bar or purchasing alcohol with a fake ID. So why does the argument not start with these more innocent cases or explore all cases together? Perhaps because people's intuitions about wrongdoers who merely steal candy bars or purchase alcohol with fake IDs are far less strong—or altogether absent. This suggests that the argument is required because people do not have equally strong intuitions across all cases of wrongdoing. But if that is so, why should we trust intuitions about the extreme cases more than intuitions about the non-extreme cases (the majority of

> Do you think that someone who steals a candy bar or purchases alcohol with a fake ID deserves to suffer punishment? Alternatively, do they merely need to return those goods (perhaps with a little extra to make up for the inconvenience created by their wrongdoing)?

cases)? This is something that the desert-based retributivist has not motivated. And if we don't have reason to trust our intuitions in extreme cases more than our intuitions in non-extreme cases, (P2) is not adequately supported.

Reply:

Even if people do not have equally strong intuitions across all cases of wrong-doing, this objection does not deny that people do have very strong intuitions about the extreme cases. If people have no intention whatsoever about the non-extreme cases, then perhaps it's okay to just go with the intuitions from the extreme cases.

But even if the intuitions in the extreme and non-extreme cases conflict, maybe what this demonstrates is that desert matters in cases of extreme wrong-doing. Perhaps this justifies a moderate position on which punishment is justified in cases of extreme wrongdoing and not justified in non-extreme cases.

Objection 2:

The above argument doesn't establish that punishments carried out by the state are justified. Desert-based retributivism relies on the concept of *moral* desert. The Russian nobleman and unrepentant Nazis are *morally* bad, and it's the moral element that generates the intuition that they deserve punishment. But there are a lot of actions the state actually does and does not prohibit. To make things more concrete, consider the following two characters:

> **Harvey:** Harvey has carefully studied workplace harassment law and knows exactly where the line is between legal and illegal behavior. He then goes out of his way to make life for the women in his workplace as miserable as possible.
>
> **Harriet:** Harriet lives near the southern border of the United States. Sometimes, she encounters undocumented immigrants in desperate need of water. She gives them water and sometimes food before they continue their journey.

Harvey acts in a morally bad way, while what Harriet does is morally good (or at least morally neutral). If either of them is deserving of punishment, it's Harvey. Yet what Harvey does is perfectly legal, while what Harriet does is illegal. And if the state were to punish either one of them, it would punish Harriet. This example demonstrates that even if moral desert can justify punishing *moral* wrongdoers, it does not necessarily justify punishing people who break the law (unless the laws align perfectly with morality).

> Can you think of crimes people are punished for that do not involve moral wrongdoing? Can you think of morally wrong acts that are not illegal?

Reply:

Perhaps Harvey is more deserving of punishment than Harriet. But this doesn't reveal a problem with the desert-based solution. Instead, it reveals that our laws don't always line up with morality, and that in at least some cases (like Harvey's and Harriet's), they should.

Objection 3:

Finally, consider the conclusion of the desert-based argument, that all wrongdoers deserve punishment. Notice that this conclusion does not say anything about the state's role in punishing. That would require a further premise:

> (C)   All wrongdoers deserve punishment.
> (P3)   If someone deserves punishment, then the state is justified in punishing them.
> (C2)   The state is justified in punishing all wrongdoers.

Even if the original argument is sound and (C) is true, why think that (P3) is true? Consider how Gandalf responds to Frodo in *The Lord of the Rings* (Tolkien 1961) when Frodo says it's a pity that Bilbo didn't kill Gollum when he had the chance:

> "Many that live deserve death. And some that die deserve life. Can you give it to them?"

Gandalf and Frodo agree that some (like Gollum) deserve death. But there's a further question of who, if anyone, is in a position to be justified in giving people what they deserve. Gandalf's question to Frodo isn't really a practical question about whether Frodo has the *ability* to give people what they deserve. Rather, Gandalf is forcing Frodo to question the link between Gollum's deserving death and someone being justified in putting Gollum to death. Similarly, some philosophers worry about the link between a wrongdoer deserving punishment and the state (or anyone else) being justified in punishing them (see, e.g., Dolinko 1991).

> How would you support (P3)? Is there a way to connect someone deserving punishment and the state being justified in punishing them?

4.2. Forfeiture-Based Justifications

Another version of retributivism justifies punishment by arguing that offenders *forfeit* their rights. Roughly, the idea is that when someone harms another person, they give up their rights. For instance, if John steals from Robin, then John forfeits his right from having his own possessions stolen. Formally, the claim can be expressed as such:

> If a person, A, violates another person B's right to X, then A forfeits A's own right to X.

Let's call this the **forfeiture claim**, since it is about forfeiting rights. Historically, the forfeiture claim was endorsed by philosophers such as Thomas Hobbes and John Locke. Why did they find this claim so attractive? These philosophers were concerned with how we come to have political rights. Take Hobbes, for example, who posits a "state of nature" in which there are no laws or government regulating people's behavior. In this situation, a rational person will realize that they need to steal and murder from others first, to prevent others from stealing or murdering them. But this leads to lots of theft and murder. The important thing to see here is that *while people in the state of nature are "free" to steal and murder, they also have no rights that protect them from theft and murder.* Given this state of nature, people will give up their freedoms to the state in exchange for rights and become more free overall (because they can pursue their lives without constant worrying about theft and murder). Importantly, rights arise out of an agreement to sacrifice certain freedoms. So when one steals or murders, they break the agreement, and thus forfeit their rights. Locke provides slightly different arguments, but overall his view is similar. Modern advocates of the forfeiture claim make similar arguments for it (see, e.g., Goldman 1994; Haksar 1986; Morris 1991).

> Consider your relationship with other people in society. Why would it be wrong for you to harm those people? Is part of your answer to that question based on whether they have harmed you?

The forfeiture claim helps address the problem of punishment. Those who do not wrong others don't forfeit their corresponding rights; those who do wrong others do forfeit these rights. This justifies punishment in the second case (punishing wrongdoers doesn't violate their rights since they've already forfeited them) and explains why those in the first case cannot be punished (since they haven't forfeited their rights, punishment would violate their rights). In premise-conclusion form, the argument can be put this way:

(P1) If an agent, A, violates an agent B's right to X, then A forfeits A's own right to X.

(P2) If A forfeits A's own right to X, then it's permissible for the state to take X from A.

(P3) If it's permissible for the state to take X from A, then the state is justified in punishing A by taking X from them.

(C) Therefore, the state is justified in punishing A by taking X from them.

Now that the argument is on the table, let's turn to some objections.

Objection 1:

Let's start with (P1), the forfeiture claim. The forfeiture claim says that someone who violates someone else's right loses that same right. So if John steals from Robin, John loses his right to his property, or his right to have others refrain from stealing his property. There are at least two worries with the reciprocal aspect of the forfeiture claim.

First, we might wonder whether John loses his rights *forever*. If so, the punishment is bound to be disproportionate to the wrongdoing. For instance, suppose John steals a candy bar from Robin. This does not give Robin the right to steal candy bars from John for the rest of John's life. Furthermore, Robin stealing something significantly more substantial than a candy bar, such as John's car or house, is also not fair. Thus, the forfeiture claim seems to justify **disproportionate punishment**—the punishment doesn't fit the crime.

Second, consider what the state would actually do in response to John stealing, say, a car. The punishment for grand theft auto often involves imprisonment. But the right to freedom of movement seems significantly different from the right to not have one's things stolen. And the forfeiture claim does not say that John forfeits this other right. Here's a related objection. Suppose a wrongdoer's crime involves something horrific like rape or torture. Even if it is true that the wrongdoer forfeits their right to not be raped or tortured, it doesn't seem that raping or torturing them as punishment is okay or good.

Reply:

What these cases suggest is that for the forfeiture claim to justify our actual practices of punishment, it must say something like "A forfeits A's own right to X, or some equivalent right." Doing the same with the other premises would lead to the conclusion that "the state is justified in punishing A by taking X, or some equivalent right, from them."

> Do you find this reply convincing? Does it solve the problem of disproportionate punishment? And if not, how would you revise the forfeiture claim so that it does?

Objection 2:

A second worry with the forfeiture-based view centers on the support for the forfeiture claim, (P1). (P1) is most plausible if rights are based on a society's agreement. But is this the most plausible view of rights? Consider part of the second paragraph of the Declaration of Independence:

> We hold these truths to be self-evident, that all men are created equal,
> that they are endowed by their Creator with certain unalienable Rights,
> that among these are Life, Liberty, and the pursuit of Happiness.

If we take this literally, then at least certain fundamental rights come from a higher power, not societal agreement. Furthermore, these fundamental rights are **inalienable**, which means that they cannot be taken away. It's also worth noting that this type of view isn't just in the Declaration. The Universal Declaration of Human Rights (UDHR) is one of the foundational documents of international law. (It's the equivalent of the Bill of Rights for American law.) It opens with the "recognition of the inherent dignity and of the equal and inalienable rights of all the members of the human family." The UDHR doesn't reference a higher power, but does affirm that we all have certain fundamental rights that can't be taken away from us.

In fact, many philosophers believe that certain fundamental rights are both universal and inalienable. For instance, John Stuart Mill (1859) argues that it's impossible to sell yourself into permanent slavery because that would involve separating yourself from your liberty, which can't be taken away from you. Similar reasoning also appears in courts, such as when a German court ruled that it's not possible to consent to being murdered and cannibalized. (And yes, this happened in 2001 when Arwin Meiwes—the cannibal—was convicted of murder, which means that the cannibalized victim had not successfully waived his rights.) If certain fundamental rights are both inalienable and universal, then nothing we do can strip others, or ourselves, of them. This means that we can't forfeit certain fundamental rights—even through explicit consent— and thus, that (P1) is false.

> It's definitely possible to waive some rights: people can waive their property rights by giving things away, and people can waive their parental rights by putting their children up for adoption. What other rights are waivable? What rights might not be waivable?

Objection 3:

The final worry concerns (P2), the claim that if A forfeits A's own right to X, then it's permissible for the state to take X from A. It's permissible for the state to take X from A precisely because A has forfeited their right to X. To give a concrete example, suppose John steals from Robin, and John thus forfeits his right to his own property. Forfeiting his right to his own property is precisely what makes it permissible for the state to steal from him. But notice that this story can be applied to actors other than the state to explain why they can permissibly steal from John as well. If John no longer has a right to his own property, then it also looks like it's permissible for Robin to steal from John. It seems that you and I could as well, if it is true that what makes stealing from John permissible is his forfeiture of his rights.

If this is correct, then one might worry that forfeiture-based retributivism allows **vigilantism**, that is, the carrying out of the law by private citizens. But is vigilantism bad? Some think vigilantism is a good thing and welcome real-life Robins, Batmans, and the like. But many think vigilantism is bad and worry that if a theory of punishment justifies the issuing of punishment by anyone, then that theory doesn't adequately justify *state* punishment.

Reply:

Some (e.g., Simmons 1994) argue that the punisher is only justified if they issue the punishment in response to the wrongdoing. They aren't justified if they just enjoy harming people who no longer have rights.

Reply to the reply:

While the reply cuts down on vigilantism from opportunistic people who enjoy harming others but don't want to do so in an unjust way, it's not clear that the opportunists make up the bulk of vigilantes. For instance, as depicted in folklore, Robin Hood doesn't violate Prince John's property rights for fun—he does so in response to wrongdoing (in this case theft) on Prince John's part.

Reply to the reply to the reply:

Even if forfeiture-based retributivism allows for vigilantism, society might prohibit vigilantism for other reasons. For instance, the risk of widespread chaos that could result from vigilantism might justify prohibiting it.

> Do you think our theory of punishment should allow for vigilantism? Should the state allow vigilantism? Why or not why?

4.3. "Justice"-Based Justifications

The last retributivist justification we'll investigate is based on the necessity of punishment for maintaining justice. **Lex talionis** is Latin for "law of retaliation," and the idea that justice requires payback can be traced as far back as 1700 BCE in ancient Mesopotamia. The Code of Hammurabi prescribes various laws, including punishments such as "an eye for an eye" and "a tooth for a tooth." Now, we can only speculate about the motivation behind the Code. But some scholars suggest that the motivation had to do with standardizing punishments in the interest of fairness, and if this was in fact the goal, then it seems reasonable to assume that the prescribed punishments were what they believed justice required.

Relatedly, others (e.g., Ross 1930) argue for the **intrinsic goodness** of punishment. Something that is intrinsically good is something that is good in and of itself; it does not have to bring about other goods in order to be good. For example, many think that happiness is intrinsically good. The core idea characterizing this view is that punishing wrongdoers is good in and of itself. To put it another way, a world in which wrongdoers are punished is better than a world in which they are not, even if nothing else in that world is different. This view means that leaving a wrongdoer unpunished is intrinsically bad, or at least non-ideal. To do so leaves the "scales of justice" unbalanced. In other words, for a society to be perfectly just, it is *obligated* to punish wrongdoers.

This memorable passage from Immanuel Kant ([1797] 1991) captures the sentiment of **justice-based justifications**:

> Even if a civil society were to be dissolved by the consent of all its members (e.g., if a people inhabiting an island decided to separate and disperse throughout the world), the last murderer remaining in prison would have to be executed, so that each has done to him what his deeds deserve and blood guilt does not cling to the people for not having insisted upon this punishment; for otherwise the people can be regarded as collaborators in this public violation of justice. (333)

We can draw two lessons from this passage. First, because society has been dissolved, executing these last criminals serves no further purpose—it doesn't deter future crime, make victims or their families happier, or render society better off in any way. Yet, purportedly, the execution is still justified. This means that punishment can be justified solely by the wrongdoing and independently of its consequence. This is the uniting feature discussed above.

Second, notice that for Kant, justice *demands* that the punishments be carried out in response to the wrongdoing of the criminals. The perfectly just state isn't merely allowed to punish wrongdoers. It is *required* or *obligated* to punish them in order to be perfectly just. This is an exceptionally strong claim. Notice that the first two arguments we investigated concluded that punishment is justified. That means that it's permissible for the state to punish wrongdoers, but also that the state does nothing wrong if it declines to punish them. This argument goes further, concluding that punishment is *required* because it is necessary for a just society.

Here's how we might put the justice-based retributivist argument:

(P1) States ought to do what justice requires.

(P2) Justice requires that wrongdoers be punished.

(P3) States ought to punish wrongdoers. (From (P1) and (P2).)

(P4) If states ought to punish wrongdoers, then states are justified in punishing wrongdoers.

(C) Therefore, the state is justified in punishing wrongdoers.

(P3) follows from (P1) and (P2). This means that (P1), (P2), and (P4) are the premises we need to focus on. We haven't talked about (P1), but let's assume that promoting justice is one of the primary jobs of the state. If we spot the justice-based retributivist (P1), that means that (P2) and (P4) are the only premises we can deny. As we've seen above, the discussion about *lex taliones* and the intrinsic goodness of justice motivates (P2). Finally, (P4) is plausible. If I ought to tell the truth, then it seems like I'm certainly justified in telling the truth. If this is all right, then it appears that the justice-based retributivist argument is sound.

We'll now turn to worries about this argument.

Objection 1:

Does justice require punishment? Our first worry concerns (P2), the claim that justice requires that wrongdoers be punished. The Code of Hammurabi, for instance, asserts that this is what justice requires, but doesn't *argue* for it. Of course, a statement of the law doesn't have to have arguments. But many arguments do rest on intuitions. For instance, take Ross's argument for the intrinsic goodness of justice. He really does invite us to think about two worlds that are exactly the same, except that in one world, the good are happy and wrongdoers are unhappy (the just world), while in the other, happiness is distributed randomly (the unjust world). He thinks many people will have the intuition that the just world is better than the unjust world.

Here's the problem. First, many people do not have Code of Hammurabi intuitions. This is why they say things like "An eye for an eye leaves everyone blind." Second, the intuitions required to support a justice-based argument would have to be much stronger than the intuitions required to support a desert-based argument. It's not just that wrongdoers deserve punishment. It's that someone, presumably the state, is *required* to punish them. To put it another way, the state does something *wrong* if it decides not to punish someone and instead shows mercy.

> Do you have the intuition that justice requires retaliation? Can you think of an example to support your intuition?

Reply:

Some people think that if the state punishes *some* wrongdoers, the state must punish *all* wrongdoers. Basically, it would be unjust if only some wrongdoers were punished, so it's all or nothing (we'll revisit this type of claim in Chapter 16). Given that we definitely want to punish some wrongdoers (e.g., the Russian noblemen and unrepentant Nazis), we then need to punish all wrongdoers. (However, it's important to note that some people agree with the all-or-nothing claim, and then use that to show that we should punish no one—we'll get to this in Chapter 16 as well.)

Objection 2:

Here's a second worry. If justice demands that wrongdoers are punished, then, on the flip side, rightdoers ought to be rewarded. Indeed, it is explicitly a part of both Ross's and Kant's views on justice that, in a perfectly just world, rightdoers need to be rewarded. Incidentally, not many people think about whether the state ought to reward good people. Even fewer think that the answer to this question is yes. And even fewer think that the state is *required* to reward good people in order to be just.

David Boonin (2008) gives an example to drive this point home. Suppose that Mary is an exceptionally virtuous person. She lives a modest life, donates to charity, and spends her time volunteering in the community. Now suppose that the state decides to reward her with a monthly stipend of $1,000 that she must spend on herself. Mary attempts to decline the reward and redirect it to others. Instead, the state attempts to force it on her, saying that she needs to be rewarded so that the state can be perfectly just. Something has clearly gone wrong here. Maybe the state interferes with Mary's autonomy, and her autonomy overrides the goodness of having a just state. But then one might worry that by imprisoning wrongdoers, the state also overrides their autonomy, and that overrides the goodness of having a just state. Instead, maybe justice doesn't require rewarding rightdoers and punishing wrongdoers. If you're not inclined to think that justice requires the state to reward rightdoers, then you probably shouldn't think it requires the state to punish wrongdoers.

> Do you think the state should reward right-doers? Do you think that the state is *unjust* if it doesn't reward rightdoers?

Reply:

Perhaps Boonin's argument shows that reward and punishment are asymmetric. It's not obligatory to reward people simply for doing the right thing. For instance, it'd be weird to ask your parents to reward you for not punching your sibling.

Reply to the reply:

While justice doesn't require rewarding people for being minimally decent, perhaps it does require rewarding them when they go above and beyond their duty. Returning to the original argument, doesn't it just seem better when good things happen to good people? We already sort of have a carrot-and-stick approach to some things: carbon taxes are imposed on companies that pollute more than their fair share, and people get tax breaks for donating to charity.

Reply to the reply to the reply:

If the carrot-and-stick approach is right, that shows that we should have punishment! We just need to add a few more carrots as well.

Objection 3:

Finally, one might worry about (P4), the claim that if the state ought to punish wrongdoers, then it is justified in doing so. In many cases, what we "ought" to do is not absolute—it is *prima facie*, and it can be overridden by other factors. Earlier, we talked about how something that is *prima facie* wrong might not be all-things-considered wrong. Something similar applies to **prima facie oughts**.

A *prima facie* ought is something that we normally should do. But sometimes there are competing factors that override it so that it is not what we all-things-considered ought to do. Consider, for instance, the claim that one ought to be honest. If there is a competing factor that outweighs it—for instance, that your friend is definitely going to be murdered if you're honest about her whereabouts—then though it's true in general that you ought to be honest, you should lie in that situation. Being honest in that situation is not what you all-things-considered ought to do. To make things more precise, let's specify 'ought' in the argument as follows:

(P1)   States (*prima facie*) ought to do what justice requires.

(P2)   Justice requires that wrongdoers be punished.

(P3)   States (*prima facie*) ought to punish wrongdoers. (From (P1) and (P2).)

(P4)   If states (*prima facie*) ought to punish wrongdoers, then states are justified in punishing wrongdoers.

(C)   Therefore, the state is justified in punishing wrongdoers.

Now that it's clear the 'ought' in (P4) is only a *prima facie* ought, (P4) seems questionable. After all, there could be an overriding factor that makes the case that the state should not punish wrongdoers, and thus, that the state would not be justified in punishing wrongdoers. To make (P4) more plausible, we would have to modify it as such:

(P4)   If states (*prima facie*) ought to punish wrongdoers, then states are justified in punishing wrongdoers (assuming there are no overriding factors).

Then the question is whether there are overriding factors. We can certainly imagine some. Take, for instance, Jean Valjean in *Les Misérables* (Hugo 1862). Suppose that it was in fact wrong for him to steal bread to feed his sister's starving children and that justice requires he be imprisoned (though perhaps not for nineteen years of hard labor). If Valjean goes to prison, even for a short sentence, his sister's children will likely starve (and it seems that they do—or at least, are not around for the rest of the novel). The badness of children starving outweighs the goodness of justly punishing him. So though the state *prima facie* ought to punish Valjean, it's not the case that the state ought to punish him all things considered.

> Can you think of factors that might outweigh the goodness of punishment?

Reply:

Not all cases are like Jean Valjean's. It's often good to imprison wrongdoers. As long as there aren't overriding factors, punishment is justified.

Reply to the reply:

It may turn out that there are far more cases like Jean Valjean's than we initially realize. (And Chapter 16 will explore some of these cases.) But more importantly, the fact that there *could* be cases like this suggests that we would need to look at the consequences of punishments before we can decide whether they are just or not. And that means that justice-based considerations are not by themselves enough to justify punishment. (We'll revisit this point in the discussion of hybrid theories in Chapter 15.)

5. Conclusion

In this chapter, we defined punishment and examined the problem of punishment. We then investigated retributivist arguments for why punishment is justified, as well as some worries associated with those arguments. In the next chapter, we'll turn to consequentialist justifications and then consider what we should think about punishment if none of these justifications are successful solutions to the problem of punishment.

Further Reading

For more on the problem of punishment, see Boonin (2008), which also contains an overview of retributivist theories and objections to them. For more on desert-based retributivism, see Moore (1993), Mundle (1954), Kleinig (1973), and Dolinko (1991). For more on forfeiture-based retributivism, see Goldman (1979), Haksar (1986), and Morris (1991). For more on justice-based retributivism, see Kant ([1797] 1991).

Chapter 15
Justifying Punishment, Part 2

1. Introduction

In the previous chapter, we discussed the **problem of punishment** and how it challenges the defender of punishment to justify punishment. We then looked closely at some **retributivist justifications** of punishment and objections to them. We're now ready to turn to the other main genre of justifications, **consequentialist justifications**. These justifications are *future-looking*, because they look to the consequences that lie ahead for justification. First, we will look at some of these justifications and the objections associated with them. Then, we'll discuss what the implications for punishment are if it turns out to be unjustified.

2. Consequentialist Justifications

Consequentialist justifications are united by one central claim: *punishment is justified because it has good consequences*. Unlike retributivist justifications from the previous chapter, which are backward-looking, consequentialist justifications are *forward-looking*. So, roughly, the consequentialist answer to the problem of punishment—which asks what justifies harming wrongdoers—is that the consequences of punishing wrongdoers are better than the consequences of not doing so.

> Before reading ahead, do you prefer the forward-looking or the backward-looking solution to the problem of punishment? Or, do you think punishment might be justified by both forward-looking and backward-looking considerations?

In this section, we'll investigate what the purported consequences of punishment are. But before we do, we need to take a brief detour to look closely at what consequentialism says.

2.1. Consequentialism

You will recall from earlier chapters that **consequentialism** says that whether an act is right depends on the consequences of that action. The most well-known consequentialist theory is **utilitarianism**, which identifies the good with happiness and which you already should be familiar with from Chapter 5. Consequentialists debate about whether happiness is the only good, whether there are multiple types of happiness, and whether there are goods other than happiness. In the context of consequentialist justifications for punishment, these debates don't matter. We'll use common sense to determine what counts as a good consequence.

> Mill has a famous quote: "It is better to be Socrates dissatisfied than a pig satisfied."
>
> What pleasures does the pig experience? Are they the same types of pleasures that Socrates could have? What does Mill's quote tell us about the varieties of pleasures and goods? Do you agree with Mill?

What might matter is the distinction between **act consequentialism** and **rule consequentialism**. Remember from Chapter 13 that, according to act consequentialism, the right action is one that produces better consequences than its alternatives, while according to rule consequentialism, the right action is the one that accords with the rules that would produce the best consequences.

One final thing before we turn to the consequences of punishment. We're not going to assume that consequentialism is true (or that it is false): our discussions of ethical theories in earlier chapters (especially Chapter 5) have shown that that's a complicated question. But we are going to presuppose that consequences are at least somewhat relevant to whether the state is justified in punishing people. Each of the following consequentialist arguments will feature the following premise:

(P1) If enacting a practice produces better consequences than not
enacting it, the state is justified in enacting that practice.

Because we're not taking a stance on whether consequentialism is true or false, none of the worries will respond to these premises by saying "in general, the consequences don't justify a practice" (i.e., "the ends don't justify the means"). However, whether the particular consequences in question—such as incapacitation or deterrence—justify punishment will be an open question to which we'll consider objections. On that note, we're now ready to turn to the (potential) good consequences of punishment.

2.2. Incapacitation

To **incapacitate** someone through punishment is to *punish them in a way that prevents them from committing future wrongs*. For instance, if John steals from Robin, then is convicted and imprisoned, the imprisonment prevents John from stealing again from Robin or anyone else. Of course, imprisonment isn't the only way to incapacitate someone. If John is a pickpocket, cutting his hands off would also incapacitate him, as would executing him.

Importantly, incapacitation is **future-directed**, which means that it looks toward future consequences. Keeping this in mind, let's consider how such a consequentialist argument might go:

(P1) If the effects of incapacitating wrongdoers through punishment produce better consequences than not punishing them, then the state is justified in punishing wrongdoers.

(P2) The effects of incapacitating wrongdoers through punishment produce better consequences than not punishing them.

(C)   Therefore, the state is justified in punishing wrongdoers.

(P1) implements consequentialist reasoning. (P2) is a claim about the consequences of incapacitation. Let's consider the ways one might respond to this argument.

Objection 1:

In *The Minority Report* (a novella by Philip K. Dick upon which the movie *Minority Report* is based), three mutants have the ability to predict future crimes. In this society, the police use their predictions to round up the would-be criminals *before* their crimes are committed. Overall, there's less crime and society is happier. But there seems to be a crucial problem: none of the people who are detained have actually committed a crime!

Suppose it's true that incapacitating wrongdoers produces better consequences than not incapacitating them because future crimes are prevented. Well, the same is true if we incapacitate would-be future wrongdoers who have not yet done anything wrong. The positive consequences for society are similar in both cases. The incapacitated person is unhappy regardless of whether they committed the crime. Perhaps those who had not committed their crime would be more unhappy than those who had committed their crimes, since they'd think their punishment was unjust. But this difference in unhappiness would not outweigh the larger social gain. Thus, (P1) seems to support punishing innocent, would-be wrongdoers.

Something similar can be said for over-punishing. For instance, suppose that imprisoning John for a year for stealing from Robin is a "fair" sentence. Also suppose that it's justified because the benefits of incapacitating John for a year outweigh the costs of imprisoning him (including the costs associated with John's unhappiness). If that's right, then punishing John for two years would also be justified, as would imprisoning him for three years, and so on. Strategies more gruesome than imprisonment might also be justified. Perhaps cutting off a serial thief's hands would be justified by the benefit to those from whom the thief would have stolen. (P1) also justifies over-punishing, in addition to punishing the innocent.

Reply 1:

One might respond by embracing punishing the innocent and over-punishing. Maybe these are the right things to do—look at the good consequences they produce!

> Do you think it's okay to punish people before they commit crimes, or over-punish people, if it leads to good consequences?

Reply 2:

One can also respond by pointing out that the worry hasn't actually shown that (P1) is false. Rather, it's only shown that it has other implications. The problem of punishment demands a justification for why it is permissible to harm wrongdoers. If (P1) (and (P2)) is true, then this argument provides that justification. Perhaps the argument has weird implications, but it still provides a justification for punishment.

Reply to the reply:

Maybe the worries about punishing the innocent and over-punishing do not directly show that (P1) is false. However, they still seem to indicate that something is wrong with the underlying rationale. Presumably, a good answer to the problem of punishment requires more than a mere justification of harming wrongdoers; it also should explain why the state would not be justified in also harming the innocent. In other words, an adequate solution needs a justification that divides cleanly between wrongdoers and rightdoers.

Here's an analogy. Suppose that someone has cancer. A treatment plan needs to do more than just kill the cancer cells. It must also not kill (too many) non-cancerous cells. This is the problem with treatments like chemotherapy and radiation: while they are effective at killing cancer cells, they often also kill too many healthy cells. That can lead to side effects like hair loss and sometimes even death. Ideally, a treatment would kill all and only the cancer cells. Likewise, even if (P1) turns out to be true, if it justifies harming too many rightdoers along with the wrongdoers, then it's not an adequate solution to the problem of punishment.

Reply to the reply to the reply:

Suppose that the reply to the reply is correct. Punishment may still be justified all things considered if the rationale behind (P1) doesn't affect too many rightdoers. Perhaps if the harm to rightdoers is minimal (closer to hair loss than death), the rationale still works.

Also, it still may be that the argument provides a solution—if combined with some additional constraint about only punishing wrongdoers, perhaps because they deserve to be harmed. (Keeping with our cancer analogy, you might think of the constraint as a sort of "shield" that protects non-cancerous cells from chemotherapy or radiation, like what you would wear over your chest if you had to get an X-ray for a broken arm.) This type of solution is called a **hybrid solution** because it requires combining elements of multiple solutions. We'll talk more about these in Section 3 of this chapter.

Objection 2:

(P2) claims that the practice of incapacitating wrongdoers through punishment produces better consequences than not punishing them. But this doesn't always seem to be true, for at least three reasons.

First, many wrongdoers do not commit future crimes. For example, young people who commit crimes are actually pretty likely to "grow out" of their criminal behavior. If that's right, then we probably shouldn't bother imprisoning most young people. In addition, it's clear that some wrongdoers are no more likely to repeat their wrongdoing than the average person in society. There are also crimes that people are unlikely to recommit. For instance, someone who negligently kills their child is unlikely to do that again.

Second, even if imprisoning a wrongdoer does lead to the goods of incapacitation, the costs may outweigh those goods. For instance, suppose someone who is convicted of a non-violent drug offense has been using their profits to support their children. The negative effects of imprisonment are likely to outweigh any positive effects gained from incapacitation.

> Can you think of other cases in which the benefits of incapacitation are either non-existent or outweighed by other factors?

Finally, in some cases, imprisonment may make the wrongdoer even more likely to commit future wrongs once released. This is especially likely in countries such as the United States where there are high recidivism rates, in part because imprisonment and other social structures do not aim to reintegrate people into society.

Reply 1:

The consequentialist can simply admit that in cases where the consequences of punishing are not better than those of not punishing, punishment is not justified.

Reply to the reply:

Taking this route means that incapacitation does not adequately solve the problem of punishment if there are too many cases where it is better to not punish than punish. Recall that a solution needs to explain why punishing the guilty (or at least most of the guilty) is justified. If the consequentialist admits that sometimes, punishing the guilty is not justified, that isn't a complete solution.

Reply 2:

Even if there are some isolated cases in which incapacitation does not lead to better consequences than letting the wrongdoer go free, adopting a *policy* of punishment in order to incapacitate is better than not adopting that policy. This is particularly plausible if most wrongdoers would continue committing wrongs if they were not incapacitated.

Also, some consequentialists can explain why we should think about the overall policy rather than individual cases. Recall the distinction between **act consequentialism** and **rule consequentialism**. Act consequentialism focuses on the consequences of individual acts, while rule consequentialism focuses on the consequences of implementing a rule—in this case, a policy on incapacitating wrongdoers. Also recall that it's simpler to follow a rule rather than evaluate every individual action, and this provides a way to respond to unusual cases.

Those motivations apply to incapacitation. It's much simpler for the state to adopt a policy of incapacitation than to research the possible consequences in every single case. Furthermore, even if there are a few cases in which the consequences of incapacitating wrongdoers produce worse consequences than letting them go free, incapacitating them still would be justified in virtue of the policy being justified. Thus, rule consequentialism explains how a policy of incapacitation would be justified even if (P2) were not true in every single case. So it can provide a full solution to the problem of punishment.

Reply to the reply:

Of course, for a policy to make sense, (P2) would have to be true in most instances of wrongdoing. So we would still need to look at exactly how often incapacitation produced better consequences than letting wrongdoers go free. We'd also have to figure out how much net value is associated with the incapacitation policy as compared to alternative policies. This is an **empirical** question—a question that requires data and studies, not just philosophical theorizing. We'll return to this issue later in Chapter 16.

2.3. Deterrence

Deterrence occurs when *someone is discouraged from performing some action.* For example, during the Cold War, the fact that Russia had nuclear weapons discouraged the United States from using its nuclear weapons for fear of global destruction, and vice versa. The mutual ability to destroy the world via nuclear war deterred both countries from using those weapons.

In the context of consequentialist justifications for punishment, *punishing wrongdoers deters others from committing those wrongs.* We can see this rationale clearly in one popular justification for the death

> Think back to when you were a child. Was there ever something that you wanted to do that your parents did not want you to do? Did they do anything to deter you from doing that thing?

penalty: executing murderers deters others from murdering. Suppose that the deterrent effect for every murderer who is executed is the prevention of two murders. Assuming that each person's death causes the same amount of disvalue on average, it is twice as bad to not execute (two deaths from murders that weren't prevented) than to execute (one death from execution). We can imagine similar deterrent effects that occur with lesser crimes and lesser punishments. For instance, the possibility of a speeding ticket and fine deters people from speeding.

Putting all of this together:

(P1) If the deterrent effect of punishing wrongdoers produces better consequences than not punishing them, then the state is justified in punishing wrongdoers.

(P2) The deterrent effect of punishing wrongdoers produces better consequences than not punishing them.

(C)   Therefore, the state is justified in punishing wrongdoers.

Like the incapacitation argument, (P1) implements consequentialist reasoning. (P2) is a claim about the deterrent effects of punishment. Let's consider the ways one might respond to this argument.

Objection 1:

Charles Dickens's *Oliver Twist* (1838) tells the story of an orphan who falls in with a gang of pickpockets. Because pickpocketing is so prevalent, the penalty for being caught is quite severe—a noose awaits all who are caught, even children. As it turns out, this was an actual punishment in nineteenth-century Britain, though most (but not all!) children who were sentenced to death had their sentences commuted or lessened to transportation—that is, they were shipped to Australia for hard labor. Perhaps it strikes you as overly harsh, and even barbaric, to hang or transport a child for pickpocketing. Could deterrent benefits really justify over-punishing a child for pickpocketing? Well, if the deterrent benefits were great enough to outweigh the child's suffering, then they would—at least if the rationale behind (P1) is correct. (As it turns out, this particular punishment did not effectively deter crime—but that issue pushes us into an objection to (P2), which we'll get to in the second objection.)

Also notice that if it deterred a lot of bad consequences, punishing an innocent person who had been framed so that people believed they were guilty would have that same deterrent effect. What this shows is that if (P1) is true, then deterrence also justifies over-punishing and punishing innocent people.

Recall the replies to Objection 1 to the incapacitation argument. How would a similar reply go here? Reply to the reply? And reply to the reply to the reply?

Objection 2:

Let's now turn to (P2), the claim that the deterrent effect of punishing wrongdoers produces better consequences than not punishing them. The deterrent effect of any particular punishment depends on a variety of factors, such as the nature of the wrongdoing, the likelihood of being caught, and other aspects of society. Sometimes, punishments are fairly effective deterrents. For instance, in the infamous Ford Pinto case, Ford realized that the Pinto had a defect that caused it to burst into flames even in minor accidents. But because they projected the costs of a recall to be greater than the costs of settling lawsuits, they opted not to recall. After they were sued, the court added extra punitive damages, which radically shifted the **cost-benefit analysis** so that it was more profitable to recall defective cars. Had these extra punitive damages been established while Ford was deciding what to do, it is likely that they would have been deterred and recalled the cars.

But other times, punishments have little to no deterrent effect. Take our earlier example from *Oliver Twist*. The threat of hanging did not actually deter any of the children from pickpocketing because that was their only source of income and food. In general, punishments will not deter people from committing crimes if those crimes are their best option. For instance, if the risk of getting caught and hanged is low enough, it might be rational for a child to pickpocket rather than face almost certain starvation (see Wright 2010). People also won't be deterred if they are not acting rationally. For instance, people who commit crimes of passion do not first perform a cost-benefit analysis. In fact, many economists argue that there is little to no deterrent effect from most of our punishments for most crimes (see, e.g., Anderson 2002).

There is another reason why deterrence isn't very effective. The type of state that attempts to deter via harsh punishments is also likely to be structured so that deterrence isn't effective. For instance, pickpockets commonly pickpocketed at the public executions of other pickpockets. The United States also provides another example of this, since it allows states to decide for themselves whether to have a death penalty. States that have abolished the death penalty have much lower homicide rates than states that retain it (see, e.g., Bowers and Pierce 1980).

Putting this all together, the worry is that *many punishments (especially the death penalty) do not actually deter people from committing crimes.* If that's right, then (P2) is false and the argument does not show that punishing wrongdoers is justified.

Reply:

One way to respond on behalf of (P2) is to argue that the facts suggest that punishments such as the death penalty actually do have a deterrent effect. Indeed, some researchers make precisely this argument (see, e.g., Becker 1968; Nagin 1998).

When we talked about the incapacitation argument, we noted that one response to the over-punishment objection appeals to rule consequentialism. In other words, since over-punishing someone would only lead to good consequences in a few isolated cases, a rule in favor of over-punishing would lead to bad consequences, so we shouldn't over-punish.

Reply to the reply:

However, this response may not work to save the deterrence argument because there's good evidence that punishment doesn't deter wrongdoing in a majority of cases. Some studies suggest that as many as 76–89 percent of criminals self-report that they are not likely to be deterred by the imprisonment of others (either because they perceive little to no risk of being caught or are completely ignorant of the punishment). If that's right, then the rule consequentialist response would not justify deterrent-based consequentialist arguments.

Reply to the reply to the reply:

The fact that criminals self-report that they are not likely to be deterred by the imprisonment of others doesn't show that deterrence doesn't work. Obviously criminals are self-selected to be people who are not deterred by punishment. What's important is how many non-criminals would have been criminals if there was no punishment.

Ultimately, Objection 2 is an empirical claim that requires studies, and it's not enough for these studies to look only at criminals. Actually, it's not enough for the studies to look at criminals and non-criminals who would be criminals if there was no punishment. We would also need to look carefully at criminals who would not have committed wrongs if there was no punishment. (And while it may initially seem implausible that these cases exist, it's important to keep in mind that the kind of society that doesn't punish may turn out to be the kind of society that has fewer instances of wrongdoing.) In summary, to know whether (P2) is true, we need to do careful empirical studies.

2.4. Catharsis

Catharsis is *the release or purging of negative emotions*—for example, hitting a punching bag after a stressful day. Often catharsis is offered as a consequentialist-type justification for punishment. According to cathartic theories, punishing wrongdoers allows victims of wrongdoing to release emotions such as anger that stem from being wronged.

Note also that, in addition to the direct victims, broader society is often an indirect victim of wrongdoing. For instance, if John steals from Robin, his actions wrong Robin. But John's actions also affect the larger community because it feels less secure or outraged on behalf of Robin. So, the cathartic benefits of punishing

John are not limited to Robin and might extend to the whole community. Thus, the consequences associated with catharsis might be quite significant. Though the wrongdoer suffers negative consequences associated with punishment, those are outweighed by the positive consequences of the cathartic release of negative emotions by the community.

This sets up our last consequentialist argument:

(P1)   If the cathartic effect from punishing wrongdoers produces better consequences than not punishing them, then the state is justified in punishing wrongdoers.

(P2)   The cathartic effect from punishing wrongdoers produces better consequences than not punishing them.

(C)   Therefore, the state is justified in punishing wrongdoers.

> Which premise implements consequentialist reasoning? Which one requires *empirical* support, such as, studies or facts about the world?

Objection 1:

People who are wronged or witness someone else being wronged often have strong emotional reactions to the wrongdoing. These usually include a desire to see the wrongdoer punished, and it's not uncommon for people to believe that seeing the wrongdoer punished will make them feel better or have a sense of resolution. Notice that if enough people mistakenly believe that someone is guilty, punishing the innocent person would still generate the cathartic effects. For instance, suppose that John is actually perfectly justified in stealing from Robin (perhaps Robin is a thief and John wants to take Robin's money and give it to charity). In this scenario, John is perfectly innocent, but everyone mistakenly believes that he has wronged Robin. Punishing him even though he's innocent would create the same cathartic effects that punishing if he were a wrongdoer would. Thus, the consequentialist rationale behind (P1) would again justify punishing the innocent.

It's also not uncommon for people to want wrongdoers to *suffer* more than they would under the standard punishment. For example, in *A Storm of Swords* (Martin 2000), Daenerys liberates the slaves in the cities of Slaver's Bay. When the slave masters revolt, it's not enough for them to be killed. She has them publicly crucified in symbolic positions even though her advisors tell her that she's being extra with the punishment. Part of her motivation is deterrence, but a large part of it is cathartic—she wants people to see that the wrongs of slavery have been rectified so that they can move on. If over-punishing (and even torturing) can generate enough cathartic

> You know the drill! How might the defender of catharsis-based consequentialist argument reply to this worry? How might someone reply to the reply?

benefit to outweigh the pain of the punished, then the rationale behind (P1) also supports over-punishing.

Objection 2:

In some countries, like Iran, the families of murder victims get to determine the wrongdoer's punishment. In fact, they can even carry out the punishment if they desire. For fans of catharsis, this seems like the ultimate dream scenario. Victims get the satisfaction not only of knowing the wrongdoer is punished but also of carrying out the sentence. However, there are also powerful stories of families who end up sparing those who murdered their family members. One particularly moving story occurred in 2014, when a mother spared the murderer of her eighteen-year-old son at the last minute and even removed the noose from the man's neck with her own hands (see Dehgan 2014). This example shows that sometimes, greater cathartic benefit occurs through forgiveness rather than punishment.

If this is right, then (P2), the claim that the cathartic effect from punishing wrongdoers produces better consequences than not punishing them, is false. As it turns out, studies on restorative justice suggest that on average, *there is greater cathartic effect from successful reconciliation than from punishment*. In fact, many people who thought they would feel better once their loved one's murderer was executed, report that their pain did not go away after the execution. This means that if we take seriously the healing of victims and the community in the wake of serious wrongdoings, sometimes letting the guilty go free should be part of the equation. Of course, this may not be true in every case, and work will have to be done to figure out exactly when letting the guilty go free will create better cathartic effects (see Armour and Umbreit 2012, for one such study on homicide survivors). But if these cases are prevalent enough, they'll show that (P2) is false and that the catharsis-based rationale does not justify punishment.

> You've seen the replies to Objection 2 of the incapacitation and deterrence arguments. Do those replies apply in the catharsis case?

As we discussed various positive consequences that might justify punishment, you may have noticed a pattern. Worry 1 of all three arguments involves the potential for over-punishing and punishing the innocent. Worry 2 concerns letting the guilty go free. Both of these are problematic since a solution to the problem of punishment is supposed to explain why the state is justified in punishing the guilty and not in punishing the innocent.

What this pattern demonstrates is that *because they are forward-looking, consequentialist justifications don't always line up with whether a person is innocent or guilty*—that, after all, is in the past. (And the retributive justifications did not run into this problem because the basis of the punishment is the wrongdoing itself, rather than the consequences.) Perhaps this is not insurmountable. We've seen possible responses on behalf of these consequentialist justifications. But forward-looking theories run into serious problems when attempting to solve the problem of punishment.

3. Theoretical Abolition

Imagine that your friend Liz wants you to go out to a party with her Friday night. You've had a long week and have no desire to go out, but you're willing to consider it if Liz can offer you a good reason for you to go. Crucially, Liz bears the **burden** of demonstrating that there is a good reason for you to go. The **presumption**, or default position, is that you'll stay in, so if Liz doesn't satisfy this burden, you won't go. Liz seizes this opportunity and throws all sorts of reasons at you: it will be fun, there will be so many people, there will be free food, you can meet new potential best friends. You successfully counter all of these reasons: it's more fun to relax at home with your cat, you're an introvert, you're not hungry, you already have too many friends. Finally, Liz runs out of reasons. Without a reason to go out, you stay home.

According to **theoretical abolitionists**, the problem of punishment operates in a similar way. Proponents of punishment are like Liz, and the burden of demonstrating why punishment is permissible is like the burden Liz has of convincing you to go out to the party. If the burden isn't met, the presumption is that punishment is impermissible, just as the presumption in the party case is that you'll stay in. Theoretical abolitionists, like you in the party situation, don't believe that the burden has been met. Thus, the presumption holds, and punishment is impermissible (and you're staying home instead of going to the party with Liz).

> Recall: **Prima facie wrongs** are actions that are self-evidently wrong, though there may be special factors that outweigh the wrongness and make performing those actions permissible all things considered.
>
> Punishment involves harming someone, which is *prima facie* wrong. Does the proponent of punishment have the burden of demonstrating that punishment is permissible? Or does the critic of punishment have the burden of demonstrating that punishment is impermissible?

Put in this way, we can now start to formulate the argument for theoretical abolition:

(P1) There is a presumption that punishment is not justified.

(P2) If there is a presumption that punishment is not justified, then there must be a successful theory of punishment (i.e., one that demonstrates how punishment could be justified) or punishment is not justified.

(P3) There is no successful theory of punishment.

(C)   Punishment is not justified.

(P1), the claim that there is a presumption that punishment is not justified, is just a restatement of the problem of punishment. So, the two crucial premises in question are (P2) and (P3).

Let's start by considering (P3). (P3) requires theoretical abolitionists to play defense. Just as you defended against all of Liz's reasons to go out, theoretical abolitionists must defend against all theories of justification. This requires the abolitionist to go through every possible justification and show that they are not successful in justifying punishment (see, e.g., Boonin 2008). In the previous chapter, we surveyed some of the most popular attempts to justify punishment, but we cannot talk about every potential justification. We're not going to attempt to go through every theory in this chapter either, so the defense of (P3) is incomplete. For example, we haven't discussed moral education theories that attempt to justify punishment by focusing on how it benefits the person being punished through moral education (see, e.g., Hampton 1984). However, our discussion of hybrid theories in the next section may help show why if the retributivist and consequentialist theories in the previous chapter do not justify punishment, it is unlikely that any similar theories will be successful. If that's right (and one was unconvinced by the retributivist and consequentialist theories), then (P3) is plausible.

(P2), the claim that if there is a presumption that punishment is not justified, then there must be a successful theory of punishment (that demonstrates how punishment could be justified) or punishment is not justified, may sound extremely plausible. However, there is a famous objection to it based on necessity. We'll turn to the **necessity objection** after our discussion of hybrid theories.

Objection 1:

So far, we've looked at retributivist and consequentialist justifications for punishment. Regardless of whether you ultimately find these justifications successful, both face significant challenges. Because consequentialist theories are essentially forward-looking, they sometimes run into problems that arise from not looking backward at the wrongdoing. For instance, sometimes consequentialist theories justify punishing the innocent or over-punishing, and sometimes they justify not punishing wrongdoers. The connection between wrongdoing and punishment isn't sufficiently tight.

Unlike consequentialist theories, retributivist theories do a fairly good job connecting wrongdoing and punishment because they're backward-looking. However, retributivist theories also face challenges because they tend not to be forward-looking. So sometimes—such as the case of the justice-based justification—the theory requires punishment even though the punishment has bad consequences for everyone. Other versions have trouble closing the gap between someone's deserving punishment and the state's being required to punish them. In each of these cases, it appears that factoring in potential consequences might help explain why some people don't need to be punished or why only the state should punish.

In light of the strengths and weaknesses of consequentialist and retributive theories, one might be tempted to create a *hybrid* theory that combines aspects of both. Here's a promising proposal for when someone should be punished:

> **Hybrid theory of punishment 1:** Punishing X is justified if and only if X deserves to be punished AND punishing X would result in good consequences.

This captures the desert-based retributivist intuition that X deserves to be punished. But it also uses consequentialist reasoning to rule out cases in which punishing X serves no purpose or has a negative overall effect.

> Earlier we considered the case of Jean Valjean, who stole bread to feed his sister's children. Under this proposal, should Jean Valjean be punished? Do you think that's the correct result?

Reply:

While hybrid proposals inherit the strengths of the two theories they combine, they also inherit the problems of both theories. For instance, those who are inclined toward retributivism want to say that wrongdoers *deserve* punishment, regardless of the consequences. The proposal has the result that there may be some cases in which murderers should not be punished. For instance, in the BBC series *Sherlock*, Sherlock Holmes calls Billy Kincaid—also known as the Camden Garrotter—the best man he knows. Kincaid donates vast sums of money to children's hospitals and has saved hundreds of lives through his charitable giving; however, he also occasionally murders people. If we accept the *hybrid theory of punishment 1*, then this casual murderer ought not to be punished because doing so would produce a net negative effect. But retributivists like Kant would balk at this result—surely the murders are sufficient for justifying punishment!

Reply to the reply:

Consider a second hybrid theory, replacing "and" with "or":

> **Hybrid theory of punishment 2:** Punishing X is justified if and only if X deserves to be punished OR punishing X would result in good consequences.

On this proposal, punishing Kincaid is justified because Kincaid deserves to be punished.

Reply to the reply to the reply:

But given this second hybrid proposal, the state is justified in punishing far more people, including people who are innocent (as long as punishing them has good consequences). In general, if there's a problem with one of the theories involved in a hybrid theory, combining it with another theory to create a hybrid isn't going to solve that problem. In fact, including that second theory often makes the problem worse, so the hybrid will be no better than the individual theories. And of course, if a theory is without a problem, there is no need for a hybrid in the first place. Thus, appealing to hybrids to object to (P3) is not likely to be a winning strategy.

Reply to the reply to the reply to the reply:

Perhaps what this discussion demonstrates is that the problem of punishment is framed in the wrong way. Rather than ask why the state is justified in punishing wrongdoers and not justified in punishing rightdoers, perhaps we should just ask whether the state is ever justified in punishing *some* wrongdoers, and then we should ensure that this justification does not justify punishing innocent people. And the answer to this question *could* be a hybrid answer: the state is justified in punishing the subset of wrongdoers who deserve punishment when punishment would benefit society. (For more on this point on reframing the problem of punishment, see Howe 2019.)

Objection 2:

Thomas Paine (1776) said that "government, even in its best state, is but a necessary evil; in its worst state, an intolerable one." This suggests that (P3) is true but rejects (P2). This **necessity objection** claims that *even if there is no solution to the problem of punishment, punishment is still justified out of necessity.* Presumably there will always be wrongdoers, and society needs a way to respond to them. The need to respond involves intentionally harming the wrongdoer. This necessity ultimately justifies punishment—not some theoretical solution.

Here's an analogy. Suppose that your friend is seriously injured and needs to get to a hospital immediately for lifesaving treatment. You don't have a cell phone and there's no one around. But there is a car parked on the street, and the keys are in the ignition. It's obviously wrong to steal the car, but you need to get your friend to the hospital. This justifies taking the car. Similarly, if the theoretical abolition argument is right, it's wrong (or at least *prima facie* wrong) to punish someone. But the need to keep society functioning might justify punishment, even though nothing else does.

Reply:

The necessity objection is compelling. However, *it only works if there are no other feasible alternatives to punishment.* (Similarly, you're not justified in stealing the car to take your friend to the hospital if an empty cab pulls up.) So, responding to the objection requires identifying feasible alternatives to punishment. As it turns out, there are such alternatives.

First, there isn't a need for punishment for the majority of crimes committed. For instance, people who commit drug offenses make up a substantial part of the prison population (see Maur and King 2007). If the goal is to have fewer people using drugs, rehabilitation combined with resources to remove the underlying causes of drug use offers a much better response than imprisonment.

Second, criminal law can focus on **restitution**—restoring what is lost to the wronged party. This works most straightforwardly in the case of theft or vandalism. Rather than sit in prison, the wrongdoer offers restitution to right the wrong (for development of a theory of pure restitution, see Boonin 2008; Barnett 1997, 1998). This obviously won't work in all cases. For instance, one can't offer restitution to someone who's been killed. But some form of restitution might be offered to the victim's family. Even if restitution is not possible, in many cases there are alternatives to punishment, such as restorative justice, aimed at bringing healing to the victims and allowing wrongdoers to own their actions and strive to do better. As we mentioned in the discussion on justice-based retributivism, though there has been some experimentation with restorative justice, those who engage in it report positive results (for more on restorative justice, see Strang 2002; Sullivan and Tifft 2001).

Reply to the reply:
Perhaps we should use rehabilitation and restitution where feasible. But there still might be a handful of serial wrongdoers who cannot reform. Punishment is still needed in these cases—and it would be justified.

Reply to the reply to the reply:
It's true that there may still be a handful of serial wrongdoers who cannot reform. Perhaps in these cases, the state is justified in resorting to imprisonment in order to incapacitate these wrongdoers. But if incapacitation is the sole motive for imprisonment, it's not clear that imprisonment in those cases counts as punishment since it is done to protect society rather than to inflict harm in response to wrongdoing.

4. Conclusion

In this chapter and the previous one, we've engaged with the problem of punishment, which asks what, if anything, justifies punishment. We considered the two main types of pro-punishment justifications—retributivist and consequentialist justifications. Finally, we investigated theoretical abolition, the position that holds that punishment is never justified. We're now ready to turn to **practical abolition**, the position that holds that even if punishment is justified in theory, it is not justified in practice.

Further Reading

For more on consequentialism in general, see Mill (1861) and Bentham (1789) (on act consequentialism) and Hooker (2000) (on rule consequentialism). For more on abolition, see Boonin (2008) and Zimmerman (2011).

Chapter 16
Injustice and Abolition

1. Introduction

We've investigated various possible solutions to the problem of punishment. We've also considered the possibility that none are successful and that punishment ought to be abolished. This chapter explores a very different type of response: even if there is a successful solution and punishment is justified *in theory*, punishment still is not justified *in practice* because of systemic injustices in the state. We'll call this **practical abolition**. The crucial idea is that the societal context in which punishment occurs can affect whether it is justified in its *actual, practiced form*.

We'll focus on the United States. But the arguments are applicable to other states as well, especially ones with a history of colonialism, slavery, or other forms of institutionalized oppression.

> Suppose that parents are justified in grounding their children when they are caught lying. While your parents ground you for lying, they never ground your sibling for it. Is *your* punishment nevertheless fair?

2. Context

All of the arguments for practical abolition have premises about the actual practice of punishment in the United States. So we'll first summarize the societal context in the United States. For more thorough and detailed accounts, see, for example, Michelle Alexander (2012), Angela Davis (2003), and Ruth Wilson Gilmore (2007, 2021).

Note: We've capitalized the 'b' in 'Black' when referring to people in a racial or cultural context because the term designates a shared history, identity, and community, rather than a color. We've also chosen not to capitalize the 'w' in white to reflect the fact that 'white' does not designate a shared history, identity, and community in the United States (contrast this with, e.g., German American or Italian American, which are capitalized). For more on this convention, see Associated Press (2020), but also know these conventions are controversial (Appiah 2020).

2.1. Laws

Sometimes, *injustice is written explicitly into the law*. For centuries, US law legalized slavery, enforced segregation, and otherwise persecuted and disenfranchised many people. In some sense, theories of punishment handle these unjust laws easily—punishment for violating them is not justified because the laws are unjust. But whether punishment is unjust in practice goes beyond whether the laws being enforced are explicitly unjust.

There also are unjust but **facially neutral laws**—ones that *appear* non-discriminatory because they do not explicitly single out particular individuals or groups. Despite appearances, facially neutral laws *are* sometimes discriminatory. For instance, the infamous crack-cocaine laws of the 1980s prescribed different sentencing ranges for those caught with crack and those caught with cocaine even though the two are pharmacologically the same drug. These laws were facially neutral: they did not explicitly single out particular individuals or groups. But Black and Hispanic people (who were mostly convicted for crack) received much longer sentences than white people (who were mostly convicted for cocaine) for using virtually identical drugs.

Finally, *the sheer number of laws creates the potential for discrimination.* There are literally tens of thousands of federal laws—not to mention state and local ones—ranging from the obvious (like the prohibition of murder) to the innocuous (like the prohibition of throwing out junk mail addressed to previous tenants). Given how many laws there are, everyone is likely guilty of some crime. The state cannot scrutinize everyone. But the state can target any individual and find *some* law they've broken. Even if all the laws are just, the fact that virtually anyone can be charged with a crime enables the discriminatory targeting of individuals or groups.

> Suppose the state wants to target individuals or groups who are peacefully protesting. It cannot simply arrest them—that would not look good. What would imposing a curfew on all protesters allow the state to do?

2.2. Policing

Police have lots of control over which laws they investigate and enforce. They are also protected from internal discipline by unions and legally protected from personal punishment and from being sued. These protections don't *guarantee* that abuses or discriminatory policing will occur, but they make such abuses more likely. For instance, the police could choose to over-police a neighborhood, going after the pettiest of offenses and harassing people over no wrongdoing whatsoever (see, e.g., *Floyd v. City of New York* for how the stop-and-frisk policy—which was ultimately ruled unconstitutional—enabled police to stop over three million Black and Hispanic people). They can also choose to under-police serious crimes, as police in the South often did when lynchings occurred (see, e.g., Equal Justice Initiative 2017).

In addition, some tools of policing result in discriminatory policing. For instance, predictive policing algorithms incorporate racial bias (see Johnson 2020). While the computer science behind these algorithms is new, the discrimination is not, and it can be seen in similar models such as the "point system" used by police departments around the country to identify people as gang members or associates. For instance, the Boston Police Department's system assigns points to people for innocent things like wearing hats of a particular color, being victimized by a gang, and being in a photograph with someone else who's scored high on the point system (see, e.g., Boston Police Department 2017 and Dooling 2019 on the predictable racial disparities generated by the system). Lastly, the use of new facial recognition technology is controversial in its own right (see Buolamwini and Gebru 2018). It is far less accurate at identifying people of color than it is at identifying white people. Even more problematically, the inaccuracy of facial recognition technology produces false positives and has already led to wrongful arrests (see Allyn 2020).

Finally, police are people. As such *they are subject to the same biases and vices as everyone else*. However, police occupy positions of authority and, as mentioned above, are institutionally protected in ways ordinary citizens are not, which makes their biases and vices especially problematic.

In summary, the context of policing includes lots of freedom, institutional protection, tools known to be discriminatory, and human biases and prejudices. These lead to abuse and unjust punishment.

2.3. Trials

Trials determine whether someone is a candidate for punishment. An unjust trial normally leads to unjust punishment. Courts are supposed to be the paradigms of fairness, but in reality, they're not.

> **First,** like police, prosecutors have lots of freedom with respect to pursuing cases and charges. This, coupled with over-legislation, means that *prosecutors can target individuals or groups*, should they choose (see Crummett 2020). It also means that prosecutors can decline pursuing cases, as they historically have when it comes to hate crimes (see, e.g., Equal Justice Initiative 2017).
>
> **Second,** because there are so many cases and such limited legal resources, people charged with crimes are pressured into *plea deals*, in which they are pressured to plead guilty in exchange for something, like a lesser sentence, so the case doesn't have to go to trial. This encourages prosecutors to overcharge defendants and threaten to seek maximum sentences should the case go to trial. On the defense side, defendants have the right to a lawyer if they can't afford one. The *public defenders* who defend them are assigned hundreds of cases and cannot provide all their clients with *zealous defenses*. (In a zealous defense, a lawyer does everything they possibly can to make sure their client wins the case.) This, too, pushes defendants to accept plea deals. Unsurprisingly, it also means that the poor (who are disproportionately people of color) receive a less zealous defense than the rich.

Third, those who go to trial have the right to a trial by a jury of their peers. But, the "peerhood" of juries is questionable. For example, it wasn't until *Norris v. Alabama* (1935) that the Supreme Court ruled that Black people could not be systematically excluded from jury service, and women couldn't serve on juries in all fifty states until 1973. The Court took until *Batson* (1986) to rule that jurors cannot be eliminated on the basis of race with peremptory challenges (challenges that both prosecutors and defendants can use during jury selection to dismiss jurors without having to offer a reason). As you can imagine, racial discrimination in jury selection is still a big problem, given how difficult it is to prove a prosecutor's internal motivations for striking a juror.

Finally, a jury's job is not merely to determine *facts* of the case, but to determine whether punishment for the crime in question is *just*. Historically, **jury nullification**—the ability of juries to refuse to convict even if evidence demonstrates that the law was broken—played an important role in checking unjust laws (especially laws regarding seditious libel and assisting runaway slaves). Today, people who are aware of nullification are systematically excluded from juries, as are people who oppose the death penalty. This exclusion skews the jury pool toward a subset of peers who are not inclined to be moved by their convictions about right and wrong. For more on jury nullification, see *US v. Dougherty*, Paul Butler (1995), and Michael Huemer (2013, 2018).

2.4. Sentencing

Ideally, *sentences*—the punishment given as a result of a trial—are perfectly proportional to the wrongdoing. But historically, sentences have varied widely. Sentencing guidelines were introduced to keep things fair. The flip side of these guidelines, as we saw earlier in the crack/cocaine sentences, is that they can normalize unfair sentencing.

Even worse, *bias* can creep into sentencing. Even with sentencing guidelines, there is variation within the sentencing range, and studies suggest sentences vary along racial lines (e.g., ACLU 2014, a report to the Inter-American Commission on Human Rights on racial disparities in sentencing, provides a comprehensive data summary). The most extreme penalty, the death penalty, is no longer mandatory. But the federal courts and states that implement it allow juries to decide whether to institute it. Unsurprisingly, the history of death penalty implementation reveals extreme racial disparities; the Death Penalty Information Center (deathpenaltyinfo.org) and the Equal Justice Initiative (eji.org) provide current statistics on racial disparities in the application of the death penalty.

Finally, psychological studies suggest that implicit bias may play a role in sentencing (see King and Johnson 2016; Bennett 2017; Richardson 2017). Outside the legal domain, evidence suggests that even when race doesn't play a role in identifying whether a rule has been broken, *race plays a role in whether harsher or lighter penalties are assigned* (see Hall and Livingston 2012 for implicit bias in American football penalties; on gender and racial disparities in school discipline see, e.g., Skiba, Michael, Nardo, Peterson 2000).

2.5. Historical Context

So far, we've talked about how injustice creeps in at the level of laws, policing, trials, and sentencing. Importantly, all of these things fall into a larger historical context of racism and discrimination in the United States. Understanding this historical context is important because it helps explain present disparities. But even more importantly, *looking at the historical contexts reveals a pattern of oppression*, and this plays into our third argument in Section 3.3.

So here's a brief and incomplete rundown of racism in the United States. This country was built by taking land from Indigenous people—who were forcibly relocated and murdered—and on the backs of slaves—people who were kidnapped from their homes and forced to labor for others, literally classified as property, assaulted in every imaginable way, and torn from their families. It took the deadliest war in US history to end slavery, and those who suffered under slavery were never meaningfully compensated. Instead, "Black codes" criminalized ordinary behavior that was legal for white citizens, so that Black citizens could be imprisoned and rented out to basically the same people who had enslaved them. (The Thirteenth Amendment, which prohibits slavery, has a clause that exempts unpaid service in the case of imprisonment.) For instance, vagrancy laws in the South required 'Negroes' to be employed or face hard labor in prison; coincidentally, the only employment opportunities involved signing contracts with former slave owners to resume the same work done under slavery for incredibly low pay. The privatization of prisons and the prison industrial complex continues today (for an account of post–Civil War to World War II "re-enslavement," see Blackmon 2008).

In addition, Jim Crow laws resulted in legal segregation, and it took until 1954 and *Brown v. Board of Education* to end legal segregation. But other methods of segregating, such as redlining and predatory loans, also kept neighborhoods segregated in practice (see, e.g., Rothstein 2017).

Furthermore, even though the Fourteenth Amendment extended the right to vote to Black men, poll taxes, literacy tests, and outright assault and murder prevented them from voting. (Here, we might like to say "prevented them from voting until the Voting Rights Act of 1965," but the reality is that many people—disproportionately Black and Hispanic people—are still prevented from voting today by unnecessary obstacles like voter ID laws.) By the way, women couldn't legally vote until 1920, Native Americans until 1924, and Asian Americans until 1952. (And of course, in practice, many members of these groups were still not able to vote until much later.) Even today, many of those with felonies on their record are unable to vote (which is especially problematic because they are excluded from having a say on policies, like whether they should have the right to vote, that directly affect them!).

Finally, *racism, sexism, ableism, and injustice are ongoing.* In addition to the wrongs against Black and Indigenous people, Hispanic and Asian Americans, as well as other racial or ethnic minorities, have suffered at the hands of the state as well. Those with disabilities (both physical and mental) are also subject to disproportionate policing and punishment. Though women are incarcerated at a lower rate than men (though the gap is narrowing), they are subject to discrimination and abuse along gendered lines: sexual abuse by agents of the state and forced medication occur at higher rates. Gendered discrimination and abuse also affect men and transgender prisoners, though in different ways (for a more detailed account of how gender structures the prison system, see Davis 2003, chap. 4). And all of these dimensions intersect with each other so that, for example, a cis Black woman is subject to different abuses than a transgender Hispanic man.

We shouldn't discount the great deal of *progress* that's been made over the course of US history. But *serious injustices still exist,* and these are part of the context in which punishment takes place in the United States.

3. The Arguments

We're now ready to turn to the arguments. Again, these arguments share two key features. First, they all claim that *in practice* punishment is not justified—even if it is *in theory.* Second, each points to features of the system—such as the ones just discussed in Section 2—that make punishment unjust in practice. The *way* a state implements punishment can make punishment unjustified, even if the problem of punishment is in theory solved.

3.1. Arbitrariness

In 1972, the Supreme Court issued a temporary moratorium on the death penalty in *Furman v. Georgia.* Though this moratorium ended four years later with *Gregg v. Georgia,* the rule established in *Furman* was not overturned and still stands: *a state's use of the death penalty can be cruel and unusual if it is issued in an arbitrary or discriminatory way.* This is true even if the death penalty *itself* is not cruel and unusual, and the wrongdoer in question *deserves* the death penalty. As Justice William O. Douglas wrote in his opinion:

> The generality of a law inflicting capital punishment is one thing. What may be said of the validity of a law on the books and what may be done with the law in its application do, or may, lead to quite different

conclusions. It would seem to be incontestable that the death penalty inflicted on one defendant is "unusual" if it discriminates against
him by reason of his race, religion, wealth, social position, or class, or
if it is imposed under a procedure that gives room for the play of such
prejudices.

While this case deals only with the death penalty, the rationale in it applies to
other punishments as well. We'll look more closely at this broader application in
Objection 2. For now, we'll look at the argument inspired by *Furman* as it applies
to the death penalty (but any other punishment can be substituted in for the death
penalty):

(P1) If a punishment is applied in an arbitrary or discriminatory
way, then *ceteris paribus,* all instances of that punishment are
all-things-considered unjustified even if the punishment is
prima facie justified.

(P2) The death penalty is applied in an arbitrary or discriminatory way.

(C) Therefore, *ceteris paribus,* all instances of the death penalty are
all-things-considered unjustified even if the death penalty is
prima facie justified.

Both (P1) and (P2) need some unpacking. Let's turn first to (P1). Recall from
Chapter 14 that *prima facie* **wrongs** are actions that are presumed wrong unless
there is a factor that outweighs that wrongness—it's *prima facie* wrong to push
you, but not all-things-considered wrong if I'm saving you from being mauled
by a tiger. *Prima facie* **justification** is the flip side of that. An act is *prima facie*
justified **if and only if** *it is presumed permissible unless there is an outweighing factor.*
So when (P1) says "even if the punishment is *prima facie* justified," it is referring
to cases in which (i) the death penalty is generally permissible and (ii) the wrongdoer in question is guilty and deserving of the death penalty. (P1) claims that an
arbitrary or discriminatory application of a penalty can outweigh the *prima facie*
justification behind a punishment. In other words, instances of that punishment
end up being all-things-considered unjustified. Finally, *ceteris paribus* is Latin for
"other things equal." It basically means that all other factors are held constant. As
applied to (P1), it means that no other factor that would make a difference (like
the wrongdoer being an escape artist who is bound to escape prison and murder
more innocent people) is in play.

(P2) is a claim about our current practices. In many cases, like *Furman,* those
who receive the death penalty and those who don't commit virtually the same
crimes. Even worse, Black defendants are far more likely to be sentenced to death
than white defendants—even when they are co-defendants for the same crime!
Even after the death penalty was reinstated with *Gregg,* studies show that the *race*
of the killer and the victim play a central role in whether the defendant receives

the death penalty: *the chances of execution are greatest when the killer is Black and the victim is white, and least when the killer is white and the victim is Black.* Scott Philips and Justin Marceau (2020) note that the execution rate is seventeen times greater when the victim is white than when the victim is Black; and Liliana Segura and Jordan Smith (2019) demonstrate how the racial disparity in executions has actually increased since *Gregg*, even though the overall execution rate has decreased.

Obviously, we *could* implement the death penalty in a fair, non-discriminatory way. On that happy day, this argument will no longer apply. But that day has not arrived, and—interestingly—very few challenge the above argument on the basis of (P2). Instead, the philosophical worries center on (P1).

Objection 1: An Ironic Implication

The above argument implies that if more people were executed—say, all who deserve the death penalty—then the death penalty would be justified. Here's how Chief Justice Warren Burger puts it in his *Furman* dissent:

> The critical factor in the concurring opinions of both Mr. Justice Stewart and Mr. Justice White is the infrequency with which the penalty is imposed. . . . It is concluded that petitioners' sentences must be set aside, not because the punishment is impermissibly cruel, but because juries and judges have failed to exercise their sentencing discretion in acceptable fashion. To be sure, there is a recitation cast in Eighth Amendment terms: petitioners' sentences are "cruel" because they exceed that which the legislature have deemed necessary for all cases; petitioners' sentences are "unusual" because they exceed that which is imposed in most cases. This application of the words of the Eighth Amendment suggests that capital punishment can be made to satisfy Eighth Amendment values if its rate of imposition is somehow multiplied. . . . The implications of this approach are mildly ironical. (61)

This is ironic since punishment is unjust *because* fewer are being executed. And it's natural to think that more executions, not fewer, would be the unjust problem!

In looking closer at the objection, we should first ask whether it casts doubt on one of the premises. The defender of the argument could respond to this worry by pointing out that strictly speaking, the objection does not directly challenge either (P1) or (P2). Thus, the defender of the argument could maintain the argument is sound and then simply accept the ironic implication.

Perhaps, however, the objection is meant to challenge (P1). If (P1) has this implication, then there must be something wrong with it. Ernest van den Haag (1978, 397) expands on Chief Justice Burger's noting of the ironic implication and argues that "if the death penalty is morally just, however discriminatorily applied to only some of the guilty, it does remain just in each case in which it is applied." The key idea in van den Haag's suggestion is that we ought to look at each case individually. If, for an individual case, there is nothing unjust about the punishment, then it is just. Nothing else is relevant.

> Suppose you are one of many people who are speeding, but the only one who is pulled over. Do you feel it is unfair for you to be ticketed? Does it make a difference if the police targeted you because your license plate is from a different state? Or because they simply don't like the way you look?

On the face of it, this objection to (P1) is compelling. Consider speeding tickets. Clearly, the state cannot issue tickets to every person every time they speed. If you drive and reflect on your own case, I suspect you know that the likelihood of getting a speeding ticket is low. Nevertheless, if you are caught, it seems that the speeding ticket is justified. At the very least, it would be strange to complain on the following grounds: "I know I was speeding, but many people speed and don't receive tickets, so it's unfair to ticket me."

Reply 1:

Suppose consequentialism is true. Then, *if* punishment is justified, this is due to forward-looking reasons—good consequences. On this picture, if we can show that executing fewer people leads to good consequences, then executing fewer people is justified. And statistics support that fewer executions have good consequences. When the death penalty was prohibited from 1972 to 1976, starting with *Furman* and ending with *Gregg*, there was no change (or change for the better) in the deterrent effects of the punishment. Thus, when it comes to the death penalty, we have a good **consequentialist** reason to get rid of it. Similarly, if getting rid of speeding tickets leads to good consequences, we should get rid of those too.

Reply 2:

Suppose instead that **retributivism** is true. Then, *if* punishment is justified, this is due to backward-looking reasons—like justice. But suppose also that backward-looking reasons merely *permit*, but do not *require*, punishing the guilty.

Stephen Nathanson (1985), in a direct response to van den Haag, concedes that in the speeding case described above, all speeders deserve tickets and that it is okay for the state to allow most speeders to escape ticketing even though they deserve it. He also concedes that ticketing the few is justified. However, Nathanson then argues that this is because *it's impossible to ticket all speeders*. Given this, it is just to ticket speeders infrequently—as long as the most egregious speeders are targeted. For example, it seems unjust to target people who speed just a mile over the speed limit when many flaunt the limit by driving over 20 mph over it. Even worse, it would be wrong to target speeders for irrelevant factors, like speeding on Tuesday, playing a song the officer disliked, or their race or gender.

The additional examples posed by Nathanson force us to consider the difference between these three potential rules regarding punishment:

(R1) Of the wrongdoers who deserve capital punishment, only the worst offenders will receive that punishment.

(R2) Of the wrongdoers who deserve capital punishment, there will be a random lottery to determine which of the unlucky few will receive that punishment.

(R3) Of the wrongdoers who deserve capital punishment, only the ones who are [fill in demographic group] will receive that punishment.

While (R1) is a permissible rule, (R2) and (R3) are not. (R2) is a purely arbitrary rule, while (R3) is an explicitly discriminatory one. And while you might not have intuitions about the permissibility of (R2), *(R3) is clearly wrong*. (For what it's worth, (R3) would be prohibited by the Fourteenth Amendment's equal protection clause.) As it turns out, the situation in *Furman* most closely resembles (R3). Here's what Justice Douglas, writing in the majority opinion, noted from a study of capital cases in Texas from 1924 to 1968:

> Application of the death penalty is unequal; most of those executed were poor, young, and ignorant . . . 75 of the 460 cases involved co-defendants, who, under Texas law, were given separate trials. In several instances where a white and a Negro were co-defendants, the white was sentenced to life imprisonment or a term of years while the Negro was given the death penalty. . . . Another ethnic disparity is found in the type of sentence imposed for rape. The Negro convicted of rape is far more likely to get the death penalty than a term sentence, whereas whites and Latins are far more likely to get a term sentence than the death penalty. (4)

While (R3) is obviously not an explicit rule, it in fact guides the application of the death penalty in the United States. Study after study suggests that *race plays a prominent role in sentencing*. So if (R3) is wrong, then the way the death penalty is applied is wrong. Applying punishments in a discriminatory way is wrong, so (P1) of the original argument stands.

Objection 2: A Slippery Slope

Like Objection 1, Objection 2 centers on an implication of (P1). Recall that (P1) is about punishment in general and says that *all* punishments that are applied in an arbitrary or discriminatory way are *ceteris paribus* unjustified even if the punishment itself is generally justified. This second worry points out that *our application of all punishments is probably somewhat arbitrary or discriminatory.* Van den Haag (1978) puts it this way: "I see no more merit in the attempt to persuade courts to let all capital-crime defendants go free of capital punishment because some have wrongly escaped it than I see in an attempt to persuade the courts to let all burglars go free because some have wrongly escaped imprisonment" (397). So if (P1) is true, all of our punishments, as currently implemented, are unjustified. But surely we are justified in punishing wrongdoers! So (P1) must be false.

Reply 1:

There are two ways of replying to this argument. The first is to apply it to the death penalty specifically, but not to other kinds of punishment, like imprisonment. This is not difficult to do since the *death penalty is different in kind from imprisonment*. It is the *most extreme* of modern punishments, and unlike imprisonment, it is *irreversible*. Some, such as Nathanson (1985), make precisely this point. The US legal system also acknowledges the difference between the death penalty and imprisonment by reserving the former for only the most serious crimes and having far more protections in place for the death penalty than for imprisonment. So one way of responding to the worry is to draw a distinction between the death penalty and other punishments, then narrow (P1) so that it only applies to the death penalty.

Reply 2:

A second way of replying involves accepting that the worry is correct and that (P1) generalizes to basically all punishments. As you may have guessed given that this chapter focuses on *abolition*, the view that punishment is unjustified, and this is an implication that many abolitionists embrace. We'll talk more about whether it makes sense to abolish all punishment because of discrimination in section 3.3.

3.2. Community Impact

Our next argument for the abolition of punishment is inspired by Paul Butler, who argues that Black jurors should refrain from convicting Black defendants of non-violent crimes—so that they won't be punished—even if it is clear that the defendants broke the law. **Jury nullification** occurs when *jurors decline to convict a defendant even when it is clear that they are guilty*. Because jurors cannot be punished for their verdicts and defendants cannot be tried for the same offense twice (double jeopardy), jury nullification is a tool that citizens can use to ensure that a defendant is not punished. Historically, jurors were entrusted with this power in part to "check" unjust laws. Some positive uses of nullification include protecting journalists who wrote negatively about the government and abolitionists who hid or aided runaway slaves. Here, jurors acted as the last line of defense against unjust laws that would have otherwise sent good people to prison. It should also

be noted that there are notoriously egregious uses of nullification: white supremacists sometimes take advantage of nullification to help those who are guilty of hate
crimes escape punishment. (We'll return to this later.)

Butler (1995) argues that many laws are unjust in their application to Black
citizens in the United States. He supports this claim by noting that historically,
numerous laws have explicitly and intentionally disadvantaged Black people. In
addition, many laws that appear non-discriminatory have a disproportionate
impact on the Black community. As he puts it:

> The unjust effect is measured in terms of the costs to the black commu-
> nity of having so many African-Americans, particularly males, incarcer-
> ated or otherwise involved in the criminal justice system. These costs are
> social and economic, and include the perceived dearth of men "eligible"
> for marriage, the large percentage of black children who live in female-
> headed households, the lack of male "role models" for black children,
> especially boys, the absence of wealth in the black community, and the
> large unemployment rate among black men. (695)

In short, *the application of many laws is doubly unjust.* Butler contends that the way
laws are applied to members of the Black community unjustly affect not only the
person charged with the crime but also the community as a whole.

Given this backdrop, Butler proposes that when Black jurors are faced with
the choice to convict a Black defendant of a non-violent crime, they should opt
to nullify, *even if the defendant is clearly guilty.* The considerations in favor of this
proposal include both justice-based and consequentialist considerations. We've
already mentioned the justice-based considerations—the law is unjust when
applied to members of the Black community. As far as consequentialist considerations go, Butler contends that the Black community is better equipped to *rehabilitate* non-violent offenders. The line between violent and non-violent offenders
is drawn to protect the community from violence.

Butler's proposal inspires our second argument for abolition:

(P1) If the law is unjust, we shouldn't punish those who break it.

(P2) The law is unjust toward the Black community and its members.

(C)   Therefore, we shouldn't punish the Black community and its
      members who break the law.

(P1) follows from basic moral principles. We don't have an obligation to enforce
unjust laws. And harming someone for the sake of enforcing an unjust law is
wrong. (P2) is defended by Butler and we've discussed it in Section 2. From these
two claims, it follows that we shouldn't punish the Black community and its members who break the law, unless there is some outweighing factor, like community
safety, which is why Butler limits the argument to non-violent crimes.

Objection 1: Just Laws

The first objection says that (P2), the claim that the law is unjust toward the Black community and its members, is false. For example, while laws permitting slavery and punishing those who help people escape freedom are obviously unjust, laws prohibiting things like murder and theft are sensible laws to apply to everyone in society. Even laws regarding speed limits and drugs might be necessary for a well-functioning society. In short, *nothing about the content of most laws is unjust toward the Black community and its members.* Thus, (P2) is false.

Reply:

This objection fails to appreciate the ways in which apparently just laws can be applied in unjust ways. The previous sections discussed the ways in which just laws can be applied in a discriminatory way, so we won't rehash them here. However, it's worth noting another distinct point Butler discusses. Democracies function by implementing the will of the (voting) majority. The **tyranny of the majority**—the idea that the majority can vote to implement laws that unfairly harm the minority—is a looming problem with democracy. Given this danger, one might think that the legitimacy of democracy requires that minorities are able to become members of the majority at some point (see Guinier 1991). This is especially pressing given that white citizens in the United States outnumber Black citizens five to one.

The tyranny of the majority is problematic when it comes to addressing concerns that disproportionally belong to minority Black communities. For example, Butler points out that if young white men were more likely to end up in prison than college, over-incarceration would receive far more attention than it currently does, and the state would respond to drug violations with rehabilitative programs rather than imprisonment. The problem with racial prejudice (both of individuals and institutions) is that it's highly unlikely that this requirement will be met since *racial prejudice enables the majority to ignore the concerns of the minority.* If this is right, this democratic concern is an additional way in which the law can be unjust even if it is not explicitly discriminatory or applied in a discriminatory fashion.

> Suppose that you have two siblings. Every weekend, your parents take you on an outing. You always want to go to the amusement park, and your two siblings always want to go to the museum. What will happen if your parents always pick the outing based on the majority preference? Is that fair?

Objection 2: Anarchy

Our second objection centers on (P1), the claim that if the law is unjust, we shouldn't punish those who break it. Earlier, we noted that, historically, jurors were meant to check unjust laws. Today, things have changed, and *defendants are actually prohibited*

In *US v. Dougherty*, the majority wrote:

> We know that a posted limit of 60 m.p.h. produces factual speeds 10 or even 15 miles greater, with an understanding all around that some "tolerance" is acceptable to the authorities, assuming conditions warrant. But can it be supposed that the speeds would stay substantially the same if the speed limit were put: Drive as fast as you think appropriate, without the posted speed limit as an anchor, a point of departure?

What is the point of this example? Do you think it's analogous to Butler's proposal?

from arguing directly for nullification (see *US v. Dougherty*). Attitudes toward jury nullification have shifted partially out of a concern about anarchy, or, more perspicuously, disorder due to widespread disregard of the law. Even though there may be instances in which it is good to decline to punish someone for violating an unjust law, (P1) is bad as a general *rule* because it leads to the erosion of law. Here, people often cite *abuses of jury nullification*, such as when white supremacist jurors nullify verdicts for white defendants who commit hate crimes. Finally, one might worry that even if the law is unjust toward the Black community and its members, releasing offenders back into the community makes things worse for that community.

Reply 1:

In general, if you can prevent someone from being unjustly harmed, you should do so. As a juror, if you believe that the law the defendant has violated is unjust (or being applied unjustly), and that they will be harmed if you vote to convict them, you should nullify. It is true that others may abuse nullification to allow those who commit heinous crimes to go free. However, those abuses likely will occur regardless of whether you nullify. In other words, whether white supremacists abuse nullification is not connected to whether Black jurors should nullify for Black defendants who commit non-violent crimes. (For more on the general permissibility of jury nullification, see Huemer 2018 and 2013.)

Reply 2:

Butler distinguishes between violent and non-violent crimes precisely because he is concerned with the welfare of the community. He raises the following points:

> **First,** obviously, the community is made worse-off if murderers roam free. But for non-violent crime, which includes theft and drug crimes, it's not clear that the community is better if offenders serve decades-long prison sentences.

Second, the community is better placed to rehabilitate these offenders than prisons are.

Third, when one considers the overall effect of various policies, it's clear that the system as a whole has failed the Black community, and that the *community*—rather than the *system*—should handle non-violent offenders.

One might worry there isn't enough evidence that communities effectively rehabilitate criminals. But to obtain the best evidence regarding whether this is effective, communities need a chance. Given that the prison system doesn't do much rehabilitation, it's probably worth trying something else.

Objection 3: Overgeneralizing

Finally, one might object that Butler's proposal is too narrow and that what he says about Black jurors and defendants ought to apply to other races. For instance, why shouldn't Hispanic or Asian American jurors nullify for Hispanic or Asian American defendants? Why shouldn't white jurors nullify for white defendants?

Reply:

First, one might distinguish between communities who have been treated unjustly by the law and those who have not. Black communities are among the former. Other communities of color are also among the former, though there is significant variation in how unjust treatment manifests itself against these communities and subcommunities. Perhaps for the most part, white communities are among the latter, though there are obviously white subcommunities who have experienced injustice. However one settles which communities are treated unjustly by the law, *(P2) is true for those treated unjustly; (P2) is false for those who haven't been treated unjustly.*

Second—and this is the response Butler offers—*it might be good for all communities to nullify for non-violent offenses,* especially if the community benefits from the offender remaining in the community and can rehabilitate effectively. The current prison system is a disaster and, in general, our society should focus on rehabilitation and reintegration, rather than imprisonment. If jurors nullified for all non-violent defenders, they would bring attention to this fact, and society likely would shift its focus.

3.3. Prisons as a Perpetuation of Injustice

Our final argument calls for the *total abolition of prisons.* Like the previous two, this argument does not claim that punishment is *never* justified; rather, it targets the practice of punishment in the United States. Inspired by the work of abolitionists like Angela Davis, Michelle Alexander, Ruth Wilson Gilmore, and others, the argument is as follows:

(P1)   Practices regarding imprisonment in the United States serve to maintain a racial caste system.

(P2)   If some practice serves to maintain a racial caste system, that practice ought to be abolished.

(C)   Therefore, practices regarding imprisonment in the United States ought to be abolished.

Fully defending (P1) requires taking a further detour into the history of racial oppression in the United States. Here, we'll highlight the finer points and direct readers to further reading. As mentioned in Section 2, the Thirteenth Amendment ended slavery and involuntary servitude—except as a punishment for a crime. Even though slavery had ended, the desire for cheap labor and the continued subjugation of Black persons did not. Many states enacted Black codes that criminalized things like vagrancy (i.e., being unemployed) for Black persons. These codes either explicitly applied only to 'Negroes' or were only enforced against them. Those who were convicted would then be "leased out" as cheap labor. Prisons, rather than those doing the labor, kept the earnings. Strictly speaking, this wasn't slavery, but for those imprisoned doing the hard labor, the conditions were nearly indiscernible. (For more on this, see Blackmon 2008.)

Black codes and hard labor (e.g., in mines) eventually faded into history, but a new incarnation of this oppression evolved after the civil rights movements in the 1960s. The "war on crime," alongside the privatization of prisons, increased the prison population by over 1,000 percent from 1980 to 2005 (see Maur and King 2007; Mauer 1999). Though they no longer perform hard labor, prisoners still work for almost nothing. (If you're sitting in a university classroom, your desk and chair may have been made by people in prisons!) Furthermore, the prison industrial complex is incredibly profitable for the individuals who have invested in private prisons, those who have contracted with either private or public prisons, and the hundreds of thousands who are employed by prisons.

Perhaps the expansion of prisons wouldn't be bad if it were a necessary response to crime. However, statistics suggest that when the War on Drugs was enacted, crime had already declined. And there are disparities that cry out for an explanation. For example, within the United States, people of all races use drugs at approximately the same rate. Yet over half of those imprisoned for drug use are Black, when Black people make up only about 13 percent of the population. Furthermore, we can compare the United States to other European countries with similar rates of crime and drug use. In doing so, we see that the United States imprisons a far higher percentage than any other country (and this includes not just comparable countries, but non-comparable countries, with the exception of maybe Russia).

The disconnect between imprisonment and crime rates coupled with the financial incentives that come at the cost to Black Americans—who in many cities are more likely to be imprisoned than go to college—support (P1). Though things are obviously better now for Black Americans than they were before, they still aren't good. Modern-day imprisonment in the United States is discriminatory. Laws forbidding felons from voting disproportionately affect Black men and also serve to continue a history of disenfranchisement. Notice that even if none of the current practices in the United States are intentionally racist (which is doubtful), disparate impact endures as a result of these policies. Black communities continue to be destroyed by over-policing, over-imprisonment, and over-exploitation. (For further reading on this topic, see Davis 2003; Alexander 2012; and Gilmore 2018, 2021.)

(P2) is plausible. Using imprisonment to maintain a racial caste system is literally a crime against humanity in the Rome Statute of the International Criminal Court (Article 7, 2011). Even if this is merely a *prima facie* wrong that can be outweighed by some good, it's clear that there is no such outweighing good here (see above for comparative international crime rates). If this premise is also true, then the conclusion holds, and prisons in the United States ought to be abolished.

Objection 1: Aren't We Over Racism?

The first objection concerns (P1). Given the progress that has been made since slavery—there's even been a Black president!—perhaps racial oppression in the United States no longer exists.

Reply:

The demographics of the US general and prison populations cry out for an explanation. Racial oppression—in light of the country's history—is a far more likely explanation than any potential competing one, such as some races being inherently more prone to criminal behavior than others. Notice that this holds even if it is true that Black people commit disproportionately more crimes than white people. If these crimes are the result of other social conditions in play, like poverty and discrimination—which are the result of a history of racism and exacerbated by imprisonment—then racial oppression is still part of the explanation.

It's also worth considering that *success stories don't entail that there is no racism*. Even when slavery was legal, there were free and successful Black people. The fact that there are poor and oppressed white people does not entail that there is no racism either. Again, even when slavery was legal, there were white indentured servants who were seriously oppressed. (P1) points to a systemic problem, and this is compatible with individual success stories.

Objection 2: Reform versus Abolition

Unlike the second argument that concerned non-violent offenders, this argument concludes that the prison system as a whole needs to be abolished. One natural response is to ask *whether reform would be better than abolition*. For instance, many believe that prisons perform an important function, at least when it comes to keeping communities safe from violent offenders. And given that other countries (which also have a history of racism) have prison systems that aren't objectionable in the same way as US prisons, it seems possible to imprison people without perpetuating a racial caste system. In light of that possibility and the "good" functions of prison, perhaps prisons should be reformed rather than abolished. Thus, (P2) is too strong and should be modified so that it calls for reform rather than abolition.

Reply:

Many people think that it is far worse to harm someone than to fail to prevent harm. For instance, part of why the standard for criminal conviction is "beyond a reasonable doubt" is because many people assent to sentiments such as "it is far worse to convict one innocent person than let ten guilty people go free." If we take these claims seriously, then it probably is better to free everyone who is in prison than maintain the current system.

Second, *the choice between keeping the current system and letting everyone go free is a false dilemma*. There are many non-punitive things that can be done to rehabilitate wrongdoers and correct the wrongs that have been committed. For instance, Davis (2003) points out that many other countries respond to drug use with voluntary rehabilitation programs rather than prison. Furthermore, effective social programs remove the need for people to resort to crime in the first place. Lastly, even in the case of violent offenders, there are often alternatives to imprisonment that are worth pursuing. One might, for instance, pursue restorative and reparative justice, as suggested in Chapter 15. Ultimately, as long as cases in which people are beyond reform are rare (which they likely are), there are many things one can do to reshape society so that prisons aren't required as a response to crime.

Finally, we should consider seriously *whether there are reforms short of abolition that can break the racial caste system*. Perhaps getting rid of the prison industrial complex, decriminalizing drugs, declining to imprison non-violent offenders, and reforming policing and courtroom practices would lead to a just system of punishment that sparingly uses prisons. Other forms of structural racism not directly connected to punishment, such as generational poverty resulting from slavery and practices like redlining, would have to be rectified as well since those conditions lead to crime and thus disproportionately affect Black communities. If all of those policies were put into place and did break the racial caste system, the defender of this argument likely would happily accept those reforms, even in lieu of abolishing prisons. But it's important to recognize that the reforms required to break the racial caste system are quite extreme. And until these policies are put into place, the current system of punishment, including imprisonment, is not justified.

> We've now discussed three arguments that punishment is unjustified in prac-
> tice: it's applied in a discriminatory way, the laws are unjust, and the prison
> system enforces a racial caste system. Which argument did you find most
> convincing and why? Which argument did you find least convincing and
> why? Overall, has your view on practical abolition changed since reading
> this chapter?

4. Conclusion

We've learned about the problem of punishment and about retributivist and consequentialist responses to it. In this chapter, we've seen that even if consequentialism or retributivism justifies punishment *in theory*, this does not automatically
mean that punishment is justified *in practice*. Next, we turn to our final topic of
the book: disability.

Further Reading

For more on the problematic context in which punishment in the United States
takes place, see Alexander (2012), Blackmon (2008), Davis (2003), Gilmore (2018,
2021), and Rothstein (2017). For more on the first argument, see *Furman v. Georgia*, Nathanson (1985), and van den Haag (1978). For the second argument, see
Butler (1995). For the third argument, see Alexander (2012), Davis (2003), and
Gilmore (2018, 2021).

Section 6

Disability

Chapter 17

What Is a Disability?

1. Introduction

Our final topic is **disability**, and the big question we examine is the relationship between disability and **well-being**. Are people with disabilities simply *different* from non-disabled people? Or do their disabilities make them *worse off*? For example, are people who are 'double-jointed' (i.e., have hypermobility) simply different? Or, does 'double-jointedness' make them worse off than non-double-jointed people? Are people with chronic migraines simply different? Or, do chronic migraines make them worse off than people without chronic migraines? The next two chapters cover opposing answers to the question of whether disability causes people to be worse off or if it is just a way of being different. But first we need to define *disability*: What exactly is a *disability*, and what is it not? This chapter is about rival understandings of what a disability is.

> Before reading ahead, what do you think a *disability* is? How would you define the term?

Defining disability is important in many contexts, which is why we've dedicated an entire chapter to the topic. For instance, perhaps you are writing a policy on requiring schools to provide accommodations for students with disabilities, or you are trying to decide whether you should attempt to make your child abled instead of disabled (e.g., perhaps you are trying to decide whether to give your deaf child a cochlear implant). While you could approach each case on an individual basis, when it comes to general policy or ethical questions, it may sometimes make more sense to talk about disability in general. At the very least, we might want to know what unites—or perhaps, defines—the conditions that warrant legal protection or generate certain ethical duties.

2. Constructing a Definition

Before looking at proposed definitions of disability, we need to consider what would count as a successful definition. There are three general things that go into making a successful definition:

1.   A successful definition should respect paradigm cases.

2. A successful definition should be unifying or explanatory.
3. A successful definition shouldn't be circular.

When talking about disability, we'll add a fourth criterion:

4. A successful definition shouldn't presuppose that having a disability is worse than not having that disability.

We'll talk in a moment about each of these criteria. But perhaps at this point you may be thinking that this discussion is extra—can't we just look the definition up in the dictionary? Well, dictionary definitions are often lacking. Consider the following definitions offered by the *Oxford English Dictionary* (*OED*):

> **Disability 1:** a physical or mental condition that limits a person's movements, senses, or activities.
> **Disability 2:** a disadvantage or handicap, especially one imposed or recognized by the law.

Consider our *first* criterion, that a successful definition should respect paradigm cases. **Paradigm cases** are central, anchoring cases. For instance, dogs and cats are paradigm cases of domestic pets, while whales and giraffes are paradigm cases of non-domestic pets. There may be in-between cases such as pigs, which can sometimes be pets but often are not. If a definition classifies a dog as a non-pet or a whale as a pet, that definition is defective. Looking at the *OED* definitions, we can see that both are defective. For instance, being tall is not a disability. But people who are extremely tall like Shaquille O'Neal are limited in plenty of movements and activities. For instance, Shaq probably cannot navigate playground equipment and likely has difficulty showering in standard-sized showers. That definition would count Shaq as disabled, but he is clearly not disabled (at least, not with respect to being tall).

> Can you think of other paradigm cases that are either wrongfully included or wrongfully excluded by the *OED* definitions?

Now consider our *second* criterion, that a successful definition should be *unifying* or *explanatory*. Definitions should explain what a word means in a way that gets at the central concept. For instance, consider the following two definitions of "pet":

> **Pet 1:** a dog or a cat or a bird in a cage or . . .
> **Pet 2:** a non-human animal kept in a home as part of the family.

While it may be strictly speaking true that a pet is a dog or a cat or a bird in a cage, Pet 1 does not get at the central concept of what a pet is. It's more like a list.

This is easy to see in light of Pet 2, which does try to explain what the concept of a pet is. When it comes to disability, there are many different kinds of disabilities:

- **physical**, such as deafness or blindness;
- **cognitive**, such as fragile X syndrome, fetal alcohol syndrome, ADHD, or dyslexia;
- **congenital** (i.e., present at birth), such as clubfoot or Down syndrome;
- **acquired**, such as dementia, traumatic brain injury, or acquired blindness (e.g., retinitis pigmentosa);
- **visible**, such as dwarfism or Crouzon syndrome; and
- **invisible**, such as autism spectrum disorder, PTSD, schizophrenia, or bipolar disorder.

The disabilities listed above can fit into more than one category. For example, Down syndrome typically presents with cognitive impairments. It is visible and congenital. Down syndrome is often accompanied by physical challenges, such as heart defects and spinal malformation. People also can have more than one disability. For instance, a person with autism spectrum disorder might also have fragile X syndrome. Note also that a physical disability such as deafness might not be visible.

A successful definition of disability should explain what unites all of these kinds of disabilities or find the central feature they share. Note that the *OED* definitions do attempt to be unifying and explanatory by saying that "limitation" or "disadvantage" explain what disability is. But the *OED* definitions are deficient because (1) limitation and disadvantage include too many non-disabilities (like height) and possibly exclude disabilities (not all people with disabilities are limited or disadvantaged, or at least they do not believe that they are), and (2) limitation and disadvantage presuppose being worse off, which violates the fourth criterion (which we'll discuss below).

> Can you think of any feature(s) that all the categories of disability share?

Now consider our *third* criterion, that a successful definition should not be *circular*. This is pretty basic; it would obviously be problematic to define 'pet' as 'whatever counts as a pet'. Sometimes definitions can be circular in a more subtle way. Consider the second *OED* definition, that says "a disadvantage or handicap, especially one imposed or recognized by the law." It can be perfectly fine to define something in terms of what's recognized by the law. For instance, it probably makes a lot of sense to define 'felon' in terms of what the law says. But if part of why we want a definition of disability is to decide what the law should say about disability rights and accommodations, then it would be circular to define disability in terms of whatever the law recognizes.

Finally, let's turn to the *fourth* criterion, which is specific to disability. This criterion calls for *neutrality*. One immediate thing to notice is that both definitions take disability to be a disadvantage or limitation. We won't immediately define *disabilities* as things that make people worse off, since that would predetermine the answer to the big question of whether disabilities do make people worse off. Rather, we will put forward a relatively neutral definition, and then we will decide whether disabilities are bad for us by looking at arguments.

Some readers might think this way of going about things is overly cautious: Isn't it obvious that disabilities do make people worse off? How would you—if you're hearing—like to be deaf? Like nearly all other hearing people, you probably have no interest in becoming permanently deaf. But reframing the question shows that it is not obvious that disabilities make people worse off. For if you're deaf, would you want to be hearing? For many people in the Deaf community, the answer is no. The argument covered in the next chapter tries to show that it is *not* obvious that disabilities make people worse off.

3. Definitions and Counterexamples

We've now talked about why we want a definition of disability and what a successful definition would look like. The final things we need to discuss before looking at proposed definitions of disability are the mechanics of a definition and counterexamples. Philosophers often propose a candidate definition and then test it via counterexamples. Recall that in Chapter 3, we learned that a **counterexample** is designed to show that *there is something wrong with a proposed definition, claim, or principle*. We're going to look closely here at counterexamples to definitions. A **counterexample to a definition** aims to show that an important condition of the definition hasn't been met—the counterexample either shows that the definition is not a *necessary condition* or not a *sufficient condition* for the thing being defined.

A **necessary condition** for X is something that must be included to get X:

- Suppose it takes five people to lift a car. If you and three friends wanted to pick up a car, your group of four people is necessary but not sufficient to move a car. Four people is required, but not enough to get you there.

- Suppose you are making chocolate chip cookies. Having chocolate chips is necessary, but not sufficient, to make the cookies—you need other ingredients as well, but you can't make chocolate chip cookies without chocolate chips.

In contrast, a **sufficient condition** for X is something that is enough for X:

- Being a woman is sufficient for being human. Being a woman isn't required for being human, but it's enough—it is one way to be human.
- Suppose you need a new cell phone. Buying an iPhone is sufficient for buying a new phone. But you don't have to buy an iPhone—you could get an Android phone instead. Getting a new iPhone is sufficient for getting a new phone.

Definitions are supposed to give *both* the necessary and sufficient conditions for the thing defined. A good definition will *include*, for example, everything that is a disability and exclude everything that is not a disability. So if we were to give a good definition of the word 'bachelor', we would want a definition that included all bachelors and excluded all non-bachelors.

> Can you think of a definition for 'bachelor' that is both necessary and sufficient for being a bachelor?

If we said a bachelor is a person who is unmarried and male, that is a definition that would seem to capture all bachelors and exclude all non-bachelors. Together, being unmarried and a man seem jointly necessary and sufficient for being a bachelor.

Similarly, a definition is *bad* when the conditions it lists are

- not sufficient for the thing being defined; or
- not necessary for the thing being defined; or, worst case,
- both.

Counterexamples, then, show that the conditions in the definition are not *necessary* or *sufficient* for the thing being defined—in our case, a disability. (Notice that this is exactly what we did in the previous section when we used Shaq's height as a counterexample to the first *OED* definition of disability.) The philosopher can then try to improve the definition by adding new conditions or qualifications, or they can jettison the definition entirely and try to come up with a new definition.

> Can you come up with definitions of any of the following: *student*, *party*, *salad*, or *chair*? Once you have a definition, can you think of any counterexamples to it?

4. Definitions of Disability

We now turn to various definitions of disability. Many of the definitions and objections come from the first chapter of Elizabeth Barnes's (2016) book *The*

Minority Body. For the reader interested in learning more about this topic, her book is one of the first we recommend (see the end of the chapter for additional recommendations).

In 1980, the World Health Organization defined a disability as "the restriction or lack (resulting from an impairment) of ability to perform an activity in the manner or within the range considered normal for a human being" (see Barnes 2016, 18; the UN still employs this definition). This is encapsulated in

medical definition 1: disability is any departure from normal functioning.

Objection 1:

But departing from the norm is not *sufficient* for disability. After all, people with perfect musical pitch or exceptional athletic ability are abnormal. Calling LeBron James disabled because he has freakish non-"normal" athletic abilities just doesn't seem right. Generally, simply being physically different from what is statistically "normal" doesn't make someone disabled. You might be different in lots of ways without having any disability. Therefore, medical definition 1 is not sufficient because it includes non-disabled people.

Objection 2:

If disability is defined in terms of normal function, then it seems like it would rule out the possibility of a worldwide disability—because then, having a disability would be normal. However, it seems possible for the majority of humankind to be negatively affected by some disease, plague, or man-made disaster. Imagine an apocalyptic movie where the Earth is covered with a chemical that causes us all to lose our fingers, go blind, or develop an exclusive taste for human brains. The new normal would be defined as blindness, fingerlessness, or brain-lust. But this just doesn't make sense. If I'm one of the humans that escaped the plague and got to keep my fingers, I would not be disabled.

Reply 1:

One might argue that 'normal' is defined by all human beings who have lived in the recorded past. Then, we can avoid the result that the fingerless humans are not disabled because they are now 'normal' or average. And we can explain why humans who have escaped from a worldwide disaster are not disabled.

Reply 2:

We might slightly change the definition to say that disabilities are *negative* departures from proper functioning. A person with perfect pitch who departs from proper function is not disabled because this is not negative; on the contrary, it often gives the gifted individual a musical advantage. This definition also deals with our other case: in a world of people who are all blind, everyone would be functioning improperly, and thus disabled. This suggests instead

> **medical definition 2**: disability is a negative departure from proper functioning. (Daniels 1985)

Objection 1:

People with a certain genetic makeup are much more likely to get cancer. Someone who has these genes negatively departs from proper functioning, as the genes significantly raise their chance of getting cancer. Nonetheless, having these genes doesn't make them disabled (see Barnes 2016, 16, who cites Turnbull and Hodgson 2005). Thus, a negative departure from normal function is not sufficient for having a disability.

Objection 2:

If we define disability as a negative departure from proper functioning, this definition *assumes* that all disabilities are negative. The reply would amend our definition so as to predetermine the answer to the big question: disabilities turn out to make people worse off by definition. In that case, the arguments of the next chapter would be about whether anything really *counts as* a disability.

For something more neutral than the medical definition, we could try the

> **ability definition 1:** disability is the lack of an ability that most people have.

Objection:

Lacking an ability most people have is not sufficient for disability. After all, most people can roll their tongues (and we suspect you're trying that now). But not being able to roll your tongue isn't a disability.

Reply:

Maybe disability is the lack of a *significant* ability that most people have; the ability to roll the tongue is not significant. Perhaps it's useful for kissing or something—though we wouldn't know. In contrast, the inability to see is the lack of a significant ability; blind people cannot drive, they sometimes have to rely on canes, and so on. This suggests instead

> **ability definition 2:** disability is the lack of a *significant* ability that most people have.

Reply to the reply:

Lacking a significant ability is not necessary for disability. Not all disabilities are correlated with the lack of a specific ability. Dwarfism (more formally, *achondroplasia*) is a condition that affects bone growth, causing an exceptionally short stature. People with this condition have a disability, but don't lack a specific ability.

Reply to the reply to the reply:

People with dwarfism in fact lack certain abilities, for example, the ability to reach high shelves.

Reply to the reply to the reply to the reply:

The ability to reach high shelves isn't clearly a significant ability. Furthermore, people who are simply short or petite also lack the same ability, but they don't have a disability.

Next up is the

> **welfare definition**: disability is anything that makes life go worse for you. (Kahane and Savulescu 2009)

Objection 1:

Making life go worse is not sufficient for disability. After all, lots of things make our lives worse, but aren't disabilities. Suppose you slip Vegemite into our sandwiches. That makes our lives go worse, but doesn't make us disabled. Or suppose your girlfriend breaks up with you. This, again, may make your life worse, but isn't a disability.

> Can you think of any ways to reply to this objection on behalf of the welfare approach?

Furthermore, the welfare definition again predetermines the answer to the big question. (Or, again, it changes our big question to the question of whether anything really is a disability.)

Let's consider another option. This next definition presupposes that we live in a society that discriminates against people with impairments:

> **social definition**: disability is the negative effects of having an impairment in a society that discriminates against the impaired.

On the social approach, having a disability isn't a natural or physical thing, like the proper function view or the ability view. Instead, having a disability is *social*. This parallels a definition of gender on which being a man or being a woman isn't a biological thing, but is rather a social thing (see Haslanger 2014, 381). While there are different versions of the social approach, the definition above is one of the most common.

Objection 1:

This view has the result that if society did not discriminate against people with impairments (or if there were no society), there would be no people with disabilities (in the social sense). This is a little odd, and it seems to miss the point. In this society, people would still be blind, deaf, and so forth, and these underlying conditions are presumably the things that we care about when we talk about disability. To put it in terms of our criteria for a successful definition of disability, this definition does not properly explain what unites disabilities.

Objection 2:

This definition focuses only on societal discrimination. It is true that many people with impairments suffer from discrimination and that the primary effects of their disability may be social. However, the underlying impairment also has non-social effects, some of which may be negative even if the impairment is not bad in itself. This definition ignores those non-social effects (which is especially problematic if those turn out to be part of what unifies disabilities).

> Can you think of other, more plausible versions of the social definitions of disability?

If disability is not to be defined in terms of the actions of the larger society, perhaps it can be defined in terms of the preferences of the *individual*:

> **group identity definition**: a disability is something a person has when and only when they identify as having a disability.

According to this definition, *a person has a disability by self-identifying as disabled.* This view parallels a theory of gender that states that gender is determined by self-identification, rather than something biological or physical. Thus, a person will count as a man or a woman by identifying as such. Similarly, a disabled person counts as disabled by identifying as such. Such a definition takes the testimony of individuals seriously, and it provides people the autonomy to determine whether or not they are disabled.

Objection 1:

Identifying as disabled is not *necessary* for a disability. After all, some people might be disabled, but do not identify as having a disability. Consider someone who is blind or deaf, but exceptionally high achieving. Because of the societal stigma associated with disabilities, they might not identify as disabled. They might even say, "I've never thought of myself as disabled." However, maybe they only say this because of the way society associates disability with a *limitation* or *lack*. They are truly disabled, but simply have an improper view of what it means to be disabled. Similarly, one could be in denial about whether they have a disability. They might have a disability, but not realize it because they don't want it to be true or are simply unaware.

Objection 2:

Identifying as disabled is not *sufficient* for disability. Some people identify as having a disability but do not have a disability. Some of these people have a medical condition called *factitious disorder*. This is a mental disorder in which people act as if they have a physical or mental illness when, in fact, they have consciously created the symptoms. These people are not disabled, but they do identify as disabled.

Another case shows that identifying as disabled isn't sufficient for having a disability. Some people are **transabled**—also known as *body integrity identity disorder*. They believe their body *ought* to be disabled. They may, for example, believe one of their limbs is not part of their body, or they desire to be blind, deaf, or disabled in some other way. Transabled individuals identify as disabled but are often otherwise physically and psychologically normal. While they want to *become* disabled, they are not disabled.

Reply:

Factitious disorder is itself a disability. Thus, in the cases described above, those who identify as having a disability "make" themselves disabled by identifying as disabled. Perhaps transabled people are disabled as well, in the same way that identifying as a woman may be enough to make someone a woman.

Reply 1 to the reply:

There is a difference between a disability and a disease. If you have a cold, you have a disease or illness, but you aren't disabled. People with factitious disorder have a disease, not a disability.

Reply 2 to the reply:

Even if factitious disorder is itself a disability, this *fails to correctly locate the source of the disability*, and thus doesn't respect the spirit of the group identity definition—giving individuals autonomy to choose their own identities. People with factitious disorder don't identify as disabled because they think that they have factitious disorder; they identify as disabled for some other reason.

> Do you think there's a difference between a disability and a disease? How would you distinguish the two? Is there some overlap between the categories (i.e., are some diseases also disabilities)?

Objection 3:

Unsophisticated creatures, like children or animals, are sometimes disabled—blind, deaf, or missing limbs. However, they are not cognitively developed enough to *self-identify* as disabled. Indeed, cognitive disabilities might prevent even adult humans from self-identifying as disabled. Thus, self-identifying as disabled is not necessary for being disabled.

Let's consider another way of defining disability, which Barnes (2014, 2016) is sympathetic to. The "communal" definition says that having a disability is closely connected to the disability rights community:

> **communal definition 1**: disability is defined by the disability rights community. The correct definition of disability is however the disability rights community defines disability.

Objection 1:

This doesn't really tell us about the nature of disability. This might tell us a way to find out (e.g., by going and asking disabled people), but it isn't, by itself, informative.

Objection 2:

What if the disability rights community doesn't *agree* on the definition? Also, can't those in the community be *wrong* about the definition? Having a disability doesn't necessarily mean you can't be wrong about the nature of disability. So, instead, we have

> **communal definition 2**: disability is whatever the disability rights community is promoting justice for. (Barnes 2016)

Here is how Barnes explains the view:

> [The disability rights community] got together and identified a form of group solidarity. Although they had a strikingly heterogeneous range of physical conditions, they perceived a commonality in how those physical conditions were stigmatized, how people treated them because of those physical conditions, how those physical conditions made it difficult to access public spaces, to complete everyday tasks, to get adequate healthcare, get full-time employment and benefits, etc. And so despite having very different bodies, it made sense to think of their experience of their bodies as having something in common, and it made sense to think of themselves as working toward a common goal. (46)

This view is different from communal approach 1, because it is not about how the community *defines* disability, but rather about what unites the people that the community *advocates* for.

Objection 1:

Can't the disability rights community be wrong about what exactly they are promoting justice for? Again, what about disabilities that are undiscovered or

undiagnosed? Is the disability rights community promoting justice for people with those conditions?

Objection 2:

This definition is not sufficient for having a disability.
What about impaired Robinson Crusoe, who has no community? Can't he be
disabled, even if the disability rights community isn't promoting justice for him?
Further, can't animals, like ducks or dogs, have disabilities without having communities? There are also disabled people who lived in the distant past, before the
disability rights community existed.

> How would you reply to
> this objection on behalf
> of the communal defini-
> tion 2 of disability?

Reply:

Maybe the disability rights community is advocating
for all disabled creatures and beings, even those who
are isolated on desert islands, those who are non-
human, and those who lived a long time ago (see Barnes
2016, 50).

> Do you think it is plau-
> sible that the disability
> rights community is
> advocating for people
> in isolation, people
> who lived a long time
> ago, and animals? Why
> or why not?

Reply to the reply:

What about people who do not experience discrimination due to their disabilities? We can imagine that Robinson Crusoe is disabled, but does not
experience discrimination because he doesn't interact with other humans.
Furthermore, maybe future societies will progress so they don't discriminate
against disabled people. Nonetheless, people could still be blind, deaf, and so
on in these societies.

Reply to the reply to the reply:

In response to this objection, Barnes broadens her definition of disability:

> **communal definition 3**: disability is whatever the disability rights com-
> munity is promoting justice for or celebrating. (Barnes 2016, 51)

This third definition allows for there to be disabilities even when the people who
have those disabilities aren't experiencing discrimination. Even if the disability
rights community is so successful that they rid the world of all discrimination,
they will still exist to *celebrate* people with disabilities. In that case, *people with
disabilities are those whom the disability rights community is celebrating.*

Objection:

This definition isn't necessary for disability. Can't there be disabilities that the
disability rights community isn't celebrating? Let's say that the community is
confused, takes blindness to be a punishment for a sin, and also believes we

shouldn't thwart divine punishment. So they don't promote justice for or celebrate blindness. (Of course, while the disability community doesn't actually take this stance, it doesn't seem *impossible* for them to be confused in this way.) Wouldn't blindness still be a disability?

Finally, consider the

> **examples definition**: disability is defined by examples. Anything that closely enough resembles the examples on a list counts as a disability. The list could include mobility impairments, blindness, deafness, rheumatoid arthritis, achondroplasia (short-limbed dwarfism), Down syndrome, Moebius syndrome, narcolepsy, leg amputation, and so on. (Barnes 2014)

> How would you reply to this objection? Do you find communal definition 3 of disability plausible? Why or why not?

Objection 1:

How do we decide what goes on the list? It seems difficult to answer this question in a way that doesn't violate the circularity criterion.

Objection 2:

The definition does not tell us what it is to "closely enough resemble" a condition on the list. Might some disabilities—including disabilities not yet discovered—not resemble conditions on the list closely at all?

Objection 3:

The definition isn't really a 'definition' because it doesn't meet the second criterion about being unifying and explanatory. It also does not provide necessary and sufficient conditions for being a disability; it doesn't tell us anything about the fundamental *nature* of disability.

Reply:

Sometimes, an examples definition is good enough if it tells us about *family resemblance*, or the cluster of features shared by most of the examples. For instance, it's difficult to come up with a good definition of 'sport'. We might be tempted to think that sports are athletic competitions. But some sports are not particularly physical (golf and race car driving) while others don't even involve scoring or direct competition (rock climbing). However, thinking about the main shared features of most of the example sports might still be helpful. Similarly, the examples definition still gives us a good enough idea of what counts as a disability, even if it isn't a definition exactly. If our list is inclusive enough, it should be possible to turn to

> Which definition of disability do you find least plausible? Why? Which do you find most plausible? Why?

our next debate: whether these things on the list make someone's life worse off, or whether they are merely different.

5. Conclusion

Definitions are difficult. Even definitions that seem simple and obviously true turn out to have counterexamples if you think hard enough. "An unmarried male" might seem to be a pretty good definition of 'bachelor'. But what about a thirteen-year-old boy? Or the pope? They are unmarried males, but they don't seem to be bachelors because they're not eligible for marriage. Even so, we still have a good grasp of what a bachelor is, and as long as we are clear on the limitations of an imperfect definition, we can think and talk and reason about bachelors without a perfect definition with those limitations in mind.

In the same way, we might not have a perfect definition of 'disability', but we can nonetheless argue and reason about disabilities as long as we keep the limitations of an imperfect definition in mind. Furthermore, some of the above definitions, even if imperfect, still shed light on the nature of disability and tell us some important facts about it. We hope that, by reading this chapter, the reader has deepened their understanding of disability enough to proceed to the next chapters, which cover two views on the relationship between disability and well-being: disabilities are mere differences, and disabilities are bad differences.

Further Reading

For a defense of the proper function view of disability, see Daniels (1985). For a defense of the welfare account of disability, see Kahane and Savulescu (2009) and Savulescu and Kahane (2011). For an overview and analysis of many definitions of disability, see Barnes (2016), especially chapter 1. Barnes offers additional criticisms of many of the accounts we consider above; we especially recommend her work on this topic. For an argument that there isn't one unified definition of disability, see Timpe (forthcoming).

Chapter 18
The Mere-Difference View

1. Introduction

In the previous chapter, we discussed the question, What is a **disability**? While we didn't settle on one definition, we hope it gave the reader a sense of the nature of disability. Now we turn to the subject of the next two chapters: Is disability a bad thing?

As we learned in Chapter 17, there are many kinds of disabilities, and it is hard to consider such a broad class of cases all at once. For that reason, many authors—especially Elizabeth Barnes—restrict the debate to physical disabilities. Because this chapter is about Barnes's argument, and we want to present it as accurately as possible, we will also focus on physical disabilities. *Physical disabilities*, like deafness, blindness, and dwarfism, contrast with *cognitive disabilities*, such as fragile X syndrome, fetal alcohol syndrome, ADHD, and dyslexia.

This debate is about the relationship between disability and a specific good: **well-being**. But what exactly is well-being? *Well-being is what is good for a person.* In other words, someone's well-being is a measure of how well their life is going.

Philosophers disagree on what defines well-being. Some argue it is pleasure or happiness; some argue that it is when your desires are fulfilled; others argue it is when you have certain "objective goods," like friendship or knowledge (see Crisp 2017 for a summary). But we don't need to commit to one of these views here; we can understand well-being through examples. Having a career you love and friends who care for you contributes to your well-being; hating your job and lacking good friends takes away from your well-being. Being healthy contributes to your well-being; having a disease like cancer takes away from your well-being.

> What are some other examples of things that contribute to well-being? What are some examples of things that take away from well-being?

Some differences between people are bad differences that take away from well-being. It is worse for you to have cancer than to not have cancer, so having cancer is a bad difference. Other differences between people are *mere* differences. Consider being a woman. Women are different from men—but not in a way that makes them automatically worse off overall. There might be some bads associated with being a woman, such as the gender wage gap, but these are due to discrimination and not essential to being a woman. There are other things, like the pain associated with pregnancy, that are closely tied to being a woman. But these small costs don't mean that it is worse to be a woman overall—there might also be costs to being a man, like the possibility of getting testicular cancer. So being a woman is a mere difference, not a bad difference.

This brings us to the main question for this chapter and the next. One way to think about the question is this: *Is disability more like having cancer or more like being a woman?* Elizabeth Barnes (2016a) summarizes the question as follows:

> The core question . . . involves the connection between disability and well-being. Is disability simply another way of being a minority—something that makes you different but not something that makes you worse off? Or is disability something that's bad for you—not merely something that makes you different, but something that makes you worse off because of that difference? (54)

This quote suggests there are two main views of disability and well-being:

1. **Bad-difference view:** having a physical disability is bad in and of itself.
2. **Mere-difference view:** having a physical disability makes you physically non-standard, but it is not bad in and of itself.

Those who argue for the bad-difference view think that having a disability is bad for someone's well-being. On this view, disabilities take away from well-being, even if a society fully accommodates people with disabilities. If you hold the other facts about someone's life fixed and remove their disability, the bad-difference view says that their life would improve.

The mere-difference view holds that disabilities don't, by themselves, make someone worse off. Even though we use the word 'mere,' the mere difference doesn't mean that having a disability is insignificant. Again, having a disability is similar to being a woman: being female is an important trait, but it doesn't, by itself, take away from well-being. This view is consistent with thinking that being disabled is bad *in our society*—if society mistreats or discriminates against people with disabilities.

Our current debate is about whether, if there were no discrimination at all against people with disabilities, they would be worse off. Everyone agrees that unfair discrimination is a bad thing, and that it hurts the well-being of those who are discriminated against. The question is about whether having a disability is bad *in and of itself.*

Here is another way to see this last point. There are two types of goods:

1. **Intrinsic goods:** things that are good in and of themselves, like pleasure or love.

2. **Instrumental goods:** things that are good because they lead to something good. Going to the gym is, for many people, an instrumental good—while it isn't always fun to be there, it leads to a good result.

Note that some things can be both intrinsically and instrumentally good. For instance, love is good in itself, and it is also instrumentally good because it makes people feel good and leads them to act kindly.

There are also two types of bads:

1. **Intrinsic bads:** things that are bad in and of themselves, like pain or murdering an innocent person.
2. **Instrumental bads:** things that are bad because they lead to something bad, like eating too many chocolate chip cookies in one sitting.

Things can also be both intrinsically and instrumentally bad. For instance, pain is intrinsically bad, and it can also lead to other bad things, like being unable to pursue activities that would make you happier. (You may recall that intrinsic goods and bads have already been mentioned at various places earlier in this book.)

The main question in the next two chapters is, *Is having a disability intrinsically bad for a person?* The bad-difference view says yes, and the mere-difference view says no.

> Before reading ahead, what view seems right to you: the mere-difference view or the bad-difference view? Why?

This chapter gives some arguments for the mere-difference view. Some readers might initially find this view surprising or puzzling. To help us better understand the mere-difference view better, these are some claims often made by those who argue for it (Barnes 2016a, 69–70):

- Society's treatment of disabled people, not disability itself, is the source of the bad effects of disability.
- Disability is not a defective departure from normal or proper functioning.
- Disability is similar to sex, gender, race, and ethnicity.
- Disability should be celebrated and preserved, because it is a valuable part of human diversity. This is often called "*disability pride.*"

> In what ways might disability be similar to race and gender? In what ways might it be different?

2. The Outweighing Argument

Elizabeth Barnes (2014, 2016a) defends the mere-difference view. Barnes defends a version of the mere-difference view where she describes disabilities as "value-neutral." This means that having a disability isn't intrinsically bad for you, but it also isn't intrinsically good for you. It's similar to other differences between people that aren't themselves positive or negative, like race or gender.

Barnes most clearly advances the third argument we will consider, the self-report argument. However, we will begin with two other arguments, so the reader can see the various ways that one might support the mere-difference view.

Here is the outweighing argument:

(P1) Being disabled provides you goods that non-disabled people lack.

(P2) These goods counterbalance whatever bads are caused by the disability.

(P3) If having a disability isn't overall bad for you, then the mere-difference view is correct.

(C)   Therefore, the mere-difference view is correct.

> Before reading ahead, can you think of any benefits that might come along with having a disability?

In defense of (P1), having a disability might even cause you to lose some goods, like the ability to hear. However, it causes you to gain other goods, like enhancement of your other senses or the ability to be a part of the Deaf community. Barnes explains that *having a disability comes with numerous goods that might not be obvious to the non-disabled—in part because those without a disability don't experience them.*

For example, Eva Kittay (2015) discusses how her disability causes her to depend on other people. Someone might think this dependence is a bad thing—what if you required someone to push you in a wheelchair in order to get around? But for Kittay, this experience of depending on others is incredibly valuable to her, and it represents a positive aspect of having a disability (2015; Barnes 2016, 95). For example, maybe needing someone to push you in a wheelchair creates a close community of friends who are aware of each other's needs.

Rosemarie Garland Thomson (2012) discusses how having a disability expands what you can know and what you can experience. People with disabilities have access to unique knowledge and experiences that the non-disabled cannot have, and they find this valuable (Barnes 2016a, 95). Thus, while disability is associated with some losses, it is also associated with positive effects, many of which might not be obvious at first blush and cannot be experienced by those without a disability.

(P2) is hard to defend because it is difficult to consider all these goods and bads and then weigh them against each other. But the thought is this: there are a lot of positive effects associated with having a disability, many that the non-disabled aren't aware of until they actually speak to people with disabilities. There is good reason to think—especially once all these additional goods are considered—that for physical disabilities, *the goods balance out the negative aspects of having a disability*. For instance, the ancient Chinese philosopher Zhuangzi (Master Zhuang) talks about a man whose "chin is sunk in his belly." The man's shoulders are above his head with his thighs pressed against his ribs, and his organs are shifted to a different place. But this man provides for himself and is ineligible for military conscription. He ends up living far longer than he would have if he hadn't had the disability (see Altmann & Van Norden 2020). This example illustrates why having a disability may not be a bad thing overall. And, in fact, if the goods are particularly good and the bads aren't so bad, then having a disability might actually be a positive thing for a person.

Objection 1:

Against (P1), one might argue that many of the goods associated with having a disability are *ones that non-disabled people can have as well*. For example, can't you have enhanced senses or be a part of the Deaf community, even if you aren't disabled?

Reply:

Some of the goods associated with disability are ones *the non-disabled can't experience at all*, for instance, the unique knowledge and unique experience of being disabled discussed by Thomson. Other goods *the non-disabled can experience, but not to the same extent*. For example, the non-disabled can of course have friendships with those in the Deaf community. However, they won't participate in the Deaf community in the same way, because they will lack the bond and mutual understanding and experience that deaf people have with each other.

Objection 2:

Premise 2 doesn't take into account *the value of the important things that those with disabilities lack*. Consider a blind person who isn't able to see the faces of her loved ones. This is a significant loss, and it's hard to see how it is outweighed by something like enhanced hearing. Or consider the joy of listening to music; a deaf person cannot experience that. Once we see the goods that people with disabilities lack, it is hard to see how those goods could be outweighed.

Reply:

It is undeniable that some people with disabilities lack significant goods. However, the objection doesn't fully take into account the goods that are gained by having a disability. Consider the example of the blind person who cannot see the faces of her friends and family. Blind people acknowledge this is bad, but also discuss significant goods associated with being blind. For example, Kim Kilpatrick (2020) has an online journal called "Great Things About Being Blind." Here, she discusses a number of positive effects of blindness, including

- the fact that she cannot judge or stereotype others based on their physical appearance;
- the fact that she does not struggle with vanity or self-consciousness about how she looks; she is not tempted to constantly "check the mirror";
- the joy of learning and of using Braille; and
- the deep bond she has with her guide dog. (See also Barnes 2016a, 95, 157.)

And there are other goods besides these—she may know her family's voices much better than most, due to enhanced hearing; she may have close friends and mutual understanding within the blind community that she couldn't have experienced otherwise. While, again, not seeing her family's faces is surely a negative thing, it is not obvious that it couldn't be balanced by these other goods.

Objection 3:

Against (P3), this argument doesn't give us a reason to think that disability isn't bad in and of itself. Instead, *it merely says that the badness of disability could be balanced by other things.* In other words, this argument doesn't establish the mere-difference view; disability could still be intrinsically bad. Consider having cancer. Having cancer could lead to good effects: a new outlook on life, perseverance through difficulty, thankfulness for what one has, and other positive life changes. But that doesn't mean having cancer is a mere difference; it is clearly a bad difference.

Reply:

This objection helps us clarify the difference between the mere-difference view and the bad-difference view. A big question we need to think about is this: *What is essential to having a disability, and what is just accidentally a part of having a disability?*

 The reason that those in this debate set aside society's poor treatment of people with disabilities, for example, is because they assume that this poor treatment is not essential to having a disability—it is a sad fact about the society we live in, but things don't have to be that way.

That said, whether this argument successfully shows that disability is a mere difference comes down to the question, *Are the good and bad effects discussed above essential to having a disability?* Or do they just happen to be associated with it? And what is essential will depend on the disability in question. For example, the inability to see the faces of one's family is essentially associated with blindness, but so is the inability to judge others based on their physical appearance.

> What goods and bads discussed above are essential to having a disability? What ones simply happen to be associated with it? How would these essential goods and the essential bads weigh against each other?

3. The Adaption Argument

Let's now move on to a second argument for the mere-difference view, the adaption argument:

(P1)   People with disabilities can adapt to their disabilities.

(P2)   If people with disabilities can adapt to their disabilities, then the mere-difference view of disability is correct.

(C)   Therefore, the mere-difference view of disability is correct.

In defense of (P1), consider two types of disabilities: congenital and acquired. Congenital disabilities are present at birth. Acquired disabilities develop later in life. When it comes to congenital (physical) disabilities, there is good evidence that people adapt very well to them; the same goes for disabilities developed very early on, for example, as an infant or young child (Bowker and Michael 2002, chap. 28). If you are born without a limb, for example, you adapt quickly and often are able to live a flourishing life without it.

Adaption to disabilities acquired later in life is more difficult. Those who develop a disability later, for example, as an adult, may go through the five stages of grief: denial, anger, bargaining, depression, acceptance. Nonetheless, those with acquired disabilities are still often able to successfully adapt after a period of time, especially with help from friends and family, a therapist, and so on. There are also effective ways that they can cope with this change, including actively seeking help for problems they encounter, keeping their eyes on the future and making plans, and using humor.

To defend (P2), consider a quote from Harriet McBryde Johnson (2003), a disability activist. She is in a wheelchair due to a neuromuscular disease. She says, speaking of herself and others who are also disabled:

> Are we "worse off"? I don't think so. Not in any meaningful sense. There are too many variables. For those of us with congenital conditions,

disability shapes all we are. Those disabled later in life adapt. We take constraints that no one would choose and build rich and satisfying lives within them. We enjoy pleasures other people enjoy, and pleasures peculiarly our own. We have something the world needs.

This quote supports the idea that, because of their ability to adapt, people with disabilities often have the same levels of well-being as they would if they didn't have a disability, as the mere-difference view states. While, especially for those who are used to living without a disability, this may take time, having a disability ultimately doesn't prevent people from "living rich and satisfying lives," as Johnson says.

> Have you ever had to adapt to a big life change or new circumstance? Did you adapt successfully? Have you ever initially thought a life change was a bad difference, then later realized it was a mere difference?

Note that the requirement for adaption—and even treatments like therapy—doesn't automatically mean that disability makes people worse off. Many things that aren't bad for us require adaptation. Consider having a new baby. Those who become parents, especially for the first time, undergo serious adaptation to a major life change. This doesn't mean that having a child is bad for their well-being. Or think about moving across the country or undergoing a career change. While adjusting to a new lifestyle might be hard at first, once you adjust, your well-being can be just as good as—if not better—than it was before the change.

Objection 1:

Against (P1), some people who have a disability might adapt. However, *this does not mean that all adapt.* As we noted above, age matters—the younger you are when you get the disability, the easier it is to adapt. Family and community also matter—those with a family have an easier time adapting than those who are single or widowed. The elderly often have an especially difficult time adapting to newly acquired disabilities (Bowker and Michael 2002, chap. 28). Thus, while this premise might be true for some people in some situations, it isn't true for all disabilities.

Reply 1:

Recall that we are only focusing on physical disabilities. The defender of the mere-difference view only claims that physical disabilities are mere differences. The argument may not apply to other kinds of disabilities.

Reply 2:

Some of the bad effects of disability, or reasons that people have trouble adapting, might not come from the disability itself, but other factors in someone's life. If someone does not have a loving family or supportive community, their life will likely be hard, whether or not they have a disability. So this objection is only successful if it can show that the disability itself is the negative difference maker, rather than these other features of someone's life.

Objection 2:

Against (P2), *adaption is not always desirable or admirable.* Successfully adapting to some life change doesn't mean your life is good. Consider hoarders, who acquire unhealthy amounts of stuff and refuse to get rid of it. They adapt to their cluttered, dirty, and dangerous environment, and they often claim that they are totally fine and even happy with the way they live. However, they are clearly worse off, living in dirt, trash, and mess. Or consider an abused woman, who adapts to her husband's frequent beatings. She might even have Stockholm syndrome, a disorder in which a victim feels trust and affection toward their abuser. She might claim that she has adapted and is doing fine, but clearly she is in a terrible situation.

Reply:

It is true that adaption is not always desirable or admirable. However, the objection does not give us reason to think that having a disability is more like being abused or being a hoarder than it is like becoming a parent or changing jobs. Many things require adaptation; some are difficult changes, but some are neutral.

Reply to the reply:

Still, the objection shows that the ability to adapt to some change doesn't entail that the change involves mere difference. Thus, this argument does not successfully establish the mere-difference view.

> Do you think this objection ultimately undermines the adaption argument? Why or why not?

4. The Self-Report Argument

Now we will turn to a third argument for the mere-difference view. This argument is defended by Barnes (2014, 2016a). She says: "What I am going to argue . . . is that the testimony of disabled people gives us good reason to think that *disability functions like gayness and maleness with respect to well-being. It is, by itself, neutral*" (2016a, 90; emphasis ours). Barnes also states that "personal testimony of disabled people who report a positive experience of disability, even in our actual, non-ideal social context, is found along a wide spectrum of what some might call the 'severity' of disability" (102). This suggests the self-report argument:

(P1) People with disabilities self-report happiness and satisfaction, and often say they wouldn't prevent their disability if they had the choice.

(P2) If so, people with disabilities view themselves as merely different, and not badly different.

(P3) We ought to trust self-reports of well-being over the opinion of outside observers.

(C)   Therefore, the mere-difference view of disability is correct.

> Do you think this is a strong argument for the mere-difference view? If not, which premise would you deny?

(P1) is supported by stories—and data—about disabled people. We've discussed a few already: recall Kim Kilpatrick's list of things that are great about being blind and Harriet McBryde Johnson's quote about how disabled people can build rich and satisfying lives via adaptation. Barnes (2016a) mentions a number of similar stories.

She talks about Dostoevsky, the famous Russian novelist. He had severe epilepsy and dealt with intense and unpredictable seizures most of his adult life. But he also said this about his experience before having a seizure:

> For several instants I experience a happiness that is impossible in an ordinary state, and of which other people have no conception. I feel full harmony in myself and in the whole world, and the feeling is so strong and sweet that for a few seconds of such bliss one could give up ten years of life, perhaps all of life.
>
> I felt that heaven descended to earth and swallowed me. I really attained God and was imbued with him. All of you healthy people don't even suspect what happiness is, that happiness that we epileptics experience for a second before an attack. (Quoted in Tammet 2007, 43)

Barnes also discusses Sarah Eyre, a writer who has multiple sclerosis (MS), a disease in which the nervous system eats away at the protective covering of nerves, causing fatigue, loss of vision, severe pain, and impaired coordination. Yet a piece where Eyre describes her experience is titled "A Few Awesome Things About Being Disabled" (2012).

(P1) isn't supported not only by specific stories but also by data. For an overview of this research, Barnes highly recommends Bagenstos and Schlanger (2007). They summarize their findings as "a massive body of research has demonstrated that people who acquire a range of disabilities typically do not experience much or any permanent reduction in the enjoyment of life" (763). So (P1) isn't only true of a few stories; it is supported by a large body of research.

(P2) says that the above stories and data mean that disabled people see themselves as *merely different, not badly different*. If disabled people do not want to prevent or change their disability, this is good evidence that they see their disability as a mere difference. They don't see their disability as a horrible, traumatic thing—even a horrible thing that has resulted in some good, like the cancer survivor. They see their disability as a unique, defining feature about them—not something that makes them worse off.

(P3) states that we should trust the testimony of individuals about their own well-being, rather than the opinion of outside observers. This especially applies when the people in question all have a unique feature that may be hard for those on the outside to understand. Barnes (2016a) puts it this way: "The non-disabled appear to be bad at predicting the impact of disability on the disabled, and tend to systematically overestimate the bad effects of disability on perceived well-being and happiness" (71). This is also supported by scientific research; Barnes recommends George Loewenstein and David Schkade (1999) for an overview of such research.

Thinking about disability as similar to race or gender might help. Suppose we are trying to evaluate the well-being of women who work for a particular company. The men at the company claim that the women are doing just fine, and that they are just as well-off as the men. The women disagree and claim that they have had bad experiences in the company and don't enjoy working there. Whose opinion should we trust? It seems like we should give the women's testimony more weight than the men's testimony. First, people are often more aware of their own well-being than outside observers. Second, the women share a key common trait that is not shared by the men—they are women! It makes sense that since the women have a unique experience and perspective, they might have evidence about their own well-being that the men can't access.

In the same way, *even if non-disabled people say that it is obviously worse to have a disability, we should give more weight to what disabled people say about themselves.* The non-disabled have never known what it is like to have a disability, and this is a good reason to think that they lack evidence that is crucial to understanding disability.

> Can you think of any cases when we should trust outside observers more than we trust people's self-reports?

Objection 1:

Against (P2), do people with disabilities really think their disability is a mere difference? They might think that having a disability isn't as bad as the non-disabled assume. But they still might think it is *slightly* worse to have a disability. Generally, both (P1) and (P2) rest on empirical claims that are difficult to evaluate.

Reply:

As mentioned briefly above, *lots of studies have actually been done to support both (P1) and (P2)*, including Loewenstein and Schkade (1999) and Bagenstos and Schlanger (2007). (See Barnes 2016a for a summary of these studies and more.)

Here are some more specific examples. Surveys showed no statistically significant difference between self-assessed well-being in patients with severe mobility disabilities and a non-disabled control group (Stensman 1985). In another study, 74 percent of paralyzed patients rated themselves as 'happy', and those who didn't attributed their unhappiness not to their disability in and of itself, but to things that aren't essential to having a disability, like their daily activities and assistance (Bruno et al. 2011).

Researchers also found that "the strongest correlations with health-related quality of life appear to be patient rated emotional adjustment to illness and patient rated handicap." "Patient rated handicap" is a person's perception of their own limitations, which is often affected by emotional and social factors, and not a patient's objective physical state (Benito-León et al. 2003).

Further, studies show that quality of life for MS patients is correlated with their experiences of depression, rather than the extent of their physical impairment. These same studies also show that depression and degree of physical impairment are not correlated with each other (Lobentanz et al. 2004).

Finally—and interestingly—researchers found that those with partial but diminished vision had more frustration and less life satisfaction than those who were completely blind (Roy and MacKay 2002). This again shows that there is no connection between the degree or severity of a disability and self-reported well-being.

Objection 2:

Against (P1), what about disabled people who are in chronic pain? It is hard to believe that these people "wouldn't prevent their disability if they had the choice." And then (P2) would not follow, because living a life of chronic pain doesn't seem like a mere difference.

Reply:

Recall again that Barnes focuses on physical disabilities. Mental disabilities, especially those associated with chronic pain, aren't a part of Barnes's argument.

Reply to the reply:

Some physical disabilities are associated with chronic pain. Rheumatoid arthritis is the swelling and inflammation of the joints—a physical disability. However, it is highly correlated with chronic pain; in fact, researchers often identify inflammation through patients' experiences of chronic pain (see Lee 2013).

> Sometimes painful activities lead to an increase in well-being—for example, an intense, painful workout. Is it plausible that, even if some physically disabled people experience chronic pain, this bad is outweighed by other goods?

Objection 3:

Against (P3), if someone is born with a disability, it's not clear that their testimony should be trusted over someone who has never had a disability. In both cases, the person hasn't experienced both states (disability and non-disability). Since they've only experienced one, they can't make a fully informed judgment about which state is better in terms of well-being.

Reply:

This might be right. Fortunately, we have testimony from people with *acquired* disabilities that confirms the first two premises. For example, Bagenstos and Schlanger (2007) surveyed the research on people with acquired disabilities, and found that they "typically do not experience much or any permanent reduction in the enjoyment of life" (763).

Here's one specific example. Barnes (2016a, 97) discusses the story of Rebecca Atkinson, a woman who slowly lost her sight as an adult. She experienced a non-disabled life for a while at first, and then she experienced many degrees of blindness. At one point, she was presented with the possibility of regaining her sight and felt conflicted about it. She said, "If this experiment of going blind has taught me anything, it's that what you lose in one place you gain elsewhere, and while a blind life is different than a sighted life, it is not lesser" (Atkinson 2007).

Objection 4:

Against (P3), *people can be wrong about their own well-being.* Consider again the example of the abused woman. If she has Stockholm syndrome—a disorder where a victim feels trust or affection to their abuser—she might insist that she is happy being with her husband. She might say that while he is a tough man, he is good to her and provides for her, so she wants to stay with him. In this case, she has been so mistreated that she is confused about her own well-being. She is wrong about what is good for her, and we should *not* trust her testimony over that of outside observers.

Philosophers talk about a related idea called **adaptive preferences**. Adaptive preferences occur when we *irrationally change our preferences to cope with a situation that is not ideal.* Some of you might remember the old fable about the fox and the "sour" grapes. A fox is walking along and sees some grapes that look yummy, but they are high up on a tree. The fox really wants to eat the grapes. He tries and tries, but he cannot reach the grapes; they are too high. He then changes his preference: he says to himself, "I don't want those grapes anyway, because they are probably sour." This expresses an adaptive preference: the fox irrationally decides he doesn't want them—probably to avoid sadness or disappointment— but he doesn't have good reason to make this change.

> Can you think of other examples of adaptive preferences?

Someone might argue that when people with disabilities testify that they are merely different, they are expressing an adaptive preference to cope with a non-ideal situation. However, they are wrong about their own well-being. Thus, (P3) is false; we should not trust the testimony of those with disabilities over outside observers.

Reply:

Adaptive preferences are irrational. However, *changing one's preferences because of one's circumstances can be rational.* Consider a child who dreamed for many years to be a famous opera singer. This child may, for a long time, strongly desire that career. However, as the child grows older, he realizes that he isn't a great singer and being an opera singer just isn't a realistic career for him. Other career options better fit his talents, so he changes his career preference (Nussbaum 2001).

The would-be opera singer, unlike the abused wife and the fox, doesn't seem irrational. In fact, it would be weird if people never changed their preferences in response to their circumstances. While it is hard to perfectly draw the line between rational and irrational cases of preference change, one suggestion is that *this change is rational when it fits well with our other rational beliefs and rational desires.* The fox is irrational because he forms an irrational belief without evidence—that the grapes are sour—in order to justify his preference. However, changing your preference about becoming an opera singer isn't irrational because this fits your evidence—you just aren't a good singer.

People with disabilities, then, may change their preferences in light of their circumstances. In fact, this might be what the adaption argument above describes—they learn to adapt to their disability. While their disability might force them to give up old passions or hobbies, it might also cause them to develop new ones that, eventually, are just as valuable to them. For example, someone who becomes injured and has to permanently use a wheelchair has to give up running, but they may develop a passion for wheelchair sports. And it is not at all obvious that this new preference is irrational. In general, it's hard to see why people with disabilities are more similar to the fox than to the would-be opera singer. Barnes (2016a, chap. 4) provides a more extensive argument that the preferences of disabled people aren't adaptive in an irrational way. Thus, (P3) stands.

> After reading this chapter, do you think the mere-difference view is plausible? Why or why not? Which argument for the mere-difference view did you think was the best? Which did you think was the worst?

5. Conclusion

We've seen three arguments for the view that disabilities make people different, but not worse off: the outweighing argument, the adaption argument, and the self-report argument. Even with these arguments, you probably still have some questions about the mere-difference view. For example: if disabilities are mere differences, wouldn't it be okay to allow—or even cause—someone to have a disability? This question inspires several of the arguments for the bad-difference view we'll examine in the next chapter.

Further Reading

The mere-difference view is defended by Barnes (2014; 2016a). Objections to the mere-difference view are raised by McMahan (2005), Kahane (2009), and Kahane and Savulescu (2016). See Barnes (2016b) for a reply to many of these objections. Views that fall in between the mere-difference view and the bad-difference view are defended by Andrić and Wündisch (2015) and Campbell and Stramondo (2017). Books and readers on the philosophy of disability include Nussbaum (2006), Davis (2006), and Kristiansen et al. (2009).

Chapter 19
The Bad-Difference View

1. Introduction

Thus far, we have talked about the definition of disability and discussed arguments for the mere-difference view of disability. In this chapter, we discuss arguments for the bad-difference view of disability, along with—you guessed it!—objections and replies.

As a reminder, two views of the relationship between **disability** and **well-being** are the

1. **bad-difference view:** having a disability is bad in and of itself (even if there were no discrimination against people with disabilities); and
2. **mere-difference view:** having a disability makes you physically non-standard, but it is not bad in and of itself.

There is a third view we haven't discussed yet. This is the **good-difference view:** being disabled is intrinsically good because it contributes to someone's well-being. Those who have disabilities are *better off* than those who don't have disabilities.

We aren't aware of any philosophers—or non-philosophers—who defend this view. It might strike some readers as even more surprising than the mere-difference view. So let's set that view aside. If we don't consider that view, then the mere-difference view and the bad-difference view are the only two live options about the relationship between disability and well-being.

In that case, if we can prove that one view is false, then we have good reason to think that the other view is true. This is what many of the arguments for the bad-difference view try to do—they try to show that the mere-difference view is false. More specifically, they use a philosophical tool called a **reductio ad absurdum**, or 'reductio' for short.

A reductio shows that a view is false by first assuming that it is true. Then, it shows that *if* that view is true, it leads to an unacceptable—or *absurd*—conclusion. Some reductios even show that the view leads to a **contradiction:** a claim that is internally inconsistent, and therefore cannot be correct, because it implies that something must be both true and false at the same time. (For instance, "it is raining and it is not raining" is a contradictory statement.) Either way, the view we initially assumed must be false.

Here are some examples. Suppose your friend claims the Earth is flat. You might use a reductio to argue against your friend's claim. Let's assume that the Earth is flat. What about all of those who have traveled around the world, by boat or plane, and ended up where they left off without turning around? That view would mean they are all lying. It would also mean that airlines are involved in some grand conspiracy and hiding it from the rest of us. It would also mean that the pictures of the Earth from space are faked. Why would people put the time and effort into faking them?

You could even argue that if the Earth is flat, this, together with other things we know to be true, leads to a contradiction. If the Earth were flat, you would be able to see Mauna Kea (the tallest peak in the Hawaiian Islands) from Kawaikini (the seventh tallest peak in the Hawaiian Islands), which is only 303 miles away. In fact, you cannot see Mauna Kea from Kawaikini. So the view that the Earth is flat, together with something else we know to be true, leads to the contradictory claim that you both can and can't see Mauna Kea from Kawaikini. But that can't be right. Therefore, the Earth is not flat. Since a flat Earth leads to both many unacceptable conclusions and a contradiction, the Earth is not flat.

Reductios are also frequently used in mathematics. For example, you can use a reductio to show that there is no smallest positive rational number. (A rational number is a number that can be represented as a fraction.) Let's assume there is a smallest rational number. We can take that number and divide it in half to get an even smaller rational number. So the original number both is and is not the smallest rational number. This is a contradiction, so we should reject the assumption we began with—that there is a smallest rational number.

> How would you use a reductio to argue that Instagram is better than Facebook? How would you use a reductio to argue that people have free will?

All six arguments in this chapter are reductio ad absurdums. *They assume that disability is a mere difference, then show that this leads to an absurd result.* A defender of the mere-difference view will then object that either the mere-difference view doesn't lead to the absurd result or that the result isn't as absurd as we thought.

Several authors, including Peter Singer (2001) and Jeff McMahan (2005), defend the bad-difference view and endorse versions of the arguments we explain below. In this chapter, we will focus mainly on arguments for the bad-difference view given by Guy Kahane and Julian Savulescu (Kahane 2009; Kahane and Savulescu 2016)—but near the end of the chapter, we also consider an argument from McMahan. After each argument, we'll consider objections and replies before moving on to the next argument.

2. The Causing Disability Argument

We start with the causing disability argument; this argument is made by Kahane and Savulescu (2016, 778):

(P1)   If disability is a mere difference, then it is permissible to cause disability.

(P2)   It is not permissible to cause disability.

(C)   Therefore, disability is not a mere difference; it is a bad difference.

(P1) is supported by the idea that if something is a mere difference, it's often permissible to change it, since that change won't make someone worse off. Consider hair color. Having blonde hair versus red hair is a mere difference. Further, most of us think that dyeing your hair isn't morally wrong. Same with painting your nails, tanning, and even more serious changes, like a career change.

> Is it permissible to change *anything* that's a mere difference? Can you think of situations where it would be morally wrong to change a mere difference?

(P2) says that it is not permissible to cause a disability. To support this premise, consider two cases from Elizabeth Barnes (2014):

> 1. Amy and her nondisabled friend Ben work in a lab. After hours one day, they are playing around with lasers. Ben is not wearing any protective eyewear, and Amy knows that if she directs the laser beam at his eyes he is at risk of permanent vision loss. Nevertheless, *Amy does not take any precautions to avoid directing the beam at Ben's eyes. Ben becomes permanently blind.* When Ben confronts Amy angrily about what she has done, Amy explains that she hasn't done anything wrong. It's not any worse to be disabled than to be nondisabled. So while she has made Ben a minority with respect to sight, she hasn't made him any worse off. (95; emphasis ours)

> 2. Cara has a six-month-old baby, Daisy. Cara values disability and thinks that disability is an important part of human diversity. Moreover, she thinks that increasing the number of happy, well-adjusted, well-educated disabled people is an important part of combating ableism (and has a justified belief that any child she raises has a good chance of ending up happy, well adjusted, and well educated). With all this in mind *Cara has Daisy undergo an innovative new pro-disability procedure. Daisy doesn't endure any pain from this, and she won't remember it. But as a result, Daisy will be disabled for the rest of her life.* (97; emphasis ours)

Cara and Amy both have done something seriously wrong. Making your friend permanently blind with a laser and making your child disabled (even if the process is painless) are morally wrong things to do. Thus, it is wrong to cause someone to be disabled.

This completes the reductio ad absurdum argument. *If the mere-difference view implies that causing disability is okay, then we should reject the mere-difference view.*

Objection 1:

Against (P1), Barnes (2014) argues that *simply because something is a mere difference doesn't mean it is permissible to cause it.* It is often wrong to interfere in other's lives, even if our interference doesn't make people worse off. If you could push a button and change someone's race or gender, it would be wrong for you to do so, even though race and gender are mere differences.

Barnes (2014) puts it this way: "We'd be inclined to say that Amy does something wrong if she carelessly (and permanently) turns Ben's hair from brown to blonde, if she carelessly (and permanently) changes Ben's height by a few inches, and so forth. Such changes aren't particularly substantial and aren't likely to make Ben worse off in the long run" (95). So (P1) is false.

Reply 1:

What if *Ben consents* to Amy's interfering? It seems okay for Amy to permanently change Ben's hair color or height with Ben's consent (maybe she's his hair stylist), but not okay for Amy to make Ben disabled, even if he consents.

> Do you agree that it is wrong for Amy to cause Ben to be disabled, even if he wants her to? Would it be wrong for Amy to cause *herself* to be disabled? Why or why not?

Reply to the reply:

Consent doesn't always mean it is okay to interfere with another's life. If someone wants you to help them engage in self-harm, or commit suicide, you should not do it, even though they consent.

Reply to the reply to the reply:

Self-harm and suicide aren't mere differences. Plausibly, if something is a mere difference, and if the person consents to having it changed, then it is permissible to cause that change. However, even if someone consents to becoming disabled, it still seems wrong for you to cause them to be disabled.

> Can you think of situations where (i) something is a mere difference and (ii) someone wants it changed, but it is still wrong to cause the change? Would it be wrong to change someone's gender if they consented to it? What about changing their race?

Reply 2:

This objection only shows that, in some cases (e.g., if there's no consent), mere differences shouldn't be caused. But, as Kahane and Savulescu (2016, 780) point out, it doesn't show it is wrong to change all mere differences in ourselves and others. So *the mere-difference view still seems to imply that it is okay to cause some disabilities*. For example, it seems okay to change mere differences in yourself. If this is right, then given the mere-difference view, it would be okay to cause *yourself* to be disabled.

Objection 2:

Let's focus on the case of Cara causing her baby Daisy to be disabled. Barnes (2014) says that, for this case, (P1) is also false. This case is different from the case of Amy and Ben because it involves a child who cannot consent, so Barnes says the interference in the child's life is wrong. She says, "Our reaction to [this case] can be justified by (and explained as a species of) these noninterference principles, rather than anything specific to disability" (98). Thus, the interference is wrong, but it isn't wrong because Cara is causing a *disability* in particular.

Reply:

If that's correct, then we should have similar intuitions about other cases of interfering. Kahane and Savulescu (2016) argue that we don't. "Few would think that removing disability from a fetus is as wrong as causing a male fetus to become female, or causing a fetus's hair color to change from red to brown, let alone causing an abled fetus to become disabled" (779). If the *interference* is what is wrong, then it would be just as wrong to remove a disability as it is to cause a disability. But these interferences aren't the same: removing a disability is permissible, if not required, and causing a disability is wrong. This is evidence that the interference itself isn't the problem.

> Barnes (2014) notes that "we think it is perfectly permissible—indeed, we think it is **morally required**—for parents to interfere with their children's development, including their physical development. Parents make choices about education, diet, health care—all sorts of things that have a dramatic effect on a child's development" (98). Do you agree? If so, why do you think some interferences seem fine, but others seem bad?

3. Preventing Disability Argument

There is a second, related, argument against the mere-difference view that is also discussed by both Barnes (2014) and Kahane and Savulescu (2016). Instead of causing disability, this argument focuses on *preventing* disability:

(P1) If disability is a mere difference, then it is permissible to fail to prevent disability.

(P2) It is not permissible to fail to prevent disability.

(C) Therefore, disability is not a mere difference; it is a bad difference.

(P1) is supported by the idea that if something is a mere difference, then we aren't required to interfere to change it. This is even more plausible than premise 1 from the causing disability argument. If you find out your child will be a girl, then it's permissible to not interfere with your child's gender, since being a girl isn't better than being a boy. Similar considerations apply to race, hair color, and other facts about people that are clearly mere differences. This premise is hard to deny.

> Can you think of any situations where we *should* interfere with something, even though it is a mere difference?

(P2) is true because we should do what we can—within reason—to prevent disabilities. Consider several examples. Suppose your friend gets into a car accident and, as a result, will lose a leg if they aren't sent to the hospital immediately. You could easily call 911 and have the ambulance there in time. But you decide not to, and they lose their leg. It seems like you've done something seriously wrong.

Kahane and Savulescu (2016) provide some additional examples:

> If someone unknowingly puts herself at great risk of becoming disabled, and a bystander who could prevent this does nothing, no issue of unconsented interference arises. Similarly, if a natural process is about to preventably turn an abled fetus disabled, noninterference, if it implies anything, implies that we should do nothing. These are implications that many will find unacceptable: many think it would be deeply wrong to let an abled fetus become disabled via a natural process (while thinking it would be good if a similar process operated in the reverse direction). (780)

In other words, *if we can prevent disabilities—in unborn children, in our friends who have gotten into accidents, and so on—we ought to.* Consider a final case from Barnes (2014):

> Cara has a six-month-old baby, Daisy, who is disabled. Cara values Daisy's happiness and well-being. Moreover, she thinks that Daisy will have a better chance of being happy, well adjusted, and well educated if she is nondisabled. With all this in mind Cara puts Daisy through a radical new treatment for infant disability. Daisy doesn't endure much pain from this, and she won't remember it. But as a result, Daisy will grow up nondisabled. (99)

This interference seems justified. If Cara can interfere to painlessly remove Daisy's disability, she should. And it's hard to see why this would be true if disabilities are mere differences.

Objection 1:

One might argue that (P1) is false because *becoming* disabled is different than *being* disabled. In the car accident example, you should still call 911 for your friend because becoming disabled is bad for your friend.

Why would becoming disabled be bad, if being disabled is not? The answer is *transition costs*. Barnes (2014) explains:

> Advocates of the mere-difference view think that being disabled is not, by itself, a harm. But there's a big difference between being disabled and becoming disabled. Many people find being disabled a rewarding and good thing. But there is an almost universal experience for those who acquire disability—variously called adaptive process or transition costs—of great pain and difficulty associated with becoming disabled. However happy and well-adjusted a disabled person ends up, the process of becoming disabled is almost universally a difficult one. (96)

Many mere differences come with high transition costs. Consider forcing someone into a new job or forcing them to adopt a child. Even though doing a different job or having a child are mere differences, there still might be significant costs associated with adapting to such a big change. Thus, even on the mere-difference view of disability, you should still do what you can to prevent people from becoming disabled, due to transition costs.

Reply:

Not all disability involves transition costs. Consider making a young child disabled, who would never know the difference. There are no transition costs, but it is still wrong to cause the child to be disabled.

This brings us to a second objection, meant to deal with cases that don't involve transition costs.

Objection 2:

Barnes (2014) suggests that, in some cases without transition costs, we still have reason to prevent disabilities because of *potential risk*. She explains how this risk might apply in the case of Cara and Daisy:

> If Cara causes Daisy to be disabled, Daisy may well grow up to be a happy, well-adjusted disabled person. But she may not. She may resent her disability, wish to be nondisabled, and be unhappy as a result. Conversely, if Cara causes Daisy to be nondisabled, Daisy is unlikely to grow up resenting her lack of disability or wishing to be disabled. And if Cara refrains from causing Daisy to be nondisabled, Daisy may well resent that choice. Causing Daisy to be disabled is *riskier* than causing Daisy to be nondisabled. (99; emphasis ours)

Barnes thus suggests that Cara should intervene because allowing Daisy to be disabled is too risky, and there's a chance Daisy might resent Cara for not intervening.

Reply:

Why is this interference risky if the mere-difference view is true?

Reply to the reply:

The interference is risky because Cara may experience ablism and discrimination if she grows up disabled.

Reply to the reply to the reply:

If discrimination and ablism are the only reasons that Cara's intervention is risky, then the mere-difference view seems to mean that Cara should not interfere to prevent Daisy's disability in a non-discriminatory society. It would also mean that, in a society without discrimination, interfering to cause disability and interfering to prevent disability are morally the same. But both of those things seem false.

> Are there reasons besides discrimination, consistent with the mere-difference view, that this interference might be risky?

Objection 3:

Against (P2), it is actually permissible to fail to prevent disability. Barnes (2014) says, "We shouldn't cause a child who would otherwise grow up to be disabled to instead grow up to be nondisabled. Doing so would be unjustified interference and could reasonably be said to communicate ableism" (103).

Reply:

Really? So Cara shouldn't prevent Daisy from being disabled, even if she can do so easily and painlessly?

Reply to the reply:

Barnes admits that many will have a strong intuition that failing to prevent disability seems wrong. However, she also thinks that we shouldn't trust many of our intuitions about disability. This is because we live in an ableist society that frequently discriminates against people with disabilities. This shapes our perception of what it is like to have a disability. If we listened to the testimony of people with disabilities about their experiences, we would realize that some of our intuitions are confused and wrong.

> Do you agree that we shouldn't trust some of our intuitions about disability? If so, how do we pick which ones to trust and which ones to disregard?

4. The Cure Argument

Another reductio of the mere-difference view is called the cure argument. Barnes (2014) explains, and ultimately rejects, the cure argument:

(P1) If disability is a mere difference, then we should not try to develop a cure for disability.

(P2) We should try to develop a cure for disability.

(C)   Therefore, disability is not a mere difference; it is a bad difference.

(P1) seems true because if something is a mere difference, it doesn't make sense to try to find a cure for it. We don't need a cure for being a woman or for having red hair. Barnes (2014) says, "If a scientist is working hard on a 'cure' for gayness, we think she is doing something dystopian and horrible. We shun her from the academic community and take away her support infrastructure. We hope she fails miserably" (109).

(P2) seems true because it seems permissible—and even good—to try to find cures for disabilities. Barnes (2014) explains, "If a scientist is working hard to develop a 'cure' for blindness, we say she is doing something good and praiseworthy. We give her grant money and government support. We hope she succeeds" (109).

Objection 1:

Barnes does not like the word 'cure'; this language does not fit well with the mere-difference view. But a cure essentially lets people have control over whether they are disabled—if someone is disabled but does not want to be, it allows them to become non-disabled. And Barnes thinks that working to develop this kind of medical technology isn't a bad thing. So (P1) is false—even if the mere-difference view is true, medical technology that gives us more control and autonomy is good.

Reply:

Does this mean it is equally good to develop technology that *causes* people to be disabled? Can the mere-difference view explain why technology that prevents disabilities seems good, but technology that causes disabilities seems bad?

Objection 2:

Barnes (2014) also thinks we have reason to doubt (P2). While the ability to control whether one has a disability isn't necessarily a bad thing overall,

> Many of us might think that technology that prevents disabilities is good and technology that causes disabilities is bad. But do you think this might be another place where we should not trust our intuitions about disability (especially if we've never had a disability)?

Barnes thinks that working to develop this in our discriminatory world may be dangerous and make ableism worse. She explains,

> There's nothing wrong with disabled people wanting to be nondisabled. And there's nothing wrong with those disabled people who want to be nondisabled seeking the means to make themselves nondisabled. But *there is something wrong with the expectation that becoming nondisabled is the ultimate hope in the lives of disabled people and their families.* Such an expectation makes it harder for disabled people—who in other circumstances might be perfectly happy with their disability—to accept what their bodies are like, and it makes it less likely that society's ableism will change. It is hard to accept and be happy with a disabled body if the expectation is that you should wish, hope, and strive for some mechanism to turn that disabled body into a nondisabled body. And it is unlikely that society will change its norms to accommodate disability if society can instead change disabled people in a way that conforms them to its extant norms. (111; emphasis ours)

She also explains how people with disabilities themselves often object to (P2). They dislike an obsession with finding a cure for disability, preferring that more time, effort, and resources be put into accessibility and fighting ableism. Thus, (P2) might be true in an ideal world, but we have reason to think that focusing on finding a cure for disability is a bad thing for our society.

5. The Aid Argument

It seems that people with disabilities should be helped or aided in a special way. Even in a society *without* ableism, we should aid those with disabilities. This suggests another argument that disability is a bad difference, rather than a mere difference, the aid argument:

(P1) If disability is a mere difference, then people with disabilities should *not* be aided for their disabilities.

(P2) People with disabilities should be aided for their disabilities.

(C)   Therefore, disability is not a mere difference; it is a bad difference.

(P1) seems true because it is hard to see why people with disabilities should be given special aid or accommodation if disability is a mere difference. Other mere differences, like having red hair or being tall, don't seem like ones people should be accommodated for. If disability is just a way of being physically different—a type of human diversity that should be celebrated—then it's not clear why there should be special government funding for those with disabilities or for parents with disabled children.

(P2) seems true because it seems like government programs to help those with disabilities are good. Given that they lack certain abilities, it seems morally just to compensate them in some way—whether this is through public or private funds. It seems like we owe something special to those with disabilities.

Objection 1:

The obvious objection to (P1) is that society is ableist. People with disabilities should be aided because society discriminates against people with disabilities. If there were no discrimination, no aid would be needed. In the same way that there are racial reparations for the past treatment of Black people and Native Americans in the United States, there should be aid for those with disabilities because of discrimination.

Reply:

It seems like aid of people with disabilities is appropriate, even if society were fully accommodating of people with disabilities. Even in a completely accessible society, it still seems just to give disabled people special help, financially or otherwise.

Reply to the reply:

In a society without ableism, aid might still be appropriate—to make up for the ways a group of people have been wronged in the past. However, in an imaginary society that never discriminated against people with disabilities at any point, aid of the disabled would not be appropriate.

> Do you think it would be morally good to compensate people with disabilities, even in a society that has always been fully accommodating of people with disabilities? If so, do you think this supports the bad-difference view?

6. The Multiple-Disabilities Argument

A final argument for the bad-difference view is given by Jeff McMahan (2005). McMahan asks us to consider *someone with not one, but multiple disabilities*. He explains that

> if disabilities were individually entirely neutral, they ought also to be neutral in combination; but they are not. If, to take the most extreme case, we consider all the abilities whose absence is regarded as a disability and imagine a human individual who lacks them all, it would be impossible to believe that that individual's life would not be worse than

the lives of most others—or that it might be worse but only because of social discrimination and lack of adequate social accommodation. (96)

One way to formalize the multiple-disabilities argument is as follows:

(P1) If disability is a mere difference, then, all else being equal, someone with multiple disabilities would have the same well-being as someone who is not disabled.

(P2) Even with all else being equal, someone with multiple disabilities would *not* have the same well-being as someone who is not disabled.

(C) Therefore, disability is not a mere difference; it is a bad difference.

(P1) means that if having a single disability is neutral and doesn't take away from well-being, then having multiple disabilities would be neutral too. "All else being equal" means you don't change other things about their life—so the person with multiple disabilities doesn't have a less supportive family or less money, for example. It's hard to see how disabilities could be individually neutral but bad in combination. *If one disability is neutral, then several disabilities put together should also be neutral.*

(P2) seems true because if you take a non-disabled person, don't change anything else about their life, but simply give them multiple disabilities, their life seems worse. Imagine a person who is deaf and blind, missing multiple limbs, has dwarfism, MS, and arthritis. It is hard to believe that they are merely different compared to someone with no disability at all.

> Before reading ahead, how would you object to this argument? Which premise would you deny?

Objection 1:

Premise 1 is false because, sometimes, when we add things together, the overall value can't be determined by the value of the individual things. In other words, "the whole is greater than the sum of its parts." Here are three examples.

1. You might really like chocolate. You might also really like corn on the cob. But that doesn't mean you will like chocolate-covered corn on the cob. Sometimes, putting two good things together leads to something gross or bad.

2. A person being locked in a cage is a bad thing. Being a murderer is also a bad thing. However, as we discussed in the chapters

on punishment, many people think that punishing murderers by putting them in jail is a good thing—because they deserve it or because it prevents future murders.

3.   If you are hiking the woods, trying to find your way back home, not knowing where you are on a map is bad and being confused about which direction is north on the map is bad. But if you're wrong about where you are on the map and which direction is north, you may end up in the right place.

Therefore, just because two disabilities are neutral by themselves doesn't mean "putting them together" in a single person is also neutral. Sometimes, when we add things together into a new whole, their value changes.

Reply 1:

Maybe some wholes have value that doesn't come from just adding up the value of the parts. However, why does this apply to the case of disability? It's not obvious why two neutral disabilities would be worse when put together.

Reply 2:

It's not obvious that this reply fully supports the mere-difference view. It is just the view that disabilities are *individually* neutral, but are bad differences when put together. This seems to concede a lot to the bad-difference view; many defenders of the mere-difference view will not be happy with this.

Objection 2:

Both (P1) and (P2) compare someone with a disability and someone without a disability "all else equal." In other words, they want to hold everything about someone's life fixed and only change their disability. However, it's impossible to do this; having a disability is such a fundamental part of someone's identity that you can't simply remove or add a disability without changing a lot of other things. Barnes (2016) puts it this way:

> Why think it's possible, for example, to hold fixed someone's personal and social circumstances while removing their disability? Thinking that it is possible seems to rely on an overly medicalized view of a disability. If disability is not just a physical condition—if it's also a social identity— then it's not clear we could, in any meaningful sense, remove a person's disability but hold their important social and personal circumstances fixed. (66)

So the problem with the argument is that we can't compare having a disability to not having a disability holding everything else equal. Thus, we don't have reason to believe that either premise is true.

Reply:

If we can't compare having a disability to not having a disability, then it's hard to see how we could make a decision between the bad-difference and mere-difference views at all. If the objection is right, then it seems like disability wouldn't be a bad difference *or* a mere difference; there would just be two states that are impossible to compare in terms of well-being. So this objection actually creates a problem for both views.

> After reading this chapter, do you think the bad-difference view is plausible? Why or why not? Which argument for the bad-difference view did you think was the best? Which did you think was the worst?

7. Conclusion

We've now seen several arguments for the bad-difference view. But note that, even if disability is a bad difference, we should still do our best to fight prejudice and discrimination against people with disabilities. We should encourage society to accommodate people with disabilities and do what we can to make their lives better or easier, to make our world a more accommodating place. So everyone in this debate—including the most passionate advocates of the bad-difference view—thinks we should fight ableism. The question is just whether, in a society free from discrimination, people with disabilities would be worse off.

It is also worth noting that some versions of the mere-difference view and the bad-difference view are more extreme than others. For example, you might think that, due to some of the arguments in this chapter, disabilities are overall bad for well-being. But maybe, because of the testimony of people with disabilities, you also think that disabilities aren't nearly as bad as we thought. This view would be a version of the bad-difference view—but the bad-difference view doesn't tell us *how bad* disabilities are. Disabilities might be bad, but only a little bad.

Another possibility is that some disabilities are mere differences, and others are bad differences. In the previous chapter, we noted that Barnes only argues that physical disabilities are mere differences; her argument is consistent with the idea that cognitive disabilities are bad differences. It's also possible that some physical disabilities are mere differences, and others are bad differences. Most defenders of the bad-difference view tend to think that all disabilities are bad differences, but we don't have to be so extreme. Maybe we simply shouldn't treat all disabilities the same—and when it comes to well-being, some disabilities detract from well-being, but others do not. We didn't have space to cover all of these possibilities in the chapter, but it is worth thinking more about them.

> How (if at all) has your view about disability and well-being changed after reading these chapters on disability?

Further Reading

The bad-difference view is defended by Singer (2001), McMahan (2005), Kahane (2009), Kahane and Savulescu (2016), and Bognar (2016). Objections to the bad-difference view are given by Barnes (2009, 2014, 2016a, 2016b). Views that fall in between the mere-difference view and the bad-difference view are defended by Andrić and Wündisch (2015) and Campbell and Stramondo (2017). Books and readers on the philosophy of disability include Nussbaum (2006), Davis (2006), and Kristiansen et al. (2009).

Bibliography

Chapter 1: General Introduction

Boonin, David, and Graham Oddie. 2009. *What's Wrong? Applied Ethicists and Their Critics.* Oxford: Oxford University Press.

Christman, Matthew. 2017. *What Is This Thing Called Metaethics?* New York: Routledge.

LaFollette, Hugh. 2014. *Ethics in Practice: An Anthology.* 4th ed. Malden, MA: Wiley-Blackwell.

Lyons, Jack, and Barry Ward. 2018. *The New Critical Thinking.* New York: Routledge.

Oderberg, David S. 2000. *Applied Ethics: A Non-Consequentialist Approach.* Malden, MA: Wiley-Blackwell.

Shafer-Landau, Russ. 2017. *The Fundamentals of Ethics.* 4th ed. Oxford: Oxford University Press.

Singer, Peter. 2011. *Practical Ethics.* 3rd ed. Cambridge: Cambridge University Press. Selections reprinted with permission of the licensor through PLSclear.

Timmons, Mark. 2019. *Disputed Moral Issues.* 5th ed. Oxford: Oxford University Press.

Section 1: Abortion

Chapter 2: The Sanctity of Life Argument

Bentham, Jeremy. 1988 [1789]. *An Introduction to the Principles of Morals and Legislation.* Amherst, MA: Prometheus Books.

Berg, Amy. 2016. "Abortion and Miscarriage." *Philosophical Studies* 174: 1217–26.

Derbyshire, Stuart W. G., and John C. Bockmann. 2020. "Reconsidering Fetal Pain." *Journal of Medical Ethics* 46: 3–6.

English, Jane. 1975. "Abortion and the Concept of a Person." *Canadian Journal of Philosophy* 5(2): 233–43.

Engelhardt, H. Tristram. 1974. "The Ontology of Abortion." *Ethics* 84(3): 217–34.

Feinberg, Joel. 1978. "Voluntary Euthanasia and the Inalienable Right to Life." *Philosophy & Public Affairs* 7(2): 93–123.

Frankfurt, Harry. 1971. "Freedom of the Will and the Concept of a Person." *The Journal of Philosophy* 68(1): 5–20.

Greasley, Kate. 2017. *Arguments about Abortion: Personhood, Morality, and Law.* Oxford: Oxford University Press.

Greasley, Kate, and Christopher Kaczor. 2017. *Abortion Rights: For and Against.* Cambridge: Cambridge University Press.

Harman, Elizabeth. 1999. "Creation Ethics: The Moral Status of Early Fetuses and the Ethics of Abortion." *Philosophy & Public Affairs* 28 (4): 310–24.

———. 2003. "The Potentiality Problem." *Philosophical Studies* 114(1–2): 173–98.

Kaczor, Christopher. 2015. *The Ethics of Abortion: Women's Rights, Human Life, and the Question of Justice*. New York: Routledge.

Kortsmit, Katherine, et al. 2020. "Abortion Surveillance—United States, 2018." *Morbidity and Mortality Weekly Report: Surveillance Summaries* 69(7): 1–29.

Lee, Patrick, and Robert P. George. 2005. "The Wrong of Abortion." In *Contemporary Debates in Applied Ethics*, edited by Andrew I. Cohen and Christopher Heath Wellman, 13–26. Malden, MA: Wiley-Blackwell.

Locke, John. 1689. "Of Identity and Diversity." *An Essay Concerning Human Understanding*. London: Thomas Bassett.

Menkiti, Ifeanyi A. 1984. "Person and Community in African Traditional Thought." In *African Philosophy, An Introduction*, edited by Richard A. Wright, 171–81. Lanham, MD: University Press of America.

Nepomanschy, Pablo A., et al. 2006. "Cortisol Levels and Very Early Pregnancy Loss in Humans." *Proceedings of the National Academy of Sciences*. 103(10): 3938–42.

Olson, Eric. 2007. *What Are We? A Study in Personal Ontology*. Oxford: Oxford University Press.

Princess Elisabeth of Bohemia. 1643. "Correspondence with Descartes." In *Women Philosophers of the Early Modern Period*, edited by Margaret Atherton, 9–21. Indianapolis: Hackett Publishing Company, 1994.

Schouten, Gina. 2017. "Fetuses, Orphans, and a Famous Violinist." *Social Theory and Practice* 43(3): 637–65.

Singer, Peter. 2011. *Practical Ethics*. 3rd ed. Cambridge: Cambridge University Press. Selections reprinted with permission of the licensor through PLSclear.

Stone, Jim. 1987. "Why Potentiality Matters." *Canadian Journal of Philosophy* 17(4): 815–30.

Swinburne, Richard. 2007. *Revelation: From Metaphor to Analogy*. 2nd ed. Oxford: Oxford University Press.

———. 2019. *Are We Bodies or Souls?* Oxford: Oxford University Press.

Tooley, Michael. 1973. "Abortion and Infanticide." *Philosophy & Public Affairs* 2(1): 37–65.

Warren, Mary Anne. 1973. "On the Moral and Legal Status of Abortion." *The Monist* 57(4): 43–61.

———. 2000. "The Moral Difference between Infanticide and Abortion: A Response to Robert Card." *Bioethics* 14(4): 352–59.

Chapter 3: Future of Value Argument

Card, R. F. 2006. "Two Puzzles for Marquis's Conservative View on Abortion." *Bioethics* 20(5): 264–77.

Cudd, Anne E. 1990. "Sensationalized Philosophy: A Reply to Marquis's 'Why Abortion Is Immoral.'" *The Journal of Philosophy* 87(5): 262–64.

Feldman, Fred. 1992. *Confrontations with the Reaper: A Philosophical Study of the Nature and Value of Death*. Oxford: Oxford University Press.

Korcz, Keith Allen. 2002. "Two Moral Strategies Regarding Abortion." *Journal of Social Philosophy* 33(4): 581–605.

Marquis, Don. 1989. "Why Abortion Is Immoral." *The Journal of Philosophy* 86(4): 183–202.

———. 1994. "A Future Like Ours and the Concept of Person: A Reply to McInerney and Paske." In *The Abortion Controversy: A Reader*, edited by Louis P. Pojman and Francis J. Beckwith, 354–68. Boston: Jones & Bartlett.

———. 2007. "An Argument That Abortion Is Wrong." In *Ethical Theory: An Anthology*, edited by Russ Shafer-Landau, 2nd ed., 400–411. Malden, MA: Wiley-Blackwell.

———. 2009. "Abortion Revisited." In *The Oxford Handbook of Bioethics*, edited by Bonnie Stienbock, 395–415. Oxford: Oxford University Press.

McInerney, Peter K. 1990. "Does a Fetus Already Have a Future-Like-Ours?" *The Journal of Philosophy* 87(5): 264–68.

McMahan, Jeff. 2002. *The Ethics of Killing: Problems at the Margins of Life*. Oxford: Oxford University Press.

Norcross, Alastair. 1990. "Killing, Abortion, and Contraception: A Reply to Marquis." *The Journal of Philosophy* 87(5): 268–77.

Reitan, Eric. 2015. "Avoiding the Personhood Issue: Abortion, Identity, and Marquis's 'Future-Like-Ours' Argument." *BioEthics* 30(4): 272–81.

Roberts, Melinda A. 2010. *Abortion and the Moral Significance of Merely Possible Persons*. New York: Springer.

Sinnott-Armstrong, Walter. 1997. "You Can't Lose What You Ain't Never Had: A Reply to Marquis on Abortion." *Philosophical Studies* 96: 59–72.

Strong, C. 2008. "A Critique of 'The Best Secular Argument Against Abortion'." *The Journal of Medical Ethics* 34(10): 727–31.

Tännsjö, Torbjorn. 2015. *Taking Life: Three Theories on the Ethics of Killing*. Oxford: Oxford University Press.

Chapter 4: The Famous Violinist Argument

Boonin, David. 2003. *A Defense of Abortion*. Cambridge: Cambridge University Press.

Finnis, John. 1973. "The Rights and Wrongs of Abortion: A Reply to Judith Thomson." *Philosophy & Public Affairs* 2(2): 117–45.

Fischer, John Martin. 1991. "Abortion and Self-Determination." *The Journal of Social Philosophy* 22: 5–11.

———. 2013. "Abortion and Ownership." *The Journal of Ethics* 17(4): 275–304.

Foot, Phillippa. 2002. *Moral Dilemmas and Other Topics in Moral Philosophy*. Oxford: Oxford University Press.

Hursthouse, Rosalind. 1987. *Beginning Lives*. Oxford: Basil Blackwell.

Kaczor, Christopher. 2015. *The Ethics of Abortion: Women's Rights, Human Life, and the Question of Justice*. New York: Routledge.

Maitzen, Steven. 2003. "Abortion in the Original Position." *The Personalist Forum* 15(2): 373–87.

Rachels, James. 1975. "Killing and Letting Die." *The New England Journal of Medicine* 292: 78–80.

Schouten, Gina. 2017. "Fetuses, Orphans, and a Famous Violinist." *Social Theory and Practice* 43(3): 637–65.

Thomson, Judith Jarvis. 1971. "A Defense of Abortion." *Philosophy & Public Affairs* 1(1): 47–66.

———. 1973. "Rights and Deaths." *Philosophy & Public Affairs* 2(2): 146–59.

———. 1995a. "Abortion." *Boston Review*. http://bostonreview.net/archives/BR20.3/thomson.html.

———. 1995b. "Reply." *Boston Review*. http://bostonreview.net/archives/BR20.4/Thomson.html.

Watt, Helen. 2016. *The Ethics of Pregnancy, Abortion and Childbirth: Exploring Moral Choices in Childbearing*. New York: Routledge.

Wilcox, John T. 1989. "Nature as Demonic in Thomson's Defense of Abortion." *New Scholasticism* 63(4): 463–84.

Section 2: Animal Ethics

Chapter 5: The Contractarian Argument

Besong, Brian. 2018. *An Introduction to Ethics: A Natural Law Approach*. Eugene, OR: Cascade Books.

Carruthers, Peter. 1992. *The Animals Issue: Moral Theory in Practice*. Cambridge: Cambridge University Press. Selections reprinted with permission of the licensor through PLSclear.

———. 2011. "Animal Mentality: Its Character, Extent, and Moral Significance." In *The Oxford Handbook of Animal Ethics*, edited by Tom L. Beauchamp and R. G. Frey, 373–406. New York: Oxford University Press. Selections reprinted with permission of the licensor through PLSclear.

Copp, David, ed. 2007. *The Oxford Handbook of Ethical Theory*. Oxford: Oxford University Press.

Dancy, Jonathan. 2004. *Ethics without Principles*. Oxford: Oxford University Press.

Hsiao, Tim. 2015. "In Defense of Eating Meat." *Journal of Agricultural and Environmental Ethics* 28(2): 277–91.

———. 2017. "Industrial Farming Is Not Cruel to Animals." *Journal of Agricultural and Environmental Ethics* 30(1): 37–54.

Hursthouse, Rosalind. 2001. *On Virtue Ethics*. Oxford: Oxford University Press.

Kant, Immanuel. (1797) 1996. *The Metaphysics of Morals*. Translated and edited by Mary Gregor. Cambridge: Cambridge University Press. Selections reprinted with permission of the licensor through PLSclear.

———. (1785) 1997. *Groundwork of the Metaphysics of Morals*. Translated and edited by Mary Gregor. Cambridge: Cambridge University Press. Selections reprinted with permission of the licensor through PLSclear.

———. (1798) 2010. "Anthropology from a Pragmatic Point of View." In *Anthropology, History, and Education*, edited and translated by Robert Louden and Gunter Zoller, 227–429. Cambridge: Cambridge University Press.

Korsgaard, Christine. 1997. "Introduction." In *Groundwork of the Metaphysics of Morals*, translated and edited by Mary Gregor, vii–xxx. Cambridge: Cambridge University Press. Selections reprinted with permission of the licensor through PLSclear.

———. 2018. *Fellow Creatures: Our Obligations to the Other Animals*. Oxford: Oxford University Press. Selections reprinted with permission of the licensor through PLSclear.

McNaughton, David. 1988. *Moral Vision*. Malden, MA: Blackwell.

Rawls, John. 1999. *A Theory of Justice: Revised Edition*. Cambridge, MA: Harvard University Press.

Regan, Tom. 2004. *The Case for Animal Rights*. Los Angeles: University of California Press.

Ross, David. 2002. *The Right and the Good*. Oxford: Oxford University Press.

Rowlands, Mark. 2009. *Animal Rights: Moral Theory and Practice*. New York: Palgrave Macmillan.

Scanlon, T. M. 1998. *What We Owe to Each Other*. Cambridge, MA: The Belknap Press of Harvard University Press. Copyright © 1998 by the President and Fellows of Harvard College. Reprinted by permission.

Swanson, Jennifer. 2011. "Contractualism and the Moral Status of Animals." *Between the Species* 14(1): 1–17.

Chapter 6: Animal Welfare and Animal Rights

Armstrong, Susan, and Richard G. Botzler. 2008. *The Animal Ethics Reader*. New York: Routledge.

Cohen, Carl, and Tom Regan. 2001. *The Animal Rights Debate*. Lanham, MD: Rowman & Littlefield.

Davis, Steven. 2003. "The Least Harm Principle May Require That Humans Consume a Diet Containing Large Herbivores, Not a Vegan Diet." *Journal of Agricultural and Environmental Ethics* 16: 387–94.

DeGrazia, David. 2002. *Animal Rights: A Very Short Introduction*. Oxford: Oxford University Press.

Frey, R. G. 1987. "Autonomy and the Value of Animal Life." *The Monist* 70(1): 50–63.

Gruen, Lori. 2014. *The Ethics of Captivity*. Oxford: Oxford University Press.

Korsgaard, Christine. 2018. *Fellow Creatures: Our Obligations to the Other Animals*. Oxford: Oxford University Press. Selections reprinted with permission of the licensor through PLSclear.

Regan, Tom. 1997. "The Rights of Humans and Other Animals." *Ethics & Behavior* 7(2): 103–11.

Rowlands, Mark. 2009. *Animal Rights: Moral Theory and Practice*. New York: Palgrave Macmillan.

Scanlon, T. M. 1998. *What We Owe to Each Other*. Cambridge, MA: The Belknap Press of Harvard University Press. Copyright © 1998 by the President and Fellows of Harvard College. Reprinted by permission.

Singer, Peter. 2002. *Animal Liberation*. New York: HarperCollins.

Sunstein, Cass R., and Martha C. Nussbaum. 2004. *Animal Rights: Current Debates and New Directions*. Oxford: Oxford University Press.

Chapter 7: Humane Farming

Chan, Rebecca, and Dustin Crummett. 2019. "Moral Indulgences: When Offsetting Is Wrong." *Oxford Studies in Philosophy of Religion* 9: 68–95.

Cuneo, Terence. 2015. "Conscientious Omnivorism." In *Philosophy Comes to Dinner*, edited by Andrew Chignell, Terence Cuneo, and Matthew Halteman, 21–38. New York: Routledge.

Driver, Julia. 2015. "Individual Consumption and Moral Complicity." In *The Moral Complexities of Eating Meat*, edited by Ben Bramble and Bob Fischer, 67–79. Oxford: Oxford University Press.

Fischer, Bob. 2019. *The Ethics of Eating Animals: Usually Bad, Sometimes Wrong, Often Permissible*. New York: Routledge.

Hooley, Dan, and Nathan Nobis. 2015. "A Moral Argument for Veganism." In *Philosophy Comes to Dinner*, edited by Andrew Chignell, Terence Cuneo, and Matthew Halteman, 92–108. New York: Routledge.

Huemer, Michael. 2019. *Dialogues on Ethical Vegetarianism*. New York: Routledge.

John, Tyler, and Jeff Sebo. 2020. "Consequentialism and Nonhuman Animals." In *The Oxford Handbook of Consequentialism*, edited by Douglas W. Portmore, 564–91. New York: Oxford University Press.

Korsgaard, Christine. 2018. *Fellow Creatures: Our Obligations to the Other Animals*. Oxford: Oxford University Press. Selections reprinted with permission of the licensor through PLSclear.

Loughnan, Steve, Nick Haslam, and Brock Bastian. 2010. "The Role of Meat Consumption in the Denial of Moral Status and Mind to Meat Animals." *Appetite* 55(1): 156–59.

McMahan, Jeff. 2002. *The Ethics of Killing: Problems at the Margins of Life*. Oxford: Oxford University Press.

McPherson, Tristram. 2015. "Why I Am a Vegan (and You Should Be Too)." In *Philosophy Comes to Dinner*, edited by Andrew Chignell, Terence Cuneo, and Matthew Halteman, 73–91. New York: Routledge.

Nozick, Robert. 1974. *Anarchy, State, and Utopia*. New York: Basic Books.

Parfit, Derek. 1982. "Future Generations: Further Problems." *Philosophy & Public Affairs* 11(2): 113–72.

Pettit, Philip. 1989. "Consequentialism and Respect for Persons." *Ethics* 100(1): 116–26.

Podgorski, Abelard. 2020. "The Diner's Defence: Producers, Consumers, and the Benefits of Existence." *Australasian Journal of Philosophy* 98(1): 64–77.

Rawls, John. 1999. *A Theory of Justice: Revised Edition*. Cambridge, MA: Harvard University Press.

Reese, Jacy. 2018. "There's No Such Thing as Humane Meat or Eggs. Stop Kidding Yourself." *The Guardian*. https://www.theguardian.com/food/2018/nov/16/theres-no-such-thing-as-humane-meat-or-eggs-stop-kidding-yourself.

Regan, Tom. 2004. *The Case for Animal Rights*. Los Angeles: University of California Press.

———. 2017. "The Radical Egalitarian Case for Animal Rights." In *Environmental Ethics: Readings in Theory and Application*, edited by Louis P. Pojman, Paul Pojman, and Katie McShane, 106–13. Boston: Cengage Learning.

Rothgerber, Hank. 2015. "Can You Have Your Meat and Eat It Too? Conscientious Omnivores, Vegetarians, and Adherence to Diet." *Appetite* 84: 196–203.

Singer, Peter. 2011. *Practical Ethics*. 3rd ed. Cambridge: Cambridge University Press. Selections reprinted with permission of the licensor through PLSclear.

Yetter Chappell, Richard. 2015. "Value Receptacles." *Nous* 49(2): 322–32.

Section 3: Environmental Ethics

Chapter 8: Future Generations

Arrhenius, Gustaf. 2000. "An Impossibility Theorem for Welfarist Axiologies." *Economics and Philosophy* 16(2): 247–66.

Arrhenius, Gustaf, and Torbjörn Tännsjö. 2017. "The Repugnant Conclusion." *Stanford Encyclopedia of Philosophy*. https://plato.stanford.edu/entries/repugnant-conclusion/.

Boonin, David. 2014. *The Non-Identity Problem and the Ethics of Future People*. Oxford: Oxford University Press.

Hare, Caspar. 2013. *The Limits of Kindness*. Oxford: Oxford University Press.

Huemer, Michael. 2008. "In Defense of Repugnance." *Mind* 117(468): 899–933.

Kavka, Gregory. 1982. "The Paradox of Future Individuals." *Philosophy & Public Affairs* 11(2): 93–112.

Korsgaard, Christine. 2018. *Fellow Creatures: Our Obligations to the Other Animals*. Oxford: Oxford University Press. Selections reprinted with permission of the licensor through PLSclear.

Neuhauser, Alan. 2019. "100,000 Americans Die from Air Pollution, Study Finds." *USA Today*. https://www.usnews.com/news/national-news/articles/2019-04-08/100-000-americans-die-from-air-pollution-study-finds.

Parfit, Derek. 1984. *Reasons and Persons*. Oxford: Oxford University Press.

Roberts, Melinda A. 2019. "The Nonidentity Problem." *Stanford Encyclopedia of Philosophy*. https://plato.stanford.edu/entries/nonidentity-problem/.

Ryberg, Jesper, and Torbjörn Tännsjö. 2004. *The Repugnant Conclusion: Essays on Population Ethics*. Dordrecht, Netherlands: Springer.

Scheinman, Ted. 2019. "The Couples Rethinking Kids because of Climate Change." *BBC*. https://www.bbc.com/worklife/article/20190920-the-couples-reconsidering-kids-because-of-climate-change.

Weinberg, Rivka. 2016. *The Risk of a Lifetime: How, When, and Why Procreation May Be Permissible*. Oxford: Oxford University Press.

Chapter 9: Environmentalism

Anderson, Elizabeth. 1993. *Value in Ethics and Economics*. Cambridge, MA: Harvard University Press. Selections reprinted with permission of the licensor through PLSclear.

———. 2004. "Animal Rights and the Values of Non-Human Life." In *Animal Rights: Current Debates and New Directions*, edited by Cass R. Sunstein and Martha C. Nussbaum, 277–98. Oxford: Oxford University Press. Selections reprinted with permission of the licensor through PLSclear.

Attfield, Robin. 1983. *The Ethics of Environmental Concern*. Oxford: Blackwell.

Baxter, William. 1974. *People or Penguins: The Case for Optimal Pollution*. New York: Columbia University Press.

Brennan, Andrew, and Yeuk-Sze Lo. 2015. "Environmental Ethics." *Stanford Encyclopedia of Philosophy*. https://plato.stanford.edu/entries/ethics-environmental/.

Callicott, James Baird. 1998. "The Conceptual Foundations of the Land Ethic." In *Environmental Philosophy: From Animal Rights to Radical Ecology*, edited by M. E. Zimmerman, J. B. Callicott, G. Sessions, K. J. Warren, and J. Clark, 2nd ed., 101–23. Upper Saddle River, NJ: Prentice Hall.

Cochrane, Alasdair. n.d. "Environmental Ethics." *Internet Encyclopedia of Philosophy*. https://www.iep.utm.edu/envi-eth/.

Leopold, Aldo. 1989. *A Sand County Almanac, and Sketches Here and There*. Special Commemorative Edition. Oxford: Oxford University Press. Selections reprinted with permission of the licensor through PLSclear.

Naess, Arne. 1973. "The Shallow and the Deep Long-Range Ecology Movement. A Summary." *Inquiry* 16: 95–100.

Regan, Tom. 2004. *The Case for Animal Rights*. Los Angeles: University of California Press.

Rolston, Holmes III. 1985. "Duties to Endangered Species." *Bioscience* 35(11): 718–26.

Scanlon, T. M. 1998. *What We Owe to Each Other*. Cambridge, MA: The Belknap Press of Harvard University Press. Copyright © 1998 by the President and Fellows of Harvard College. Reprinted by permission.

Zimmerman, Michael E., J. Baird Callicott, George Sessions, Karen J. Warren, and John Clark. 1998. *Environmental Philosophy: From Animal Rights to Radical Ecology*. Upper Saddle River, NJ: Prentice Hall.

Chapter 10: Wild Animals

Anderson, Elizabeth. 2004. "Animal Rights and the Values of Non-Human Life." In *Animal Rights: Current Debates and New Directions*, edited by Cass R. Sunstein and Martha C. Nussbaum, 277–98. Oxford: Oxford University Press. Selections reprinted with permission of the licensor through PLSclear.

Animal Ethics. 2020. "Vaccinating and Healing Sick Animals." https://www.animal-ethics.org/wild-animal-suffering-section/helping-animals-in-the-wild/vaccinating-healing-sick-injured-animals/.

Bostrom, Nick, and Toby Ord. 2006. "The Reversal Test: Eliminating Status Quo Bias in Applied Ethics." *Ethics* 116(4): 656–79.

Carpendale, Max. 2015. "Welfare Biology as an Extension of Biology: Interview with Yew-Kwang Ng." *Relations* 3(2): 197–202.

Clark, Stephen R. L. 1979. "The Rights of Wild Things." *Inquiry* 22: 171–88.

Creegan, Nicola Hoggard. 2013. *Animal Suffering and the Problem of Evil*. Oxford: Oxford University Press.

Crummett, Dustin. 2017. "The Problem of Evil and the Suffering of Creeping Things." *International Journal for Philosophy of Religion* 82(1): 71–88.

Dawkins, Richard. 1995. *River Out of Eden: A Darwinian View of Life.* New York: Basic Books. Copyright © 1995. Reprinted by permission of Basic Books, and imprint of Hachette Book Group, Inc.

Donaldson, Sue, and William Kymlicka. 2011. *Zoopolis: A Political Theory of Animal Rights.* Oxford: Oxford University Press.

Hale, Benjamin. 2016. *The Wild and the Wicked: On Nature and Human Nature.* Boston: MIT Press.

John, Tyler, and Jeff Sebo. 2020. "Consequentialism and Nonhuman Animals." In *The Oxford Handbook of Consequentialism*, edited by Douglas W. Portmore, 564–91. New York: Oxford University Press.

Leopold, Aldo. 1989. *A Sand County Almanac, and Sketches Here and There.* Special Commemorative Edition. Oxford: Oxford University Press. Selections reprinted with permission of the licensor through PLSclear.

McMahan, Jeff. 2016. "The Moral Problem of Predation." In *Philosophy Comes to Dinner: Arguments About the Ethics of Eating*, edited by A. Chignell, T. Cuneo, and M. C. Haltemann, 268–95. New York: Routledge.

Ng, Yew-Kwan. 1995. "Towards Welfare Biology: Evolutionary Economics of Animal Consciousness and Suffering." *Biology and Philosophy* 10: 255–85.

Paez, Eze. 2020. "A Kantian Ethics of Paradise Engineering." *Analysis* 80(2): 283–93.

Pearce, David. 2007. "The Abolitionist Project." https://www.hedweb.com/abolitionist-project/index.html.

———. 2015. "A Welfare State for Elephants? A Case Study of Compassionate Stewardship." *Relations* 3(2): 153–64.

Regan, Tom. 2004. *The Case for Animal Rights.* Los Angeles: University of California Press.

Scudellari, Megan. 2019. "The Promise of Gene Drives." *Nature.* https://www.nature.com/articles/d41586-019-02087-5.

Tennyson, Alfred. 1850. "In Memoriam A.H.H. OBIIT MDCCCXXXIII: 56." *Representative Poetry Online* (University of Toronto Libraries). https://rpo.library.utoronto.ca/poems/memoriam-h-h-obiit-mdcccxxxiii-56.

Tomasik, Brian. 2017. "Habitat Loss, Not Preservation, Generally Reduces Wild Animal Suffering." *Essays on Reducing Suffering.* https://reducing-suffering.org/habitat-loss-not-preservation-generally-reduces-wild-animal-suffering/.

———. 2019. "How Many Wild Animals Are There?" *Essays on Reducing Suffering.* https://reducing-suffering.org/how-many-wild-animals-are-there/.

Section 4: Charitable Giving

Chapter 11: The Obligatory View

Barry, Christian, and Gerhard Øverland. 2013. "How Much for the Child?" *Ethical Theory and Moral Practice* 16: 189–204.

Cullity, Garrett. 2004. *The Moral Demands of Affluence.* Oxford: Oxford University Press.

Gabriel, Iason. 2017. "Effective Altruism and Its Critics." *Journal of Applied Philosophy* 34(4): 457–73.

GiveWell. 2019. "2019 GiveWell Cost-effectiveness Analysis—Version 5." https://docs.google.com/spreadsheets/d/1d255LKz11L3V-OgOEns9WvJzpnVeaLTcEP1HD4lC478/edit#gid=791021775.

Hillebrandt, Hauke. 2015. "Bednets Have Prevented 450 Million Cases of Malaria." *Giving What We Can.* https://www.givingwhatwecan.org/post/2015/12/bednets-have-prevented-450-million-cases-of-malaria/.

Illingworth, Patricia, Thomas Pogge, and Leif Wenar, eds. 2010. *Giving Well: The Ethics of Philanthropy.* Oxford: Oxford University Press.

Kamm, Frances. 2000. "Does Distance Matter Morally in the Duty to Rescue?" *Law and Philosophy* 19(6): 655–81.

MacAskill, William. 2016. *Doing Good Better: Effective Altruism and a Radical New Way to Make a Difference.* London: Guardian Faber.

Singer, Peter. 1972. "Famine, Affluence, and Morality." *Philosophy & Public Affairs* 1(3): 229–43.

———. 2009. *The Life You Can Save: How To Do Your Part to End World Poverty.* New York: Random House. Reprinted by permission. An updated 2019-edition of this book is now available free of charge, as an eBook or audiobook, from www.thelifeyoucansave.org.

———. 2011. *Practical Ethics.* 3rd ed. Cambridge: Cambridge University Press. Selections reprinted with permission of the licensor through PLSclear.

———. 2016. *Ethics in the Real World: 82 Brief Essays on Things That Matter.* Princeton, NJ: Princeton University Press.

Sonderholm, Jorn. 2012. "World Poverty, Positive Duties, and the Overdemandingness Objection." *Politics, Philosophy, and Economics* 12(3): 308–27.

Timmerman, Travis. 2015. "Sometimes There Is Nothing Wrong with Letting a Child Drown." *Analysis* 75(2): 204–12.

Unger, Peter. 1996. *Living High and Letting Die: Our Illusion of Innocence.* Oxford: Oxford University Press.

Wenar, Leif. 2010. "Poverty Is No Pond: Challenges for the Affluent." In *Giving Well: The Ethics of Philanthropy,* edited by Patricia Illingworth, Thomas Pogge, and Leif Wenar, 104–32. Oxford: Oxford University Press.

Wisor, Scott. 2011. "Against Shallow Ponds: An Argument against Singer's Approach to Global Poverty." *Journal of Global Ethics* 7(1): 19–32.

Wolf, Susan. 1982. "Moral Saints." *Journal of Philosophy* 79(8): 419–39.

World Health Organization (WHO). 2020. "Children: Reducing Mortality." https://www.who.int/news-room/fact-sheets/detail/children-reducing-mortality.

Chapter 12: The Supererogatory View

Arthur, John. 2016. "Famine Relief and the Ideal Moral Code." In *The World of Philosophy: An Introductory Reader,* 1st ed., edited by Stephen M. Kahn, 354–60. Oxford: Oxford University Press.

Garcia, Jorge. 1996. "The Heart of Racism." *The Journal of Social Philosophy* 27(1): 5–45.

Gilligan, Carol. 1982. *In a Different Voice: Psychological Theory and Women's Development.* Cambridge, MA: Harvard University Press.

Held, Virginia. 2006. *The Ethics of Care.* New York: Oxford University Press.

Hursthouse, R. 1999. *On Virtue Ethics.* Oxford: Oxford University Press.

Johnson, James D., Carolyn H. Simmons, Amanda Jordav, Leslie Maclean, Jeffrey Taddei, Duane Thomas, John F. Dovidio, and William Reed. 2002. "Rodney King and O. J. Revisited: The Impact of Race and Defendant Empathy Induction on Judicial Decisions." *Journal of Applied Social Psychology* 32: 1208–23.

Kagan, Shelly. 1989. *The Limits of Morality.* Oxford: Oxford University Press.

Noddings, Nel. 1982. *Caring: A Feminine Approach to Ethics and Moral Education.* Berkeley: University of California Press.

Norcross, Alastair. 2000. "Contractualism and the Ethical Status of Animals." *Southwest Philosophy Review* 17: 137–43.

Nozick, Robert. 1974. *Anarchy, State, and Utopia.* New York: Basic Books.

Nussbaum, Martha C. 2006. *Frontiers of Justice: Disability, Nationality, and Species Membership.* Cambridge, MA: Harvard University Press.

O'Neill, Onora. 1986. *Faces of Hunger: An Essay on Poverty, Development and Justice.* Boston, MA: Allen & Unwin.

———. 1987. "Rights, Obligations, and World Hunger." In *Poverty and Social Justice: Critical Perspectives: A Pilgrimage Toward Our Own Humanity,* edited by Francisco Jiménez, 86–100. Tempe, AZ: Bilingual Press.

Pojman, Louis P. 1992. *Life and Death: Grappling with the Moral Dilemmas of Our Time.* Boston: Jones & Bartlett.

Pojman, Louis P., and James Fieser. 2012. *Ethics: Discovering Right and Wrong.* 7th ed. Boston: Wadsworth.

Singer, Peter. 1972. "Famine, Affluence, and Morality." *Philosophy & Public Affairs* 1(3): 229–43.

———. 2009. *The Life You Can Save: How to Do Your Part to End World Poverty.* New York: Random House. Reprinted by permission. An updated 2019-edition of this book is now available free of charge, as an eBook or audiobook, from www.thelifeyoucansave.org.

———. 2011. *Practical Ethics.* 3rd ed. Cambridge: Cambridge University Press. Selections reprinted with permission of the licensor through PLSclear.

Slote, Michael. 2004. "Famine, Affluence, and Empathy." In *What's Wrong? Applied Ethicists and Their Critics,* edited by David Boonin and Graham Oddie, 2nd ed., 146–54. Oxford: Oxford University Press. Selections reprinted with permission of the licensor through PLSclear.

———. 2007. *The Ethics of Care and Empathy.* New York: Routledge. Selections reprinted with permission of the licensor through PLSclear.

———. 2010. *Moral Sentimentalism.* Oxford: Oxford University Press. Selections reprinted with permission of the licensor through PLSclear.

Timmons, Mark. 2013. *Moral Theory: An Introduction.* Lanham, MD: Rowman & Littlefield.

Trawalter, Sophie, Kelly M. Hoffman, and Adam Waytz. 2016. "Racial Bias in Per-
    ceptions of Others' Pain." *PLOS ONE* 11(3): [e48546]. doi:10.1371/journal.pone.
    0048546.

Chapter 13: Charity Skepticism

Berkey, Brian. 2018. "The Institutional Critique of Effective Altruism." *Utilitas* 30(2):
    143–71.
Brzozowski, Diane. 2003. "Lifeboat Ethics: Rescuing the Metaphor." *Ethics, Place, and
    Environment* 6(2): 161–66.
Buck Cox, Susan Jane. 1985. "No Tragedy of the Commons." *Environmental Ethics* 7: 49–62.
Chang, Ha-Joon. 2006. *The East Asian Development Experience: The Miracle, The Crisis,
    and the Future*. Chicago: University of Chicago Press.
Clough, Emily. 2015. "Effective Altruism's Political Blind Spot." *Boston Review*. https://
    bostonreview.net/world/emily-clough-effective-altruism-ngos.
Corbett, Steve, and Brian Fikkert. 2012. *When Helping Hurts: How to Alleviate Poverty
    without Hurting the Poor . . . and Yourself*. Chicago: Moody Publishers.
Hardin, Garrett. 1968. "The Tragedy of the Commons." *Science* 168(3859): 1243–48.
———. 1974a. "Commentary: Living on a Lifeboat." *BioScience* 24(10): 561–68.
———. 1974b. "Stimulus/Response: Lifeboat Ethics: The Case against Helping the
    Poor." *Psychology Today* 8(4): 38–43, 123–26.
Herzog, Lisa. 2016. "Can 'Effective Altruism' Really Change the World?" *openDem-
    ocracy*. https://www.opendemocracy.net/en/transformation/can-effective-altruism-
    really-change-world/.
Hillebrandt, Hauke. 2015. "Effective Altruism, Continued: On Measuring Impact."
    Boston Review. http://bostonreview.net/blog/hauke-hillebrandt-giving-what-we-can-
    effective-altruism-impact.
Lupton, Robert D. 2012. *Toxic Charity: How Churches and Charities Hurt Those They Help,
    and How to Reverse It*. New York: HarperCollins.
Lutts, Ralph. 1984. "Garrett Hardin: Dilemmas and Taboos." *The Environmentalist* 4:
    287–93.
MacAskill, William. 2015. *Doing Good Better: How Effective Altruism Can Help You Help
    Others, Do Work That Matters, and Make Smarter Choices about Giving Back*. New York:
    Random House.
Malthus, Thomas Robert. 1789. *An Essay on the Principle of Population*. London: J.
    Johnson.
McMahan, Jeff. 2016. "Philosophical Critiques of Effective Altruism." *The Philosopher's
    Magazine* 73(2): 92–99. http://jeffersonmcmahan.com/wp-content/uploads/2012/11/
    Philosophical-Critiques-of-Effective-Altruism-refs-in-text.pdf.
Miller, Kenneth R. 2018. *The Human Instinct: How We Evolved to Have Reason, Con-
    sciousness, and Free Will*. New York: Simon & Schuster.
Nagel, Thomas. 1970. *The Possibility of Altruism*. Oxford: Oxford Clarendon Press.
Nell, Onora. 1975. "Lifeboat Earth." *Philosophy & Public Affairs* 4(3): 273–92.

Nussbaum, Martha. 1997. "If Oxfam Ran the World." *London Review of Books* 19(17). https://www.lrb.co.uk/the-paper/v19/n17/martha-nussbaum/if-oxfam-ran-the-world.

Okeyere-Manu, Beatrice. 2016. "Overpopulation and the Lifeboat Metaphor: A Critique from an African Worldview." *International Studies in the Philosophy of Science* 30(3): 279–89.

Ryberg, Jesper. 1997. "Population and Third World Assistance." *Journal of Applied Philosophy* 14(3): 207–19.

Singer, Peter. 2010. *The Life You Can Save: How to Do Your Part to End World Poverty.* New York: Random House. Reprinted by permission. An updated 2019-edition of this book is now available free of charge, as an eBook or audiobook, from www.the lifeyoucansave.org.

———. 2011. *Practical Ethics.* 3rd ed. Cambridge: Cambridge University Press. Selections reprinted with permission of the licensor through PLSclear.

Sober, Elliott, and David Sloan Wilson. 1998. *Unto Others: The Evolution and Psychology of Unselfish Behavior.* Cambridge, MA: Harvard University Press.

Southern Poverty Law Center (SPLC). n.d. "Garrett Hardin." https://www.splcenter. org/fighting-hate/extremist-files/individual/garrett-hardin.

Srinivasan, Amia. 2015. "Stop the Robot Apocalypse." *London Review of Books.* https://www.lrb.co.uk/the-paper/v37/n18/amia-srinivasan/stop-the-robot-apocalypse.

Timmons, Mark. 2019. *Disputed Moral Issues: A Reader.* 5th ed. Oxford: Oxford University Press.

Weathers, Scott. 2016. "Can 'Effective Altruism' Change the World? It Already Has." *openDemocracy.* https://www.opendemocracy.net/en/transformation/can-effective-altruism-change-world-it-already-has/.

Section 5: Punishment

Chapter 14: Justifying Punishment, Part 1

Boonin, David. 2008. *The Problem of Punishment.* New York: Cambridge University Press.

Code of Hammurabi. Translated by L. W. King. *The Avalon Project.* https://avalon.law. yale.edu/ancient/hamframe.asp.

Declaration of Independence. 1776. https://www.archives.gov/founding-docs/declaration-transcript.

Dolinko, David. 1991. "Some Thoughts about Retributivism." *Ethics* 101(3): 537–59.

Dostoevsky, Fyodor. (1862) 1990. *The Brothers Karamazov.* Translated by Richard Pevear and Larissa Volokhonsky. New York: Farrar, Straus, and Giroux.

Goldman, Alan H. 1994. "The Paradox of Punishment." In *Punishment,* edited by A. John Simmons, Marshall Cohen, Joshua Cohen, & Charles R. Beitz, 30–46. Princeton, NJ: Princeton University Press.

Haksar, Vinit. 1986. "Excuses and Voluntary Conduct." *Ethics* 96(2): 317–29.

Hobbes, Thomas. 1904. *Leviathan: Or, The Matter, Forme & Power of a Commonwealth, Ecclesiasticall and Civil*. London, UK: University Press.

Hugo, Victor. 1862. *Les Misérables*. London, UK: Dodd, Mead.

Kant, Immanuel. (1797) 1991. *The Metaphysics of Morals*. Translated by Mary Gregor. New York: Cambridge University Press. Selections reprinted with permission of the licensor through PLSclear.

Kleinig, John. 1973. *Punishment and Desert*. The Hague: Martinus Nijhoff.

Lippke, Richard L. 2001. "Criminal Offenders and Rights Forfeiture." *Journal of Social Philosophy* 32 (Spring): 78–89.

Locke, John. (1689) 1963. *Two Treatises of Government*. Cambridge: Cambridge University Press.

Mill, John Stuart. (1859) 2011. *On Liberty* (Cambridge Library Collection - Philosophy). Cambridge: Cambridge University Press. Doi: 10.1017/CBO9781139149785.

Moore, Michael. 1993. "Justifying Retributivism." *Israel Law Review* 27: 15–49.

Morris, Christopher W. 1991. "Punishment and Loss of Moral Standing." *Canadian Journal of Philosophy* 21(1): 53–80.

Mundle, C. W. K. 1954. "Punishment and Desert." *The Philosophical Quarterly* 4(16): 216–28.

Primoratz, Igor. 1989. *Justifying Legal Punishment*. London: Humanities Press International.

Ross, W. D. 1930. *The Right and the Good*. Oxford: Oxford University Press.

Simmons, A. John. 1994. "Locke and the Right to Punish." In *Punishment*, edited by A. John Simmons, Marshall Cohen, Joshua Cohen, and Charles R. Beitz, 219–60. Princeton, NJ: Princeton University Press.

Tolkien, J. R. R. (1961) 1994. *Lord of the Rings: The Fellowship of the Ring*. New York: Houghton Mifflin Company.

Universal Declaration of Human Rights. 1948. https://www.un.org/en/about-us/universal-declaration-of-human-rights.

Chapter 15: Justifying Punishment, Part 2

Anderson, David A. 2002. "The Deterrence Hypothesis and Picking Pockets and the Pickpockets Hanging." *American Law and Economics Review* 4(2): 295–313.

Armour, Marilyn Peterson, and Mark S. Umbreit. 2012. "Assessing the Impact of the Ultimate Penal Sanction on Homicide Survivors: A Two State Comparison." *Marquette Law Review* 96(1): Article 3.

Barnett, Randy. 1997. "Restitution: A New Paradigm of Criminal Justice." In *Punishment and Rehabilitation*, edited by Jeffrie G. Murphy, 2nd ed., 211–31. Belmont, CA: Wadsworth.

———. 1998. *The Structure of Liberty: Justice and the Rule of Law*. Oxford: Clarendon Press.

Becker, Gary S. 1968. "Crime and Punishment: An Economic Approach." *Journal of Political Economy* 76(2): 169–217.

Bentham, Jeremy. 1789. *An Introduction to the Principles of Morals and Legislation*. London: Clarendon Press.

Boonin, David. 2008. *The Problem of Punishment*. New York: Cambridge University Press.

Bowers, William J., and Glenn L. Pierce. 1980. "Deterrence or Brutalization: What Is the Effect of Executions?" *Crime and Delinquency* 26(4): 453–84.

Dehgan, Saeed Kamali. 2014. "Iranian Mother Who Spared Her Son's Killer: 'Vengeance Has Left My Heart.'" *The Guardian*, April 25, 2014. https://www.theguardian.com/world/2014/apr/25/interview-samereh-alinejad-iranian-mother-spared-sons-killer.

Dick, Philip K. (1956) 2016. *The Minority Report and Other Classic Stories By Philip K. Dick*. New York: Kensington Publishing Corp.

Dickens, Charles. (1838) 2008. *Oliver Twist*. London: Penguin Books Limited.

Hampton, Jean. 1984. "The Moral Education Theory of Punishment." *Philosophy and Public Affairs* 13(3): 208–38.

Hooker, Brad. 2000. *Ideal Code, Real World*. Oxford: Oxford University Press.

Howe, Alex. 2019. "Regaining Traction on the Problem of Punishment: A Critique of David Boonin's Use of the Entailment Test." *Res Publica* 25: 261–72.

Martin, George R. R. 2003. *A Storm of Swords*. New York: Random House Publishing Group.

Mauer, Marc, and Ryan S. King. 2007. "A 25-Year Quagmire: The War on Drugs and Its Impact on American Society." *The Sentencing Project*. https://www.sentencingproject.org/wp-content/uploads/2016/01/A-25-Year-Quagmire-The-War-On-Drugs-and-Its-Impact-on-American-Society.pdf.

Mill, John Stuart. (1861) 2012. *On Utilitarianism*. New York: Dover Publications, Inc.

Nagin, Daniel S. 1998. "Criminal Deterrence Research at the Outset of the Twenty-First Century." *Crime and Justice* 23: 1–42.

Paine, Thomas. (1776) 2011. *Common Sense*. (n.p.): The Capitol Net Inc.

Strang, Heather. 2002. *Repair or Revenge: Victims and Restorative Justice*. Oxford: Clarendon Press.

Sullivan, Dennis, and Larry Tifft. 2001. *Restorative Justice: Healing the Foundations of Our Everyday Lives*. Monsey, NY: Willow Tree Press.

Wright, Valerie. 2010. "Deterrence in Criminal Justice: Evaluating Certainty v. Severity of Punishment." *The Sentencing Project*. https://www.sentencingproject.org/wp-content/uploads/2016/01/Deterrence-in-Criminal-Justice.pdf.

Zimmerman, Michael J. 2011. *The Immorality of Punishment*. N.p.: Broadview Press.

Chapter 16: Practical Abolition

ACLU. 2014. "Racial Disparities in Sentencing." https://www.aclu.org/sites/default/files/assets/141027_iachr_racial_disparities_aclu_submission_0.pdf.

Alexander, Michelle. 2012. *The New Jim Crow: Mass Incarceration in the Age of Colorblindness*. Revised ed. New York: The New Press.

Allyn, Bobby. 2020. "'The Computer Got It Wrong': How Facial Recognition Led to False Arrest of Black Man." *NPR*. June 24, 2020. https://www.npr.org/2020/06/24/882683463/the-computer-got-it-wrong-how-facial-recognition-led-to-a-false-arrest-in-michig.

Appiah, Kwame Anthony. 2020. "The Case for Capitalizing the *B* in Black." *The Atlantic*. June 18, 2020. https://www.theatlantic.com/ideas/archive/2020/06/time-to-capitalize-blackand-white/613159/.

Associated Press. 2020. "AP Changes Writing Style to Capitalize "B" in Black." https://apnews.com/71386b46dbff8190e71493a763e8f45a.

Batson v. Kentucky. 476 U.S. 79 (1968).

Bennett, Mark W. 2017. "The Implicit Racial Bias in Sentencing: The Next Frontier." *Yale Law Journal* 126: F. 381. https://www.yalelawjournal.org/forum/the-implicit-racial-bias-in-sentencing#_ftnref68.

Blackmon, Douglas. 2008. *Slavery by Another Name: The Re-enslavement of Black People in America from the Civil War to World War II.* New York: Doubleday.

Boston Police Department. 2017. "Gang Assessment Database." Rules and Procedures, Rule 335. March 23, 2017. https://www.documentcloud.org/documents/6219626-BPD-Rule-335-Gang-Assessment-Database.html.

Bowers, William J., and Glenn L. Pierce. 1980. "Deterrence or Brutalization: What Is the Effect of Executions?" *Crime and Delinquency* 26(4): 453–84.

Buolamwini, Joy, and Timnit Gebru. 2018. "Gender Shades: Intersectional Accuracy Disparities in Commercial Gender Classification." *Proceedings of Machine Learning Research* 81: 1–15.

Butler, Paul. 1995. "Racially Based Jury Nullification: Black Power in the Criminal Justice System." *Yale Law Journal* 105(3): 677–725.

Crummett, Dustin. 2020. "Prosecutorial Discretion and Republican Non-Domination." *Ethical Theory and Moral Practice* 23: 965–85.

Davis, Angela. 2003. *Are Prisons Obsolete?* New York: Seven Stories Press.

Dooling, Shannon. 2019. "Here's What We Know about Boston Police's Gang Database." *WBUR.* July 26, 2019. https://www.wbur.org/news/2019/07/26/boston-police-gang-database-immigration.

Equal Justice Initiative. 2017. *Lynching in America: Confronting the Legacy of Racial Terror.* 3rd ed. https://lynchinginamerica.eji.org/report/.

Floyd v. City of New York. 959 F Supp. 2d 540 (2003).

Furman v. Georgia. 408 U.S. 238 (1972).

Gilmore, Ruth Wilson. 2007. *The Golden Gulag: Prisons, Surplus, Crisis, and Opposition in Globalizing California.* 2nd ed. Berkeley: University of California Press.

———. 2021. *Change Everything: Racial Capitalism and the Case for Abolition.* Chicago: Haymarket Books.

Gregg v. Georgia. 428 U.S. 153 (1976).

Guinier, Lani. 1991. "No Two Seats: The Elusive Quest for Political Equality." *Virginia Law Review* 77(8): 1413–1514.

Hall, Erika V., and Robert W. Livingston. 2012. "The Hubris Penalty: Biased Responses to 'Celebration' Displays of Black Football Players." *Journal of Experimental Social Psychology* 48(4): 899–904.

Huemer, Michael. 2013. *The Problem of Political Authority.* London: Palgrave Macmillan.

———. 2018. "The Duty to Disregard the Law." *Criminal Law and Philosophy* 12(1): 1–18.

International Criminal Court. 2011. Rome Statute, Article 7. https://www.icc-cpi.int/resource-library/documents/rs-eng.pdf.

Johnson, Gabrielle M. 2020. "Algorithmic Bias: On the Implicit Biases of Social Technology." *Synthese.* doi.org/10.1007/s11229-020-02696-y.

King, Ryan D., and Brian D. Johnson. 2016. "A Punishing Look: Skin Tone and Afro-centric Features in the Halls of Justice." *American Journal of Sociology* 122(1): 90–124.

Maur, Marc. 1999. *Race to Incarcerate*. New York: New Press.

Maur, Marc, and Ryan King. 2007. "Uneven Justice: State Rates of Incarceration by Race and Ethnicity." *The Sentencing Project*. July 1, 2007. https://www.sentencingproject.org/publications/uneven-justice-state-rates-of-incarceration-by-race-and-ethnicity/.

Nathanson, Stephen. 1985. "Does It Matter If the Death Penalty Is Arbitrarily Administered?" *Philosophy & Public Affairs* 14(2): 149–64.

Norris v. Alabama. 294 U.S. 587 (1935).

Philips, Scott, and Justin F. Marceau. 2020. "Whom the State Kills." *Harvard Civil Rights-Civil Liberties Law Review* 55(20). http://dx.doi.org/10.2139/ssrn.3440828.

Richardson, L. Song. 2017. "Systemic Triage: Implicit Racial Bias in the Criminal Courtroom." *Yale Law Journal* 126: 862. https://www.yalelawjournal.org/article/systemic-triage-implicit-racial-bias-in-the-criminal-courtroom.

Rothstein, Richard. 2017. *The Color of Law: A forgotten history of how our government segregated America*. New York: Liveright Publishing.

Segura, Liliana, and Jordan Smith. 2019. "Counting the Condemned." *The Intercept*, 2019. https://theintercept.com/2019/12/03/death-penalty-capital-punishment-data/.

Skiba, Russell J., Robert S. Michael, Abra Carroll Nardo, and Reece Peterson. 2000. "The Color of Discipline: Sources of Racial and Gender Disproportionality in School Punishment." https://files.eric.ed.gov/fulltext/ED468512.pdf.

US v. Dougherty. 473 F.2d 1113 (1972).

Van den Haag, Ernest. 1978. "The Collapse of the Case against Capital Punishment." *National Review* March 31, 397.

Section 6: Disability

Chapter 17: What Is a Disability?

Barnes, Elizabeth. 2014. "Valuing Disability, Causing Disability." *Ethics* 125: 88–113.

———. 2016. *The Minority Body*. Oxford: Oxford University Press. Selections reprinted with permission of the licensor through PLSclear.

Daniels, Norman. 1985. *Just Health Care*. Cambridge: Cambridge University Press.

Haslanger, Sally. 2014. *Resisting Reality*. Oxford: Oxford University Press.

Kahane, Guy, and Julian Savulescu. 2009. "The Welfarist Account of Disability." In *Disability and Disadvantage*, edited by Kimberley Brownlee and Adam Cureton, 14–53. Oxford: Oxford University Press.

Savulescu, Julian, and Guy Kahane. 2011. "Disability: A Welfarist Approach." *Clinical Ethics* 6: 45–51.

Timpe, Kevin. (forthcoming). "Denying a Unified Concept of Disability." *The Journal of Medicine and Philosophy*.

Turnbull, Clare, and Shirley Hodgson. 2005. "Genetic Predisposition to Cancer." *Clinical Medicine* 5 (5): 491–98.

United Nations. 2004. "The United Nations and Disabled Persons—The First Fifty Years." https://www.un.org/esa/socdev/enable/dis50y10.htm.

Chapter 18: The Mere-Difference View

Andrić, Vuko, and Joachim Wündisch. 2015. "Is It Bad to Be Disabled? Adjudicating between the Mere-Difference and the Bad-Difference Views of Disability." *Journal of Ethics and Social Philosophy* 9(3): 1–16.

Altmann, John, and Bryan W. Van Norden. 2020. "Was This Ancient Taoist the First Philosopher of Disability?" *The New York Times*, July 8, 2020. https://www.nytimes.com/2020/07/08/opinion/disability-philosophy-zhuangzi.html.

Atkinson, Rebecca. 2007. "Do I Want My Sight Back?" *The Guardian*, July 17, 2007. https://www.theguardian.com/lifeandstyle/2007/jul/17/healthandwellbeing.health.

Bagenstos, S., and Schlanger, M. 2007. "Hedonic Damages, Hedonic Adaptation, and Disability." *Vanderbilt Law Review* 60(3): 745–97.

Barnes, Elizabeth. 2014. "Valuing Disability, Causing Disability." *Ethics* 125: 88–113.

———. 2016a. *The Minority Body*. Oxford: Oxford University Press. Selections reprinted with permission of the licensor through PLSclear.

———. 2016b. "Reply to Guy Kahane and Julian Savulescu." *Res Philosophica* 93(1): 295–307.

Benito-León, Julián, José Manuel Morales, Jesús Rivera-Navarro, and Alex Mitchell. 2003. "A Review about the Impact of Multiple Sclerosis on Health-Related Quality of Life." *Disability and Rehabilitation* 25(23): 1291–1303.

Bowker, John H., and John W. Michael, eds. 2002. *Atlas of Limb Prosthetics: Surgical, Prosthetic, and Rehabilitation Principles*. 2nd ed. Rosemont, IL: American Academy of Orthopedic Surgeons. (Original work published 1992)

Bruno, Marie-Aurélie, Jan L. Bernheim, Didier Ledoux, Frédéric Pellas, Athena Demertzi, and Steven Laureys. 2011. "A Survey on Self-Assessed Well-Being in a Cohort of Chronic Locked-in Syndrome Patients: Happy Majority, Miserable Minority." *BMJ Open* 1(1): 1–9.

Campbell, Stephen M., and Joseph A. Stramondo. 2017. "The Complicated Relationship between Disability and Well-Being." *Kennedy Institute of Ethics Journal* 27(2): 151–84.

Crisp, Roger. 2017. "Well-Being." In *Stanford Encyclopedia of Philosophy*. https://plato.stanford.edu/archives/fall2017/entries/well-being/.

Davis, Lennard J. 2006. *The Disability Studies Reader*. 2nd ed. New York: Routledge.

Eyre, Sarah. 2012. "A Few Awesome Things about Being Disabled." *xoJane*, May 17, 2012.

Johnson, Harriet McBryde. 2003. "Unspeakable Conversations." *The New York Times Magazine*, February 16, 2003.

Kahane, Guy. 2009. "Non-identity, Self-Defeat, and Attitudes to Future Children." *Philosophical Studies* 145: 193–214.

Kahane, Guy, and Julian Savulescu. 2016. "Disability and Mere-Difference." *Ethics* 126: 774–88.

Kilpatrik, Kim. 2020. "Great Things about Being Blind." http://kimgia3.blogspot.com.

Kittay, Eva. 2015. "Dependency." In *Keywords in Disability Studies*, edited by Rachael Adams and Benjamin Reiss, 54–58. New York: NYU Press.

Kristiansen, Kristjana, Simo Vehmas, and Tom Shakespeare. 2009. *Arguing about Disability: Philosophical Perspectives.* New York: Routledge.

Lee, Yvonne C. 2013. "Effect and Treatment of Chronic Pain in Inflammatory Arthritis." *Current Rheumatology Reports* 15(300): 1–8.

Lobentanz, I. S., S. Asenbaum, Karl Vass, C. Sauter, Gerhard Klösch, Harald Kollegger, W. Kristoferitsch, and Josef Zeitlhofer. 2004. "Factors Influencing Quality of Life in Multiple Sclerosis Patients: Disability, Depressive Mood, Fatigue and Sleep Quality." *Acta Neurologica Scandinavica* 110(1): 6–13.

Loewenstein, George, and David Schkade. 1999. "Wouldn't It Be Nice? Predicting Future Feelings." In *Well-Being: The Foundations of Hedonic Psychology*, edited by Daniel Kahneman, Ed Diener, and Norbert Schwarz, 85–105. New York: Russell Sage Foundation.

McMahan, Jeff. 2005. "Causing Disabled People to Exist and Causing People to Be Disabled." *Ethics* 116: 77–99.

Nussbaum, Martha C. 2001. "Symposium on Amartya Sen's Philosophy 5: Adaptive Preferences and Women's Options." *Economics and Philosophy* 17(1): 67–88.

———. 2006. *Frontiers of Justice: Disability, Nationality, and Species Membership.* Cambridge, MA: The Belknap Press of Harvard University Press.

Roy, Archie W. N., and Gilbert F. MacKay. 2002. "Self-Perception and Locus of Control in Visually Impaired College Students with Different Types of Vision Loss." *Journal of Visual Impairment & Blindness* 96(4): 254–66.

Stensman, R. 1985. "Severely Mobility-Disabled People Assess the Quality of Their Lives." *Scandinavian Journal of Medical Rehabilitation* 17(2): 87–99.

Tammet, Daniel. 2007. *Born on a Blue Day: Inside the Extraordinary Mind of an Autistic Savant.* New York: Simon & Schuster.

Chapter 19: The Bad-Difference View

Andrić, Vuko, and Joachim Wündisch. 2015. "Is It Bad to Be Disabled? Adjudicating between the Mere-Difference and the Bad-Difference Views of Disability." *Journal of Ethics and Social Philosophy* 9(3): 1–16.

Barnes, Elizabeth. 2009. "Disability, Minority, and Difference." *Journal of Applied Philosophy* 26(4): 337–55.

———. 2014. "Valuing Disability, Causing Disability." *Ethics* 125: 88–113.

———. 2016a. *The Minority Body.* Oxford: Oxford University Press. Selections reprinted with permission of the licensor through PLSclear.

———. 2016b. "Reply to Guy Kahane and Julian Savulescu." *Res Philosophica* 93(1): 295–307.

Bognar, Greg. 2016. "Is Disability Mere Difference?" *The Journal of Medical Ethics* 42: 46–49.

Campbell, Stephen M., and Joseph A. Stramondo. 2017. "The Complicated Relationship between Disability and Well-Being." *Kennedy Institute of Ethics Journal* 27(2): 151–84.

Davis, Lennard J. 2006. *The Disability Studies Reader.* 2nd ed. New York: Routledge.

Kahane, Guy. 2009. "Non-identity, Self-Defeat, and Attitudes to Future Children." *Philosophical Studies* 145: 193–214.

Kahane, Guy, and Julian Savulescu. 2016. "Disability and Mere-Difference." *Ethics* 126: 774–88.

Kristiansen, Keistjana, Simo Vehmas, and Tom Shakespeare. 2009. *Arguing about Disability: Philosophical Perspectives*. New York: Routledge.

McMahan, Jeff. 2005. "Causing Disabled People to Exist and Causing People to Be Disabled." *Ethics* 116: 77–99.

Nussbaum, Martha C. 2006. *Frontiers of Justice: Disability, Nationality, and Species Membership*. Cambridge, MA: The Belknap Press of Harvard University Press.

Singer, Peter. 2001. "Ethics and Disability: A Response to Koch." *Journal of Disability Policy Studies* 16: 130–33.

Glossary

Abortion: the intentional termination of a pregnancy, resulting in the death of the fetus.

Act consequentialism: a form of *consequentialism* that says the right action is the one which produces better consequences than its alternatives.

Adaptive preference: a change in preference to cope with a new situation.

All-things-considered wrong: an action that is overall wrong once all the relevant factors are taken into account.

Analysis: an analysis specifies what does and does not fall under a concept by giving the most central components of that concept; for example, "an unmarried man" is an analysis of 'bachelor'.

Animal ethics: the area of ethics that examines whether our treatment of animals is permissible.

Anthropocentric: human-centered.

Applied ethics: the area of ethics that tries to give answers to the practical moral questions we ask in everyday life.

Argument: a group of claims, some of which are premises and at least one of which is the conclusion. The premise(s) support the conclusion.

Argumentation: the activity of presenting and analyzing arguments.

Argument from analogy: an argument that uses observed similarities between two things to infer an unobserved similarity.

Argument from cases: an argument that uses carefully selected cases designed to bring out a particular judgment or to argue that a certain view best explains the correct judgments about those cases.

Argument from elimination: a type of argument that starts by listing all of the possible options, then eliminates all of the options except one, so concludes that the last standing option must be correct.

Argument from marginal cases: an argument which claims that proposed properties (e.g., intelligence) do not make humans morally more important than animals, since some humans lack those properties.

Argument from wonder: a genre of arguments that uses positive emotions toward the environment to generate environmentalist conclusions.

Bad-difference view: having a disability is bad in and of itself.

Biting the bullet: a metaphor for accepting a wild implication of an argument rather than attempting to explain why the argument does not have that implication (or just rejecting the argument).

Blame questions: questions about whether a person who performs an action is deserving of praise, blame, or neither.

Broad morality: further ethical questions that are not answered just by figuring out what is right and wrong.

Burden, or burden of proof: the requirement to provide evidence demonstrating that one's position is correct.

Case of the miners: a case given by Michael Slote (2004) to support care ethics (and the supererogatory view of charitable giving). Slote claims, against utilitarianism, that we should use resources to save trapped miners rather than install safeguards that would save more lives in the long run.

Catharsis: the release or purging of negative emotions.

Ceteris paribus: Latin for "other things equal."

Collective action: an action taken by a group of people (e.g., fighting global climate change).

Conclusion: the main point of an argument, or the claim the premises of an argument support.

Consequentialism: the view that the morality of an action is determined by its consequences. *Utilitarianism* is an important version, which says the key consequence that matters is happiness.

Consequentialist justifications of punishment: Forward-looking justifications of punishment, which hold that punishment is justified because of its good consequences.

Contractarianism: the view that morality is what would be agreed upon by rational agents who decide what rules we should follow.

Contractarian argument: an argument originated by Peter Carruthers (1992) which tries to show that our use of animals is not wrong because the correct moral theory, contractarianism, doesn't give them moral standing.

Contradiction: a claim that is internally inconsistent, and therefore cannot be correct, because it implies that something must be both true and false at the same time.

Cost-benefit analysis: a mathematical method for weighing the risks and rewards of a course of action; one kind of cost-benefit analysis is an *expected utility calculation*.

Contractualism: synonymous with *contractarianism*.

Counterexample: an example designed to show that there is something wrong with a proposed definition, claim, or principle.

Counterexample to a definition: an example which shows that an important condition of the definition hasn't been met—the counterexample either shows that the definition is not a *necessary condition* or not a *sufficient condition* for the thing being defined.

Culling: the "humane" killing of wild animals through actions like hunting, usually aimed at reducing their population size.

Cultural relativism: a popular version of moral relativism that says that morality depends on the rules of a culture or society.

Deterrence: occurs when someone is discouraged from performing some action.

Desert: what someone deserves.

Diner's defense: a more sophisticated variant of the *logic of the larder*. It claims that consuming humanely raised meat may be okay even if farmers are wrong to kill humanely raised animals.

Disability: It's complicated. See Chapter 17.

- **Medical definition 1:** disability is any departure from normal functioning.

- **Medical definition 2:** disability is a negative departure from normal functioning.

- **Ability definition 1:** disability is the lack of an ability that most people have.

- **Ability definition 2:** disability is the lack of a significant ability that most people have.

- **Welfare definition:** disability is anything that makes life go worse for you.

- **Social definition:** disability is the negative effects of having an impairment in a society that discriminates against the impaired.

- **Group identity definition:** a disability is something a person has when and only when they identify as having a disability.

- **Communal definition 1:** disability is defined by the disability rights community (and the correct definition of disability is however the disability rights community defines disability).

- **Community definition 2:** disability is whatever the disability rights community is promoting justice for.

- **Communal definition 3:** disability is whatever the disability rights community is promoting justice for or celebrating.

- **Examples definition:** disability is defined by examples, and anything that closely enough resembles the examples on a list counts as a disability; the list could include mobility impairments, blindness, deafness, rheumatoid arthritis, achondroplasia (short-limbed dwarfism), Down syndrome, Moebius syndrome, narcolepsy, leg amputation, and so on.

Disproportionate punishment: the punishment doesn't fit the crime.

Divine command theory: a normative moral theory which says that morality depends on the commands of God.

Earning to give: taking a high-paying job so that one can donate more money to charity.

Effective altruism: a social movement, informed by Peter Singer's work, that encourages individuals to do as much good as they can while stressing the use of reason and evidence to determine what will do the most good. Effective altruists heavily stress donations to effective charities.

Emotion: a feeling. In many cases, emotions can be more or less apt/appropriate (e.g., feeling outrage toward someone lighting a cat on fire).

Empirical: involving observations about the world.

Environmental ethics: the branch of ethics that deals with our interaction with the natural environment.

Environmental fascism: a derogatory term for the *land ethic* coined by Tom Regan because it cares only about the ecosystem as a whole and not about the individual humans and other animals who live in it.

Environmentalism: in a broad sense, a social movement concerned with preserving the environment. In the narrower sense used in this book, the philosophical view that we should care about the environment (ecosystems, biodiversity, natural beauty, etc.) for its own sake, apart from how caring impacts people or animals.

Ethics: the area of philosophy that studies right and wrong, good and bad; ethics is often broken into three subareas—*applied ethics, normative ethics,* and *metaethics.*

Ethics of care (or 'care ethics'): a version of virtue ethics. It claims that an action is obligatory if and only if a caring person would perform the action, permissible if and only if a caring person might perform the action, and wrong if and only if a caring person would not perform the action. Michael Slote's version identifies being caring with being empathetic.

Expected utility calculation: a mathematical method for weighing the risks and rewards of a course of action; a kind of *cost-benefit analysis.*

Facially neutral law: laws that appear non-discriminatory because they do not explicitly single out particular individuals or groups.

Factory farms: large, industrial farms that attempt to produce animal products as cheaply as possible, generally at the expense of the animals' well-being.

Fetus: the zygotic, embryonic, and fetal stages of an organism.

Forfeiture claim: if person A violates another person's right to something, then A forfeits A's own right to that thing. For example, if I kill someone, I lose my own right to live.

Free agreement: one of T. M. Scanlon's two contractarian principles to ensure fair rules; this one says that agents' priority must be to agree on rules for society in a free and unforced way.

Future-directed: something that looks toward future consequences.

Future-directed desires: desires about the future.

Future generations: generations of people who do not currently exist but will in the future.

Future like ours: a future that has value but is also full of the rich and varied experiences that most adult humans have (including moral experiences).

Future of value: synonymous (for purposes of this book) with *future like ours*.

Future of value argument: a pro-life argument that claims that killing is wrong because it deprives the victim of future experiences, and that abortion is wrong since it deprives a fetus of future experiences.

Gene drives: attempts to genetically re-engineer wild animal populations. So far, many of these attempts have focused on ways to prevent mosquitoes from spreading malaria and other diseases.

Genus-species relationship: when one thing is a type of another; for example, a rose is a type of flower.

Good-difference view: having a disability is intrinsically good, because it contributes to someone's well-being, and those who have a disability are better off than those who do not.

Gradients of bliss: the replacement of pain with experiences that feel better by the same amount; the experiences that used to be painful now feel good, but the experiences that used to feel good now feel really good.

Hedonistic utilitarianism: the view that we should take actions that maximize pleasure and minimize pain.

Humane farming: farming animals while giving them nice lives (at least until they are killed, in the case of animals farmed for meat).

Hybrid solution: combines elements of multiple solutions.

If and only if (iff): operates similarly to an "="; what's on the right should pick out exactly what the left picks out. For example, someone is a bachelor if and only if they are an unmarried male. Analyses make use of "if and only if," but typically one side will "explain" the other even though both pick out the same things.

Impersonal wrongs: wrong actions that don't wrong anyone; also known as "victimless crimes."

Inalienable: cannot be taken away.

Incapacitate: with respect to punishment, punishing a person in a way that prevents them from committing future wrongs.

Inference to the best explanation (IBE): a type of argument that counts a theory's or principle's explanatory power as evidence for the truth of that theory or principle.

Inherent value: value possessed due to the kind of thing you are; for Tom Regan, the basis of moral rights.

Institutional critique (of effective altruism): the criticism that effective altruism focuses too much on individual charitable donations and not enough on institutional reform.

Instrumental bad: bad because of leading to something bad.

Instrumental good: good because of leading to something good.

Interventionism: the idea that we should intervene in the natural world on a large scale to help the animals in it avoid suffering and death.

Intrinsically bad: bad in and of itself (e.g., suffering).

Intrinsically good: good in and of itself (e.g., happiness).

Intuitions: an "intellectual seeming" regarding, for example, a judgment about a case or the truth of a claim or principle.

Jury nullification: declining to convict a defendant even when it is clear that the defendant is guilty.

Justice-based justifications: a kind of retributivist justification on which we ought to punish wrongdoers because doing so is intrinsically good (good in and of itself).

Kantian ethics: an ethical theory developed by Immanuel Kant. It claims that actions are permissible if and only if they are *universalizable* and treat everyone as an end in themselves, not as a mere means.

Killing: actively taking a life.

K-select: animals that are K-selected have relatively small numbers of offspring which they take pretty good care of, and many of their offspring survive (like human beings, dogs, cats, etc.).

Land ethic: the view, defended by Aldo Leopold, that "a thing is right when it tends to preserve the integrity, stability, and beauty of the biotic community. It is wrong when it tends otherwise."

Legal questions: questions about whether some action is legal or illegal.

Letting die: passively failing to intervene to prevent someone's death.

Lex talionis: Latin for "law of retaliation"; the idea that justice requires payback, for example, "an eye for an eye" and "a tooth for a tooth."

Lifeboat argument: an argument from Garrett Hardin claiming that people in wealthy nations are analogous to passengers in a lifeboat who cannot save the drowning people around them without sinking their own boat.

Logic of the larder: an argument that it's okay to eat farmed animals, since they wouldn't even exist if people didn't farm them for meat.

Logic of the logger argument: an argument which claims that wild animals generally have bad lives on balance, and concludes it would be better if lots of wild animals didn't exist at all.

Mere addition paradox: a paradox leading to the *repugnant conclusion*, so named because one of its main assumptions is that "merely adding" people to the world who have lives worth living will not make the world worse.

Mere addition principle: suppose that all the same people who exist in world X also exist in world Y, and world Y also has some additional people who don't exist in world X. Everyone who exists in world X is better off in world Y. And the people who only exist in world Y have lives worth living. If this is true, then world Y is better than world X.

Mere-difference view: having a physical disability makes you physically non-standard, but it is not bad in and of itself.

Merely conscious beings: beings who are not aware of themselves as distinct individuals with pasts and futures. Peter Singer's *replaceability argument* suggests that it's okay to kill them, provided you replace with other equally happy animals.

Metaethics: the area of ethics that tries to answer fundamental questions about the nature of morality, for example: What does it mean for an action to be 'right' or 'wrong'? Is morality objective?

Money-pump argument: an argument for transitivity. It aims to show that by following intransitive preferences (i.e., you prefer A to B, B to C, but C to A), you are inevitably led to make a series of trades that leaves you much worse off.

Moral claim: a claim that involves a substantive moral position, for example, one about whether an action is justified by a future consequence.

Moral particularism: a *normative moral theory* on which there are no neat and universal moral principles about what makes a right action right and what makes a wrong action wrong.

Moral pluralism: a *normative moral theory* on which there are several different, equally fundamental moral principles, and an action is right if and only if it strikes the right balance between them.

Moral standing: to have moral standing is to be a being to whom others owe obligations.

Morally forbidden: synonymous with *morally impermissible*.

Morally impermissible (or 'impermissible'): something one ought not to or should not do.

Morally obligatory (or 'obligatory'): something one ought to or should do.

Morally permissible (or 'permissible'): something that one is morally allowed to do, but not required to do.

Morally required: synonymous with *morally obligatory*.

Narrow morality: the part of morality dealing with right or wrong, or what we owe to each other.

Natural law theory: a *normative moral theory* on which an action is right if and only if it accords with natural laws given by reason.

Natural rights: rights we have in virtue of the kind of being that we are, for example, the right to life.

Necessary condition: a necessary condition for X is something that is required for X; it *must* obtain in order for X to obtain.

Necessity objection: a notable objection to the theoretical abolition of punishment; the claim that even if there is no solution to the problem of punishment, punishment is still justified out of necessity.

Negative rights: rights not to be interfered with, for example, the right not to be killed, robbed, or abused.

Non-anti-egalitarianism: if all the same people exist in world Y and world Z, but world Z has more happiness, a higher average happiness, *and* a more equal distribution of happiness, then world Z is better than world Y.

Non-identity problem: a puzzle introduced by Derek Parfit which suggests that it is not wrong to bring a less happy, but still happy, person into existence rather than a different, more happy, person.

Non-moral claim: a claim that does not involve morality, for example, the claim that cats are a different kind of animal than dogs.

Normative ethics: the area of ethics that tries to construct theories that account for the rightness or wrongness of certain actions, motives, and/or character traits.

Normative moral theory: a theory in *normative ethics* that tries to get at the most basic or fundamental reason certain actions, attitudes, or character traits are good, bad, right, or wrong.

Objection: a criticism of an argument, usually focused on a premise being implausible or false, or the premises not leading to or supporting the conclusion.

Obligatory view (of charitable giving): helping the poor (through charitable donations) is a moral requirement.

Ought implies can: the principle that you ought to do something, then you are able to do it. For example, you don't have an obligation to find parents for all the orphans in the world since that's impossible for you to do.

Overpopulation: the world having too many people for the environment to support.

Paradigm cases: Central, anchoring cases that guide the construction of definitions.

Paradox: an argument that seems persuasive, but leads to a very implausible conclusion.

Personhood argument: a pro-choice argument which says that only persons have a right to life, and that since fetuses are not persons, they do not have a right to life.

Pluralistic consequentialism: form of *consequentialism* which says that multiple things have value. (This contrasts with *utilitarianism*, a form of consequentialism which says that only happiness has value.)

Positive rights: rights to receive something, for example, the right to be fed, clothed, or housed.

Practical abolition: the position that even if punishment is justified in theory, it is not justified in practice because it is embedded in an unjust context.

Precautionary principle: a principle which says that in cases of uncertainty, we should err on the side of caution when the stakes are high.

Preference utilitarianism: the view that we should maximize desire satisfaction and minimize desire frustration.

Premise: the claim(s) of an argument that support the conclusion.

Preservation:

- of ecosystems: for example, avoiding habitat destruction, and preventing the introduction of invasive species

- of biodiversity: for example, keeping endangered species from going extinct

- of natural beauty: for example, the Grand Canyon, or waterfalls, or redwood forests

Presumption: the default position.

Prima facie: Latin meaning "at first glance."

Prima facie **justified:** something that is normally permissible to do, but this could be overridden by other factors.

Prima facie **ought:** something that we normally ought to do, but could be overridden by other factors.

Prima facie **wrong:** something that is normally wrong to do, but this could be overridden by other factors. For example, lying is *prima facie* wrong, but it seems okay to lie to save someone's life.

Principle of equal consideration of interest (PEC): a moral principle stating that we should give equal weight to the like interests of all those affected by our actions.

Principled argument (for charitable giving): an argument from Peter Singer which claims that since you are obligated to prevent very bad things from happening when you can do so without sacrificing anything nearly as important, you are obligated to donate to charity.

Problem of punishment: the question of how we justify punishment, given that it involves harming someone.

Pro-choice position: abortion is usually or always permissible.

Pro-life position: abortion is usually or always wrong.

Punishment: intentionally harming someone because they've committed a wrong, in order to communicate condemnation of their wrongful act.

Reasonable rejection: one of T. M. Scanlon's two contractarian principles to ensure fair rules; a rule that there is a good basis for a rational agent to reject will not be included.

Reductio ad absurdum: an argument which shows that a claim leads to an absurd statement or contradiction and thus must be false.

Replaceability argument: an argument from Peter Singer suggesting that some animals may be "replaceable," so that it's permissible to kill them and replace them with another, equally happy animal.

Repugnant conclusion: for any world full of happy people, a world full of people whose lives were just barely worth living would be better, provided that the latter world contained enough people.

Restitution: restoring what is lost to a wronged party; often thought of as an alternative to punishment.

Retributivist justifications of punishment: backward-looking justifications of punishment which hold that punishment is justified because of a wrongdoing.

Rights: legitimate claims on others; rights allow you to legitimately demand that others do or not do certain things.

R-select: animals that are r-selected have as many offspring as possible, and only a fraction survive (like mice, insects, most fish, etc.).

Rule consequentialism: a form of *consequentialism* which says that the right action is the one that accords with the rules that would produce the best consequences if people generally followed them.

Sanctity of life argument: a traditional pro-life argument that uses the wrongness of killing humans to support the wrongness of killing human fetuses.

Self-conscious beings: beings who are aware of themselves as distinct individuals with pasts and futures.

Self-defeating: pursuing a goal is self-defeating if intentionally pursuing it prevents you from getting it.

Self-interest: what is best for one's self.

Sentience: the ability to have conscious experiences. Particularly relevant in ethics is the ability to feel pain.

Shallow pond argument: an argument which claims that donating to charity is relevantly analogous to saving a child drowning in a pond in front of you. Since you should save the child, you should also donate.

Speciesism: prejudice against animals (i.e., prejudice on the basis of species, allegedly similar to racism and sexism).

State: government.

Status quo bias: an irrational preference for an option because it preserves the way things are.

Stream of consciousness: a person's thoughts, feelings, and experiences perceived as a continuous flow.

Subject-of-a-life: an individual with psychological states, such as beliefs, desires, emotions, or sensations. For Tom Regan, the basis for possessing inherent value.

Sufficient condition: a sufficient condition for X is something that is enough for or guarantees X.

Supererogatory: morally good but not obligatory.

Supererogatory view (of charitable giving): helping the poor (through charitable donations) is a nice thing to do, but you are not morally required to help the poor.

Theoretical abolition: the view that punishment is not justified because there is no successful solution to the *problem of punishment*.

Theories of punishment: views that try answer the *problem of punishment*, and explain why punishment is sometimes justified (e.g., retributivist and consequentialist justifications).

Thought experiment: an imaginary story; often designed to support a philosophical view or theory.

Tragedy of the commons: the idea that when resources are shared in common without appropriate regulation, people will use resources at an unsustainable rate, eventually making everyone worse off.

Transabled: someone who believes they ought to be disabled.

Transitivity: if Y is better than X, and Z is better than Y, then Z is better than X.

Triage policy: a medical policy of directing resources to where they will do the most overall good, often with the result that some sick people won't get medical care (e.g., if you can't save everyone, you concentrate on how you can save the most lives overall).

Tyranny of the majority: the idea that the majority can vote to implement laws that unfairly harm the minority.

Universalizability: an action is universalizable if and only if you could consistently will that everyone perform that type of action.

Utilitarianism: the view that we should maximize the balance of happiness over unhappiness in the world.

Value receptacles objection to utilitarianism: an objection which claims that utilitarianism fails to respect the inherent value of individuals, instead treating them as valuable only as "receptacles" for happiness.

Veil of ignorance: a thought experiment by John Rawls that asks us to figure out what's fair by imagining the rules we would construct if we did not know what place in society we would occupy.

Viability: the point at which the fetus can survive outside the womb.

Vice: a negative character trait that disposes someone to act in similar ways across various circumstances (e.g., dishonesty, cowardliness, and foolishness).

Vigilantism: the carrying out of the law by private citizens (e.g., what superheroes do).

Virtue: a positive character trait that disposes someone to act in similar ways across various circumstances (e.g., honesty, courage, and wisdom).

Virtue ethics: an ethical theory which says an action is obligatory if and only if a virtuous person would perform the action, permissible if and only if a virtuous person might perform the action, and wrong if and only if a virtuous person would not perform the action.

Voluntaristic rights: rights arising from someone voluntarily assuming an obligation, such as through promises, agreements, or contracts, for example, the right to a contractor's labor.

Well-being: what is good for a person.

Wrong (adj): impermissible.

Wrong (n): an impermissible action.

Wrong view (of charitable giving): helping the poor (through charitable giving) is immoral.